Guide to Sources in American Journalism History

Recent Titles in
Bibliographies and Indexes in Mass Media and Communications

American Journalism History
Wm. David Sloan, compiler

Guide to Sources in American Journalism History

Edited and Compiled by
Lucy Shelton Caswell

**Prepared under the auspices
of the American Journalism Historians Association**

Bibliographies and Indexes in
Mass Media and Communications, Number 2

GREENWOOD PRESS
New York • Westport, Connecticut • London

Library of Congress Cataloging-in-Publication Data

Caswell, Lucy Shelton.
　Guide to sources in American journalism history.

　(Bibliographies and indexes in mass media and com-
munications, ISSN 1041-8350 ; no. 2)
　"Prepared under the auspices of the American Journalism
Historians Association."
　Includes index.
　1. Journalism—United States—History—Sources—Biblio-
graphy. I. American Journalism Historians Association.
II. Title. III. Series.
Z6951.C35　1989　[PN47.31]　　016.071′3　　89-11857
ISBN 0-313-26178-4 (lib. bdg. : alk. paper)

British Library Cataloguing in Publication Data is available.

Library of Congress Catalog Card Number: 89-11857
ISBN: 0-313-26178-4
ISSN: 1041-8350

First published in 1989

Greenwood Press, Inc.
88 Post Road West, Westport, Connecticut 06881

Printed in the United States of America

The paper used in this book complies with the
Permanent Paper Standard issued by the National
Information Standards Organization (Z39.48-1984).

10 9 8 7 6 5 4 3 2 1

Contents

Preface   vii

Research Strategies in Journalism History

Laying a Foundation for the Study of Journalism History:
The Organization of the American Journalism Historians
Association
Michael D. Murray   1

The History of Historical Writing
Wm. David Sloan   15

New Directions for Research in Journalism History
John J. Pauly   31

Research Methods in Journalism History

Bibliographies for Journalism History: A Selection
Jean Ward and Kathleen A. Hansen   47

Databases for Historical Research
Kathleen A. Hansen and Jean Ward   63

The United States Newspaper Program
Gary Charbonneau   81

Oral History
Maurine H. Beasley   91

Archival and Manuscript Sources

Guide to Archival and Manuscript Sources   99
    ALABAMA   100
    ARIZONA   101

CALIFORNIA	102
COLORADO	113
CONNECTICUT	114
DELAWARE	121
DISTRICT OF COLUMBIA	122
FLORIDA	137
GEORGIA	139
ILLINOIS	143
INDIANA	145
IOWA	148
KANSAS	155
KENTUCKY	156
LOUISIANA	157
MAINE	157
MARYLAND	158
MASSACHUSETTS	159
MICHIGAN	164
MINNESOTA	172
MISSOURI	184
MONTANA	184
NORTH CAROLINA	187
NEBRASKA	189
NEW HAMPSHIRE	190
NEW JERSEY	191
NEW YORK	193
NORTH DAKOTA	209
OHIO	210
OKLAHOMA	223
OREGON	224
PENNSYLVANIA	227
SOUTH CAROLINA	230
TENNESSEE	232
TEXAS	233
UTAH	238
VIRGINIA	238
VERMONT	243
WASHINGTON	243
WISCONSIN	249
Index	277

Preface

As the first book-length project under the aegis of the American Journalism Historians Association (AJHA), the *Guide to Sources in American Journalism History* has been a cooperative effort. Credit for its inspiration must go to James Startt of Valparaiso University. The chair of the AJHA Research Committee, Thomas A. Schwartz of The Ohio State University, gave encouragement and wise council. Research Committee members reviewed the essay chapters and provided insightful comments for the authors. The contributors themselves brought outstanding subject expertise to the project and were conscientious and cooperative throughout.

The Ohio State University Libraries Advisory Committee on Research provided a seed grant to facilitate the initial collection of information about repositories and The Ohio State University School of Journalism and its director, Walter Bunge, also supported the project. Finally, sincere thanks go to Paulette Tiggs, Luther Boren, Ingrid Hubbard and Diane Terry for their production assistance.

Lucy Shelton Caswell

Research Strategies
in Journalism History

Laying a Foundation for the Study of Journalism History: The Organization of the American Journalism Historians Association

Michael D. Murray

Much of what scholars are able to produce is based on the availability of resources and their familiarity with what is accessible from archives and special collections. In addition, the knowledge we are able to advance is often tied directly to institutional and group support and the current effort is no exception. The establishment of the American Journalism Historians Association (AJHA) in 1982 contributed greatly to prospects for the enhancement of the study of journalism and mass communication history in the United States. AJHA offered the first specialized professional society with national scope to endorse scholarship in the area. As a founding member and past president, the author is proud to offer some background on how the group came to be formed along with information on its activity during this period of infancy.

The development of AJHA rested on a desire to meet a need that was not being met. Journalism history was generally viewed as one of the least developed and most widely overlooked areas of mass communication scholarship and teaching. The history of the organization can be traced to a series of conversations between David Sloan and Gary Whitby in the 1970s. Sloan, then a doctoral candidate at the University of Texas, was teaching at the University of Arkansas. Whitby, also a college instructor, had been asked to develop courses in journalism history and enrolled in two of Sloan's classes. Whitby subsequently decided to pursue a doctorate at the

University of Iowa. He continued to work in the field of journalism history and the two scholars discussed the need for a national organization devoted exclusively to the history of mass media. At the 1981 national meeting of the Association for Education in Journalism (AEJMC), they further developed their ideas for a national group.

Also in 1981 Sloan met Donald Avery at a mass communication symposium in Fort Worth, Texas, where they discussed mutual concerns regarding the need for a national journalism history organization. These discussions were mentioned in a letter proposing an association sent by Sloan in December 1981, to seven scholars. Recipients of that letter included Avery and Whitby, C. Richard King, Darwin Payne, Perry Ashley, John Erickson, and Sharon Murphy, because each had expressed an early interest in the foundation of such an organization. The purpose of Sloan's letter was to solicit advice and request future assistance. He articulated the following objectives for the new group: "to foster greater interest in history, to encourage livelier scholarship and to provide an outlet for it, to give support to journalism historians, and to make journalism history a more integral part of the college curriculum."[1]

Sloan suggested that a board should form to give direction to the organization and that an advisory editor be appointed to serve as administrator of a proposed journal to implement organizational goals. In his letter, Sloan asked that the seven recipients consider plans for publication of the journal and for an initial convention which would include a paper competition and panel presentations. Many of the proposals in this first mailing had been discussed in some detail with those expressing an early interest. Sloan noted that Gary Whitby had already expressed some optimism that typesetting for a journal could be done at his institution. Sloan also mentioned the hope of obtaining funds for operating expenses and start-up funds from his university. He concluded his letter by stating that although a considerable amount of work would be required for such endeavors to take shape, the organization was definitely needed to inject vitality into the field. He concluded, "The future, we hope, is bright. I look forward to working alongside you."[2]

Correspondence accompanying the first letter included the announcement of an organizational meeting anticipated for October 1-2, 1982, at Central Arkansas University in the Ozarks. The meeting place was changed to Southern Methodist University due to an offer by Darwin Payne of S.M.U. to host the conference. When the nationwide call to interested scholars was made in the spring of

1982, the announcement mentioned that it would be the first national meeting devoted exclusively to journalism history. Sloan again expressed the desire to meet with interested scholars as part of a planning process to form a national organization of journalism historians.[3] The announcement described the organization of research sessions, panel discussions and proposed topics for sessions such as "New Directions of Journalism Historiography" and "Graduate Education in Journalism History." From the outset, AJHA founders interpreted the term "journalism history" broadly and welcomed scholarship on innovative research topics.

Don Avery, then at Southern Illinois University, supervised a paper competition judged on a "blind" review as announced in the early mailing. Because *Journalism History*, a well-known publication of the California State University, Northridge Foundation in cooperation with the C.S.U. Department of Journalism, had a somewhat irregular publishing schedule at that time, early consideration was given to scholarly publishing prospects due to the need for an additional publication outlet. Gary Whitby, formerly editor of the *Journal of Communication Inquiry*, planned the first AJHA journal issue tentatively organized around papers accepted for presentation at the first meeting. All of these early efforts were inclusive and urged "as many history teachers as possible [to become] involved in planning and directing the organization and its activities."[4]

At the outset Sloan and the others received additional inquiries and expressions of support for the concept of a new group and a new journal. Among them were letters from Sidney Kobre who founded and published the *Journal of Journalism History* while on the faculty of Florida State University, and Harold Davis who expressed a desire to contribute as soon as he concluded his administrative service as vice president for academic affairs at his home institution, Georgia State University.[5] Also expressing an early interest were Barbara Cloud of the University of Nevada-Las Vegas; Alf Pratte, then of Shippensburg State; Mitchell Stephens, New York University; Robert E. Lance, Arizona State University; Sharon Murphy, then of Southern Illinois University; Maurine Beasley, University of Maryland; Mike Buchholz, then of Oklahoma State University; Chris Miller, Loyola of New Orleans; J. William Snorgrass, Florida A. and M.; Reg Westmoreland, North Texas State University; and Bruce Underwood, Iona College.

Convention host Darwin Payne sent out meeting notices on September 9, 1982, and subsequently handled details on the schedule, transportation and housing for the AJHA organizational conference in Dallas, Texas. The meeting was held in the Umphrey Lee Student Center at S.M.U. and was attended by thirty scholars from ten states. The improvement of teaching techniques at the undergraduate level was a major topic of discussion and papers were presented on topics ranging from the Civil War press to the status of women in journalism. For example, Dr. Lewis Gould, chairman of the Department of History at the University of Texas, discussed "Attitudes of First Ladies Toward News Coverage." As important as the scholarly presentations and panels were, the deliberations concerning prospects for the association itself were of equal importance.

A major theme of the conference's business meeting was the priority of having the organization work closely with other academic and professional groups, particularly the Association for Education in Journalism and Mass Communication, to foster interest in journalism and mass communication history. The need to increase awareness of the role of the First Amendment in developing a national identity was also stressed. In this regard, two resolutions were passed recommending that departments of journalism make journalism history a required course.[6] Gary Whitby presented tentative plans to publish a bi-annual journal to include papers from the meeting in the first issue. He also outlined plans to provide an additional outlet for diverse historical research, making the point that this effort would not duplicate existing publications in the field.

A slate of officers was presented and nominations were taken from the floor to form the basis for a mail ballot to the general membership. David Sloan was asked to serve as secretary and the mail ballot produced the new leadership of the newly formed organization, with Don Avery serving as the first president and J. William Snorgrass, vice president.

Members of the board of directors with terms of office based on vote totals were Darwin Payne (1985); Maurine Beasley (1985); Mike Buchholz (1985); Sidney Kobre (1984); Jo Ann Dickerson (1984); Robert Lance (1984); Lloyd Chiasson (1983); Barbara Cloud (1983); and Michael Murray (1983). Because of other demands, Maurine Beasley was unable to serve the board at that time and was replaced by the next highest vote-getter, Harold Davis.

The first meeting was regarded by Sloan as a tremendous success. In a letter to *Clio* editor Marion Marzolf, Sloan reflected on his initial expectation that perhaps eight to ten scholars with a strong interest in history would gather in Dallas — enough to form the nucleus for an organization which in four or five years could begin to build and broaden its influence. Surprisingly, forty-seven journalism professors from twenty-seven states had indicated a strong interest in AJHA. The fact that thirty scholars attended the initial meeting is all the more impressive when one considers that planning for it did not begin until March before the fall meeting. The actual program consisted of eleven presented papers and three panels. Minutes of the first business meeting followed the mail ballot and included additional information on planning for the 1983 meeting. Initially the convention host served as chief executive of the organization, a policy which centralized decision-making for the organization for the next two years.

Before long, board members were urging others to join the organization which resulted in its growth to approximately forty-five journalism historians. With a forth-coming publication sponsored by AJHA, members were asked to consider the need for a dues structure. The result was the establishment of an annual $10 regular membership fee. In a mailing accompanying election information, David Sloan expressed optimism that the organization could make the field of history the most vital area in journalism education.[7] With differing interests among new members, activity in all areas of journalism history was encouraged.

Three individuals were unable to attend the first meeting, but showed great support. President Don Avery and Harold Davis offered advice on how the organization might proceed in an orderly manner through establishing by-laws and operating procedures. Barbara Cloud offered to host a convention at the University of Nevada-Las Vegas. Efforts were being made to build on the success of the first meeting in developing membership and, at the same time, maintaining high academic standards regarding programs and paper competitions.

The participation of well-known scholars such as Sidney Kobre helped to establish the organization very early. With many organizational details accomplished in its first year, AJHA held its second national meeting in Tuscaloosa, Alabama, October 6-7, 1983, with the University of Alabama serving as host institution. The second conference turned out to be one of the largest meetings ever held for the sole purpose of studying journalism history with sixty scholars in attendance.[8] Four standing committees (Education, Elections, Publications, and Research) with a total committee membership of twenty-five were established. Faculty membership dues were boosted to $15 which included a one-year subscription to the new journal, *American Journalism.* Graduate student membership was free in an effort to attract younger scholars. The organization was intent on maintaining a modest dues structure to insure maximum participation of its nearly one hundred members, many of whom were involved in committee work or the journal.

While the organization was growing in size and prestige, the leadership was beginning to come to grips with questions relating to operational matters, conducting paper competitions, and the logistics of executing what was quickly becoming a major annual meeting. Key questions included planning for both the conference itself and the business meeting, which had been established as an integral part of the overall convention; the need for a registration fee and means to meet the additional costs incurred by having guest speakers; the role students would play; and the need to recognize research contributions, including outstanding student papers.

The Research Committee, headed by Jim Stovall, studied topics for future consideration and ways to continue to upgrade the quality of research presented at the meeting. Stovall was assisted by Jim Startt, Art Kaul, Nancy Roberts, and Joe McKerns. The Publications Committee chaired by Charles Marler considered projects such as the establishment of a newsletter, a membership brochure, a membership survey and sponsoring a variety of books and monographs in the field of journalism history. Committee members Warren Barnard and Tom Schwartz supported these efforts and made recommendations on how they might be implemented. Finally, the Education Committee led by John Pauly offered a variety of proposals regarding paper competitions and panel presentations and suggested scheduling lectures by those particularly well-known as master teachers in the field.

A proposal specifying that the vice president of the organization would automatically assume the presidency each year at the end of the annual meeting was presented by the Election Committee. That group also recommended that the board be elected at the annual business meeting by secret ballot and that for the 1985 meeting, the convention would be hosted by a vice president to be elected in 1983. Thus began a short-lived policy of electing a vice president who would assume the presidency and also serve as convention host. This dual responsibility was not binding and was later dropped. Serving subsequently as president were J. William Snorgrass (1983); Barbara Cloud (1984); Michael Murray (1985); Joseph McKerns (1986); Thomas Connery (1987); and Margaret Blanchard (1988). In addition to those mentioned earlier, board members included: Perry Ashley, Mike Buchholz, Lloyd Chiasson, Thomas Schwartz, Maurine Beasley, John Pauly and Sidney Kobre.

In the first issue of the organization's newsletter *S.O.N., Something Old/Something New*, editor Alf Pratte could report AJHA members at more than eighty schools and boast qualifications for bulk mailing privileges with over two hundred names on the distribution list.[9] The initial publication of the newsletter (Spring-Summer 1984) included a call for the next annual meeting at Florida A. & M. University in Tallahassee on October 3-6, 1984. Once again, a dual emphasis on teaching as well as scholarship dominated planning. John Pauly, chair of the Education Committee at that time, requested that members forward course outlines in journalism history for distribution at the meeting. The Spring-Summer 1984 *S.O.N.* also included a prospectus of the organization's journal, *American Journalism*, and a list of its advisory board which included Maurine Beasley, Maryland; Douglas Birkhead, Louisiana State; James Carey, Illinois; John Erickson, Iowa; Russell Blaine Nye, Michigan State; Sam Riley, Virginia Tech; and William David Sloan, Alabama.

One early effort used to insure wide participation and assistance with both the journal and the organization in general was the mailing of a questionnaire asking members to specify their areas of specialization and, later, to provide a brief bibliography of their work. The intent was to broaden input during the initial phases of the organization in an effort to avoid the formation of what was termed a "self-perpetuating" group, one in which only a few members would take part.[10] Most of the early correspondence warned against exclusivity and encouraged relations with other groups. In this regard both secretary David Sloan and journal editor Gary Whitby communicated directly with officers of other organizations, clarifying objectives to assure that there was no misunderstanding about the desire to work together to achieve common purposes.[11] This strategy was effective in diffusing concerns about competition and avoiding any antagonistic spirit about a new organization cropping up among the more established groups.

In this cooperative spirit the first issue of the AJHA newsletter also reported on a regional meeting of the AEJMC History Division held at the National Press Building in Washington and coordinated by Maurine Beasley, an active member of AJHA and the Society of Professional Journalists Sigma Delta Chi. Similarly, a February meeting of the West Coast Journalism Historians was noted in the newsletter with participants including board member Robert Lance of Arizona State University and AJHA Vice President Barbara Cloud, chairperson of the Department of Communication Studies at the

University of Nevada-Las Vegas, in attendance. Although there was consensus on most important issues, AJHA members experienced differences from time to time as was evidenced early regarding the choice of the name for the organization. In a preliminary report of the 1983 annual meeting, a change of name was considered since the issue had been raised and discussed at the convention. The argument was advanced that the words "American" and "Journalism" were too confining and did not account for the broader interests of the membership and allow for further growth. It was said that a name change while the organization was still in its beginning stages would be better, before the group became more widely accepted. On the other hand, those expressing a desire for focus, specificity, and the maintenance of inroads already made with the founding of the new group argued for continuance of the name American Journalism Historians Association. Three alternate names were suggested: American Media Historians Association, Communication History Association, and Journalism Historians Association. Additional arguments were considered, a mail ballot was taken and the decision was made to continue with the original name.[12] J. William Snorgrass hosted the 1984 meeting at which over fifty scholars took an active role. A total of thirty-seven participants were on the program consisting of seven panel sessions and the presentation of fifteen scholarly papers. Also at that meeting, Gary Whitby was recognized for his work in establishing *American Journalism.* Harold Davis was elected executive secretary and David Sloan was asked to take over as editor of *American Journalism.*

The Education Committee recommended in 1984 that the organization consider inviting a noteworthy historian to speak at subsequent meetings. The by-laws were amended to eliminate the requirement that the AJHA president automatically be chairman of the annual convention, although the incoming vice president had already volunteered to host the 1985 meeting. Another innovation was the publication of *Convention Proceedings* by Warren Barnard of Indiana State University and the detailed convention coverage by newsletter editor Alf Pratte of Brigham Young University, who was asked to remain in that position. Sharon Bass of the University of Kansas was selected to assist the organization with graphics for the journal and to serve as a consultant in other publishing projects.

As 1984 drew to a close, outgoing president J. Snorgrass estimated a membership approaching one hundred fifty faculty members from every state in the Union. Incoming president Barbara Cloud called it a transition period for the organization: "We are past the embryonic stage and one of our big tasks will be to develop a set of by-laws befitting an established organization, by-laws flexible enough to be responsive to members' needs but structured enough to provide a mechanism for meeting those needs."[13]

Following the earlier recommendation, President Cloud invited Dr. Daniel Czitrom of Mount Holyoke College, author of *The Media and the American Mind,* to address the 1985 convention in Las Vegas. The talk was funded by a grant from the Nevada Humanities Committee and the University of Nevada-Las Vegas. Dr. Cloud also established the precedent of offering convention participants the opportunity for insights into local journalism history by inviting H.M. Greenspun, publisher of the *Las Vegas Sun,* to deliver a luncheon address. Greenspun, whose encounters with Senator Joseph R. McCarthy are well-known, decried the loss of "gutsy journalism," pointing to fear of litigation and management by committee as the chief reasons for a decline in aggressive reporting.[14]

Both panel and research sessions in Las Vegas focused on the Western press. In addition, a special session on archival materials and a panel on depictions of journalists in popular culture highlighted the conference. In organizational matters, Roy Atwood of the University of Idaho was asked to draft proposals related to membership status and a scholarship was announced to honor the memory of Robert E. Lance who had died January 3 at the age of 49. Professor Lance who taught journalism history at Arizona State University and specialized in the history of the western press had been a member of the editorial board of *American Journalism.*

The membership selected St. Paul, Minnesota as the 1987 meeting location and also decided that meeting sites should be selected two years in advance beginning with the 1986 convention. Members were asked to propose a new name for the AJHA newsletter. More significantly, the announcement was made that *American Journalism* would increase its publication frequency to four issues per year. Rising circulation, an increase in the number of high-quality manuscripts submitted for publication, and changes in both editorial and production operations justified the increase.

The ties between AJHA and other groups were strengthened considerably with the election of Joseph McKerns as vice president. McKerns, then deputy director of the School of Journalism at Southern Illinois University-Carbondale, had been recently named editor of *Journalism Monographs,* a publication of the Association for Education in Journalism and Mass Communication. In addition, AJHA board member Maurine Beasley of the University of Maryland was appointed chairperson of the Historic Site Committee of the Society of Professional Journalists Sigma Delta Chi. Other active members included Hiley H. Ward of Temple University, editor of *Media History Digest*, published by *Editor and Publisher*, and Sidney Kobre, the author of more than fifteen books in the field who was responsible for an organizational survey of journalism history teachers.

In honor of AJHA's 1986 meeting in St. Louis, Missouri's Governor designated September 28-October 4, as Journalism History Week in the state.[15] In issuing the proclamation, Governor John Ashcroft cited the role of the field of journalism history in informing and educating the public on the function of the American press, especially the importance of the First Amendment. This theme was reinforced by the convention keynote speaker, Dr. Craig R. Smith, President of the Freedom of Expression Foundation. In his talk at the Old Courthouse in downtown St. Louis, Smith contrasted the limitations of the broadcast media to that of the newspaper press and called for reform to free the airwaves of restriction from editorialization. Two eminent scholars, both of midwestern institutions, were asked to provide a dialogue on the oral tradition and contemporary culture. Father Walter Ong, S.J., University Professor of Humanities at St. Louis University, spoke on "Plato, Writing, Print and Computers" and Professor James Carey, Dean of the College of Communications at the University of Illinois and former president of AEJMC, on "Journalism and the Oral Tradition."

At the Las Vegas meeting board members had voted to honor Sidney Kobre, author of *The Development of American Journalism* (1969) and *Reporting News in Depth* (1982), at the 1986 convention in St. Louis with an award to acknowledge his contributions to journalism history education. Professor Kenneth Kobre, a photojournalist and author of the well-known text *Photojournalism: A Professional Approach*, was asked to make the presentation to his father. Most appropriately, the award was presented at the historic Old Courthouse, location of both the Dred Scott Decision and the purchase of the first Pulitzer newspaper, the *St. Louis Post-Dispatch.*

In a brief talk to those gathered, Sidney Kobre discussed the relationship between the work of the historian and good reporting methods.[16] He pointed out how the principles and methods of Joseph Pulitzer had provided him with an example of the importance of being involved in the community "campaigning for better conditions for the reader, tackling their problems, ranging from getting a better bus system to the establishment of a two-year community college."[17] Dr. Kobre praised AJHA in helping him to establish and maintain contact with those having similar interests, pointing out that in his home town of Baltimore, a city with over two million residents, there were only one or two people with whom he could discuss journalism history or trends in the media.

Following the practice of having a local journalist address the meeting, James Lawrence, editor of the editorial page of the *St. Louis Post-Dispatch* and a Pulitzer employee for almost fifty years, discussed his career at the conference luncheon. Lawrence referred to the importance of scholarship and mentioned the work of Dr. Daniel Pfaff of Pennsylvania State University, a Pulitzer scholar and active AJHA member in attendance at the luncheon.

The increased size and level of participation at the St. Louis meeting established the need for concurrent sessions which meant that, for the first time, members had to choose between conference presentations — an unfortunate by-product of organizational growth. In spite of the increased size of the group, an informal tone was maintained. Members actively sought to host future meetings and offered service to fulfill leadership roles. New board members included Professor James Startt of Valparaiso University and Professor Charles Marler of Abilene Christian. Dr. Startt had served as chair of the Research Committee and handled paper submissions for both the Las Vegas and St. Louis meetings and Professor Marler had worked with Sidney Kobre in organizing and publishing a survey of teachers in journalism history of behalf of the association. In addition, a student-paper award had been established earlier and Deborah Shannon, a graduate student at the University of Texas, received the award in 1986 from Research Committee chairman James Startt, for her paper on the Western press.

Just prior to his death in 1987, Dr. J. William Snorgrass was re-elected to the AJHA board. A distinguished scholar and author of many works on the history of the Black press, Snorgrass had served AJHA both as president and as its first historian. A scholarship was established at his university to honor his many contributions to journalism history and AJHA also established an award in his name for a scholarship in minority journalism.

The concurrent programming of sessions and panels from the St. Louis meeting was continued the following year in St. Paul, Minnesota. AJHA president Joseph McKerns convened a dinner meeting of the Board of Directors on September 30, 1987, the opening of the sixth annual conference, on the campus of the College of St. Thomas, organized by convention host Thomas Connery of that school. Connery also arranged for the keynote speaker, Dr.

Paul L. Murphy, Professor of History and American Studies at the University of Minnesota since 1970, whose talk centered on American civil liberties.

A luncheon address was delivered by WCCO-TV anchorman Dave Moore, author of *A Member of the Family*, who for twenty-five years had been one of the Twin Cities' leading television newsmen. Moore, a critic of broadcasting, entertained the luncheon guests with stories from his book and warned against the continued growth of entertainment values and the corporate mentality of broadcast executives or what he termed "conglomermania."[18]

Papers on the "Historical Origins of the New Journalism," oral history, and journalism ethics highlighted this conference with panels on "Women and the First Amendment," and innovative research-in-progress sessions on the "American Media During the Depression" filling out the agenda. The meeting also included an invited presentation on foreign correspondents by Michael Emery, professor and chair of the Department of Journalism at California State University, Northridge, well-known as co-author of *The Press and America.*

The organization also voted to endorse the publication of a guide to sources in American journalism history to be edited by Lucy Caswell of Ohio State and asked that Barbara Cloud take over as editor of the re-named newsletter, *The Intelligencer.* As the meeting closed, president Thomas Connery announced his intention to follow-up on earlier recommendations concerning the need to revise the organization's constitution and by-laws and a spring meeting date was set with those objectives in mind.[19] In April 1988 Connery presided over a meeting for that purpose in St. Louis. At this writing, board members are considering reorganization proposals because AJHA has outgrown its initial structure. In six years the AJHA has achieved considerable recognition for a very important but traditionally undervalued area of journalism scholarship and education. Its members are among the most distinguished in the field conducting academic research, sharing this work as part of nationally-recognized meetings, and supporting superior scholarship as evidenced by this volume and *American Journalism.* Those responsible for this fast-paced growth and development can only hope that the organization will continue to prosper and fulfill its mission of making journalism and mass communication history a preeminent field of inquiry.

1. Memo from David Sloan, December 9, 1981. All personal correspondence cited in this article is part of the American Journalism Historians Association archives in the possession of the author, the organization's historian.

2. Undated letter from David Sloan. Letter to author from Sloan, July 20, 1988.

3. Ibid., 2.

4. Letter from Sidney Kobre, May 22, 1982. Letter from Harold Davis, March 31, 1982.

5. Release to Jerome Walker, managing editor of *Editor and Publisher,* from Alf Pratte, October 5, 1982. Sloan to AJHA Officers, January 5, 1983.

6. 1983 Preliminary Report, David Sloan to membership. Undated.

7. Letter to Marion Marzolf, October 7, 1982.

8. Membership mailing from David Sloan. Undated.

9. *Something Old/Something New,* Spring-Summer 1984, 1.

10. Donald Avery letter to David Sloan, October 7, 1981.

11. Whitby to Warren Francke, November 2, 1982. Sloan to James Swartz, April 9, 1985.

12. *1983-83 AJHA Report,* compiled by David Sloan and Donald Avery, 6.

13. Barbara Cloud, "1985 Outlook Good," *AJHA Proceedings,* February 1985, 1.

14. "Greenspun Decries Loss of Gutsy Journalism," *Las Vegas Sun,* October 6, 1985, 5.

15. "Missouri Governor Sets Up History Week," *Something Old/ Something New,* Summer 1986, 2.

16. "Good Journalism Historians Must Be Good Reporters," *The Intelligencer,* Winter 1985, 4.

17. Ibid. See also, "Journalist, Author Receives Historical Award," *St. Louis Globe-Democrat,* October 3, 1986, 10A.

18. Author's notes, address by Dave Moore, WCCO-Channel 4 News, Minneapolis-St. Paul, October 2, 1987.

19. "Board Meets," *The Intelligencer,* June 1988, 3.

The History of Historical Writing

Wm. David Sloan

In 1801 Noah Webster, the lexicographer and Federalist newspaper editor, toyed with the idea of compiling a history of American journalism. As with his dictionary, he wished to make a contribution to the distinctiveness of the American nation and its heritage, showing how it differed from the British and, in the process, how Americans were naturally superior. In the end, Webster did nothing more than collect material for his study, but the fact that he thought seriously about writing a history indicated an early interest among Americans in their nation's press and in its past. Even though Webster's project never reached fruition, it was only nine more years before another newspaper editor, Isaiah Thomas, published a solidly researched, detailed history.

That work, *The History of Printing in America* (1810), may fairly be claimed to be the first book-length study of any aspect of mass communication published in the United States. It is not surprising that it was a historical study. History is not only one of civilization's most universal disciplines, but also one of its oldest. The ancient Hebrews and the Greeks were telling history before the invention of writing, and the desire to keep alive the memory of the past exists with all peoples. In mass communication, therefore, it is not surprising that history should be the oldest form of research.

Like Webster, Thomas also was a Nationalist historian, as were many nineteenth-century historians who followed them. They believed that the central story of history was the continuing growth of liberty and improvement of humanity. In that story, America played a central role, for in America one could see history fulfilled. It was the nation chosen to lead the human race to perfection. In the Nationalists' history, the press was especially important, for it was one of America's key institutions. It had helped the citizens throw off tyrannical British rule, it helped safeguard the rights of a free people, and it provided information to help enlighten a whole nation.

Similarly, the Romantic historians, who began to write about journalism around the middle of the nineteenth century, believed in America as the chosen nation. They differed from the Nationalists mainly in how they told the story. Whereas Nationalists had emphasized large issues and institutions in building their explanations, Romantic historians took people, individuals, as the means of constructing their narratives. The preeminent Romantic historian was James Parton, the "Father of American Biography." Along with his books on other major American figures, twice he turned to journalism for his subjects, in 1855 for *Life of Horace Greeley* and in 1864 for *Life and Times of Benjamin Franklin.* Greeley he viewed as a leader in not only journalism but national politics as well, and Franklin he presented as a surpassingly competent businessman and the very best editor in the American colonies. Like Parton, other Romantic historians told history as human drama and achievement, written with the artist's sensitive feel for style.

During Parton's lifetime, however, a major change took place in journalism, and with it came a new perspective on journalism history. The popular "penny" press, originated by Benjamin Day's *New York Sun* in 1833, began to supplant the polemical, six-cent party newspapers. It appealed to the mass audience with a lower price and an emphasis on news, sensationalism, and entertainment. While partisan in politics, the penny press nevertheless was published autonomously from parties. Journalists and historians suddenly began to think of such journalism as the proper sort of journalism and of the history of journalism as the development of practices that had led to this modern profession.

The leader in this new journalism was the *New York Herald.* It was only natural that a member of its staff should write one of the most important historical works on the history of American newspapers. The author was Frederic Hudson, the *Herald's* managing editor; and his book, *Journalism in the United States, From 1690 to 1872,* was published in 1873. It was the first survey of journalism history written after the appearance of the penny press. A narrative detailed with character profiles of journalists and various newspaper episodes, it placed them all within the story of the origin and continuing progress of those practices associated with the penny press. Many journalism histories since Hudson's have used his developmental perspective and much of his material.

While Developmental historians had a different outlook than Nationalist and Romantic historians, they resembled them in one important feature. Most historians of all three schools were or had been working journalists and could draw on their personal experiences for their research. Those who were not journalists were educated men of means. During a time when few members of the general public had access to the types of material necessary for historical research, it was incumbent on historians to possess their own libraries or to have cultivated acquaintances and accumulated experiences they could use as sources. In the last half of the nineteenth century, therefore, one finds numerous articles and books written by journalists about people they had known and episodes in which they had participated. Whitelaw Reid of the *New York Tribune*, for example, told the life of the paper's founder in *Horace Greeley* (1879). Parke Godwin and John Bigelow, both of the *New York Evening Post*, wrote separate biographies of that newspaper's great poet-editor, each entitled *Life of William Cullen Bryant*, in 1883 and 1890 respectively. Such works as Joseph Buckingham's *Personal Memoirs and Recollections of Editorial Life* and *Specimens of Newspaper Literature, 1779-1861, With Personal Memoirs, Anecdotes, and Reminiscences*, published in 1852 and 1882 respectively, and Beman Brockway's *Fifty Years in Journalism*, in 1891, exemplified another tendency of these historians, that of writing autobiographies and memoirs to tell of the interesting people and events they had known.

The Developmental perspective has continued as the strongest since Hudson's original work, but the twentieth century can truly be called the age of the professional historian. The volume of works has multiplied infinitely, and college journalism professors and practicing journalists have contributed the bulk of them. The growth of journalism as a huge industry with a well-established, large body of professional journalists in its work force has accounted for the increase in the number of historical studies. As the news media field grew in size and took on the characteristics of a substantial, respectable institution, it became more and more acceptable as a subject for legitimate historical study. As the number of journalists working in the field increased, they began to think of themselves more and more as members of a profession, and their interest turned naturally to the history of their profession. Likewise, the growth of journalism encouraged the founding of college training programs. Even though most programs in the first half of the twentieth century emphasized instruction in practical skills, some universities encouraged their faculty members to do research, and some of those professors turned to history.

Along with the emergence of the professor as historian there occurred another trend of major importance. That was the appearance of scholarly research publications produced by academicians. In the nineteenth century, histories appeared as books or as articles in magazines such as *North American Review* and *Harper's New Monthly Magazine*. Frequently based on admirable research, they were written in a narrative style that appealed to a literate audience among the general populace. Today, popular and trade magazines still print occasional historical articles, and many books on journalism history are published each year aimed at a popular audience; but they provide the outlets for a minority of historical studies. In 1924, the medium for publication changed. In that year, the fledgling American Association of Teachers of Journalism (now the Association for Education in Journalism and Mass Communication) began publishing the *Journalism Bulletin* (now *Journalism Quarterly*). It was intended as an outlet for essays and research articles by professors. With time it became a refereed, footnoted research journal. Over its life, it probably has published almost as many articles on journalism history as most other publications combined. It presented limitations to historians, however, such as restrictions on article lengths which made the development of a narrative difficult, and in 1974 the Department of Journalism at the University of California-Northridge began publication of *Journalism History*, which specialized in research articles and essays on the state of historical study. In 1982 a group of professors formed the American Journalism Historians Association. The following year it began publishing *American Journalism*, a quarterly journal emphasizing longer articles than either *Journalism Quarterly* or *Journalism History* allowed. Since these journals are oriented toward an academic audience, in 1980 the trade publication *Editor and Publisher* initiated a quarterly magazine entitled *Media History Digest* aimed at the professional and general audience. Studies of the print media have predominated in the aforementioned journals. In 1957 the *Journal of Broadcasting* began publication and has printed a number of historical articles on electronic media. Along with such journals focusing on journalism, journals outside the field also publish articles on journalism history. The number of articles appearing, however, somewhere other than in *American Journalism*,

Journalism History, and *Journalism Quarterly* are comparatively few.

The fact that most journalism historians have been either journalism professors or professional journalists has had two distinctive effects on the study of history. First, the Developmental perspective continued its strong hold throughout most of this century. That was natural, since professional journalists identified closely with their profession and accepted its practices as the proper ones. Likewise, most professors came out of a background in professional journalism and retained that perspective when writing history. Both sets of historians considered the history of journalism to be the chronology of how the press had progressed and how "proper" journalism had been practiced at particular times in the past.

The second effect was in the level of sophistication that these historians brought to their research. Most had not been trained in historical methods, and their research revealed the inadequacy of their methods. Perhaps because they had worked as journalists, they tended to apply the techniques of journalism to historical study. That resulted in attempts to research subjects in short time spans, superficial collection and examination of materials, and writing that tended simply to piece together collections of facts with little analysis or insightful explanation. Such efforts compared unfavorably with research which trained historians outside journalism conducted — and which historians must undertake for meaningful results. Few journalism historians have been willing to devote several years to one subject and to mine the primary sources beyond the perfunctory ones of newspaper pages, or had the inclination or talent to write historical narrative in a style that deviates from the mechanical approach of news writing.

Fortunately, some very useful reference works are now being published to assist the historian in the search for material. This particular book, *Guide to Sources in American Journalism History,* provides an invaluable tool in the quest for primary sources. Using those sources is mandatory, and such a guide is thus indispensable. Of secondary sources and the body of literature published on particular historical topics, journalism historians, unfortunately, too often have possessed little more than a cursory knowledge, so that all too commonly they have relied on such items as survey history textbooks for references to specialized historical topics, when in most instances a number of books and articles have been written on the topics. Familiarity with the historical literature is essential. Two works published by Greenwood Press will prove helpful.   Researchers will find Richard A. Schwarzlose's *Newspapers: A Reference Guide* (Greenwood Press, 1987) particularly useful. It lists almost 1,700 books about the newspaper field, many of which are on history. Even more detailed is *American Journalism History: An Annotated Bibliography* (Greenwood Press, forthcoming) which will include more than 2,600 books and articles.

Considerable blame for the methodological inadequacy of journalism historians may be placed on the nature of graduate training. Until the 1940s, history occupied a prominent place in graduate programs, but in recent decades the emphasis has shifted to the social and behavioral sciences. Training in mass communication research has been directed at such methods as experiments and surveys, neither of which has much applicability for the study of history. Most textbooks on methods have given little more than passing notice to historical research; and most teachers of methods, trained as they are in social and behavioral aspects of communication, have little comprehension of historical practice. The result is that graduate research courses spend little time on historical research methods. When ninety-five percent of the class is devoted to methods for conducting non-historical research such as experiments in attitude change, it is not surprising that students have not mastered historical methods, or, as frequently happens, that they have been convinced that historical research is not really quite legitimate in communication study. Yet, scholars who consider themselves journalism historians have little excuse for not being acquainted with historical methods. Manuals such as Louis Gottschalk's *Understanding History* and Jacques Barzun and Henry F. Graff's *The Modern Researcher* have been available for years. Although the manuals have not dealt specifically with journalism history, the methods they explain can be adapted quite easily to journalism.

Unfortunately, in historical research in journalism, one can virtually count on one hand the useful works. The most detailed discussion of methods remains Lucy Maynard Salmon's *The Newspaper and the Historian*, published in 1923. Considering newspapers as invaluable sources for historical research, it offered guidelines that historians should apply when considering the validity and reliability of newspapers. That work was followed some two decades later by one of the most useful articles addressing a particular aspect of newspaper research, Frank Luther Mott's "Evidences of Reliability in Newspapers and Periodicals in Historical Studies," published in 1944 in *Journalism Quarterly*. Like Salmon's work, it listed characteristics of newspapers which the historian should consider as indications of how reliable individual papers may be as historical sources.

Textbooks on communication research methods occasionally included discussions of historical methods, but in general their treatments were cursory. The first text dealing exclusively with communication history research was John Stevens and Hazel Dicken Garcia's *Communication History*, published in 1980. While calling for more rigorous application of research methods, its main effort was to urge historians to use new interpretative perspectives in explaining the past. Among the better works discussing historical method was Guido H. Stempel III and Bruce H. Westley's *Research Methods in Mass Communication*, published in 1981, to which various authors contributed chapters, including two on history. One of them, David Paul Nord and Harold L. Nelson's "The Logic of Historical Research," consisted simply of a personalized essay on the nature of history. Mary Ann Yodelis Smith's chapter on "The Method of History" offered suggestions on methodology, including formulating research questions, determining the authenticity of research material, and analyzing the data. Because of the limited number of pages which could be allotted to the chapter, however, Professor Smith was unable to provide detailed guidance on those topics.

Despite journalism historians' traditional failings in methodology, for various reasons journalism scholars and publishers in recent years have shown a growing interest in research methods. One result is a forthcoming book entitled *Historical Methods in Mass Communication*, an entry in the series of advanced textbooks published by Lawrence Erlbaum Associates. Its senior author, James D. Startt, is a professor of history at Valparaiso University who specializes in historical methods. The book is the first applying the full range of historical methods to journalism research. As such, it offers the potential finally to make historical methods generally familiar to journalism historians.

While blissfully ignoring research methods, journalism historians in the twentieth century have given increasing attention to the interpretative approaches that they might use to explain the past. For the most part, their recommendations have concentrated on examining the media within their cultural or social context. It may seem odd, however — although it is not surprising — that no historian ever wrote a treatise explaining the dominant, Developmental interpretation historians have provided for journalism. That no historian writing from that perspective, which has accounted for about fifty to sixty per cent of all works on journalism history, would explain it is natural. Developmental historians were so accustomed to thinking of journalism history as the chronicle of progress from seminal practices to the advanced present, that they thought such an explanation was only natural. They did not have an inkling, as far as I can detect, that their explanation was simply a perspective and was only one among several possible ways one can look at the past.

It was precisely the Developmental interpretation's pervasiveness, however, that prompted a few historians to call for new approaches. Although the pleas for taking sociological/cultural perspectives appear to have come as a reaction to the dominance of the Developmental interpretation, those historians pleading for change, like their Developmental counterparts, never seemed to have grasped what the perspective really was that underlay traditional journalism history. They recognized only certain of its features and called it by such names as "great man" history, or "whig" history, or simply "history" history. The suggestions for taking a sociological/cultural approach can be traced through several prominent essays.

The line had its origin in a chapter written by Robert E. Park, "The Natural History of the Newspaper," for the book *The City*, published in 1925. A sociologist, Park argued that the history of newspapers was not the story of how individuals had willed papers to take on certain characteristics. He spoke instead of the "natural history" of newspapers in their sociological, economic, and political settings and implied that their growth had parallels to biological evolution. "The newspaper," he said, "like the modern city, is not wholly a rational product. No one sought to make it just what it is. In spite of all the efforts of individual men and generations of men to control it and to make it something after their own heart, it has continued to grow and change in its own incalculable ways.

"The type of newspaper that exists is the type that has survived under the conditions of modern life .... The natural history of the press is the history of this surviving species. It is an account of the conditions under which the existing newspaper has grown up and taken form .... The struggle for existence, in the case of the newspaper, has been a struggle for circulation."[1]

Park's interpretative approach was applied most fully to newspaper history in Alfred E. Lee's *The Daily Newspaper in America: The Evolution of a Social Instrument*, published in 1937. Like Park, Lee also was a sociologist who believed that impersonal, automatically acting social forces, rather than great individuals, had determined the historical changes that molded the nature of the newspaper. To explain the historic changes in newspapers, he, like Park, also resorted to the biological theory of evolution, which a number of sociologists had attempted to adapt to theories of social change. American newspapers, Lee said, had gone through an evolutionary growth marked throughout history by a process of invention of or variation from methods, selective elimination of less effective methods, and transmission of effective methods to other newspapers.

The third prominent contribution to the sociological interpretation was made by Sidney Kobre, a journalist with a doctoral degree in sociology who would become one of the most prolific historians the journalism field had produced. In a 1945 article entitled "The Sociological Approach in Research in Newspaper History," Kobre recommended that historians should place their emphasis on the political, economic, geographical, technological, cultural, and social factors and chronology of the internal workings of the press. They should not treat the press, he said, as an isolated institution but should relate it to society. His sociological approach, like that of Park and Lee, was to study the newspaper as a changing, evolving social institution.

While not using the word "sociological," the eminent political historian Allan Nevins, a journalist who had risen to the position of president of the American Historical Association, called on journalism historians to give more consideration to the press in its role in American democracy and politics. In a 1959 article entitled "American Journalism and Its Historical Treatment," Nevins suggested that journalism history should be studied in terms of its "relation to the workings of democratic government," for "a vigorous democracy and a vigorous free journalism have the closest interrelationships, so that one cannot exist without the other. This interdependence is the central theme in the history of the press in any free country."[2]

Although blessed with the names of these prominent scholars, the suggestions for taking new approaches to history did not gain many adherents among historians. By the 1970s, however, the intellectual milieu was ripe for change. A number of younger historians with only short tenures in newspaper offices, and therefore with less devotion to the trade than their predecessors possessed, were ready to divorce themselves from the pro-journalism, trade-oriented Developmental interpretation. Educated in mass communication theory but not enamored of the quantitative research methods that served as its handmaiden, instructed in qualitative methods but not informed in historical ones, they awaited a new explanation. The revelation came in the form of an article by James Carey in the inaugural issue of the journal *Journalism History*. Entitled "The Problem of Journalism History" and published in 1974, it became the most conspicuous of recent works.[3] Because of its prominence and its influence, it deserves special attention.

Carey suggested that historians could best explain journalism as a form of "consciousness" in what he called "cultural" history. In studying journalism history, he wrote, "we are principally studying a way in which men in the past have grasped reality."[4] Journalism was important in the process because it was one of the primary means by which people formed their ideas and awareness of the world. "Consciousness" pervaded journalism, beginning with how journalism was practiced and continuing with how it operated on the minds of the audience. That is, journalists used certain practices because of the ideas they held. Journalism then affected the audience's "attitudes, emotions, motives ... expectations ... imagination ... structure of feeling," etc., for journalism "is essentially a state of consciousness, a way of apprehending, of experiencing the world."[5]

Carey's idea generated much interest and widespread acclamation. Essayists and devotees of Carey, who found him to be intellectually stimulating and personally appealing, flocked to him as journalism history's philosophical leader. It is no exaggeration to say that the name "Carey" and the term "cultural" took on a special significance. Many were the historians who invoked those words to imbue their articles and conference papers with respectability. Yet in spite of such recognition, Carey's cultural approach has led to few solid historical studies in my opinion.

There are a number of reasons for the interpretation's failure to produce fruits. On a most elementary level, some historians who acknowledged it failed to understand it. Without analyzing what Carey proposed, they appear to have assumed that he meant simply that the press should be examined in the context of its cultural/social milieu (as good historians always have done). While Carey made his meaning clear, part of the fault for the misunderstanding nevertheless can be cast on his selection of terms. In historical study the term "cultural" traditionally had been used to refer to the social and cultural context in which the past took place. Carey altered the word "cultural" to mean something else, specifically "the organization of social experience in the consciousness of men manifested in symbolic action."[6] The concept which he proposed — ideas, how people grasp reality, and so forth

— usually has been designated by historians as either the "history of ideas" or "intellectual history." Its most notable advocate was the philosopher R.G. Collingwood, who said that the primary task of historical study is to discover the thoughts that motivated actions.[7] Stating the concept in another way, the British historian F.M. Powicke wrote that "historical events ... cannot be separated from what we call mind."[8] In the field of communication, it resembles general semanticists' concept of "perception of reality." They assume that an individual's perception of reality is determined by the verbal messages one receives, an assumption quite similar to Carey's. His selection of the word "cultural" therefore muddied his idea.

A second reason for the weakness of the research that the "cultural" approach generated has little to do with the approach itself. It stems from the nature of the relationship that existed between Professor Carey and his followers. Many held him in such high esteem that they accepted his proposal without evaluating it critically. Having not examined it for possible weaknesses, they therefore did not recognize those that it had. When they later considered applying it to historical research, those weaknesses either posed difficult barriers to surmount or created flaws which could not be cured. Among a circle of journalism historians, acceptance of Carey's proposal also discouraged consideration of critiques or alternatives to it.

The most difficult problem the concept presents, however, is this: how does the historian discover past "consciousness"? There is little "evidence" other than the content of the media. It is an unjustified leap of scholarly faith, however, to assume that because a news report (the primary fact of Carey's research material) appeared in print it "forged" (to use Carey's word) the consciousness of an individual. It is a second leap then to assume that because journalism constructed the consciousness of one individual the historian can conclude that the consciousness of any other individual also was affected. The problem in Carey's approach is the same one that all historians confront: one must have evidence. In attempting to analyze the relationship between journalism and human thought, however, the problem is simply much more vast. What evidence is necessary for the historian to determine that a newspaper report influenced human thinking? If the historian could find evidence that one person's consciousness had any relationship to journalism, the historian then would need to find evidence for a second person, and a third, and a fourth .... Since "cultural" historians have tended to deal with the consciousness of the aggregate population, one has to ask how many individual consciousnesses must the historian discover before making the jump to the aggregate? What evidence is available for one individual? In journalism history, anyone who has attempted to do research knows that few people have left records indicating that what they read in a newspaper influenced their thinking. It is true that many statements remain expressing fear that weaker or less principled minds might be affected adversely by sensational or partisan newspaper material. But they provide no evidence, relying instead only on the type of intuition that "cultural" historians have wound up having to lean on. As a result, their studies have concentrated on the material appearing in the media, and then they have made the leap of faith to forged consciousness. They have done little more than what mediocre historical research has always done: collect items from newspapers to discover what people said. Such "reaction" history has been lamented for years by historians aware of what good historical research requires. "Cultural" historians have simply added to that problem by assuming without evidence that media content somehow equates with forged human consciousness.

Another disquieting method has tended to be popular with "cultural" historians. To a greater extent than most other historians, they have taken an *a priori* approach to the past. Convinced that the "cultural" theory provides the best explanation of the past, they have begun with the theory rather than with the particular facts of the past. Thus they have used the theory to determine the selection of material to be considered and the meaning to give to particular facts. In other instances, unfortunately, the preeminence of theory has had even worse consequences. Some historians have built their studies on a meager number of primary sources or on nothing more than a few secondary sources. Such, it appears, they assume to be adequate to prove how history molded itself to their theory. History has become separated from the concrete reality of the past, and some historians speak of the "symbolic meaning of communication" as the essence of the past. That line of thinking has led to a specious assumption. If the symbol is preeminent, then we must wonder if a real past, made up of real, particular events, facts, and people, ever existed. Despite what these "cultural" historians have implied, both scientists and philosophers as well as most historians assure us that objective reality does exist — and that it must exist if we are to be able to study it.

Despite its shortcomings, Professor Carey's essay had some exceedingly positive benefits. It encouraged historians to reconsider traditional historical approaches, and it contributed to vigorous discussions about the state of historical study. It also offered a proposal for one way of approaching journalism history which seems, to this author at least, quite useful. The challenge is to determine how it can be applied using acceptable methods of historical research and to recognize that it offers only one among many ways of looking at the past.

Along with Carey's cultural approach, a number of other influences have been working actively in journalism history in recent years. Among the most noticeable has been an increased emphasis on women's and minority history. More aware of female and minority issues today, historians have been quite prolific in addressing their role in journalism in the past. The minority groups receiving most attention have been Black, Native American, and Mexican-American journalists. Most historians have approached these subjects admiringly, using as their thesis that although historians have overlooked the subject, these people performed well under difficult circumstances and made contributions not only to journalism, but also to their own group and to American life. A central theme in women's history has been to document the accomplishments of women journalists, and a substantial number of works have dealt with the particular conditions that female journalists faced and the unique influence they brought to journalism because of their perspectives as women. Most historians who have studied female journalists were women, and several have made substantial contributions to the field. Some of the more notable work is typified by that of Susan Henry on colonial newspaper printers, Sherilyn Cox Bennion on frontier women, and Maurine Beasley on twentieth-century journalists.

Historians of minority journalism have concentrated primarily on bringing attention to individuals and media activities that traditional Anglo-American-oriented history has overlooked. Foremost among the studies have been those of Black journalists. Historians began to study them in the late nineteenth century, and today the field comprises a substantial body of both reference works and historical studies covering subjects from the first Black American newspaper (*Freedom's Journal*, founded in 1827) to contemporary media. Study of Native American and Spanish-language journalism is a much more recent phenomenon. Those subjects began to receive substantial attention from journalism historians only in the 1970s. After much early activity, studies of Native American journalism now being produced have diminished in number. On the other hand, it is not unlikely that as Mexican-Americans begin to make up larger proportions of the United States population, studies of Spanish-language journalism will increase.

Continuing research on women and minority groups cannot help but add to the vitality of journalism history. With time, studies of those subjects probably will become more detached (as has happened with the study of Black journalism history), and the contributions that the research makes to historical understanding will grow more insightful.

Predicting the future is difficult, whether one is an astrologer or a journalism historian. Assessing present conditions is a little easier. In reflecting on the study of journalism history during the last two decades or so, one notes encouraging signs. The appearance of new journals specializing in journalism history, the publication of a number of research and reference books dealing with the study of journalism history, the founding of the American Journalism Historians Association, the vitality of historians' reflection on their craft — all are positive signs about its health. Historians do need to be more aware of various facets of historiography and to devote more effort to mastering historical research methods. Even in those areas, however, the last few years have shown reassuring improvement. It is not being too hopeful to think that within the next decade the study of history, the oldest form and the cornerstone of mass communication research, will ascend to its rightful place as the capstone of modern scholarship.

1. Robert E. Park, "The Natural History of the Newspaper," in Park, Ernest W. Burgess and Robert D. McKenzier, *The City* (Chicago: University of Chicago Press, 1925), 80.

2. Allan Nevins, "American Journalism and Its Historical Treatment," *Journalism Quarterly*, 36 (Fall 1959): 411.

3. James W. Carey, "The Problem of Journalism History," *Journalism History*, 1 (1974): 3-5, 27.

4. Ibid., 5.

5. Ibid., 4-5

6. Ibid., 5.

7. R.G. Collingwood, *The Idea of History* (Oxford: Clarendon Press, 1946).

8. F.M. Powicke, *History, Freedom and Religion* (1938): 6.

9. The works of these three historians are too numerous to list in their entirety, but the following are representative:
   Susan Henry's articles have been based to a large extent on her doctoral dissertation, "Notes Toward the Liberation of Journalism History: A Study of Five Women Printers in Colonial America" (Syracuse University, 1976). Her underlying

approach is explained most cogently in "Colonial Woman Printer as Prototype: Toward a Model for the Study of Minorities," *Journalism History*, 3 (1976): 20-24.

Sherilyn Cox Bennion has been the most prolific historian of the female frontier journalist. In numerous articles she has pointed out the importance of this topic for historical study. Typifying her body of work are such articles as "Early Western Publications Expose Women's Suffrage Cries," *Matrix*, 64 (Summer 1979): 6-9; "Women Suffrage Papers of the West, 1869-1914," *American Journalism*, 3 (1986): 125-141; and "A Working List of Women Editors of the 19th Century West," *Journalism History*, 7 (1980): 60-65.

Maurine Beasley's work has focused primarily on the professional performance of female journalists. Her body of research includes such works as *Eleanor Roosevelt and the Media: A Public Quest for Self-Fulfillment* (Urbana: University of Illinois Press, 1987) and "A 'Front Page Girl' Covers the Lindberg Kidnaping: An Ethical Dilemma," *American Journalism*, 1 (1) (1983): 63-74.

Selected Bibliography

Altschull, J. Herbert. "The Journalist and Instant History: An Example of the Jackal Syndrome." *Journalism Quarterly*, 50 (1973): 389-96.

Bashin, Bryan Jay. "How TV Stations Are Trashing History." *Columbia Journalism Review* (May/June 1985): 51-54.

Beasley, Maurine, and Richard R. Harlow. "Oral History: Additional Tool for Journalism Historians." *Journalism History*, 7 (1980): 38-39.

Boyce, D.C. "Public Opinion and Historians." *History, the Journal of the Historical Association*, (June 1978): 214-28.

Dahl, Folke. "On Quoting Newspapers: A Problem and a Solution." *Journalism Quarterly*, 25 (1948): 331-38.

Endres, Kitty. "Oral History: Preserving a Multimedia Past." *Matrix*, 65 (Spring 1980): 8-10.

Henry, Susan J. "Private Lives: An Added Dimension for Understanding Journalism History." *Journalism History*, 6 (1979): 98-102.

Housman, Robert T. "Journalism Research in Relation to Regional History." *Journalism Quarterly*, 13 (1936): 402-406.

Kobre, Sidney. "The Sociological Approach to Research in Newspaper History." *Journalism Quarterly*, 22 (March 1945): 12-22.

Lee, Alfred E. *The Daily Newspaper in America*. New York: Macmillan, 1937.

Mott, Frank Luther. "Evidences of Reliability in Newspapers and Periodicals in Historical Studies." *Journalism Quarterly*, 21 (1944): 304-10.

Nevins, Allan. "American Journalism and Its Historical Treatments." *Journalism Quarterly*, 36 (Fall 1959): 411-422, 519.

Rapport, Leonard. "Fakes and Facsimiles: Problems of Identification." *American Antiquarian*, 42 (January 1979): 13-58.

Salmon, Lucy Maynard. *The Newspaper and the Historian*. New York: Oxford University Press, 1923.

Schwarzlose, Richard A. "A Plea from Amid the Letter Boxes."*Journalism History*, 1 (1974): 50-51.

Startt, James D., and Wm David Sloan *Historical Methods in Mass Communication.* Hillsdale NJ: Lawrence Erlbaum, 1989.

Stempel, Guido H. III, and Bruce H. Westley, eds. *Research Methods in Mass Communication.* Englewood Cliffs NJ: Prentice-Hall, 1981.

Taft, William H. *Newspapers as Tools for Historians.* Columbia MO: Lucas Brothers, 1970.

Ward, Jean. "Interdisciplinary Research and Journalism Historians." *Journalism History*, 5 (1978): cover, 17-19.

New Directions for Research in Journalism History

John J. Pauly

Though historians have often relied on journalistic records, their research has rarely done justice to journalism as an activity in its own right. Historians are, of course, among the first to recognize the shortcomings of newspapers, magazines, and broadcasts as documentary records. But those same scholars too often fail to address a larger intellectual problem: their own tendency to treat journalism as a secondary phenomenon, a mere reflection of other, more real issues such as "public opinion." For the historian a forage through the press may provide some undependable facts, lively quotes, or colorful descriptions of notable events. Too rarely does it provide an occasion for studying journalism as an institutionalized ritual by which society each day calls itself into existence.

Here, then, is the special task (and the special opportunity) of the journalism historian. For at least two centuries now, journalism has documented the making and unmaking of modern societies. It has told of all the strategies by which societies identify themselves, offer models of reality, set the bounds of normal behavior, dramatize conflicts between competing groups, legitimize power, and chart the future. The goal of this essay is to help historians listen to journalism's stories more carefully. My approach, though surely not the only one, leans heavily on the work of an unlikely band of Americans – sociologists such as Erving Goffmann, Hugh Duncan, and Anselm Strauss, the literary critic Kenneth Burke, the anthropologist Clifford Geertz, the cultural historian Robert

Darnton, the philosopher Richard Rorty, and the mass communication theorist James Carey.[1] Despite significant differences in approach and temper, these thinkers share a concern with meaning, interpretation, myth, and story — that whole ensemble of symbolizing practices anthropologists call *culture.* Journalism offers an ideal site for studying culture because it is modernity's center stage, the place where groups contend over the meaning of persons, places, events, and policies.

One advantage of a cultural approach is that it enables journalism historians to break the intellectual shackles forged, perhaps inadvertently, by the early classics of the field. Like most Americans, journalism historians have been captivated by the quest for freedom. They have cheered the victories of the "free press," memorialized its heroes, and celebrated the codification of press freedom in the law of the land.[2] The history-law axes have even mapped the occupational sociology of journalism history, as when American universities advertise for faculty to teach history-law, assuming a close tie between the two. A cultural approach, while it recognizes legal studies as intrinsically worthwhile and important, draws on sociological and literary methods to articulate more forcefully journalism's character as a symbolizing practice. From the vantage of cultural studies, law cannot claim to be the final or decisive result of historically realized natural rights. Law is simply one aspect of the sociology of the press, or, even better, one of the literatures modern people create in order to explain journalism to themselves.

One reason for recasting the terms of journalism history is to demonstrate that much work remains to be done. For too long historians glumly assumed that they could do little but add details to the earlier work of Mott, Emery, Bleyer, Kobre, and others. Journalism history is beginning to overcome the cloying and premature sense of closure. Our prospects are exciting if we choose to understand journalism in its full complexity, not as a reflection of "ideas" whose real home is elsewhere nor as a mere vehicle for transmitting more or less accurate "information," but as a form of cultural midwifery through which society is born and nurtures itself. Journalism historians need not imagine their work as a dreary trek through an archival swamp or a goose-step down the narrow road to certainty. It can as easily be an amble through the woods, in search of the wellsprings of our humanity.

A cultural approach treats journalism history as one form of communication history. By communication I mean the social processes by which human beings constitute, maintain, and celebrate shared models of reality.[3] I take it as given that humans live largely within the webs of significance spun by their own acts of communication. This emphasis on symbolmaking underscores humans' propensity (and biological need) to *produce* reality through language, as well as language's propensity to produce particular forms of humanity. Humans literally make sense using symbols, and are subsequently made over by their symbols, so that language provides a very model of how our humanness operates in the world.

Given the abstruse irrelevance of much communication theory, perhaps journalism historians can be forgiven for paying so little attention to it. After all, journalism only vaguely resembles the senders, receivers, messages, channels, and feedback loops of conventional communication theory, no matter how obscurely theorists try to clarify that model with boxes, circles, and arrows. Just who, for example, is the "sender" of a newspaper story? The reporter? Editor? Publisher? Source? What is the "message" that a news story carries? In one sense there is no message, for each story is but one result of a complex, ongoing collaboration between organizational routines, budget constraints, social pressures, professional aspirations, and literary conventions. Moreover, all the "facts" in a message are inextricably embedded in stories. Even when journalists publicly proclaim their devotion to "information," they remain storytellers, and their work resounds with the echoes of other stories that the society tells itself. As a result the "receiver" may interpret a published or broadcast story in an astonishing variety of ways. The same investigative expose, for different audiences, might signify the triumph of shoe-leather research methods, an invasion of privacy, the potential promotion of a newsroom rival, the possibility of a Pulitzer Prize, a crisis in the ethics of the profession, or the beginning of a criminal prosection or civil suit. To define communication in such a story as the information that a sender intentionally transmits to a receiver is to miss most of the action.

Rather than force their work into the little boxes of communication theory, journalism historians need methods that respect the open-ended and indeterminate quality of the communication process. Historians might better imagine their research as successive takes on or replays of the scene of communication — from different angles, through different lenses, at different speeds, with different actors in view, and under rather different styles of off-camera direction. In each take the historian rehearses the possibilities of a different language of interpretation. The three key terms or takes that I suggest that historians use are *product, practice,* and *commentary.* Each term captures a distinctive aspect of journalism without denying other aspects. Because these terms identify commonalities that journalism shares with other forms of mass communication and popular culture, they allow the historian to borrow insights and methods from related fields.

Understanding journalism as a *product* is not as simple as it first seems. Because journalism has long been a manufactured good, historians must contend with its character as a commodity. Analyzing journalism as a commodity means acting, for the moment, as though it were contentless. Such contentless analysis highlights journalism's technological and industrial character, as a manufactured good analogous to other goods. For journalism the relevant technologies have included printing presses, platemaking techniques, typewriting and typesetting machines, the telegraph and telephone, paper and film, cameras, satellites, and computers. These technologies and others have defined deadlines for finishing stories, spaces and times for displaying stories, routines for competently preparing stories, and aesthetic standards for judging the work of others. Such technological analysis by historians should also consider the social and aesthetic conventions that Lewis Mumford calls *technics,* which modern societies have often mechanized even in the absence of machines. A list of the technics that have played a crucial role in the history of journalism would include "inventions" such as shorthand, the interview, the inverted pyramid story form, the beat, the cutaway shot, and the voice-over.

Because powerful modern technologies ultimately "legislate" their own forms of social order, part of the historian's task is to explain how and why journalism's technologies of production, dissemination and consumption assume their characteristic organizational form.[4] For example, Raymond Williams, in a brief survey of the history of television technology, notes that the individual technical components of television were available long before society imagined television as a technological system. Williams argues that that is the typical pattern for virtually all communication systems. Each is the product of a "crucial community of selected emphasis and support," the result of using invention to dream new forms of society.[5] Following Williams' lead historians need to understand journalism's technologies as the projection of imagination, desire, and, at times, the will to power.[6]

As part of their contentless analysis, historians must explain the economics of journalism, too. A thorough economic analysis of a news organization or magazine should account for internal operations as well as the external legal, business, and regulatory environments within which organizations operate.   Such an analysis might include studies of wages and material costs, budgets, resource allocation, income sources, expenses, marketing and sales strategies, pricing policies, labor relations, and technologically inspired efficiencies such as standardization or work speed-ups. Finally, historians need to study general economic conditions, competition within an organization's market, the effect of laws and regulation, demographic and income shifts, and transformations in cognate industries or trades.   The lack of available or extant internal records has unfortunately hindered   historical studies of the economics of periodicals or broadcast organizations.[7] Nevertheless, some historians have pieced together a picture of economic practices using data such as trade journals and convention reports, autobiographies, and legislative committee investigations.[8]

Contentless analysis can suggest surprising parallels between the business practices of journalism and those of other organizations in the economy.   For example, in trying to explain journalists' increasing use of the inverted pyramid story in the nineteenth century, historians have often fallen back on a vague technological determinism. They have said the telegraph encouraged the inverted pyramid form as a way to compress stories and make them cheaper to transmit.   Or they have argued that the inverted pyramid was a natural evolution, a response to readers' new taste for ever more up-to-date news. But one might, hypothetically at least, treat the inverted pyramid as a technic adapted to the commercial daily newspaper's search for profits. The inverted pyramid offered editors managerial flexibility by making reporters standardized, interchangeable parts. Equipped with a standardized narrative model, any reporter could be counted on to do a minimally competent story (that is, one within the editor's range of tolerance). The inverted pyramid's simplicity allowed news organizations, then as now, to hire low-paid, easily replaceable workers.

Despite the value of such economic insights, everyone knows that journalism is more than a contentless commodity.   It is also a symbolic product, and technological and economic analysis cannot fully explain journalism as a *style* of imagination or storytelling. Continuing with the example of the inverted pyramid, a historian might note that that form has been an aesthetic convention, with pleasures of its own, as well as a tool of managerial control. A story "told right," under deadline pressure, with a hint of grace or imagination snuck past the copyeditor, can be intrinsically satisfying for a journalist, even when organizational imperatives have dictated the story's slant or tone. Because journalism is only partially (even if sometimes decisively) determined by available technology, economic pressures, and managerial demands, the historian must find terms of analysis that explain journalism's pleasures as a *narrative* form.

Until recently the most common method for studying stories was content analysis.[9] Though arithmetic data, and perhaps even inferential statistics, have their place in journalism history, content analysis only marginally illuminates narrative form. The problems with content analysis are many and well-documented.[10] That technique requires the researcher to identify themes or topics that can be counted in a representative sample of stories. Though it allows the researcher to generalize over massive bodies of data, content analysis usually misses the way journalism actually works. Themes or topics do not exist in the abstract but are embedded in narrative structures. The presence of a "theme," or even of a measure of its positive, neutral, or negative treatment, says little about how that theme was woven into a story, or about its connections to a culture's other forms of storytelling. Historians are likely to consider the social scientist's operational definition of such themes arbitrary or, at worst, disconnected from the definitions of both journalist and audience The very nature of news renders futile the social scientist's attempts to identify a representative sample of stories. There is no "natural" or "normal" agenda of daily stories against which to judge divergence from the mean (beyond an organization's conscious decision to set the size of the hole for different types of news). At best content analysis often documents trends that could be discovered through other, less expensive, forms of research. Content analysis hopes to minimize the interpretive biases of individual readers or viewers by devising methods of interjudge reliability. But in the end the content analysis researcher, like everyone else, must interpret, inventing an explanation of what the presence or absence of a theme or topic means. The statistics themselves offer no sure guide to how to construct such an interpretation.

Despite all of these problems, some historical researchers have profitably used content analysis. Their studies typically employ that method as one form of evidence with a full awareness of its limits.[11] For example, for his recent history of media coverage of the Vietnam War, Daniel Hallin constructed an extraordinarily elaborate coding scheme for identifying themes in news programs.[12] He coded forty-nine variables, such as "Primary Subject of Story," "Film of Demonstrations and Organizing," and "Type of Reference to Casualties," often with dozens of subvariables in each category.

Because of the cumbersomeness of his categories and the potential cost of training other coders, Hallin did all the coding himself. He accepts the possibility of some coding bias in order to examine the entire sample of stories. In the end he uses his profile of the most common story types to confirm his other evidence. As in Hallin's study, modestly defended content analysis might help answer important questions about large-scale patterns of coverage.

Journalism historians, noting that statistical analysis merely changes the form interpretation takes, might well opt for more traditional styles of analysis. But recent developments in literary and social theory have heightened researchers' sensitivity to the ways in which writers write and readers read.[13] In general historians need to account more carefully for journalism's narrative qualities. They might begin by noting that style is in part a matter of genre and shared craft sense. In other words, apprentice journalists learn to write the types of stories journalists write. Journalism returns time and again to recurring and standardized genres such as the speech, police report, human interest story, and feature profile. Aspiring reporters learn that repertoire from classroom training, editors' criticisms, colleagues' examples and advice, and their own observation of the organization's performance. Generic form lends itself to commodity as well as narrative analysis, for popular story types perform an important marketing function reducing producers' risks and uncertainty by capitalizing on previously successful narrative strategies.

Beyond noting its reliance on genres, historians must probe journalism's connections to other forms of social imagination and discourse. Any individual work constantly betrays its ties to other languages, codes, and forms of culture, a quality literary critics call *intertextuality*. In effect, intertextuality is about the ways in which texts comment on each other. For example, the historian Robert Darnton, reflecting on his own early experience as a *New York Times* reporter, has noted that journalists write with a sense of their membership in an occupational group. That world of significant others, Darnton says, may be editors, colleagues in the organization, or even former masters of the craft to whose status journalists aspire.[14] In practice, then, reporters may write with rather different audiences in mind — that detail included to keep the editor quiet, this turn of phrase to impress a newsroom colleague, an ironic twist there to remind the cognescenti of a Great Reporter of the Past or to satisfy the reporter's sense of self. The text tells not only of its topic, but of the identity moves of the author and the social worlds that validate those moves.

Understanding intertextuality necessarily implicates the historian in an act of reading. There is no one shared and indisputable way in which all historians can (or should) conduct such reading — a fact which bothers the advocates of content analysis. Whatever the differences in styles of reading, however, the conscientious historian will likely proceed through several steps. First, the historian must carefully describe the text itself, noting its scene, actors, acts, plot, patterns of motivation, and logic.[15] Second, the historian must note patterns of figurative language, such as recurring symbols or tropes that structure the text. Third, the historian must connect the world of the text to the society that produced it and that the text purports to articulate. Finally, the historian must allow a place for the reader's role in creating and recreating the text, for meaning is possible only because of conventionalized understandings between writer and reader, ranging from shared ideologies to familiar genres to taken-for-granted conventions such as story length or placement.[16]

The stages I have identified roughly duplicate the hermeneutic method favored by Paul Ricoeur and others.[17] The steps are not entirely discrete. They simply trace the interpreter's moves from surface detail to structural analysis to intertextual connections to relevant worlds at large. There are no guarantees, no statistical assurances, about the reliability of the final result. Each interpretation simply meets another. If a "better" interpretation emerges from that encounter, we necessarily fall back again on metaphors to describe why it is better — because it illuminates the world, or resonates with our experience, or because it works, fits, or feels right. In such a system it is easier to spot bad or careless interpretations than to settle on a single best interpretation. Better interpretations display what social scientists call convergent validity or triangulation. The historian marshalls multiple forms of independent evidence to confirm the interpretations, but always aware that the question "What counts as evidence of what?" necessarily remains somewhat open.[18]

My description of journalism as a product has implicitly assumed the analysis of single artifacts. But journalism is also an ongoing process in which single stories or programs are simply moments or markers. Such processes of journalism might be usefully described as *practices*, in at least two senses of that term. First, the term *practice* calls attention to the ways in which journalism has actually been done, rather than how it has been idealized.[19] Second, the term *practice* alerts the historian to the routines by which journalism, as an occupation habitually enacts its characteristic way of doing things. The contemporary sociological studies of newsmaking, identified with the work of Gaye Tuchman, Herbert Gans, Todd Gitlin, Edward Epstein, Mark Fishman, and others, have meticulously traced the economic, technical, and social processes through which newswork gets done.[20] That method has also been successfully used to study television entertainment programs and popular music, and might be adapted in part to historical studies.[21]

The search for practices leads the historian into the social and mental worlds inhabited by both writers and readers of journalism. Too often biographical studies of journalists have accepted at face value the high-minded public explanations journalists offer for their own work. Historians must treat such explanations as social practices in their own right, as acts of identity-building and maintenance that say much about journalists' occupational conceptions but that may be tangential to journalists' everyday work. Historians must also beware, however, of an opposite but analogous error: treating journalists too mechanically, as organizational functionaries who keep the assembly line moving.[22] Journalists are neither the pillars of civilization nor mere cogs in the news machine, even when they work in a mechanical fashion. What journalists do, what their work means to them, how they dramatize their work for outsiders — that is the knot of questions the journalism historian must untangle.[23]

The practices of readers of journalism deserve closer attention as well. The act of reading a newspaper or watching a television program carries social meanings of its own, both for the actor and for others who assess the actor's behavior and motives. Readers and viewers are, in part, engaged in strategic social acts regardless of the content of what they read or view.[24] In other words, the very act of reading — and beyond that, of reading journalism — can be significant.[25] At different times and places, reading, viewing, or listening to the news has offered a way for elected officials to monitor public opinion, consumers to stay fashionable, citizens to keep informed, immigrants to affirm their Americanness, moral reformers to confirm their faith in human debauchery, husbands to shield themselves from their families, workers to take symbolic control of their lives, and sports fans to celebrate their enthusiasms.[26]

At this point analysis of product and practice may merge indistinguishably in the historians' research. Consider the case of a historian (assume she's a woman, for grammatical simplicity) who investigates a series of newspaper stories. Following the steps I cited earlier, she interprets the stories as products, considering their commodity form (length, placement, timing, costs of development, legal limits) as well as their narrative form (cast of characters and sources, plot, patterns of figuration, genre). She also examines, ideally, other "reports" of the same event, such as government investigations, letters, diaries, autobiographies of participants, police records, and magazine, trade journal, and union accounts. Because each account is a narrative in its own right, she must scrutinize each as carefully as the original stories. (The sheer time required for historical research now becomes evident.) But even her simplest reading of the news stories — for example, as a purported representation of something that happened — leads her to consider matters of journalistic practice. Why did reporters consider those happenings as news events worth covering? How did the reporters gather information and choose to constitute the events in particular narrative form? What sources did reporters rely on and why? Where did the stories fit into the imaginative landscapes inhabited by different groups of readers? Each news story, in a sense, marks an arbitrary end to the writing process and an arbitary beginning to the reading process. Each story speaks of its nominal subject — an event, policy, person — but each also tells of the ongoing practices of reality-building and, if the historian listens closely, of the struggle for cultural authority.[27]

This example aptly illustrates how the analysis of product and practice both entail symbolic interpretation. Rather than reducing narrative to content, or social practice to function and structure, the historian must learn to interpret both product and practice as symbolic action. Interpreting meaning-making as social behavior requires the journalism historian to rework the traditional distinction between primary and secondary materials. That distinction properly requires historians to use all available archival materials and to assess such materials for their authenticity and reliability. But historians misuse the primary-secondary distinction if they attempt to privilege private stories as inherently more reliable. Primary sources such as letters and diaries are symbolic behaviors that demand every bit as much interpretation as newspapers or newscasts. All documents, even statistical records, are ultimately stories requiring interpretation. Their reliability is, to a discomforting degree, a matter of context (reliable on what sorts of questions) and convention (reliable by whose standards).[28] Historians often assume that private documents are better guides to thoughts and behaviors that could only be known privately, such as motives. Yet motives are socially constructed, so that explanations of private behavior are inevitably shaped by the forms of public discourse.[29] The assumed superiority of primary documents rests on two arguable assumptions: first, that some final, factual account of events exists against which the inadequacy of public accounts can be measured; and second, that people speak their lives more authentically in private than in public, that humans do not stage their private acts as fully or as frequently as they do their public acts.

The observation that there are no privileged, automatically reliable accounts of reality leads the historian to the final level of analysis, which I have called *commentary*. If the study of product and practice account for the forms of reality that journalists make, then commentary accounts for what everyone (including journalists) makes of what journalists make. Journalists not only accomplish their work but also step back to reflect on what that work means. Journalism's self-reflexive commentary is one of the least studied areas of historical research.[30] Though journalism has produced numerous professional, trade, and union journals, there have been almost no systematic studies of those journals in their own right, as stages on which successive generations of journalists have dramatized their quest for identity.

Beyond becoming more aware of journalists' interpretations of themselves, their organizations, and their readers, historians should investigate the ways in which other groups use the institution of journalism as something to think with.[31] Diverse groups have seized upon the products and practices of journalism to comment on everything from the twilight of authority in modern politics, to the degradation of modern morals, to the subversion of democracy by the wealthy and powerful. Such commentaries on journalism respond in part to the performance or style of the press itself, but they also often articulate vague but widely shared feelings about the state of society as a whole. Thus historians cannot assume that all talk about journalism is about journalism alone, for such talk may voice larger concerns by its allusions, tropes, and occasions.

At this point journalism historians can be forgiven if they feel that they have wandered into a hall of mirrors in which it is nearly impossible to establish a frame of reference or gauge the depth of field. The historian's first immersion in the research materials is likely to produce a combination of giddy exhilaration and sheer panic. But the research process is not as totally open-ended as I have made it sound. For one thing historians necessarily work with whatever materials are extant; availability and access limit the possible range of investigations. Similarly the choice of topic also answers to personal preferences. Journalism historians may enter the research maze at nearly any point; my comments only offer a rough sketch of how to proceed once inside. Thus historians can, and have, chosen to study news stories about particular events, people, places, and issues; the people who make or — more frequently — pay for the making of such stories; the groups that use or feel used by journalists; the identities journalists create for themselves or for other groups in society; the organizations that journalists work for and that work on them; and the whole tumultuous process in which journalists and citizens alike try to figure out what it all means, what to praise and what to pray for, what to regulate and what to ignore.

Ultimately journalism history offers a way to map the discourse not just of journalism but of the society as a whole. Journalism historians might do better to think of themselves not as writing the history of one specialized area of mass communication, but as following journalism, somewhat idiosyncratically, as one path into the history of public life. That reorientation might give historians a better sense of the scope and significance of their research. For example, the enormous literature on freedom of the press too often misses a general point it might make about American life: the extent to which virtually all groups in the United States deploy the term *freedom* to describe their own preferred forms of depredation and liberation. A careful reading of public talk about freedom of the press, if conducted in the context of press practices and the law of the press, might make this point well. The discourse of freedom is one of the characteristic ways in which Americans try to discipline and rationalize changing circumstances, and the debate over press freedom has been an important form of that discourse.[32] At various moments the phrase "freedom of the press" has signified the ready availability of cheap printing presses, a common carrier style of operation, access to news, an attitude of skepticism toward established power, the prerogative of a class of powerful news organizations, the chance to speak one's mind, or the social responsibility of a class of professional journalists. Anyone who writes about freedom of the press chooses from and eventually adds to this image repertoire. In studying press freedom, the social scientist's method of operational definition is literally senseless. The best journalism historians can do, and it would be a great deal indeed, is to interpret the phrase "freedom of the press" as a strategic symbolic practice by which Americans habitually talk not only about journalism but also about the very nature of their own society.

In the end each journalism historian adds one more voice to the hubbub. And someone else comes along to talk about it.

1. For those unfamiliar with this approach, the following sources provide a good introduction: Erving Goffman, *The Presentation of Self in Everyday Life* (Garden City NY: Anchor Books, 1959) and *Stigma* (Englewood Cliffs NJ: Prentice-Hall, 1963); Hugh Duncan, *Communication and Social Order* (New York: Bedminster Press, 1962); Anselm Strauss, *Mirrors and Masks* (Mill Valley CA: Sociology Press, 1969); Kenneth Burke, *Permanence and Change*, rev ed. (Berkeley: University of California Press, 1984), and *Attitudes Toward History*, 3rd ed. (Berkeley: University of California Press, 1984); Clifford Geertz, *The Interpretation of Cultures* (New York: Basic Books, 1973); Robert Darnton, *The Great Cat Massacre* (New York: Basic Books, 1984); Richard Rorty, *Consequences of Pragmatism* (Minneapolis: University of Minnesota Press, 1982); and James W. Carey, "A Cultural Approach to Communication," *Communication*, 2 (1975): 1-22.

2. Others have commented on this historiographical tendency. See, for example, James Carey, "The Problem of Journalism History," *Journalism History*, 1 (1974): 3-5, 27, and Joseph McKerns, "The Limits of Progressive Journalism History," *Journalism History*, 4 (1977): 88-92.

3. For discussions of this perspective, see James W. Carey, "A Cultural Approach to Communication"; Clifford Geertz, "Thick Description: Toward an Interpretive Theory of Culture," in *The Interpretation of Cultures*: 3-30; Kenneth Burke, "Terministic Screens," in *Language as Symbolic Action* (Berkeley: University of California Press, 1966): 44-62; and Anselm Strauss, "Language and Identity," in *Mirrors and Masks*: 15-30.

4. The observation about technology "legislating" social life comes from Langdon Winner, *Autonomous Technology* (Cambridge MA: MIT Press, 1977).

5. Raymond Williams, *Television, Technology and Cultural Form* (New York: Schocken Books, 1975): 18.

6. Susan J. Douglas's recent book, *Inventing American Broadcasting, 1899-1922* (Baltimore: Johns Hopkins University Press, 1987), demonstrates the complex relations between invention, political and economic control, and social imagination.

7. Once a new group of records has been discovered or organized, however, it can lead to a long and productive line of research. For an account of how just such a discovery shaped his own work, see Robert Darnton, *The Literary Underground of the Old Regime* (Cambridge MA: Harvard University Press, 1982): vi-viii.

8. Two classic sources of economic data that are still extremely valuable to historians are S.N.D. North, *History and Present Condition of the Newspaper and Periodical Press of the United States* (Washington DC: U.S. Census Bureau, 1881), and Alfred M. Lee, *The Daily Newspaper in America* (New York: Macmillan, 1937). For a fine example of how a careful researcher can draw economic evidence from scattered sources, see Ted Curtis Smythe, "The Reporter, 1800-1900. Working Conditions and Their Influence on the News," *Journalism History*, 7 (1980): 1-10. Arthur J. Kaul and Joseph P. McKerns, "The Dialectic Ecology of the Newspaper," *Critical Studies in Mass Communication*, 2 (1985): 217-233, attempts to place newspaper economics in a wider historical context.

9. On the techniques of content analysis, see Klaus Krippendorf, *Content Analysis* (Beverly Hills CA: Sage, 1980), and Guido H. Stempel III, "Content Analysis," in

Research Methods in Mass Communication, Stempel and Bruce H. Westley, eds. (Englewood Cliffs NJ: Prentice-Hall, 1981): 119-131.

10. For a fine discussion of the problems of applying content analysis to historical studies, see Roberto Franzosi, "The Press as a Source of Socio-Historical Data: Issues in the Methodology of Data Collection and Newspapers," *Historical Methods,* 20 (Winter 1987): 5-16.

11. David Paul Nord has provided exemplary models of historical reasoning from statistics in two recent articles: "Working-Class Readers: Family, Community, and Reading in Late Nineteenth-Century America," *Communication Research,* 13 (1986): 156-181, and "A Republican Literature: A Study of Magazine Reading and Readers in Late Eighteenth-Century New York," *American Quarterly,* 40 (1988): 42-64.

12. *The "Uncensored War"* (New York: Oxford University Press, 1986).

13. For an example of how this consciousness has touched historical studies in general, read Hayden White, *Tropics of Discourse* (Baltimore: The Johns Hopkins University Press, 1978). A recent call for the incorporation of such perspectives into mass communication history is George Lipsitz, "'This Ain't No Sideshow': Historians and Media Studies," *Critical Studies in Mass Communication,* 5 (June 1988): 147-161.

14. "Writing News and Telling Stories," *Daedalus,* 104 (1975): 175-197.

15. Kenneth Burke invented what he called the *pentad* to identify the key terms humans use to describe their actions and motives. *A Grammar of Motives* (Berkeley: University of California Press, 1969): xv-xxiii. The terms of that pentad are actor, act, actor, scene, purpose, and agency — the same terms, a journalist might note, as the who, what, when and where, why, and how of a news story.

16. For an interesting application of theories of reading to mass communication, see Linda Steiner, "Oppositional Decoding as an Act of Resistance," *Critical Studies in Mass Communication,* 5 (1988): 1-15.

17. Jack Lule has used hermeneutic methods to analyze news in the American press about the Soviet Union. See "News as Myth: A Hermeneutic Approach to U.S. News of the Soviet Union" (Ph.D. diss., University of Georgia, 1987). For an example of Burkean analysis, see Lule's "The Myth of My Widow: A Dramatistic Analysis of News Portrayals of a Terrorist Victim," *Political Communication and Persuasion,* 5 (1988): 101-120.

18. Clifford Geertz has called this piling up of perspectives "thick description." See Geertz, "Thick Description: Toward an Interpretive Theory of Culture," in *The Interpretation of Cultures:* 3-30.

19. Ideas, of course, can be read as a social practice, too — -the practice of ideology. In American journalism calls for press freedom often legitimize more narrow and controversial organizational practices, using languages of praise that are widely shared in the society. On journalism's use of "professionalism" for just such purposes, see Douglas Birkhead, "The Power in the Image: Professionalism and the Communications Revolution," *American Journalism,* 1 (Winter 1984): 1-14. For a warning about the dangers of accepting press mythology at face value, see John C. Nerone, "The Mythology of the Penny Press," *Critical Studies in Mass Communication,* 4 (December 1987): 376-404.

20. Gaye Tuchman, *Making News* (New York: Free Press, 1978); Herbert Gans, *Deciding What's News* (New York: Random House, 1979); Todd Gitlin, *The Whole World Is Watching* (Berkeley: University of California Press, 1980); Edward

Epstein, *News from Nowhere* (New York: Random House, 1973); Mark Fishman, *Manufacturing the News* (Austin TX: University of Texas Press, 1980). A convenient introduction to the literature is W. Lance Bennett, *News, the Politics of Illusion*, 2nd ed. (New York: Longman, 1988).

21. For a wonderful study that combines production and narrative analysis, see Todd Gitlin's book on entertainment television, *Inside Prime Time* (New York: Pantheon, 1983). For examples of production analysis and useful bibliographic citations, see Richard A. Peterson, *The Production of Culture* (Beverly Hills CA: Sage, 1976). Joli Jensen offers a perceptive critique of typical production approaches in "An Interpretive Approach to Cultural Production," in *Interpreting Television*, Willard D. Rowland Jr. and Bruce Watkins, eds. (Beverly Hills CA: Sage, 1984): 98-118.

22. The newsmaking literature sometimes displays this exaggerated sense of the mechanicalness of the newsroom, in part because much sociology conventionally deals with group life through static concepts like role, structure, and function rather than more complex, ambiguous concepts such as process or interaction. For a discussion of the interactive approach, see Strauss, *Mirrors and Masks:* 44-88.

23. In an exciting line of continuing research, James S. Ettema and Theodore L. Glasser have been studying the processes by which investigative reporters do their work. For early results, see Ettema and Glasser, "On the Epistemology of Investigative Journalism," *Communication*, 8 (1985): 183-206.

24. Two studies that deal explicitly with reading/viewing as intrinsically important acts are Janice Radway, *Reading the Romance* (Chapel Hill NC: University of North Carolina Press, 1984), and Charles Frazer, "The Social Character of Children's Television Viewing," *Communication Research*, 8 (1981): 307-322.

25. Whatever their methodological shortcomings, the functionalist studies of what missing the daily newspaper means, typically conducted during newspaper strikes over the last forty years, express this common recognition of journalism's place in everyday life. See, for example, Bernard Berelson's "What 'Missing the Newspaper' Means," reprinted in *The Process and Effects of Mass Communication*, Wilbur Schramm, ed. (Urbana IL: University of Illinois Press, 1961): 36-47.

26. For a discussion of the theoretical issues involved in studying people's use of mass communication, see James W. Carey and Albert L. Kreiling, "Popular Culture and Uses and Gratifications: Notes Toward an Accommodation," in *The Uses of Mass Communications. Current Perspectives on Gratifications Research*, Jay G. Blumler and Elihu Katz, eds. (Beverly Hills CA: Sage, 1974): 225-248.

27. For an excellent example of how to read journalism as a cultural text, see Richard Lentz, "Sixty-Five Days in Memphis: A Study of Culture, Symbols, and the Press," *Journalism Monographs*, no. 98 (August 1986).

28. I am using the word reliable here in the general sense of "trust." Social science notes two senses of the word trust — validity, or the ability of a measure to measure what it intends to, and reliability, or the ability of a measure to measure in a consistent fashion. My use of the word reliability partakes of both social science meanings, for historical arguments often entail simultaneous disagreements about validity and reliability.

29. Burke, *Permanence and Change:* 19-36, is his classic first formulation of this approach to motives. But also see Strauss, *Mirrors and Masks:* 45-54.

30. For two recent examples of studies of journalism's commentaries on itself, see David L. Eason, "On Journalistic Authority: the Case of Janet Cooke," and John J. Pauly, "Rupert Murdoch and the Demonology of Professional Journalism," in

Media, Myths, and Narratives: Television and the Press, James W. Carey, ed. (Newbury Park CA: Sage, 1988): 205-227 and 246-261.

31. Robert Darnton discusses the ways in which cultural history explicates people's attempts to think with different artifacts in *The Great Cat Massacre* (New York: Basic Books, 1984): 3-7. For an attempt to apply a similar approach to analyzing public talk about American cities, see Anselm Strauss, *Images of the American City* (New Brunswick NJ: Transaction Books, 1976).

32. Following Kenneth Burke's approach, journalism historians might interpret the phrase "freedom of the press" as a style of "symbolic bridging," a way to accommodate experience to our models of reality by using old words for new things, and new words for old things. See Burke, *Attitudes Toward History*: 224-225. At this point, no matter what sort of press Americans get, they — or at least the journalists who work in it — are likely to consider it "free."

Research Methods
in Journalism History

Bibliographies for Journalism History: A Selection

Jean Ward and Kathleen A. Hansen

For journalism historians, the bibliographic trail takes the researcher off the main highway and into countless byways, lanes and even alleys. Each journalism history subject intersects inevitably with numerous topics and subtopics that relate in important and interesting ways to the journalism of the past. Thus, while bibliographic tools are important for all historians, journalism historians inevitably go beyond the standard tools and take excursions into a wide variety of bibliographic sources across many disciplines.

For the most part, this chapter concentrates on bibliographies as secondary sources for journalism historians. The numerous reference tools that help historians locate special collections, of which this volume is an example, are not included here. However, many of the bibliographies in this chapter include references to such collection guides, making the task of locating these references a fairly straightforward one.

On the whole, the efficient journalism historian assumes that useful bibliographies are available and are profitably consulted early in the research process. Because of the interdisciplinary nature of communication history, it is almost certain that at least one bibliography will treat the journalism scholar's topic.

For items not in the historian's own campus library, two national electronic catalogs are available to identify the holdings of major research and public libraries. Librarians can search for the titles requested by scholars and learn which collections around the country own the volumes. The two systems are RLIN (Research

Libraries Information Network) produced by the Research Libraries Group, and OCLC (Online Computer Library Center) produced by OCLC, Inc.

The compilation and enumeration of scholarly materials has a long and rich history. In the second century A.D., for example, Galen produced a classified record of his own works. Medieval monastic scholars and librarians cooperated to produce bibliographies as guides to their collections. The sixteenth century Swiss physician and scholar Konrad Gesner, popularly known as the "father of bibliography," compiled a twenty-volume guide to world literature titled *Bibliotheca Universalis.* Organized subject bibliography as an aid to scholarly communication was well established by the end of the nineteenth century.[1]

Shera envisions the contemporary bibliographic system as a pyramid.[2] Adopting his perspective in the American context, at the base of the pyramid is the 754-volume listing of North American library holdings, the *National Union Catalog: Pre-1956 Imprints,* and its ongoing companion series, *National Union Catalog: A Cumulative Author List.* Through this catalog, scholars can learn the existence and location of more than nine million works published throughout the world and available in at least one of a thousand research libraries in North America. Another item at the base of the pyramid is the U.S. national enumerative bibliography, *American Book Publishing Record* and cumulations, a list of books published in the U.S. since 1876.

As one proceeds through the middle levels of the pyramid, bibliographies grow increasingly specialized and selective. Bibliographies may be based on the date of publication, location of publication, quality of material, subject matter, type or nature of published material, or other characteristics. At the apex of the pyramid, the scholar finds the bibliographic essay, the most specialized and scholarly of the contributions to bibliography. At this point, the roles of the bibliographer and the historian merge.

Several examples of bibliographic work at the apex include such essays as one finds in the specialized communication history journals. *American Journalism* and *Journalism History* regularly publish bibliographic essays that are rich in sources for communication history researchers. Examples of such essays are included in the bibliography of this chapter. The work of the scholar as bibliographer also is visible in books published on a variety of journalism subjects. Two examples, cited fully in this chapter bibliography, are the extensive bibliographies in Agee, Ault and Emery's *Introduction to Mass Communication* (1988) and Head and Sterling's *Broadcasting in America: A Survey of Electronic Media* (1987). Such bibliographies often include historical sources even though the books are not strictly or exclusively about communication history.

Bibliographies of Bibliographies

Some often-neglected tools at the mid-level of the pyramid are those that identify published bibliographies. The journalism historian seeking comprehensiveness consults these standard tools early in the research process. Prominent and relevant for journalism historians are these: Besterman's *World Bibliography of Bibliographies* (1965-1966), and its successor, Toomey's *World Bibliography of Bibliographies, 1964-1974* (1977); Henige's *Serial Bibliographies and Abstracts in History* (1986); Sheehy's *Guide to Reference Books* (1986); and the many tools that lead to more specialized and regularly updated bibliographies. Some tools in this final category include: *America: History and Life* (July 1964 to present); *Bibliographic Index* (1937 to present); and *Writings on American History* (1902 to present).

General U.S. History

The work of U.S. journalism scholars necessarily relates closely to the broader context of U.S. history. The scholar finds bibliographic assistance in such standard works as: Beers' *Bibliographies in American History: Guide to Materials for Research* (1942, reprint 1975), and its update, *Bibliographies in American History 1942-1978* (1982); Cassara's *History of the United States of America: A Guide to Information Sources* (1977); Fitzgerald's *American History: A Bibliographic Review* (1985); Freidel and Showman's *Harvard Guide to American History* (1974); *Historical Documentary Editions* (1986); Kaminkow's *U.S. Local Histories in the Library of Congress: A Bibliography* (1975), and its *Supplement and Index* (1976); MacDonald's *Documentary Source Book of American History 1606-1926* (1926, reprint 1969); and U.S. Library of Congress' *A Guide to the Study of the United States of America* (1960) and its *Supplement, 1956-65* (1976).

Manuscript and Archive Collections

Locating collections of primary research materials is an early critical task for many journalism history studies. Some ordinary bibliographies may lead the scholar to a variety of primary research collections. In addition, published guides to manuscript and archive collections, such as the few cited here, also are useful:

Carnegie Institution's *[Guides to Manuscript Materials for the History of the United States]* (1906-1943, reprint 1965) which lead the scholar to U.S. manuscript materials in French, Roman and Italian, Cuban, Mexican, German, Russian, Spanish, Swiss and Austrian archives; *Guide to the National Archives of the United States* (1974); Hamer's *A Guide to Archives and Manuscripts in the United States* (1961); the National Historical Publications and Records Commission's *Directory of Archives and Manuscript Repositories in the United States* (1978); and the *National Union Catalog of Manuscript Collections 1959/61--* (1962 to present); and *Women's History Sources: A Guide to Archives and Manuscript Collections in the U.S.* (1979). Guides to manuscript and archive materials in electronic form are included in the database chapter of this volume. Historians wishing to contact historical societies directly can locate them by using *Directory of Historical Societies and Agencies in the United States and Canada* (biennial).

Mass Communication Bibliography

More specific still in the mid-levels of the bibliographic pyramid are the standard bibliographies for the field of mass communication scholarship. Since 1962, Blum has been the leading bibliographer in mass communication. Her current work, with F. Wilhoit, is *Mass Media Bibliography: Reference, Research and Reading* (1989). Others in this category include: Brigham's *History and Bibliography of American Newspapers, 1690-1820* (1947, reprint 1962); Cannon's *Journalism: A Bibliography* (1924, reprint 1967); Danielson and G.C. Wilhoit's, *A Computerized Bibliography of Mass Communication Research, 1944-1964* (1967); Dunn and Cooper's *A Guide to Mass Communication Sources* (1981); Hansen and Parsons' *Mass Communication: A Research Bibliography* (1968); Price's *The Literature of Journalism: An Annotated Bibliography* (1959); Price and Pickett's *An Annotated Journalism Bibliography, 1958-1968* (1970); and Wolseley and Wolseley's *The Journalist's Bookshelf: An Annotated and Selected Bibliography of United States Print Journalism* (1986).

Union Lists and Bibliographies About Chronological Periods

Union lists are useful for the scholar because they help to identify the existence and location of primary research materials such as newspaper or magazine collections. In addition, specialized bibliographies lead the scholar to materials about a communication topic in a particular chronological period. Many of these references can be identified through some of the sources listed in this chapter. Some examples of these are: Adams' *American Independence, The Growth of an Idea: A Bibliographical Study of The American Political Pamphlets Printed Between 1764 and 1776 Dealing with the Dispute Between Great Britain and Her Colonies* (1965, reprint 1980); *Check List of American 18th Century Newspapers in the Library of Congress* (1936, 1968); Ford's *Check-List of American Magazines Printed in the Eighteenth Century* (1889, reprint 1972); Gregory's *American Newspapers, 1821-1936: A Union List of Files Available in the U.S. and Canada* (1937); and Jacobs' *Antebellum Black Newspapers* (1976).

Regional Bibliographies

Another category of specialized bibliographies is regional. Again, many of these can be located by using the tools mentioned in this chapter. Some examples include: Ligenfelter and Gash's *The Newspapers of Nevada: A History and Bibliography, 1854-1979 (1984)*; Norton's *Religious Newspapers in the Old Northwest to 1861: A History, Bibliography, and Record of Opinion* (1977); Winther's *A Classified Bibliography of the Periodical Literature of the Trans-Mississippi West (1811-1957)* (1961), and its supplement with Van Orman, *A Classified Bibliography of the Periodical Literature of the Trans-Mississippi West: A Supplement (1957-1967)* (1970).

Media Industries and Communication Professions Bibliographies

An outstanding example of this type of scholarly work is Schwarzlose's *Newspapers: A Reference Guide* (1987). Broad in scope and deep in specific sources, this book includes narrative and annotated references on topics such as newspaper history and biography, historical anthologies, bibliographies, checklists such as Milner's *Newspaper Indexes: A Location and Subject Guide for Researchers* (1977-1982), indexes, newspaper chronologies and major newspaper research collections. Many sources included in Schwarzlose are not included in this chapter. The newspaper history scholar should refer to his book for additional references.

Bibliographies about the other media professions and industries still await the kind of treatment given newspapers. In advertising, an example is: Polley's *Information Sources in Advertising History* (1979). Materials in broadcasting include: *Broadcasting Bibliography: A Guide to the Literature of Radio and Television* (1984); Cassata and Skill's *Television: A Guide to the Literature* (1985); Einstein's *Special Edition: A Guide to Network Television*

Documentary Series and Special News Reports, 1955-1979 (1987); Hill and Davis' *Religious Broadcasting 1920-1983* (1984); Kittross' *A Bibliography of Theses and Dissertations in Broadcasting: 1920-1973* (1978); Lichty and Topping's *American Broadcasting: A Sourcebook on the History of Radio and Television* (1975); McCavitt's *Radio and Television: A Selected, Annotated Bibliography* (1978), and its *Supplement One: 1977-1981* (1982); McNeil's *Total Television: A Comprehensive Guide to Programming from 1948-1980* (1980); Pitts' *Radio Soundtracks: A Reference Guide* (1976); Rose's *Radio, Television, and Broadcasting: An Annotated Bibliography* (1947); Smith's *Television Network News: A Guide to Sources in English* (1984); and Sparks' *A Bibliography of Doctoral Dissertations in Television and Radio* (1971).

The graphics area is covered in: Bigmore's *A Bibliography of Printing* (1880-1886); and Greco's *The Graphic Arts Bibliography* (1984). Public relations titles include: Bishop's *Public Relations: A Comprehensive Bibliography* (1974) and Cutlip's *A Public Relations Bibliography* (1965). Magazine bibliography includes: Edgar's *A History and Bibliography of Magazines: 1810-1820* (1975); Hoffman, Allen and Ulrich's *The Little Magazine: A History and Bibliography* (1946); Paine and Paine's *Magazines: A Bibliography for Their Analysis, with Annotations and Study Guide* (1987); Richardson's *History of Early American Magazines, 1741-1789* (1967); and Schact's *A Bibliography for the Study of Magazines* (1968). One aspect of photo communication and social criticism is covered in Dixon's *Photographs of the Farm Security Administration: An Annotated Bibliography 1930-1980* (1983).

Special Topic or Subject Bibliographies

Many communication history topics are covered in one or more bibliographies or source guides devoted specifically to that subject. Again, the scholar can use many of the general bibliographic tools mentioned in this chapter to identify these sources. For example, race, ethnicity and the U.S. media are treated in: Arndt and Olson's *The German Language Press of the Americas: History and Bibliography, 1732-1968* (1961, 1964, 1976); Bush and Fraser's *American Indian Periodicals in the Princeton University Library: A Preliminary List* (1970); Danky and Hady's *Native American Periodicals and Newspapers, 1829-1982: Bibliography, Publishing Record and Holdings* (1984); Snorgrass and Woody's *Blacks and Media: A Selected, Annotated Bibliography 1962-1982* (1985); and Wynar and Wynar's *Encyclopedic Directory of Ethnic Newspapers and Periodicals in the United States* (1976).

Media, politics and society topics are included in such special bibliographies as: Brightbill's *Communications and the United States Congress: A Selectively Annotated Bibliography of Committee Hearings, 1870-1976* (1978); Cantirl's *Public Opinion, 1935-1946* (1951); Childs' *A Reference Guide to the Study of Public Opinion* (1934); Hausman's *Criticism of the Press in U.S. Periodicals, 1900-1939: An Annotated Bibliography* (1967); Klejment and Klejment's *Dorothy Day and the Catholic Worker: A Bibliography and Index* (1985); McCoy's *Freedom of the Press: An Annotated Bibliography* (1968), and his *Freedom of the Press, A Bibliocyclopedia: Ten Year Supplement (1967-1977)* (1979); McKerns' *News Media and Public Policy: An Annotated Bibliography* (1985); Silha Center's *Two Bibliographies on Ethics* (1986); and Swindler's *A Bibliography of Law on Journalism* (1947).

Historiography is covered in Kinnell's *Historiography: An Annotated Bibliography of Journal Articles, Books and Dissertations* (1987); and Stephens' *Historiography: A Bibliography* (1975). Women in U.S. history are covered in such special bibliographies as: Danky and Hady's *Women's Periodicals and Newspapers from the 18th Century to 1981* (1982); Krichmar's *The Women's Rights Movement in the United States, 1848-1970: A Bibliography and Sourcebook* (1972); and Leonard, Drinker and Holden's *The American Woman in Colonial and Revolutionary Times, 1565-1962* (1962, reprint 1975).

Early bibliographies of books published in North America are included in titles such as Evans' *American Bibliography* (1903-1959) which covers the years 1639 to 1800; Kelly's *American Catalogue of Books: Original and Imprints* (1938); Roobach's *Bibliotheca Americana* (1849); and Shipton and Mooney's *National Index of American Imprints Through 1800: The Short-Title Evans* (1969).

Bibliographies about communication technologies include: Shearer and Buxford's *Communications and Society: A Bibliography on Communications Technologies and Their Social Impact* (1983); and Shiers and Shiers' *Bibliography of the History of Electronics* (1972).

Biographies

The study of historic figures has traditionally played a prominent role in the work of journalism historians. Numerous tools help the scholar to identify biographical information, including bibliographies of biographical sources. For instance, Kaplan's *A Bibliography of American Autobiographies* (1962) has hundreds of index entries for "Journalists." Standard biographical reference tools also may include bibliographies. For instance, Ashley's

American Newspaper Journalists, 1873-1900 (1983) and his *American Newspaper Journalists, 1901-1925* (1984) include signed biographical sketches of each person along with bibliographies of works by and about the journalists. A continuation of Ashley's work is *Who Was Who in Journalism 1925-1928* (1978). Others include Abrams' *Journalist Biographies Master Index* (1979) and *Foremost Women in Communications* (1970).

Published bibliographies, as well as informally-circulating bibliographies shared by communication researchers, have played an important role in the development of journalism history scholarship. As the information explosion continues, these resources undoubtedly will increase in the significance they hold for the serious scholar. Existing resources are rich and those available in a variety of disciplines enhance the depth of scholarship and speed the task of surveying existing knowledge on journalism history topics.

1. Jesse H. Shera. *Introduction to Library Science* (Littleton CO: Libraries Unlimited, 1976): 108-109.

2. Ibid., 109.

Selected Bibliography

Abrams, Alan E. *Journalist Biographies Master Index.* Detroit: Gale, 1979.

Adams, Thomas Randolph. *American Independence, The Growth of an Idea: A Bibliographical Study of the American Political Pamphlets Printed Between 1764 and 1776 Dealing with the Dispute Between Great Britain and Her Colonies.* Providence RI: Brown University Press, 1965; reprint, Austin TX: Jenkins and Reese, 1980.

Agee, Warren K., Phillip H. Ault, and Edwin Emery. *Introduction to Mass Communications.* 9th ed. New York: Harper and Row, 1988.

America: History and Life. Santa Barbara CA: Clio Press, 1964--. Quarterly.

American Book Publishing Record. New York: Bowker, 1876--. Annual.

Arndt, Karl J. R., and May E. Olson. *The German Language Press of the Americas: History and Bibliography, 1732-1968.* 3 vols. Munich: Verlag Dokumentation, 1961, 1965, 1976.

Ashley, Perry J., ed. *American Newspaper Journalists, 1873-1900.* Vol. 23, *Dictionary of Literary Biography,* Detroit: Gale, 1982.

_____. *American Newspaper Journalists, 1901-1925.* Vol. 25, *Dictionary of Literary Biography.* Detroit: Gale, 1984.

Beers, Henry. *Bibliographies in American History: Guide to Materials for Research.* New York: Wilson, 1942. Reprint. New York: Octagon, 1975.

_____. *Bibliographies in American History, 1942-1978.* Woodbridge CT: Research Publications, 1982.

Besterman, Theodore. *World Bibliography of Bibliographies.* 5 vols. 4th ed. Lausanne: Societas Bibliographica, 1965-1966.

Bibliographic Index: A Cumulative Bibliography of Bibliographies. New York: Wilson, 1937--. Triannual.

Bigmore, Edward C. *A Bibliography of Printing.* 3 vols. London: B. Quaritch, 1880-1886.

Bishop, Robert L. *Public Relations: A Comprehensive Bibliography._*Ann Arbor: University of Michigan Press, 1974.

Blum, Eleanor. *Basic Books in the Mass Media.* 2d ed. Urbana: University of Illinois Press, 1980. (First edition, 1972).

_____ and Frances Wilhoit. *Mass Media Bibliography: Reference, Research and Reading.* Urbana: University of Illinois Press, 1989.

_____. *Reference Books in the Mass Media.* Urbana: University of Illinois Press, 1962.

Brigham, Clarence S. *History and Bibliography of American Newspapers, 1690-1820.* 2 vols. Worcester MA: American Antiquarian Society, 1947; reprint, Hamden CT: Archon, 1962.

Brightbill, George D. *Communications and the United States Congress: A Selectively Annotated Bibliography of Committee Hearings, 1870-1976.* Washington DC: Broadcast Education Association, 1978.

Broadcasting Bibliography: A Guide to the Literature of Radio and Television. Washington DC: National Association of Broadcasters, 1984.

Bush, Alfred L., and Robert S. Fraser. *American Indian Periodicals in the Princeton University Library: A Preliminary List.* Princeton: Princeton University Press, 1970.

Cannon, Carl L. *Journalism: A Bibliography.* New York: New York Public Library, 1924; reprint, Detroit: Gale, 1967.

Cantril, Hadley, ed. *Public Opinion, 1935-1946.* Princeton: Princeton University Press, 1951.

Carnegie Institution. *[Guides to Manuscript Materials for the History of the United States].* 23 vols. Washington DC: Carnegie Institution, 1906-1943; reprint, Millwood NY: Kraus Reprint, 1965.

Cassara, Ernest, ed. *History of the United States of America: A Guide to Information Sources.* Detroit: Gale, 1977.

Cassata, Mary, and Thomas Skill. *Television: A Guide to the Literature.* Phoenix AZ: Oryx Press, 1985.

Check List of American 18th Century Newspapers in the Library of Congress. Washington DC: U.S. Government Printing Office, 1936. New rev. enl. ed. Westport CT: Greenwood Press, 1968.

Childs, Harwood. *A Reference Guide to the Study of Public Opinion.* Princeton: Princeton University Press, 1934.

Cutlip, Scott M. *A Public Relations Bibliography.* 2d ed. Madison WI: University of Wisconsin Press, 1965.

Danielson, Wayne A., and G. C. Wilhoit. *A Computerized Bibliography of Mass Communication Research, 1944-1964.* New York: Magazine Publishers Association, 1967.

Danky, James P., and Maureen E. Hady. *Native American Periodicals and Newspapers, 1829-1982: Bibliography, Publishing Record and Holdings.* Westport CT: Greenwood, 1984.

_____. *Women's Periodicals and Newspapers from the 18th Century to 1981.* Boston: G.K. Hall, 1982.

Directory of Historical Societies and Agencies in the United States and Canada. 12 vols. Madison WI: American Association for State and Local History. Biennial.

Dixon, Penelope. *Photographs of the Farm Security Administration: An Annotated Bibliography 1930-1980.* New York: Garland, 1983.

Dunn, M. Gilbert, and Douglas W. Cooper. "A Guide to Mass Communication Sources." *Journalism Monographs* 74 (November 1981).

Edgar, Neal L. *A History and Bibliography of American Magazines: 1810-1820.* Metuchen NJ: Scarecrow, 1975.

Einstein, Daniel. *Special Edition: A Guide to Network Television Documentary Series and Special News Reports, 1955-1979.* Metuchen NJ: Scarecrow, 1987.

Evans, Charles. *American Bibliography.* 14 vols. Chicago: Blakely Press, 1903-1959.

Fitzgerald, Carol B. *American History: A Bibliographic Review* Westport CT: Meckler, 1985.

Ford, Paul L. *Check-List of American Magazines Printed in the Eighteenth Century.* No. 24 in Historical Printing Club series. 1889; reprint, New York: Macmillan, 1972.

Foremost Women in Communications. New York: Foremost Americans Publishing Co., 1970.

Freidel, Frank, and Richard Showman, eds. *Harvard Guide to American History.* 2 vols. Rev. ed. Cambridge MA: Harvard University Press, 1974.

Greco, Albert N., ed. *The Graphic Arts Bibliography.* New York: New York University, 1984.

Gregory, Winifred. *American Newspapers, 1821-1936: A Union List of Files Available in the U. S. and Canada.* New York: Wilson, 1937.

Guide to the National Archives of the United States. Washington DC: U.S. Government Printing Office, 1974.

Gutierrez, Felix. "Spanish-Language Media in America: Background, Resources, History." *Journalism History* 4(2) (Summer 1967): 34-41, 65-67.

Hamer, Philip M. *A Guide to Archives and Manuscripts in the United States.* New Haven CT: Yale University Press, 1961.

Hansen, Donald A., and J. Herschel Parsons. *Mass Communication: A Research Bibliography.* Santa Barbara CA: Glendessary Press, 1968.

Hausman, Linda W. "Criticism of the Press in U.S. Periodicals, 1900-1939: An Annotated Bibliography." *Journalism Monographs* 4. (August 1967).

Head, Sydney W., and Christopher H. Sterling. *Broadcasting in America: A Survey of Electronic Media.* 5th ed. Boston: Houghton Mifflin, 1987.

Henige, David. *Serial Bibliographies and Abstracts in History.* Westport CT: Greenwood Press, 1986.

Hill, George H., and Lenwood Davis. *Religious Broadcasting 1920-1983.* New York: Garland, 1984.

Historical Documentary Editions. Washington DC: National Historical Publications and Records Commission, 1986.

Hoffman, Frederick John H., Charles Allen, and Carolyn F. Ulrich. *The Little Magazine: A History and Bibliography.* Princeton: Princeton University Press, 1946.

Huntzicker, William E. "Historiographical Essay: Historians and the American Frontier Press." *American Journalism* 5(1) (1988):28-45.

Jacobs, Donald M., ed. *Antebellum Black Newspapers.* Westport CT: Greenwood Press, 1976.

Kaminkow, Marion J. *U.S. Local Histories in the Library of Congress: A Bibliography.* Baltimore: Magna Carta Books, 1975.

_____. U.S. Local Histories in the Library of Congress: Supplement and Index. Baltimore: Magna Carta Books, 1976.

Kaplan, Louis, comp. *A Bibliography of American Autobiographies.* Madison WI: University of Wisconsin Press, 1962.

Kelly, James. *American Catalogue of Books: Original and Imprints.* New York: P. Smith, 1938.

Kinnell, Susan K. *Historiography: An Annotated Bibliography of Journal Articles, Books, and Dissertations.* Santa Barbara CA: ABC-Clio, 1987.

Kittross, John M., comp. *A Bibliography of Theses and Dissertations in Broadcasting: 1920-1973.* Washington DC: Broadcast Education Association, 1978.

Klejment, Anne, and Alice Klejment. *Dorothy Day and the Catholic Worker: A Bibliography and Index.* New York: Garland, 1985.

Krichmar, Albert, et al. *The Women's Rights Movement in the United States, 1848-1970: A Bibliography and Sourcebook.* Metuchen NJ: Scarecrow, 1972.

Leonard, Eugenie A., Sophie H. Drinker, and Miriam Y. Holden. *The American Woman in Colonial and Revolutionary Times, 1565-1800.* Philadelphia: University of Pennsylvania Press, 1962; reprint, Westport CT: Greenwood Press, 1975.

Lichty, Lawrence H., and Malachi C. Topping. *American Broadcasting: A Sourcebook on the History of Radio and Television.* New York: Hastings House, 1975.

Ligenfelter, Richard E., and Karen R. Gash. *The Newspapers of Nevada: A History and Bibliography, 1854-1979.* Reno: University of Nevada Press, 1984.

McCavitt, William E. *Radio and Television: A Selected, Annotated Bibliography.* Metuchen NJ: Scarecrow, 1978.

_____. *Radio and Television: A Selected, Annotated Bibliography: Supplement One: 1977-1981.* Metuchen NJ: Scarecrow, 1982.

McCoy, Ralph E. Freedom of the Press: An Annotated Bibliography. Carbondale: Southern Illinois University Press, 1968.

_____. Freedom of the Press: A Bibliocyclopedia: Ten Year Supplement (1967-1977). Carbondale: Southern Illinois University Press, 1979.

MacDonald, William, ed. *Documentary Source Book of American History 1601-1926. 1926.* Reprint. New York: Macmillan, 1969.

McKerns, Joseph P. "Media Ethics: A Bibliographical Essay." *Journalism History* 5(2) (Summer 1978): 50-55.

_____. *News Media and Public Policy: An Annotated Bibliography.* New York: Garland, 1985.

McNeil, Alex. *Total Television: A Comprehensive Guide to Programming From 1948-1980.* New York: Penguin, 1980.

Marzolf, Marion, Ramona D. Rush, and Darlene Stern. "The Literature of Women in Journalism History." *Journalism History* 1(4) (Winter 1974-75): 117-128.

Marzolf, Marion. "The Literature of Women in Journalism History: A Supplement." *Journalism History* 3(4) (Winter 1976-77): 116-123.

Mather, Anne. "A History of Feminist Periodicals, Part One." *Journalism History* 1(3) (Autumn 1974): 82-85.

_____. "A History of Feminist Periodicals, Part Two." *Journalism History* 1(4) (Winter 1974-75): 108-111.

_____. "A History of Feminist Periodicals, Part Three." *Journalism History* 2(1) (Spring 1975): 19-27, 31.

Milner, Anita C. *Newspaper Indexes: A Location and Subject Guide for Researchers.* 3 vols. Metuchen NJ: Scarecrow, 1977-1982.

National Historical Publications and Records Commission. *Directory of Archives and Manuscript Repositories in the United States.* Washington DC: National Archives, 1978.

National Union Catalog: Pre-1956 Imprints. 684 vols. London: Mansell, 1968-1980. Plus 70-vol. supplement, 1980-1982.

National Union Catalog: A Cumulative Author List. Washington DC: U.S. Library of Congress, Card Division, 1956--. Annual.

National Union Catalog of Manuscript Collections 1959/61--. Hamden CT: Shoe String, 1962--. Annual.

Norton, Wesley. *Religious Newspapers in the Old Northwest to 1861: A History, Bibliography, and Record of Opinion.* Athens: Ohio University Press, 1977.

Paine, Fred K., and Nancy E. Paine. *Magazines: A Bibliography for Their Analysis, with Annotations and Study Guide.* Metuchen NJ: Scarecrow, 1987.

Pitts, Michael R. *Radio Soundtracks: A Reference Guide.* Metuchen NJ: Scarecrow, 1976.

Polley, Richard W. *Information Sources in Advertising History.* Westport CT: Greenwood Press, 1979.

Price, Warren C. *The Literature of Journalism: An Annotated Bibliography.* Minneapolis: University of Minnesota Press, 1959.

Price, Warren C., and Calder M. Pickett. *An Annotated Journalism Bibliography, 1958-1968.* Minneapolis: University of Minnesota Press, 1970.

Pride, Armistead S. "The Black Press to 1968: A Bibliography." *Journalism History* 4(4) (Winter 1977-78): 148-154.

Richardson, Lyon N. *History of Early American Magazines, 1741- 1789.* New York: Hippocrene Books, 1967.

Roobach, Orville. *Bibliotheca Americana.* New York: O.A. Roobach, 1849.

Rose, Oscar, ed. *Radio, Television, and Broadcasting: An Annotated Bibliography.* New York: Wilson, 1947.

Schact, J. H. *A Bibliography for the Study of Magazines.* Urbana: University of Illinois Press, 1968.

Schwarzlose, Richard A. *Newspapers: A Reference Guide.* Westport CT: Greenwood Press, 1987.

Shearer, Benjamin F., and Marilyn Buxford. *Communications and Society: A Bibliography on Communications Technologies and Their Social Impact.* Beverly Hills CA: Sage, 1983.

Sheehy, Eugene P. *Guide to Reference Books.* 10th ed. Chicago: American Library Association, 1986.

Shiers, George, and May Shiers. *Bibliography of the History of Electronics*. Metuchen NJ: Scarecrow, 1972.

Shipton, Clifford K., and James E. Mooney. *National Index of American Imprints through 1800: The Short-Title Evans*. Worcester MA: American Antiquarian Society, 1969.

Silha Center for the Study of Media Ethics and Law. *Two Bibliographies on Ethics*. Minneapolis: University of Minnesota, 1986.

Smith, Myron J. *U.S. Television Network News: A Guide to Sources in English*. Jefferson NC: McFarland & Co., 1984.

Snorgrass, J. William, and Gloria T. Woody, comps. *Blacks and Media: A Selected, Annotated Bibliography 1962-1982*. Tallahassee: Florida A. & M. University Press, 1985.

Sparks, Kenneth R. *A Bibliography of Doctoral Dissertations in Television and Radio*. 3d ed. Syracuse NY: School of Journalism, Syracuse University, 1971.

Stephens, Lester D. *Historiography: A Bibliography*. Metuchen NJ: Scarecrow, 1975.

Stevens, John D. "Journalism Manuscripts in the Michigan Historical Collections." *Journalism History* 2(2) (Summer 1975): 57.

Stevens, John D. "Museum of Cartoon Art Offers Possibilities for Research." *Journalism History* 3(3) (Autumn 1976): 89.

Swindler, William F. *A Bibliography of Law on Journalism*. New York: Columbia University Press, 1947.

Toomey, Alice F. *World Bibliography of Bibliographies 1964-1974*. 2 vols. Totowa NJ: Rowman & Littlefield, 1977.

United States. Library of Congress. General Reference and Bibliography Division. *A Guide to the Study of the United States of America*. Washington DC: Government Printing Office, 1960.

_____. *Supplement, 1956-1965*. Washington DC: Government Printing Office, 1976.

Walrath, Ronald. "The Media Collection of the Minnesota Historical Society." *Journalism History* 1(1) (Spring 1974): 26-27.

Who Was Who in Journalism, 1925-1928. Detroit: Gale, 1978.

Winther, Oscar. *A Classified Bibliography of the Periodical Literature of the Trans-Mississippi West (1811-1957)*. Bloomington: Indiana University Press, 1961.

_____, and Richard Van Orman. *A Classified Bibliography of the Periodical Literature of the Trans-Mississippi West: A Supplement (1957-1967)*. Bloomington: Indiana University Press, 1970.

Wolseley, Roland E., and Isabel Wolseley. *The Journalist's Bookshelf: An Annotated and Selected Bibliography of United States Print Journalism*.

Indianapolis: R.J. Berg, 1986. (Former editions 1939, 1943, 1946, 1951, 1955, 1961).

Women's History Sources: A Guide to Archives and Manuscript Collections in the U.S.. New York: Bowker, 1979.

Writings on American History, 1902-1961. 49 vols. Millwood NY: Kraus-Thomson, 1904-1978.

_____, 1962-1973. 4 vols. Millwood NY: KTO Press, 1976.

_____, 1973/74--. Millwood NY: Kraus-Thomson, 1974--. Annual.

Wynar, Lubomyr, and Anna Wynar. *Encyclopedic Directory of Ethnic Newspapers and Periodicals in the United States.* 2d ed. Littleton CO: Libraries Unlimited, 1976.

Databases for Historical Research

Kathleen A. Hansen and Jean Ward

Like other scholars, some historians doubtless have looked ahead to a time when information would be at their computer-connected fingertips. Seated at their office computer terminals, they would collect much of their wished-for data without struggling to find travel money to visit distant archives, without endless hours in libraries, reading and copying from ancient records. This futuristic fantasy for scholarly research is in its infancy, especially for historians. For the most part, the archival material and ancient records have not been transferred to electronic systems, so historians will continue to travel and to copy. There are, however, some collections which can be located through electronic services and recent scholarship on the subject by other historians can be identified and retrieved electronically.

The development of computer systems capable of fast and comprehensive information retrieval is just beginning to make major contributions to historical scholarship. Primary sources, such as vital statistics, tax records and census data, began to be created in electronic form in the mid-1960s. Only as these electronic files accumulate will they be useful to historical researchers. However, many bibliographic sources that historians use are available in electronic database form, especially those sources that have been compiled since the mid-1960s.

A database is simply a machine-readable file of information stored in a computer and accessible through either a telephone-computer link or via a compact disc. These files may consist of a number of different types of information. For example, bibliographic databases consist of citations to journal articles, books, technical reports, conference papers, government documents, popular press materials and other such sources. Some bibliographic files include both citations and short abstracts of the item cited.

Another type of database is the full-text file. These files include the complete text of each article included in the database. For instance, the full-text file includes the complete text of an article in the *New York Times*, whereas the bibliographic file includes only the citation to the same article, or the citation plus a brief abstract. Since most full-text files go back only to 1980 or so, their usefulness for historians currently is limited. In the future such files will be enormously important in speeding and expanding the work of media historians.

A third type of database that will be very useful to future media historians is the numeric database. Numeric files include demographic information culled from census reports and other sources, financial information about media companies, and media audience information.

Historians in major research or population centers have easy access to database information. Public, academic and special libraries have professional staff who are equipped to search these files at the scholar's request. Since there are more than 4,000 different databases, the expertise of the library staff is critical to successful searches. Most professional searchers will request that the researcher be present during the search, since the continual flow of information during an interactive search presents decision points that the scholar is best equipped to make.

Researchers should understand the distinction between producers of databases and vendors of databases. A database producer creates the content of the electronic file and is responsible for the information in the file. The vendor, on the other hand, sells access to the information in producers' databases. Nearly all vendors provide access to numerous databases from a variety of producers. Further, popular databases often are available through a number of vendors. A small number of database producers vend the files they have created. Some major database vendors include: DIALOG, which provides access to over two hundred different databases (full-text, bibliographic and numeric) and DIALOG's major competitor, BRS; NEXIS, one of the largest full-text systems with news and financial information; VU-TEXT, another full-text system with national and regional newspapers; and DOW JONES NEWS RETRIEVAL, a business and financial information service. The researcher can ask the librarian to do the search using the most cost-effective vendor that supplies the needed database.

Historians who have their own computers and communications equipment and software might be interested in learning to search databases independent of a professional searcher. Some database vendors offer training seminars for a fee. Because there are so many different vendors and their search protocols all differ, few historians are likely to take this route. The future expansion of simplified "gateway" programs that allow the searcher to bypass many of these complexities may increase scholars' independent searching. In addition, the expanding availability of databases on disc, known as CD-ROM technology, means that many files can be searched by novices. Historians of the future will be more independent searchers of electronic files than historians of today.

Databases have presented a challenge to the notion of free access to information in libraries and research centers. The fees associated with database searching can be intimidating. Unless the researcher has a grant or is affiliated with an institution that provides free searches, cost becomes an important issue. Searching through a library or research center provides several advantages. The institution has contracts with the major vendors that provide access to as many as two hundred electronic files through a central service. In addition, the institution may have contracts with some database producers that vend their databases independently.

Fees for online searching are based on a number of elements. The producer of the database charges a royalty fee. The "online" time, or time that the searcher is hooked into the computer, is charged at a per-minute rate. Telecommunication charges are billed for use of the telephone-satellite link between the main computer and the local terminal. Finally, there is a fee for each record (citation, article, numerical table) that is printed. For instance, a bibliographic file called "America: History and Life" charges $65.00 per connect hour and $.15 per citation printed. For a ten-minute search that locates thirteen citations, then, the charge to the searcher would be $8.45 plus telecommunication costs. While paying such fees may seem unwarranted to some researchers, others willingly trade the time they save for the service and royalty fees.

Databases on disc present a different type of cost accounting. The library or subscribing institution pays a large fee for purchase of the information on a compact disc, which is then kept in-house and can be searched on local equipment as many times as patrons wish. In many instances the researchers do their own searching. The library may charge a small fee for use of the equipment and disc to recover some of the costs in purchasing the subscription to the disc.

Since database searches usually involve some cost to the researcher, it is crucial that the search be effectively structured to take advantage of the efficiency of the system. The researcher's first step is to conduct a manual literature search in printed indexes and abstracts in order to become acquainted with the structure of information for the subject being researched. The researcher can identify possible search terms and subject headings that might be useful in the database search itself. Also, the manual literature search may yield some citations that could be used as search leads in the electronic files. Following the manual search, the researcher should review and evaluate material collected as part of that search process.

Next, the researcher needs to identify the appropriate goals for the database search. Should the search uncover the location of collections of primary sources? Bibliographic information from scholarly sources? Full-text materials from periodicals? Demographic information about residents of a particular geographic area? This process will help the researcher to identify the appropriate place (such as library, archive or historical society) from which to request the search and to choose databases in which to search.

Having clarified the goals for use of the database, the researcher is prepared for the reference interview with the professional who will conduct the search. During this interview, the searcher will ask the historian what material is in hand already and what additional information is desired. The historian and the searcher must agree on the boundaries of the search, such as time period, place, topic, discipline and so forth. What emerges from this discussion are the key vocabulary choices that describe the subject and clues for selecting the best databases to meet the information need. The searcher may ask the historian if comprehensiveness of the search is valued, even at the expense of retrieving numerous irrelevant items, since the most comprehensive searches are likely to retrieve material irrelevant to the scholarly project. Once into the search, the historian and the searcher can respond to the information being displayed on the screen by narrowing or expanding the search vocabulary or boundaries. For example, if the search recovers three hundred items from the database, obviously the search vocabulary needs to be refined, thereby reducing the number of items being recovered to those most closely related to the scholarly project. If the search uncovers just a few choice items, these may be printed immediately on the searcher's printer before disconnecting from the database. If more citations or records are found, the historian may request that these be printed "offline" -- that is, the searcher will disconnect from the database after requesting that the material be printed overnight and mailed. Offline printing usually saves some money because per-minute fees are not assessed during the printing process.

Media history is inherently interdisciplinary. Scholarship in the field draws upon general history, economics, political science, sociology, law, international relations, rhetoric, biography, popular arts, literature, and other fields. Databases allow historians to tap simultaneously into sources in a variety of fields. In contrast to printed reference works that concentrate on one field, database searches can bring to the scholar a variety of materials originating in relevant fields. For example, one vendor of databases provides a means for searching as many as twenty files concurrently, which means that the historian can seek material from twenty disciplines with one search. A similar manual search would require use of twenty different printed indexes and a variety of subject headings.

Comprehensiveness and currency are additional advantages to using database services. Unlike many printed indexes and abstracts, databases are updated monthly, weekly or even daily. Thus, historians can be assured that their literature searches represent the most complete and current review of relevant, available material.

As the development of databases grows, historians increasingly will recognize that some information is available only in electronic form. Currently, many sources exist both in print and in databases. The future for public records, numeric sources and major daily newspaper content is likely to be largely electronic. To the extent that some research projects would never be practical using printed sources, database access allows historians to conceptualize and carry out imaginative and pathbreaking research.

To take advantage of database search power, historians need at least a rudimentary understanding of the Boolean logic on which text database searching is based. In order to find the needed information, the computer must match the historian's search terms with the occurrence of those same terms in the database files. Boolean logic makes possible the matching and combination of many terms (by using AND, OR or NOT as term connectors), and the extraction from the file of any and all items that fit the search logic. For instance, the historian could combine such terms as (reconstruction AND slavery), AND (newspaper press OR telegraph) for a search in a bibliographic file. The database search would encompass a variety of disciplines, yielding citations that include all of the elements represented by the search terms.

Database files are at the immediate command of the researcher. They are never at the bindery, checked out to another user, on reserve or otherwise inaccessible. Database systems allow for simultaneous use by hundreds of users. For citation databases, however, the researcher may need a variety of methods for retrieving the source material identified by the database search.

For historians, most databases do not go back far enough into the past to meet many needs. For example, historians working in public records will still find it necessary to work in paper records. Manuscript and archival materials will not be online, although directories that assist the historian in locating those materials may be available in database form. The two national online catalogs, RLIN and OCLC, include information about the location of manuscript and archive collections. Many archives are now developing in-house databases that catalog their holdings at the folder or item level, as well. The actual archival records themselves, however, will still be in paper form. Therefore, historians working in the Colonial period, for example, will find little other than citations of other scholars' work or guides to archival collections in databases. As more material is stored long term in electronic form, full-text databases and public record databases will become more useful for historians.

Historians may well become alarmed at the destruction of original materials in favor of storing them electronically. For instance, as electronic storage of daily newspapers becomes standard, the availability of those newspapers in paper or microfilm form may become limited. Historians certainly recognize that the "text" is not the only significant aspect of a newspaper's coverage of, say, the 1988 presidential election. The display, graphics, placement and surrounding material all play a role in understanding the "meaning" of coverage. All these aspects are lost in the database record of a newspaper's presentation of the story.

Another disadvantage of the electronic systems is that, for the most part, they will continue to exist only so long as they contribute to profits in the private sector of the economy. Producers and vendors of databases may not be compelled by historians' needs and may simply destroy electronic files that are not perceived as profitable. Comparable paper files may not exist, either because the database never had a paper counterpart or because the paper version was abandoned or destroyed when the electronic version was established. Scholars disturbed by these prospects are organizing to prevent destruction of valued electronic files.

The cost of database use limits browsing and serendipity as search methods. Users of printed indexes and abstracts, for example, frequently encounter references under subject headings they had not expected to use. Scanning the printed versions of bibliographic references has no practical equivalent in the electronic realm.

Since browsing and serendipity are impractical in electronic searches, historians recognize that a search is only as good as the strategy on which it is based. All variant uses of a term (say, "radio" and "wireless") must be anticipated when the terminology for the search is established. Imprecision of terminology plagues those who search in social sciences and humanities databases, since terminology in those disciplines is less precise than in the physical sciences.

Bibliographic Databases

Databases that give the scholar a relevant set of citations currently are viewed as the most useful for historians. This section of the chapter provides examples of what historians might expect to retrieve from a variety of databases.

America: History And Life

Historians doubtless are familiar with the print counterpart to this database, the three-part series that gives article abstracts and citations, indexes to book reviews and American history bibliographies. The database is updated three times yearly and covers American and ethnic studies, folklore, history, historiography, methodology, popular culture and urban affairs. Having been started in 1964, it is one of the "oldest" of databases. It abstracts and indexes more than 2,000 journals in the sciences and humanities; in addition it covers monographs and dissertations relevant to U.S. and Canadian history.

The powers of Boolean searching in this database are illustrated by one scholar's search for citations on the history of the peace movement and opinion or attitude change. The database identified 970 citations that included the phrase "political attitude" and 217 citations including the phrase "peace movement." When these two phrases were combined with the logical operator AND, the search was narrowed to twenty citations that included both of the phrases, yielding a manageable bibliography of relevant articles.

Historical Abstracts

This index and abstract reference service covers the history of the world, excluding the U.S. and Canada, from 1450 to the present. Articles are abstracted from more than 2,000 journals in thirty languages and from ninety countries. Its print counterpart bears the same name as the database, which began in 1973.

Arts & Humanities Search

Corresponding to Arts & Humanities Citation Index, this database adds about 9,000 items every fortnight in art, social sciences and humanities. Its bibliographic citations cover 1,300 journals in the arts, humanities, science and social sciences. Among the subjects to be found in these citations are those from architecture, art, dance, film, history, literature, music, philosophy, theatre, theology, television and radio. In addition to the general history citations, communication historians might consult it for citations on film, television and history or for assistance with a topic on the popular music industry and its relations with the radio industry. The database began in 1980.

Social Scisearch

Since 1972, this database has been available as a multidisciplinary search service covering 1,500 journals in the social sciences and additional related items from 3,000 journals in biomedical, natural and physical sciences. Selected monographs are included as well. An unusual feature of this database is that it can be searched to learn the cited references of an author. This capability is useful for assessing the impact of an author on his or her scholarly field, for example. Another innovative use of this database is to use it to discover if a particular scholarly work has been cited in a specific context. For example, the historian seeking citations on the peace movement and public opinion located 817 references to opinion researcher Hadley Cantril's *Public Opinion, 1935-1946.* By combining the term PEACE with Cantril's name, she reduced the total relevant references to five. These five citations could not have been retrieved through any other method.

Six media-related databases are cited below as examples of the kinds of bibliographic sources available to communication historians. While these services have begun only recently, historians doubtless recognize that recent media content may include material of historical interest. For example, in searching for information on the role of newspapers on the western frontier, the historian may locate recent news stories that give accounts of a newspaper's founding and of the community at the time the paper began.

Newspaper Abstracts

With coverage back to 1984 for most titles, this file offers comprehensive indexing and concise abstracting of more than twenty major U.S. and international newspapers, including the *New York Times, Wall Street Journal* and *Los Angeles Times.* The database is updated weekly with more than 10,000 new records. In addition, it is possible to order a full-text, copyright-cleared copy of any article located through a search in the database from the UMI Article Clearinghouse, so historians who do not have access to particular newspapers can still get copies of the articles needed.

Index To Black Newspapers

Editorial material from ten prominent Black newspapers is indexed in this database, which began in 1979. The researcher will receive citations, abstracts and a code distinguishing articles as review, commentary and editorial. A corresponding print index has the same title as the online version. Newspapers in the database are: *Amsterdam New York News, Atlanta Daily World, Baltimore Afro-American, Bilalian News* (Chicago), *Chicago Defender, Cleveland Call & Post, Norfolk Journal & Guide, Los Angeles Sentinel, Michigan Chronicle, New Pittsburgh Courier,* and *St. Louis Argus.*

The Information Bank

This file, going back to 1969, contains abstracts of all news and editorial matter from the final Late Edition of *The New York Times* newspaper and selected material from approximately ten other newspapers and thirty-nine magazines published in the U.S., Canada, and Europe. Items covered include general news articles, forecasts, analyses, surveys, biographies, features, columns, and editorials. Maps, charts, photographs, diagrams, and other graphics are noted but captions are excluded. The database is updated daily, with 180,000 new items added each year.

Television Script Archive

A network television script archive at the Annenberg School of Communications Library in Philadelphia can be searched using a specialized database. The collection includes more than 24,000 scripts from almost all series, movies made for television, specials and pilots aired during prime time from 1976 to the present. The collection grows at the rate of 1,500 scripts a year. The database and the archive are available to researchers upon written application.

Primetime Radio Classics

Information about radio programs of the 1930s, -40s and -50s is available through this database which has two major types of material available.   About 25,000 titles are available, with information on characters, casts, sponsors, program times and inclusive broadcast dates included in the material. In addition, a listing of 450 episodes of vintage programs can be ordered on cassette.

Magill's Survey Of Cinema

The database includes articles on more than 1,800 important films, as well as brief abstracts and credit listings for many other films.   The complete text articles that cover the more significant films include the film title, date, origin, cast and credit listings, rating by the Motion Picture Association of America, abstract, critical essay, citation to noteworthy reviews, awards given, qualitative ratings, running time and video availability. Updated every two weeks, the database entries cover 1902 to the present.

Magazine Index

Historians should find numerous uses for this online index to magazine content, particularly since it covers the period of 1959 to March 1970 and 1973 to the present.   Historians examining magazine coverage of, to cite a few examples, political issues, war and peace, public opinion, and popular culture trends will find citations to articles in 435 popular magazines. One could examine all magazine articles written by Marshall McLuhan, as well as all articles written about McLuhan, for instance.   In addition, the Magazine Index contains full texts of records from more than one hundred magazines, beginning in 1983. With more than 2.5 million records, it is updated monthly.

Inasmuch as media history is a highly interdisciplinary enterprise, historians of mass communication frequently consult references from relevant fields such as law, humanities, politics, philosophy, public affairs, ethnic studies and women's studies. A selection of relevant databases illustrates the value of searching in fields outside communication history.

Index To Legal Periodicals

Articles from 476 legal periodicals published in English are included in both the online and print versions of this index. The database also includes statutes, case notes and book reviews. Updated twice a week, this database covers August 1981 to the present and averages 14,400 new items each year.

Legal Resource Index

This index covers more than 750 law journals, six law newspapers and selected legal monographs, with new records added monthly since it began in 1980. Legal Resource Index also provides law articles from other online files, including *Magazine Index, National Newspaper Index* and *Trade and Industry Index.* In addition to periodical articles, it indexes book reviews, case notes, letters to the editor, transcripts, biographical items and editorials considered useful for locating secondary information useful in law.

Humanities Index

Since February 1985, this database corresponding to the print version of same name has been available for reference to 294 English-language periodicals covering art, classical studies, area studies, folklore, history, journalism, language and literature, literary and political criticism, performing arts, philosophy, photography, religion and theology.

U.S. Political Science Documents

Abstracts and index items from 150 major U.S. political science journals provide access to research results in political, social and policy sciences. The database began in 1975 and is updated quarterly.

Philosopher's Index

This database provides indexes and abstracts from 1940 to the present, with quarterly updates covering books and more than 270 journals of philosophy and related disciplines. The database corresponds to the printed publication that bears the same title. Of particular interest to communication historians will be its material on the philosophy of such disciplines as history and law.

Eighteenth Century Short Title Catalog

Covering a time span of 1701 to 1800, this service is produced by The British Library to provide access to books, lists, advertisements, songs and other printed materials from the Eighteenth Century. It has about 180,000 citations, chiefly in English, covering Great Britain, North America, India and other British possessions of the 18th century.

Religion Index

Four databases covering related areas are encompassed by the title above. They are: *Religion Index Database, Religion Index One, Religion Index Two* and *Research in Ministry.* The databases cover 1949 to the present, with monthly updating. The databases cover some materials that do not appear in the print indexes with corresponding titles. They include 350 journals in which all articles are covered and another 350 journals reviewed for entries relevant to religion. Broadly interdisciplinary, the indexes cover literature of religion and theology and relevant areas of archaeology, anthropology, social science, medicine, psychology, ethics, art, church history, ethnology, music and canon law. About seventy percent of the database consists of journal articles, with the remaining thirty percent being monographs, proceedings and theses.

American Statistics Index

Covering 1973 to the present, this index corresponds to the printed version of the same name. Some publications issued in the 1960s are covered, as well. Included are citations and abstracts referring to the social, economic, demographic and other statistical data collected and analyzed by the U.S. government.

Pais International

Public policy is a major focus of this database, which combines two print publications, *PAIS Bulletin* and *PAIS Foreign Language Index*. Contents relevant to communication historians include material on business, economics, international relations, government and social and political sciences. The foreign language index portion goes back to 1972, while the PAIS Bulletin goes back to 1976. About sixty percent of the items indexed were published originally in English and most entries have a sentence or two in English noting the contents of the entry. Printed material in all formats is covered, including books and periodical articles; government documents; committee hearings; pamphlets; reports of public and private organizations.

CIS/INDEX

Congressional Information Service/Index to Congressional Publications and Public Laws gives a detailed index and lengthy abstracts of significant publications issued by nearly 300 Congressional committees and subcommittees. It covers 1970 to the present with about 15,500 items added each year. CIS/INDEX would be helpful to historians researching federal actions and contemplated actions in relation to mass communication businesses, for example, and to those examining freedom of information questions over time.

Full Text Databases

Researchers find full text databases convenient, since these files contain the complete text of files which can be printed during or immediately following the database search. Naturally, records from full text files are more expensive to retrieve than those from bibliographic files. Some examples of full text databases useful to communication historians are given below.

AP News

About five hundred news stories a day are filed in this full text database, which goes back to 1977. U.S. and international news reports are included, covering government, financial, political, sports and entertainment topics.

Magazines ASAP

Magazine Index, cited above in bibliographic databases, covers about four hundred magazines. In this online service, about one hundred of the magazines in the Magazine Index are selected for indexing and full text electronic storage. Complete articles, editorials, columns and reviews can be received online.

American Marketplace

The full text of a newsletter on U. S. population data is available electronically. Data from and analyses of the 1980 census are available, along with important related developments in federal bureaus. Updated fortnightly.

Legi-Slate

This database has two major sections. One, dating to 1979, contains all bills and resolutions of the U.S. Congress and the Texas State Legislature, along with recorded votes, committee meeting schedules and actions taken. Researchers use it to track bills in the legislature and committees, since it has comprehensive data on each bill and actions related to it. The second section of the database includes regulatory information consisting of abstracts of such documents as *Federal Register* announcements by government agencies, Sunshine Act meetings, presidential documents and rules and regulations.

LEXIS

LEXIS is a rich full text data base having numerous component files that cover varied aspects of legal information. Generally, it contains federal and state court reported cases, constitutions, codes, rules, regulations, and government agency decisions. The component databases include the LEXIS COMMUNICATIONS

LIBRARY, segments of which go back to 1929. It includes, for example, volumes of the FCC Commission Reports dealing with frequency allocations, sponsorship identification, equal time, and fairness doctrine material.

Westlaw

Westlaw full text databases contain material from 1932 to the present and largely correspond to relevant West Publishing Company printed products. They include the full text of cases from the federal and appellate courts of fifty states, a complete Federal Tax library, the text of the U.S. code and varied specialized legal libraries. Of particular interest to some communication historians is the WESTLAW COMMUNICATIONS DATA BASE, containing full text and headnotes of communication cases from the Supreme Court since 1880, Courts of Appeals since 1891, District Courts since 1789 and the Court of Claims since 1929, along with the full text of Federal Communications Commission reports since 1965. It also includes selected law review articles and relevant sections of federal codes and the *Federal Register.*

Numeric Databases

Another major category of information in database files is numeric and statistical data. Historians may find that these files are more valuable in the future as more and more information begins to be stored and kept in these electronic systems. Some of the currently-available files that might be useful are discussed here.

Americanprofile

This file includes demographic and economic data from the 1970 and 1980 U.S. census, current year updates, five-year projections of selected demographic characteristics, and some proprietary statistics including mobility, auto registration data, and private sector employees. The file also includes more than 160 key statistics describing the commercial environment in ZIP code areas. The file is produced by Donnelley Marketing Information Services and is updated annually.

Cendata

Produced by the U.S. Census Bureau, this file contains the full text and numeric data from Census Bureau economic and demographic reports from 1980 to date. The reports cover such materials as business, population, and housing reports updated daily.

Politics Online

For historians tracking the relationship between media and politics, this file may prove very useful. It consists of information on contributions made to U.S. congressional candidates by Political Action Committees. Included are the amounts of individual and aggregated contributions by PAC, committee assignments of current members of Congress, the percentage of votes each legislator received in elections, and ratings of their voting records by fifty-two organizations (e.g. ACLU, Common Cause). The file is produced by Information for Public Affairs.

Access to Other Information in Databases

A number of databases do not easily fit into the categories discussed above, or they cross categories. Many of these files combine directory or reference materials with bibliographic information. Several such "unusual" files are mentioned here.

Biography Index

This file contains references to biographies available in current books of biography, autobiography, critical studies, and biographical fiction; about 2,600 periodicals; newspaper obituaries; bibliographies; and other printed materials. Both current and historical persons are included. Information includes the name of the person, dates of birth (and death), profession, and the names and dates of biographical source publications that list the individual. The file corresponds to the printed *Biography Index.* It covers 1984 to date and is updated twice a week.

Biography Master Index

The electronic counterpart to *Biography and Genealogy Master Index,* second edition and its annual updates, this file provides a master index to biographical information in more than seven hundred source publications and 1,150 publication editions, including English-language general and geographical who's who-type publications, major biographical dictionaries, handbooks, and directories. Both current and historical persons are included. The file is updated irregularly.

Books In Print

This is the major source of information on books currently published and in-print in the United States. The file corresponds to the several *Books in Print* publications. However, the electronic version, through its Boolean searching capability, allows for searches that are not possible in the print version. For example, a researcher seeking books on labor/management history and conflict by midwest publishers combined those search elements to identify the seventeen citations that fit his needs. Only an electronic search could have uncovered these books efficiently. Records in this file include basic bibliographic information (author, title, publisher, date), LC or ISBN number, and price. The file is updated monthly by the producer, R. R. Bowker.

Book Review Index

Gale Research Company has produced this file since 1969. All reviews of books or periodicals appearing in more than 380 journals are indexed in this database. Coverage includes books in literature, fine arts, history, social science, and education. Each record lists author, book or periodical title being reviewed, document type and source of the review. The file is updated three times a year.

Database Of Databases

Detailed information on publicly-available databases is included in this file, updated irregularly. All databases described are accessible either through an online service or a batch processor, or they are available for direct lease or purchase on tape, diskette, or other medium. Gale Research Company produces the file.

Dissertation Abstracts Online

The definitive subject, title, and author guide to virtually every American dissertation accepted at an accredited institution since 1861, this file is updated monthly by University Microfilms International. In addition, citations for thousands of Canadian dissertations and an increasing number of papers accepted abroad are included. Abstracts are available for a large majority of the dissertations accepted after January 1980.

ERIC

ERIC is a traditional bibliographic file, covering educational materials from the Educational Resources Information Center from 1966 to date. It has particular use for journalism historians, however, because it includes citations for papers read at a number of important professional meetings, including Association for Education in Journalism and Mass Communication, International Communication Association, and Speech Communication Association. Many items can be purchased from the ERIC Document Reproduction Service in paper copy or microfiche. The file is produced by the U.S. Department of Education, and is updated monthly.

Guide To Microforms In Print

This file contains references to about 125,000 publications currently available on microfiche or microfilm. Books, monographs, periodicals and selected other types of documents such as dissertations are included. This is a current file updated monthly. It corresponds to the printed guide by the same name, and is produced by Meckler Publishing Co..

RLIN

Produced by the Research Libraries Group, RLIN (Research Libraries Information Network) is a shared catalog service that includes records of books, journal and archive holdings for many major research collections. Such prestigious collections as those at Stanford, Columbia, Yale and the New York Public Library are included along with many other research collections. With a search in RLIN, the historian can see a list of libraries that own the book the researcher needs. Interlibrary loan may be used to borrow many of the items listed.

OCLC

Another shared catalog network, OCLC (Online Computer Library Center) includes catalog information for 3,800 member libraries and another 2,500 adjunct members. Many medium- and small-sized public and college libraries are included. As with an RLIN search, the historian must have the author and title of the book before searching.

LC/Line

Covering 1968 to the present, LC/LINE provides extensive coverage of the monographic literature, serials, maps, manuscripts, and other materials cataloged by the U.S. Library of Congress (LC). Historians will be particularly interested in access to manuscript collections offered by this database. It is a product of SDC Information Services, updated semiannually.

Premarc Database

All records from the Library of Congress shelflist not previously put into LC's own MARC system (their online catalog) from 1897 to the present are included. The system includes 5 million records, and 1.8 million MARC records. The database is updated quarterly by Carrollton Press Inc.

Scorpio

This database, produced by the Library of Congress, consists of several files of information on federal legislation, programs, and agencies.   The LEGISLATIVE INFORMATION FILES contains citations, with abstracts and digests, to public bills and resolutions introduced in Congress from the 93rd Congress (1973/74) to date. It is updated daily. The GENERAL ACCOUNTING OFFICE FILES contain citations to documents on U.S. federal agencies and their programs submitted to or produced by the GAO, updated annually. The BIBLIOGRAPHIC CITATION FILE contains citations, with short abstracts, to periodical articles, pamphlets, and U.S. Government and United Nations publications from 1976 to date. It is updated weekly.   Of particular interest to historians is the COPYRIGHT HISTORY MONOGRAPHS FILE, which contains citations to documents registered or renewed for copyright protection. Literary works, works of performing and visual arts, and sound recordings from 1978 to date are included.   For each record, the author and copyright claimant, title of work, dates of creation and copyright filing, registration number, and related works are listed.   It is updated weekly.   SCORPIO includes several other files, including LC MARC, PREMARC, and the NATIONAL REFERRAL CENTER MASTER FILE.

The databases cited in this chapter by no means exhaust the electronic sources available to historians. With more than 4,000 databases in existence and additional files being created constantly, the possibilities for creatively using databases in historical research seem unlimited. Database searching is taking its place as a new and exciting research method that supplements traditional historical methods. As with these traditional methods, successful database searching requires the contribution of librarians and archivists. The research partnership among these participants will continue to enrich the contributions of communication historians.

The United States Newspaper Program

Gary Charbonneau

One of the principal sources for almost any project in journalism history is the newspaper itself. Unfortunately, American newspapers have been the subject of much neglect by publishers and librarians over the years. Part of the neglect has to do with some of the physical characteristics of newspapers. *En masse*, they are bulky and heavy. Storing them on library shelves is often difficult, because bound newspapers are usually too large to be stood upright. They take up a good deal of space, a precious commodity in most libraries. As a result, newspaper backfiles frequently have been relegated to piles in basements and broom closets, thus limiting public access.

While this situation is regrettable, what happens to newspapers even under the most user-friendly storage conditions is absolutely tragic. After the Civil War, newspapers ceased being printed on durable but expensive rag paper and began to be printed on cheaper pulp paper. The chemical process used to produce pulp paper leaves behind an acid residue which causes the paper to self-destruct. This problem is not unique to newspapers. Indeed, an entire century of publications of all types is beginning to disintegrate on the shelves of the nation's libraries. The extremely poor quality of the paper used for newsprint means that newspapers are the species most in danger of immediate physical extinction. Yesterday's news is becoming tomorrow's crumbling "yellow snow."

The deteriorating physical condition of most newspapers is a serious concern for the scholar. Somewhat less serious, perhaps, is the haphazard nature of much newspaper bibliography. Fortunately, some of the tools for identifying newspaper titles and locating newspaper files have been excellent. One thinks, for example, of Clarence Brigham's monumental *History and Bibliography of American Newspapers, 1690-1820*. Originally published in eighteen installments in the *Proceedings of the American Antiquarian Society* from 1913 to 1927, the bibliography was reissued by the Society in two volumes in 1947. The work was reissued again in 1962 by Archon Books with additions and corrections through 1961.

Brigham's bibliography was a model of its kind. Arranged alphabetically by state and city, it gave lengthy histories of each paper and listed the holdings of each title in a number of major national repositories as well as many local repositories. If there was any problem with Brigham's work, it was that it stopped with 1820. There were several reasons for this, but, as Brigham noted, it was "chiefly because the bibliography had to stop somewhere and to extend it into later decades might cause the entire undertaking to fall under its own weight."[1]

To cover the years after 1820, Winifred Gregory, working under the auspices of the Bibliographical Society of America, compiled her *American Newspapers, 1821-1936*, published by the H.W. Wilson Company in 1937. Gregory's work differed considerably in appearance from Brigham's. The historical descriptions of the titles she listed were far less extensive, consisting primarily of notes about major title changes, relationships with other titles, and suspensions of publication. Most listings were accompanied by no descriptions at all save for information about beginning and ending dates (if known) and frequency of publication. Listings of repositories were, however, far more extensive than Brigham's. This reflected the fact that newspapers published after 1820 were more likely to have survived than papers published before that date and were far more numerous to begin with.

For many years after Brigham and Gregory, a number of fine newspaper bibliographies were published dealing with some limited subset of the universe of American newspaper titles. Many covered newspapers published in a given state or locality and a few dealt with papers issued by or for particular ethnic communities. No attempt was made to compile another bibliography covering the entire country. Meanwhile, the papers themselves continued to fall victim to fire, flood, and, above all, to their own acidity.

Concerned about the lack of comprehensive bibliographic work being done for newspapers, the Committee on Bibliographical and Research Needs of the Organization of American Historians (OAH) proposed in 1969 that Gregory's bibliography be updated. From 1973 to 1975, OAH received financial support from the National

Endowment for the Humanities (NEH) to plan the update. At first, a traditional printed bibliography in book form was contemplated, but a new technology was emerging which was beginning to make the printed bibliography obsolescent. That technology was, of course, the computer. Computers made it less expensive to record and structure bibliographic data. More important, they made it relatively easy to correct errors, to add new information, and to share information among remote sites.

By the mid-1970s, the Library of Congress and other agencies had already made considerable strides toward solving the technical and organizational problems involved in coding and sharing bibliographic information in machine-readable form. To take advantage of this progress, the Organization of American Historians began to work closely with the Library of Congress to develop a plan for a computerized catalog of the nation's newspapers. With additional funding from the National Endowment for the Humanities, a pilot project was conducted in Iowa to determine the kinds of problems which might be encountered in a project of this scope and to develop solutions to those problems.

Building on the experience derived from the Iowa pilot project, the National Endowment for the Humanities and the Library of Congress began to develop a long-term plan for cataloging and preserving newspapers. This plan called for a decentralized approach to compile a new and completely comprehensive catalog of newspapers on a state-by-state basis with central coordination assured by NEH funding and Library of Congress technical oversight. In addition, the National Endowment would provide funds to preserve a portion of each state's newspapers for posterity. These objectives have been incorporated into a major National Endowment project called the United States Newspaper Program, or USNP.

Before the program could get under way, several important technical details had to be resolved. One such detail was the question of just how the bibliographic data was to be recorded. At the time that the US Newspaper Program was being initiated, the American library community was in the process of changing the standard national rules for cataloging. The result was a new cataloging code known as *Anglo-American Cataloguing Rules*, 2nd edition or, more popularly, *AACR2*. The general principles of *AACR2* were subsequently incorporated, along with some practical changes, into a newspaper cataloging manual to guide library catalogers working with newspapers. A second detail involved the method by which newspapers were to be preserved. Ideally, one would like to preserve the physical papers themselves. Given the brittle condition of so many old newspapers, this has not proven to be feasible; therefore, it was decided that all preservation carried out under USNP auspices would involve preservation of the *intellectual content* of newspapers through archival quality microfilming.

The general approach of the United States Newspaper Program is one that involves distributing the work to agencies in individual states. Each state is expected to progress through three phases. In Phase I, a feasibility study is conducted which has as its purpose the estimation of the scope of the work involved (How many newspapers are there in the state? Where and under what conditions are they housed?) and the development of a proposal to carry out the work. Phase I is funded by the National Endowment for the Humanities with a grant of up to $10,000. At the end of this phase, the state submits a proposal to the Endowment. If the proposal is accepted, the state receives a second and far more substantial grant for Phase II, the cataloging of the state's newspapers. This grant requires that the state carry out a modest amount of local fundraising to supplement the NEH grant. Finally, the state prepares a plan and receives funding for Phase III, microfilming. Because of the enormous need in this area, the Endowment has announced that it cannot afford to fund the filming of more than a portion (generally about ten to fifteen percent) of a state's previously unfilmed titles. In addition, during Phase III a state must match NEH funding dollar-for-dollar from local resources. Originally, each state was expected to have completed Phase II before proceeding to Phase III. More recently, state projects have been expected to undertake Phase II (cataloging) and Phase III (microfilming) simultaneously. This avoids the need to handle papers twice, which was not only time-consuming and expensive, but also sometimes resulted in the destruction of brittle papers by catalogers before they could be turned over to microfilmers.

Before any cataloging was done at the state level, the US Newspaper Program first began cataloging at several "national repositories," so called because of the size of their collections (at least 2,000 titles) and because they had a tradition of collecting newspapers published in all areas of the country. The cataloging records produced by these national repositories could be used subsequently by the various state projects, thus reducing the amount of work that would need to be done at the state level. In addition, by beginning with a relatively small number of national repositories, it was possible to further refine the goals and methodologies of the program before expanding it to the states. The first six national repositories to participate were: the New York Historical Society; the American Antiquarian Society; the Center for Research Libraries; the Western Reserve Historical Society; the State Historical Society of Wisconsin; and the Kansas State Historical Society. The Library of Congress participated as a seventh national repository although, as a federal agency in its own right, it did not receive funding from the National Endowment.

Cataloging at the national repositories began early in 1983. In the spring of that same year, planning grants were awarded to sixteen state projects. Numerous additional state projects have been funded since that time. Although the program is now well under way, its scope and cost are such that the National Endowment for the Humanities does not anticipate completion until some time in the middle of the first decade of the next century.

The bibliographic information compiled by the United States Newspaper Program is being entered and stored in the database of the Online Computer Library Center (OCLC), the nation's largest "bibliographic utility." It is a non-profit enterprise which receives its revenue by providing the computer resources which enable libraries to share bibliographic data. Today, most North American libraries of any size participate in OCLC or a similar bibliographic utility. They buy cataloging records from these utilities either in the form of traditional catalog cards (printed at and distributed from OCLC's offices in Dublin, Ohio) or in the form of magnetic tapes which can be loaded into a library's local computer catalog. In turn, the libraries allow the utilities to share the bibliographic records they have created with other libraries which might need them.

Two types of Newspaper Program records are entered into OCLC. One is the bibliographic record which contains the traditional kinds of information associated with library cataloging -- title, place of publication, publisher, extent of published run, etc. The other record is the union list (holdings) record. The union list records shows which repositories hold a title and show the extent of their holdings. They may also carry some additional local information such as call number. The union list record for each title held by a repository is linked by the computer to the appropriate bibliographic record.

Because of certain coded information in the bibliographic and holdings records, it is possible for OCLC to produce newspaper bibliographies in print, microfiche or on computer tape. The National Endowment for the Humanities requires that each state project purchase from OCLC one of these paper, fiche, or tape "off-line products" at the completion of its cataloging work. The off-line product thus constitutes a new and up-to-date state newspaper bibliography. Each state project is free to distribute the bibliography as it sees fit. At least one state has considered having the major libraries in the state load the magnetic tape product into their local computer catalogs.

In addition to the state-level off-line products, OCLC has been producing the *United States Newspaper Program National Union List.* Actually, this title is a bit of a misnomer; because of limitations in the program used to pull the list from the OCLC database, it includes some foreign newspapers as well. The first edition of the *National Union List* appeared in June, 1985. The second appeared in June, 1987, and incorporated titles cataloged for the Newspaper Program in the intervening two years. It is available in two formats: as a multi-volume paperback, and as a set of microfiche in a vinyl binder with a printed guide. It may be presumed that OCLC will issue further editions as demand warrants and as its computer resources permit.

The *National Union List* consists of a master list of newspapers arranged alphabetically by "main entry." For newspapers, the main entry is the title. Qualifiers (usually in the form of place of publication) are added to the end of titles that are not unique. Various indexes provide alternative access to the main entry list. At the present time there are indexes for beginning date of publication, place of publication, language and intended audience.

Most users of th*e National Union List* will probably wish to begin their search using one of the indexes rather than the main entry master list. This may be because they have no specific title in mind when they begin the search, or it may be because they are not certain of the exact title. In this connection, it must be pointed out that the cataloging manual used by participants in the US Newspaper Program adheres in most essentials to a major principle of the *Anglo-American Cataloguing Rules,* 2nd edition. That principle calls for recording as the main entry the title of the newspaper exactly as it appeared on the paper. When the title changes, as it often does, a second record is made for the new title. This practice is somewhat at odds with the approach traditionally taken by newspaper bibliographers, who have usually omitted title words having to do with either place of publication or frequency. To the traditional newspaper bibliographer, *The Times, The Daily Times,* and the *Tinytown Times* would probably have been a single title requiring a single entry -- for *The Times* -- under the listing of titles published in Tinytown. Variations in title might not have been noted, and the title shown in the bibliography might never actually have appeared in that form on the banner of the paper. The US Newspaper Program would see them as three separate titles requiring three separate records, and so they would appear in the *National Union List*. With the wisdom of hindsight it is possible to argue that it would have been better to deviate from *AACR2* to accommodate the needs of newspaper users, few of whom have a fussy interest in a paper's precise title. In addition, the number of additional cataloging records required because of literal adherence to the cataloging rules has been substantial, adding considerably to the expense of the Newspaper Program without yielding much useful data in return.

The index of intended audience terms was devised as a way of providing a kind of subject access to newspapers. Many papers have been published for people belonging to particular ethnic groups or of particular political or religious persuasions. A controlled vocabulary of ethnic, political, and religious terms was developed under the auspices of the State Historical Society of Wisconsin. Early in the project, however, USNP philosophy regarding intended audience terms shifted. This may have been due in part to technical difficulties: The field in an OCLC holdings record which contained these terms could only be viewed by the cataloging agency which created the record. This meant that each cataloging agency had to redo the intellectual work required to assign an index term even when the basic cataloging work had already been done by some other agency. In addition, the possibility existed that two different cataloging agencies could index the same paper under entirely different terms.

Whatever the reason, the use of intended audience terms was discontinued after July, 1986. It was replaced by the use of Library of Congress subject headings, familiar to users of most library catalogs. These are carried in the bibliographic records, not the holdings records, and can thus be viewed even by the agencies which did not originally create the records. Unfortunately, many of the index terms in the State Historical Society of Wisconsin list are not in the controlled vocabulary of Library of Congress subject headings. Because of this, subject access to titles cataloged after July, 1986, is generally limited to ethnic terminology, with access by political or religious terminology no longer available.

One index to the data which may be conspicuous to some by its absence is an index to editors. Some of the bibliographic records created by the US Newspaper Program do contain information about editors, but most do not. Program participants are permitted to enter information about editors if they already have such information readily available, but the National Endowment for the

Humanities has discouraged extensive work to identify and list editors because of the time and expense involved. Although the OCLC *National Union List* contains no index by editor, it would be possible to create such an index, incomplete though it might be, by computer processing of a state's magnetic tape "offline product."

The bibliographic data in the *National Union List* should be readily understood by anyone who can decipher the information on a library catalog card, but the holdings data merit a brief explanation here. Each bibliographic listing is followed by one or more holdings listings which indicate in somewhat cryptic fashion which issues are held in each repository. Repositories are identified by three-letter codes assigned to them by OCLC. Each repository code is followed by general information (specific only as to the year or years held) about the holdings in that repository. To identify the repository by name, it is necessary for the user to consult a separate "Key to Institution Codes." This key also gives the address and phone number of each repository.

More specific holdings information is given for each repository in a subsidiary "level two" record. The "level two" record might, by means of a four-character code, identify a shelving location within a repository. It also shows in greater detail than the "level one" record what the repository has. Level two holdings reports have the format: yyyy:m:d, where "yyyy" is the year of publication, "m" is the month of publication expressed as a number from one to twelve, and "d" is a specific date. Thus, an issue for July 5, 1863 would be shown as 1863:7:5. Angle brackets -- <3:7:5> -- might be used to set off major groups of holdings and improve legibility. Because the available funding from the National Endowment has not permitted state projects the luxury of full collation, users of the *National Union List* must approach the data with care. Many, if not most, long runs indicated as complete may actually be expected to have a few issues missing. The user is sometimes warned of this fact by means of a note: "Scattered issues wanting." Sometimes a run is less than fifty percent complete, in which case the note reads, "Scattered issues."

The holdings data also indicate whether the holdings are in original newsprint or in microform. If the holdings are in microform, the type of microform (positive or negative, service copy or master) is specified. At one time, the holdings record also identified, by means of a code, the publisher of the microform reproduction. It was decided that this information was of limited utility, and it is no longer being recorded.

One feature of both the master list and the indexes in the *National Union List* is that the record identification number of each record in the OCLC database is shown. Those records can be viewed directly by anyone with access to the database. Most large American libraries and many smaller ones as well have computer terminals capable of searching OCLC. A few are beginning to offer the user tha ability to dial into the database from home or office using a personal computer. The online file in OCLC is more complete and up-to-date than the print or microfiche *National Union List,* so where an especially comprehensive search is needed, it may be desirable to search the database directly rather than to rely on the paper or fiche version. A few caveats are in order, however: First, the records displayed in OCLC include a variety of computer codes used by catalogers and may be somewhat difficult for the uninitiated to decipher. Second, the database, which includes records for all types of library materials in addition to newspapers, is enormous (approaching 18,000,000 records at this writing) and has outgrown the capacity of its indexing system to make searching as quick and easy as one would like. Third, the syntax needed to search the system is not menu-driven, so one may need some preliminary instructions from a librarian in order to begin.

The cataloging work now being carried out under the auspices of the United States Newspaper Program will eventually result in the creation of a new national bibliography of American newspapers. The bibliography will be both reasonably definitive and reasonably comprehensive. Because the information is being carried in a computer database, it is easy to maintain and modify. While praising this new national bibliography, it is necessary to point out a few of the things it does *not* do. It does not provide information about the many newspapers for which no issues have survived. It does not provide a list of the titles that were in publication at a given date. It does not, except to a very limited extent, provide information about editors or publishers. It does not provide indexes to the contents of individual papers, although in some cases notes are included to identify the existence of such indexes published elsewhere. Despite these limitations, students of American journalism history now have a new and increasingly powerful bibliographic tool at their disposal, thanks to the U.S. Newspaper Program.

1. Clarence Brigham, *History and Bibliography of American Newspapers* (Hamden CT: Archon Books, 1962), I, p. x.

Oral History

Maurine H. Beasley

A useful way for the journalism historian to look at oral history is to recognize the ways in which it is similar to and at the same time different from journalism itself. Obviously both fields depend on personal interviews. Journalists get a great deal of their information from human sources, usually by asking questions to elicit factual information that is then packaged in a news story. Oral historians also ask questions - indeed, the substance of oral history consists of personal interviews. Yet the oral historian and the journalist operate from different perspectives and mind sets.

Journalists frequently want answers in a hurry. They often seek facts to flesh out a preconceived package of material that fits into the general formula of a news or feature story. Their emphasis is on the five w's - the who, what, when, where, why of newswriting. Even when they conduct interviews in depth, they generally are seeking specific pieces of information to weave into a profile or article pegged to a current news event.

Oral historians, on the other hand, are not particularly interested in the contemporary. Their intent is broader: to construct a document that will stand the test of time and can be used for a variety of purposes. They are not necessarily looking for the "straight" answer or the "quotable quote." Yet both journalists and oral historians are interested in the same end - recording truthful material for those who want to use their products.

Oral history usually is thought of as a relatively new subspecialty of the field of history. While this is true in a sense - the birth of the electronic recorder signaled the start of what we label oral history - in other ways this definition is misleading. The study of history itself originated with Herodotus, often called the "Father of History." His long account of the wars between the Greeks and the Persians was based primarily on oral testimony. Thus, the use of oral sources has a long and rich tradition in historical writing, although professional historians long have relied largely on written records.

In some ways the term oral history lends itself to confusion. It is not oral, since the aim is to create a written record. At the same time it is not actual history, if we use the definition of Allan Nevins, the Columbia University historian who pioneered in establishing oral history collections. According to Nevins, history is "any integrated narrative, description or analysis of past events or facts written in a spirit of critical inquiry for the whole truth."[1] Oral history fails to fit this definition because it is not per se a critical inquiry, even though it may be used for this end. In general, oral history is simply the tape-recording of reminiscences about which the narrator can speak from first-hand knowledge. Some see it as the sole domain of the professionally-trained interviewer; others view it as a fruitful pursuit for individuals of widely-varying background. There is agreement, however, that oral history is not merely the tape-recording of speeches, conferences, or community events, as valid as these may be in creation of a historical record.[2]

The chief object of oral history is preparation of a transcript of questions and answers. The questions are asked by an interviewer who has carefully planned them in advance after becoming familiar with the background of the subject. In the questioning, the interviewer assumes a neutral role. The purpose is to elicit information from the subject without interjection of the adversarial stance sometimes taken by news reporters. This does not mean, however, that the interviewer lacks the power to influence the interview to a considerable extent, a fact that must be recognized. For this reason familiarity with established oral history procedures is a necessity for interviewers interested in producing a credible record.

Who is a suitable subject for an oral history? In 1938 Nevins wrote of the need to make "a systematic attempt to obtain, from the lips and papers of living Americans who have led significant lives, a fuller record of their participation in the political, economic, and cultural life of the last sixty years." He gave this as the rationale for establishment of Columbia University's vast oral history program.[3] Yet oral history definitely has not been limited to interviews with those whose lives appear "significant," according to elitist criteria. In many instances oral history projects have been set up by community agencies, such as public libraries and historical societies, to chronicle the lives of ordinary individuals. According to Donald A. Ritchie, former president of the Oral History Association, today there is a consensus "that all types of interviewees are legitimate, and that the most useful projects are those which cast their nets the widest."[4]

Ritchie cautions, however, that individual researchers may operate less responsibly than interviewers associated with archival projects. Whereas journalists often resort to the use of confidential sources, oral historians are committed to making a verifiable record. Authors who call themselves oral historians but then do not deposit their interviews for public inspection are not meeting the standards of the field.[5]

Whereas journalists are warned not to show their notes to their sources because of time pressure as well as fear that sources will want to change their comments to appear to advantage in print, oral historians operate under different constraints. Transcripts of interviews are shown to their interviewees to be checked for accuracy before being placed in public repositories. Legal releases must be obtained from the subjects before their transcripts can be accepted. Sometimes the actual tapes of the interviews also are deposited.

Ritchie suggests that those who want to use oral history techniques extensively associate themselves with archival repositories at the start of their project. In this way archives will be spared the possibility of being flooded with transcripts and tapes which may or may not meet standard criteria for oral history. Also, a co-operative arrangement may be of tangible benefit to the researcher. Archives may be willing to lend assistance, such as equipment, legal release forms, and transcription services, in return for guarantees of additions to their collections.[6]

Both journalists and oral historians face the problem of eliciting information from sources who occasionally may want to conceal the truth for self-serving motives. Both sometimes encounter individuals who mislead because of faulty memories. Faced with such difficulties in the interview situation, journalists and historians operate somewhat differently. Journalists by virtue of their training are likely to ask the "hard" question that attempts to pin the subject down and, if possible, force the subject into an admission of error. Oral historians may occasionally correct subjects if they know, for example, that they are giving wrong dates, but their main aim is to let subjects tell their own stories with a minimum of intrusion. Sometimes this is regarded as a defect of oral history, a reason for not taking it seriously. But it should be noted that documents, the main source for standard historical research, are not necessarily accurate renditions of reality. They also can mislead and falsify. Just as oral history is most useful when it is supported with the written record, documents should be checked against oral accounts.[7]

In recent years interest in oral history has grown phenomenally. The use of recorded historical information dates back to the turn of the century when the Smithsonian Institution sent anthropologists to visit Native American tribes to record their music, language, and narratives on phonograph records. During the Depression of the 1930s the federal Works Progress Administration (WPA), in an attempt to create jobs for unemployed professional persons, hired writers and historians to conduct interviews with individuals such as former slaves, tenant farmers, ordinary citizens, and those on the lower socioeconomic level who rarely had received attention from scholars. Initially greeted with skepticism by those who disdained the testimony of deprived groups, the volumes of published interviews stemming from the WPA project today are seen as important sources of historical information. One popular oral historian, Studs Terkel, worked as a WPA interviewer during the Depression.[8]

During the World War II era the use of recording devices - first heavy wire recorders and later more compact equipment - spurred the development of the contemporary oral history movement, which now relies on the small cassette recorder. Numerous projects related to activities of the federal government are sponsored by all branches of the military, by Presidential libraries, by the Smithsonian, and by agencies as diverse as the Central Intelligence Agency and the U.S. Forest Service.[9]

As we become a society that relies less and less on intimate written documents such as letters and diaries and more and more on instant communication such as telephone calls and electronic mail, it is likely that oral history will become an increasingly important research tool. In some ways it has strength that far outweighs the traditional value placed on research done with the written documents. As one author on oral history expressed it, "Subjectivity, which, if distorted by memory, is a potential weakness of the oral document, can also be its strength....spoken memories and ruminations are the essential human stuff of our time, for they reveal inner sources and motives."[10]

For this reason the use of oral history is related to another trend in historical writing - psycho-history. How does one get at inner feelings? Obviously a great deal more is involved than merely relying on oral history transcripts; yet oral history, particularly if it is placed within a context, provides one way to help understand human behavior, character, and personality. Who can say that an oral history conducted with Hitler, for example, would not be of tremendous value to historians even though it obviously would be highly subjective?[11]

How does one do oral history? A good way to begin is to visit a library or archive which is sponsoring an oral history project. There are hundreds of these ranging from those affiliated with government at all levels to those run by universities, foundations, museums, libraries, and private businesses. Examination of existing oral histories and exploration of the possibility of affiliating with projects already under way will enable one to quickly become familiar with the field.

In general, standard oral history techniques fall into three categories: pre-interview preparation, the interview itself, and post-interview activities. Brief guidelines for each category follow:

- Preparation

Keep a file on each person to be contacted, noting the kind and amount of information being sought.

Request an interview by either letter or telephone call, noting on a log each contact with the subject.

Set up a pre-interview appointment to establish rapport and ask to borrow personal papers to use as background.

Ask the subject to sign a legal release giving the tape and transcript to the sponsoring agency.

Make sure recording equipment is working properly prior to the interview.

Prepare a list of questions to be asked.

Record "header" information in advance including the name of interviewer and interviewee, date and location of interview and approach to the subject (biographical, topical, or thematic).

- Interview

Maintain good eye contact and concentrate on what is being said.

Take notes, jotting down spelling of names and other material that might cause difficulty in transcription.

Ask the questions prepared in advance, but be willing to make adjustments based on answers given in the interview.

Begin with brief questions requiring detailed answers.

Bring up triumphs before asking about failures and steer the interviewee back to the main point if he or she strays away from it.

- Post-interview Activities

Play back the interview immediately to make sure it was recorded properly.

Complete the documentation to go with the interview: a data sheet listing the subject's name, address, telephone number, birthdate, birthplace and the name of the interviewer; an interviewer's statement with comments on the interview setting, the appearance of the subject, and value of the interview; and a list of topics covered in the interview for a table of contents.

Transcribe the interview as soon as possible and return to the interviewee if there is a need for more information.

Edit the transcript.

Submit the transcript to the interviewee for review before depositing the material.[12]

As in all fields, numerous questions and problems arise. How long should the interview be? Generally sixty to ninety minutes is sufficient at one sitting. Sometimes subjects prove so interesting that interviewers return for additional sessions. How much editing should be done? The answer probably is as little as possible. Should you deposit papers obtained from the interviewee with the interview? Yes, if you have the subject's permission to do so. But as in all things there are exceptions to each rule. Excellent sources of information on oral history are the *Newsletter* of the Oral History Association and its *Oral History Review*, both of which contain discussions of professional problems confronting the oral historian. The executive secretary of the Oral History Association is Anne G. Campbell, P.O. Box 926, University Station, Lexington, Kentucky, 40506. Interviewers needing assistance with the transcription of oral history tapes might consider using Tapescribe, a service of the Center for Oral History at the University of Connecticut, Box U-103, Storrs CT 06268.

1. Allan Nevins, *Gateway to History*, rev. ed. (Garden City NY: Doubleday, 1962), 39.

2. Willa K. Baum, *Oral History for the Local Historical Society* (Nashville TN: American Association for State and Local History, 1971), 7.

3. Nevins, 8.

4. Donald A. Ritchie, "The Oral History/Public History Connection," in Barbara J. Howe and Emory L. Kemp, eds., *Public History: An Introduction* (Malabar FL: Robert E. Krieger Publishing Co., 1986), 64.

7. Ibid., 65.

8. Donald A. Ritchie, "Oral History in the Federal Government," *Journal of American History* 74 (Sept. 1987), 587-97.

9. Ibid., 590.

10. James Hoopes, *Oral History: An Introduction for Students* (Chapel Hill: University of North Carolina Press, 1979), 17.

11. Ibid., 18.

12. Maurine Beasley and Richard R. Harlow, "Oral History: Additional Research Tool for Journalism Historians," *Journalism History* 7 (Spring 1980), 38-39.

Selected Bibliography

Baum, Willa K. *Oral History for the Local Historical Society.* Stockton CA: Conference of California Historical Societies, 1969. Rev. ed. Nashville TN: American Association for State and Local History, 1971.

Beasley, Maurine, and Richard R. Harlow. "Oral History: Additional Research Tool for Journalism Historians." *Journalism History* 7 (Spring 1980): 38-39.

Benison, Saul. "Oral History: A Personal View." In *Modern Methods in the History of Medicine,* ed. Edwin Clarke. New York: Oxford University Press, 1971.

Colman, Gould P. "Oral History - An Appeal for More Systematic Procedures." *American Archivist* 28 (January 1965): 79-83.

Davis, Cullom, Kathryn Back, and Kay MacLean. *Oral History: From Tape to Type.* Chicago: American Library Association, 1977.

Grele, Ronald J., ed. *Envelopes of Sound: Six Practitioners Discuss the Theory, Method and Practice of Oral History and Oral Testimony.* Chicago: Precedent, 1975.

Harris, Ramon I., Joseph H. Cash, Herbert T. Hoover, and Stephen R. Ward. *The Practice of Oral History: A Handbook.* Glen Rock NJ: Microfilming Corporation of America, 1975.

Hoopes, James. *Oral History: An Introdution for Students.* Chapel Hill: University of North Carolina Press, 1979.

Lewis, Oscar, et al. *Four Men - Living the Revolution: An Oral History of Contemporary Cuba.* Urbana: University of Illinois Press, 1977.

Mason, Elizabeth B., and Louis M. Starr, eds. *The Oral History Collection of Columbia University.* 1979 ed. New York: Columbia University, 1979.

Moss, William W. *Oral History Program Manual.* New York: Praeger, 1974.

Nevins, Allan. *The Gateway to History.* Garden City NY: Doubleday, 1962.

Raines, Howell. *My Soul Is Rested: Movement Days in the Deep South Remembered.* New York: Putnam, 1977.

Ritchie, Donald A. "Oral History in the Federal Government," *Journal of American History* 74 (September 1987): 587-95.

_____. "The Oral History/Public History Connection." In *Public History: An Introduction,* Barbara J. Howe and Emory L. Kemp, eds. Malabar FL: Robert E. Krieger Publishing Co., 1986: 57-68.

Starr, Louis M. "Oral History." *Encyclopedia of Library and Information Science* 20. Reprint. New York: Columbia University, 1978.

Terkel, Studs. *Hard Times: An Oral History of the Great Depression.* New York: Pantheon, 1970.

_____. *Working: People Talk About What They Do All Day and How They Feel About What They Do.* New York: Pantheon, 1974.

Vansina, Jan. *Oral Tradition: A Study in Historical Methodology.* London: Routledge, 1961.

Archival and Manuscript Sources

Guide to Archival and Manuscript Sources

The inspiration for a list of repositories holding primary research materials of interest to journalism historians came from James Startt, a history professor at Valparaiso University. His idea was to model such a guide on *Sources in British Political History 1900-1951* compiled by Chris Cook (London: Macmillan, 1975). Startt chaired the Research Committee of the American Journalism Historians Association (AJHA) when he first mentioned the project in 1986. At AJHA's annual meeting that fall, the members endorsed the Research Committee's recommendation that the project be undertaken. Because guides already existed for some aspects of mass communication history, the scope of the AJHA project was defined as archival and manuscript sources documenting the news function of print and electronic media in the United States.

In November 1987, a data collection form was sent to more than 650 repositories including members of the Association of Research Libraries, state and local historical societies, libraries listed as having journalism holdings in several special collections guides, and repositories suggested by AJHA members. In January 1988, a follow-up mailing was sent to a selective list of approximately one hundred institutions. Responses were received from 172 repositories in thirty-four states. The information which follows is necessarily defined by those responses. Some institutions included very complete descriptions of their holdings; some, a list of names; and some did not reply at all.

Researchers are strongly encouraged to augment information available in this volume with searches of the *National Union Catalog of Manuscript Collections* and the two major bibliographic utilities, RLIN (Research Libraries Information Network) and OCLC (Online

Computer Library Center). See the chapters by Hansen and Ward in this volume for further information on these sources.

The guide which follows is arranged alphabetically by state and then alphabetically by repository name. Other institutional information included (if available) is the complete address, telephone number, contact person, hours of operation, availability of photocopy services, and types of finding aids including OCLC and/or RLIN and published guides. Individual collections are listed alphabetically under the repository name. Where available, collection entries include personal dates, type of collection and inclusive dates, size, availability on microfilm, biographical notes, major correspondents, availability of a register or other finding aid, collection identification code, and restrictions on the collection's use. All materials are in English unless otherwise noted. Occasionally the list of correspondents in large collections exceeded the space available and some were omitted. In general, however, all information provided about correspondents was included.

The scope of this guide has been interpreted broadly in order not to exclude germane collections. Several repositories submitted lists of their newspaper holdings and this information was omitted because it will be covered by the US Newspaper Program. This guide is not as detailed as Professor Startt's model, but it is a beginning which can be refined and enhanced in the future. The hope of the American Journalism Historians Association is that it will foster many new research projects.

A final caution for potential users of the materials described in the following list: Most of the repositories have limited hours and virtually none of the items may be charged out. The prudent researcher will make arrangements with the repository well in advance of a visit to ensure the best and most efficient use of his or her time.

ALABAMA

University of Alabama

• William Stanley Hoole Special Collections Library, The University of Alabama, PO Box S, Tuscaloosa AL 35486-9784. 205-348-5512. Joyce Lamont, Curator. 8 am-5 pm M-F; 6-10 pm Th. Photocopy services. Unpublished finding aids in library.

Ayers, Harry Mell, 1885-1964. Papers 1918-1965: ca. 36,960 items. Newspaper editor and publisher in Anniston AL. Correspondence, letters to the editor, editorials and other papers relating to local state and national political campaigns and elections, education, civil rights, China and current affairs.

Boone, James Buford, 1909-   Papers 1935-1968: 5 ft. Journalist and publisher in Tuscaloosa AL. Correspondence, writings, scrapbooks, memorabilia, photographs, phonorecords and audiotapes relating to Boone's career as a journalist in Alabama and Georgia. Information on Autherine Lucy and integration of University of Alabama 1956. RESTRICTED: Until one year after the death of George C. Wallace.

Dennis, Jere Clemens, 1862-   Papers 1841-1935: ca. 2,900 items. Newspaper printer, editor and proprietor. Edited or was affiliated with *Birmingham Labor Advocate* 1890-1893, 1900-1905.

Garner, Thomas Henry, 1869-1944. Papers 1887-1913: ca. 178 items. Editor of *Tuscaloosa Gazette*. Correspondence.

Gilmore, Eddy Lanier King, 1907-1967. Papers 1940s-1960s: ca. 46 boxes. Associated Press correspondent; assigned to Moscow bureau 1942; chief of AP Moscow bureau 1945. Pulitzer Prize for international affairs reporting 1947.

Mayfield, Sara, 1905-1979. Papers 1905-1972: ca. 3,945 items. Author and foreign correspondent. Letters, Black folk songs and phonorecords, plays, novels, short stories, news stories and articles. Includes ca. 175 papers, principally press releases, from 1945 Inter-American Conference on Problems of War and Peace in Mexico. RESTRICTED: Permission of family required for use.

ARIZONA

Arizona State University

• Special Collections, Arizona State University Library, Tempe AZ 85287. 602-965-6519. Marilyn Wurzburger, Librarian. 8 am-5 pm M-F. Photocopy services.

Fisher, Francis McCracken (Mac). Collection 1935-1939, 1941: 3 boxes. North China correspondent for United Press. Dispatches, journals, newspapers, magazines.

Smedley, Agnes. Collection 1936-1949: 46 vols. Reporter for *Frankfurter Allgemeine Zeitung* and *Manchester Guardian*. Lecture notes, clippings, newspapers, periodicals, photos.

Steele, A.T. Collection 1932-1945: 18 linear ft. Worked for *New York Herald Tribune*; also wrote for *New York Times, Chicago Daily News*, Associated Press. Articles and documents dealing with events in China 1932-1949. Dispatches, clippings, pamphlets.

CALIFORNIA

California Historical Society

• Historic Resources Center, California Historical Society, 4201 Wilshire Blvd, Suite 202, Los Angeles CA 90010. 213-937-1848. 1-4 pm T-F.

CHS/Ticor Collection. 40,000 photographs 1880-1940. Many photos of 1910 bombing of *Los Angeles Times*.

• Edward C. Kemble Collections on Western Printing and Publishing, California Historical Society, 2099 Pacific Ave., San Francisco CA 94109. 415-567-1848. Glenn E. Humphries, Curator. 1-5 pm, W-Sa. Photocopy services. See also Glenn E.Humphries, comp., "Printing, Publishing, and Ancillary Trades: A Checklist of Manuscript and Archival Holdings in the Edward C. Kemble Collections on Western Printing & Publishing, California Historical Society Library, San Francisco," *California History* 66:1 (March 1987), 55-67.

Alta California. Records 1849-1850: 1 vol. Account book of first daily newspaper in California. V.F865.1.A7.

Antioch Ledger. Records 1871-1875: 1 folder. Correspondence from editor and publisher Joshua P. Abbott to typefounders and advertisers. MS. 3439.

Argonaut Publishing Company. Records 1880-1905: 2 vols. Transfer journal and dividend records. MS. 64.

Brown, Beriah. Papers 1863-1865: 1 folder. Records of a disagreement over the *San Francisco Daily Republic*, precursor of the *San Francisco Examiner*. MS. 2406.

Ewer, Ferdinand C., 1816-1883. Diary 1826-1860: 1 vol. Journalist associated with *Pacific News, Sacramento Transcript, San Francisco Sunday Dispatch, Alta California.* Editor of *The Pioneer*, a literary magazine. V. MS. 21.

Gordon, David Everett, 1830?-1913. Letters 1855-1856: 1 folder. Correspondence about founding of *Trinity Journal* between Henry J. Seaman and Gordon. MS. 369A.

Hart, Jerome A., 1854-1937. Papers: 18 boxes and 43 scrapbooks. Assoc. editor, 1880-1891, and editor, 1891-1907, of the *Argonaut.* Financial records, drafts of writings, business correspondence, receipts, clippings, photographs. MS. 951.

Hearst, William Randolph, 1863-1951. Papers 1931-1942: 2 folders. Correspondence to and from Hearst regarding the *San Francisco Examiner, New York Evening Herald,* and *Chicago Herald.* MS. 978.

Henderson, Alexander B. Correspondence 1888-1893: 1 folder. Managing editor, *San Francisco Examiner.* Includes correspondence from William Randolph Hearst on managing the newspaper. MS. 487.

Kester, Frank, 1888-1981. Papers 1888-1980: 4 boxes. Marine editor, *Oakland Tribune* 1921-1942. Typescripts of columns, photographs, 18-folder typescript autobiography. MS. 3588.

Knowland, Joseph R., 1873-1966. Papers 1889-1961: 16 boxes. Publisher of *Oakland Tribune.* Includes rough-draft of autobiography (1961). MS. 3154.

Paul, Almarin Brooks. Reminiscences 1823-1883: 1 vol. Correspondent for *Saint Louis Herald,* and *San Francisco Evening Bulletin.* Publisher of *True California.* MS. 3010.

Reineger, Novella. Papers 1968: 1 folder. Documentation of the Mailers' Union strike against San Francisco Newspaper Printing Co., publisher of the *San Francisco Chronicle* and *San Francisco Examiner.* MS. 2050.

Shinn, Milicent Washburn, 1858-1940. Papers 1880-1925: 3 folders. Editor, *Overland Monthly* 1883-1894. Business and personal correspondence. Descriptive guide available. MS. 1960.

Santa Barbara Historical Society

• Gledhill Library, 136 E. De la Guerra St., PO Box 578, Santa Barbara CA 93101. 805-966-1601. Michael Redmon, Librarian. Noon-4 pm T-F. Photocopy services.

Storke, Thomas. Collection: 6 boxes. Materials relating to *Santa Barbara Daily News* and *Santa Barbara News-Press.*

Stanford University

• Dept. of Special Collections and University Archives, Stanford University Libraries, Cecil H. Green Library, Stanford CA 94305. 415-723-4054. Margaret Kimball, Manuscripts and Archives Librarian. 9 am-5 pm M-F; 9 am-noon Sa. Photocopy services. Registers available. Collection level records on RLIN.

Allen, Peter C., 1915-   Student Demonstration Papers 1965-1971: .75 linear ft. Editor of *Stanford Review* 1946-1952, Director of News and Publications 1952-1961; later Publications Service 1961-1965, University Editor 1965-1976, University Editor Emeritus 1977-   . Research notes, reports, Stanford news releases about campus demonstrations assembled by Allen.

Bierce, Ambrose, 1842-1914? Papers 1872-1913: 2 linear ft. Writer for various English publications.   Returned to United States and became editor of the *San Francisco Argonaut*. Author of several works and journalist for *San Francisco Examiner*. Correspondence, photographs, address books. Includes 15 letters by Bierce, and letters to him from Charles Warren Stoddard (his publisher), H.L. Mencken, Percival Pollard, George Sterling, Charles Warren Stoddard.

Bliven, Bruce, 1889-1977. Papers 1906-1985: 8 linear ft. Editor of *New Republic*, writer and lecturer.   Correspondence, notes, printed materials, photographs and clippings.

McEwen, Arthur, 1851-1907. Papers ca. 1900: 2 items. California journalist, editor and publisher.   Copyprint of original photograph with notes about McEwen's career.

Russell, Isaac, 1897-1927.   Papers 1898-1827: 8 linear ft. American journalist with the *New York Times, Collier's, New Masses,* and *Harper's Weekly*.   Also labor mediator and editor. Correspondence, manuscripts, published articles and clippings, government and legal documents, photographs and ephemera. Correspondents include Clarence Darrow, Bernard DeVoto, Wallace Irwin, David Starr Jordan, Theodore Roosevelt, Upton Sinclair, Ida M. Tarbell, Melvin Vaniman, Ray Lyman Wilbur, and the Wright brothers.   Major stories include coverage of the Titanic, the Wright brothers and Pancho Villa.

• Hoover Institution Archives, Stanford University, Stanford CA 94305. 415-723-3563. Elena S. Danielson, Asst. Archivist.8:15 am-4:45 pm M-F. Photocopy services. Collection-level descriptions for all collections on RLIN. Registers for most large collections.

Abel, Elie. Misc. papers 1941-1978: 4 boxes. American journalist. Speeches, writings, correspondence and printed matter relating to world politics and the press. Drafts of *Special Envoy to Churchill and Stalin, 1941-1946* by E. Abel and W. Averell Harriman (pub. 1975). CSUZ84035-A.

Allen, Benjamin Shannon, 1883-1963. Papers 1910-1967: 6 boxes. American journalist. Correspondence, press releases, clippings, photographs relating to Commission for Relief in Belgium, U.S. Food Administration and U.S. Fuel Administration during World War I, and of National Committee on Food for the Small Democracies and Finnish Relief Fund during World War II, to political conditions in the U.S., and to Herbert Hoover. CSUZ54001-A.

Allen, Niel R., 1894-1959. Papers 1919: 1 box. Second lieutenant, U. S. Army and editor, *Pontanezen Duckboard,* Camp Pontanezen, Brest, France. Correspondence, account books, contracts, newspaper clippings, notes. CSUZ59001-A.

Bennett, Milly, 1900-1960. Papers 1915-1960: 16 boxes. American journalist. Correspondent in China 1926-1927, the Soviet Union 1931-1936, Spain 1936-1937. Memoirs, news dispatches other writings, correspondence, clippings and photographs. CSUZ82073-A.

Bouton, Stephen Miles, 1876- Papers 1918-1962: 6 boxes. Correspondent in Berlin 1911-1916, 1919-1934. Memoirs, dispatches, newspaper columns and correspondence. CSUZ83014-A.

Brown, Elizabeth Churchill. Papers 1943-1984: 41 boxes. American journalist. Memoirs, correspondence and printed matter relating to American politics, especially during 1950s; Sen. Joseph McCarthy; American communism. Includes some papers and memoirs of Constantine Brown, journalist and husband of E.C. Brown. Also includes some letters and writings of Earl Browder. CSUZ84010-A.

Browne, Louis Edgar, 1891-1951. Papers 1917-1956: 2 boxes, 3 reels microfilm. Correspondent of *Chicago Daily News* in Russia and Turkey 1917-1919. Dispatches, correspondence, printed matter, photographs. CSUZ69033-A.

Burrill, Harvey D. Typescript dispatches 1918-1919: 1 box. Newspaper correspondent in England and France for *Syracuse Journal.* World War I. CSUZ69057-A.

Campaigne, Jameson Gilbert, 1914-1985. Papers 1945-1986: 13 boxes. Journalist. Editor *Indianapolis Star* 1960-1969. Correspondence, newspaper columns and other writings, printed matter, photographs. CSUZ86020-A.

Chamberlain, John, 1903-   Papers 1943-1985: 141 boxes. American journalist. Writings, correspondence, printed matter. CSUZ86004-A.

Chester, Edmund Albert, 1897-1973. Papers 1933-1947: 4 scrapbooks. Chief, Latin American Dept. Associated Press 1936-1940; director, Shortwave Broadcasting and Latin American Relations, Columbia Broadcasting System 1940-1948. Photographs, clippings, correspondence, press releases, memorabilia. CSUZ79065-A.

Cooley, John K., 1917-   Papers 1960-1962: 1 box. *Christian Science Monitor* correspondent in North Africa. Dispatches, radio broadcast transcripts, memoranda, transcripts of interviews, press releases, printed matter. CSUZ63001-A.

Crozier, Brian. Papers 1936-1985: British journalist and author. Chairman, Forum World Features 1965-1974; director, Institute for the Study of Conflict 1970-1979. Writings, correspondence, memoranda, book reviews, printed matter. CSUZ85035-A.

De Toledano, Ralph, 1916-   Papers 1940-1971: 6 boxes. Journalist and author. National reports editor, *Newsweek* 1948-1960; syndicated columnist 1960-   Correspondence, memoranda, reports, drafts and published copies of writings, printed matters. Includes 98 letters from Whittaker Chambers about the Alger Hiss case. RESTRICTED: Whittaker Chambers' letters may not be used without written permission from Ralph De Toledano. CSUZ71030-A.

Dennis, Lawrence, 1893-   Papers 1921-1975: 24 boxes. Editor, *Weekly Foreign Letter* 1938-1942, and *Appeal to Reason* 1946-1972. Correspondence and writings. Includes copies of newsletters edited by Dennis and subscription records. CSUZ84036-A.

Dorrian, Cecil. Papers 1912-1926: 1 box, 6 envelopes. War correspondent *Newark Evening News* 1914-1926. Clippings, writings, postcards, photographs. CSUZXX223-A.

Evans, Henry S. Papers 1942-1970: 2 boxes, 1 scrapbook. Publicist. Director, Midwest Bureau, Chinese News Service, national director, U.S. People for the United Nations. Memoranda, transcripts and analyses of radio news broadcasts, press releases. CSUZ70012-A.

Fertig, Lawrence. Papers 1943-1978: 9 boxes, 2 motion picture film reels, 9 phonotapes. American economics journalist; Hearst newspaper syndicated columnist 1944-1967. Speeches and writings, correspondence, printed matter, sound recordings, motion picture film. CSUZ78112-A.

Fodor, Nandor, 1895-   Papers 1921-1945: 1 box. Hungarian correspondent in U.S. and Great Britain 1923-1939; Secretary to British newspaper publisher Lord Rothermere 1928-1937. Correspondence, clippings, photographs. CSUZ80031-A.

Gadsby, Henry Franklin, 1868-   Papers 1897-1950: 18 boxes. Canadian journalist and political satirist. Writings, correspondence, printed matter, memorabilia. CSUZ78096-A.

Gould, Randall Chase, 1898-1979. Papers 1895-1975: 16 boxes. American journalist in Far East 1923-1949; editor, *Shanghai Evening Post and Mercury* 1931-1941, 1945-1949. Correspondence, writings, clippings, photographs. Includes photographs of Japanese bombing of Shanghai in 1937. CSUZ69086-A.

Hardt, Fred B. Mimeographed letters 1914-1915: 1 box. German Kriegs-Presseburo official, Munich. CSUZXX330-A.

Hart, Jeffrey Peter, 1930-   Papers 1961-1985: 6 boxes. American newspaper columnist; senior editor, *National Review*. Correspondence, writings. CSUZ81103-A.

Irwin, William Henry, 1873-1948. Papers 1890-1942: 6 boxes, 2 scrapbooks. American journalist. Correspondence, writings, printed matter. Includes drafts of fiction and other writings by Irwin and correspondence with Herbert Hoover. CSUZ48011-A.

Kanner, Heinrich, 1864-   Typescripts 1914-1917: 2 boxes. Austrian journalist; editor, *Die Zeit* (Vienna). Includes partial translation by Robert Hopwood. CSUZ25001-A.

Lapham, Lewis H. Papers 1971-1981: 59 boxes. Managing editor and editor, *Harper's Magazine* 1971-1981. Correspondence, writings, printed matter. CSUZ82023-A.

Lauzanne, Stephane Joseph Vincent, 1874-　　Papers 1898-1954: 2 boxes, 18 scrapbooks. Editor, *Le Matin* (Paris) 1920-1940. Writings, transcripts of radio broadcasts, clippings. CSUZ67010-A.

LaVarre, William, 1898-　　Papers 1922-1978: 12 boxes. Author and journalist; chief, American Republics Unit, U. S. Dept. of Commerce 1941-1943; editor-in-chief, *American Mercury* 1957-1958. Memoirs, letters, memoranda, clippings, periodical issues, lists, notes, financial records. CSUZ77033-A.

Liepins, Olberts, 1906-　　Papers 1948-1972: 1 box. Latvian journalist. Correspondence, clippings, writings, reports. CSUZ75088-A.

Lilienthal, Alfred M. Papers 1936-1983: 140 boxes. American anti-Zionist author; editor and publisher, *Middle East Perspective* 1968-　　Speeches and writings, correspondence, notes, memoranda, press releases, serial issues, conference papers, interviews, studies, clippings, photographs, sound recordings. RESTRICTED: Closed until processed. CSUZ82070-A.

Losh, William J., 1896-1973. Papers 1917-1967: 3 boxes. American journalist. Diaries, correspondence, photographs, memorabilia, printed matter. Includes material relating to 1925 trial of John Scopes in Dayton TN and U.S. politics during Harding and Coolidge administrations. CSUZ75023-A.

Lyons, Eugene, 1898-　　Papers 1919-1980: 19 boxes, 5 audiotapes, 12 phonorecords. Correspondent in Soviet Union 1928-1934; senior editor, *Reader's Digest* 1952-1968. Correspondence, noted printed matter and photographs. CSUZ85006-A.

Martin, William, 1888-1934. Typescript notes 1915-1933: 5 boxes. Paris correspondent of the *Journal de Geneve*. Interview summaries. CSUZXX420-A.

Mason, Frank E., 1893-1979. Papers 1915-1975: 4 boxes. Berlin correspondent and president, International News Service. Correspondence, reports, dispatches. Includes a copy of the logbook of the submarine that sank the Lusitania in 1915, and correspondence with Georgii Chicherin and Karl von Wiegand. CSUZXX007-A.

Metcalfe, John C., 1935-1949: 13 boxes. *Chicago Tribune* reporter; investigator for U.S. House of Representatives Un-American Activities Committee. Diary, correspondence, reports, notes, pamphlets, clippings. CSUZ72069-A.

Metzger, H. Peter. Papers 1945-1981: 30 boxes. Science editor, *Rocky Mountain News*; president, Colorado Committee for Environmental Information. Writings, clippings, reports, studies, letters. CSUZ81083-A.

Moley, Raymond, 1886-   Papers 1912-1976: 247 boxes, 3 audiotapes. Political scientist and journalist. Advisor to Franklin D. Roosevelt 1932-1933; asst. secretary of state 1933; contributing editor *Newsweek* 1937-1968. Correspondence, diaries, reports, memoranda, speeches, notes. RESTRICTED: Correspondence between R. Moley and Richard M. Nixon closed. Eligible to be opened upon the death of the latter. CSUZ69008-A

Monday, Mark. Papers 1961-1978: 4 boxes, 3 film reels, 15 phonorecords. American journalist. Correspondence, news dispatches, reports, bulletins, pamphlets, leaflets, clippings and photographs relating to Minutemen and other right-wing paramilitary groups in U.S. and to the Irish republican movement in Northern Ireland. CSUZ74063-A.

Montrose, Sherman. Papers 1942-1947: 1 box, 2 scrapbooks. War correspondent during World War II. Correspondence, press copy, memoranda photographs, clippings. CSUZXX248-A.

Muggerage, Malcolm, 1903-   Diaries 1924-1964: 3 boxes. British journalist and author; editor, *Punch* 1953-1957. Typewritten transcript. CSUZ80084-A.

Newspaper Enterprise Association. Misc. records 1919-1921: 1 box. Correspondence, dispatches, memoranda, clippings. Consists mainly of communications from Jack Mason, Far Eastern Bureau correspondent, to Alfred O. Anderson, president, Newspaper Enterprise Assoc. CSUZ83028-A.

Norton, Robert, 1896-1974. Papers 1935-1948: 4 boxes. Editor, *China Today*. Correspondence, speeches, clippings, photographs. CSUZ77015-A.

Nossal, Frederick, 1927-   Papers 1944-1979: 69 boxes, 2 scrapbooks. Canadian journalist; Far Eastern correspondent 1959-1971; information officer, World Bank, 1971-1979. Drafts, dispatches, clippings, serial issues, photographs, slides. CSUZ80010-A.

Peroutka, Ferdinand. Papers 1938-1981: 17 boxes, 41 audiotapes. Czech journalist; chief, Czechoslovak Desk, Radio Free Europe 1950-1964. Correspondence, memoranda, printed matter. CSUZ84052-A.

Petruskevich, Ivan, 1875-1950. Papers 1910-1941: 6 boxes, 5 microfilm reels. Ukrainian journalist. Diaries, correspondence, speeches, memoranda, clippings. CSUZXX261-A.

Rieffel, Aristide, 1859-1941. Papers 1890-1941: 36 boxes. French journalist and pacifist. Correspondence, writings, pamphlets, clippings, photographs. CSUZ76065-A.

Schoenberner, Franz, 1892-   Papers 1899-1970: 4 boxes, 1 phonotape. German journalist and author; editor, *Simplicissimus* 1929-1933. Writings and correspondence. CSUZ72020-A.

Seegers, Scott, d. 1976. Papers 1932-1978: 22 boxes. Staff writer, *Reader's Digest* 1968-1976. Writings, correspondence, notes serial issues. CSUZ80180-A.

Stanfield, Boris, 1888-   Interview 1976: 1 audiotape. Russian-American journalist; reporter for *Izvestiia* 1917-1920. CSUZ76111-A.

Sullivan, Mark, 1874-1952. Papers 1883-1952: 62 boxes, 10 scrapbooks. Editor, *Collier's Weekly* 1912-1919; columnist, *New York Herald Tribune* 1923-1952. Correspondence, diaries, speeches, memoranda and printed matter. CSUZ55007-A.

Thompson, Charles T. Papers 1898-1917: 2 boxes. Correspondent for Associated Press. Correspondence, writings, clippings, photographs, printed matter. CSUZ67027-A.

Todd, Carlos, d. 1977. Printed newspaper articles 1959-1960: 1 box. Columnist, *The Times of Havana.* CSUZ78021-A.

Todd, Laurence, 1882-   Typescript memoirs 1954: 1 box. Federated Press labor reporter 1919-1933; TASS correspondent, 1933-1952. CSUZ60026-A.

United Press is on the air. 3 phonorecords. Radio series ca. 1942. CSUZXX645-A.

Viereck, George Sylvester, 1884-1962. Misc. papers 1903-1960: 2 boxes, 32 scrapbooks. German-American poet, playwright, journalist. Correspondence, writings, clippings. Portions in German. CSUZXX273-A.

Volkov, Leon, 1914-1974. Papers 1948-1974: 7 boxes. Editor and journalist, *Newsweek* 1953-1974. Diaries, correspondence, speeches and writings, reports, clippings, press excerpts, printed matter. CSUZ77088-A.

Von Wiegand, Karl H. Papers 1911-1961: 83 boxes. Hearst newspaper foreign correspondent 1917-1961. Correspondence, dispatches, writings, photographs, clippings, printed matter. CSUZ750792-A.

Wilson, Philip Whitwell, 1875- Printed writings 1907-1937: 17 binders. British journalist. Includes daily columns by P. W. Wilson in *London Daily News* 1907-1917. CSUZXX277-A.

Wilson, Richard C., 1902-1972. Papers 1941-1972: 9 boxes. Editor, *The Far Easterner* 1953-1972. Correspondence, American Red Cross reports, card files on individuals, club membership lists, printed matter. CSUZ72057-A.

Yalman, Ahmed Emin, 1889- Papers 1912-1973: 24 boxes. Turkish journalist; editor, *Vakit* 1917-1922; *Vatan* 1922-1926 and 1940-1961; *Tan* 1936-1939. Correspondence, memoirs, clippings, printed matter, photographs. CSUZ82089-A.

University of California, Los Angeles

• Dept. of Special Collections, University Research Library, UCLA, 405 Hilgard Ave., Los Angeles CA 90024-1595. 213-825-4879. Anne Caiger, Manuscripts Librarian. 9 am-5 pm M-Sa. Photocopy services. UCLA oral histories on RLIN.

Ainsworth, Edward Maddin, 1902-1968. Papers ca. 1945- 74 boxes, 3 oversize pkgs. Writer and journalist. Literary manuscripts, correspondence, articles, clippings and photographs. Register available.

Borough, Reuben Warriner, 1883- Oral history transcript: 439 pp. Newspaper man reminisces in 1968 about his work and participation in Los Angeles politics.

Dickson, Edward A. Oral history transcript: 811 pp. 1983 interviews with Ann Sumner, Wilhelmina Dickson, Edward H. Dickson and others about Edward A. Dickson's newspaper publishing career.

Douglas, George. Papers 1911-1935: 39 letters and 3 manuscripts. Book page editor for William Randolph Hearst newspaper chain in San Francisco area.

Forman, Henry James, 1879-1966. Papers ca. 1917-1957: 8 boxes. Literary editor and author. Clippings and literary manuscripts. Register available.

Forman, Henry James, 1879-1966. Oral history transcript: 513 pp. Reminiscences in 1961 of his career and prominent writers he knew. Includes bibliography of works by Forman.

McWilliams, Carey, 1905-   Oral history transcript: 522 pp. *Nation* editor discusses his life, writings on Ambrose Bierce, and involvement with the Sleepy Lagoon and Hollywood Ten defenses and the ACLU. Taped in 1981.

Penzoldt, Sylvia R. Papers: 10 boxes. Newspaper woman and writer of children's short stories and poems. Manuscripts, correspondence, photographs, scrapbooks, clippings and diaries concerning her career.

Richardson, James Hugh, 1894-1963. Papers ca. 1917-1962: 4 boxes and 5 oversize pkgs. Newspaperman. Correspondence, photographs, manuscripts, clippings, scrapbooks and memorabilia. List available.

Sakai, Yoneo, 1900-1978. Papers 1848-1979: 62 boxes. Editor, journalist, war correspondent. Special correspondent for *Tokyo Shimbun* 1947, contributing radio program "Amerika Dayori" until 1952. Joined *Sankei Shimbun* in 1964. Correspondence manuscripts published works, notebooks, diaries. RESTRICTED: Unpublished material may not be photocopied or quoted without the permission of Ruby Sakai.

Savage, George Walden, 1903-   Papers 1927-1961: ca. 680 pieces. Owner-publisher of various Owen's Valley newspapers including the *Independence Inyo-Independent*, the *Lone Pine Progress Citizen*, and the *Bishop Inyo-Register*. Also owner-publisher of *South Pasadena Review*. Scrapbooks, correspondence, clippings, photographs and related printed material concerning

Savage's career as a journalist and newspaper publisher and the Japanese War Relocation Center at Manzanar CA.

Sumner, Anna Emily. 1904-   Oral History transcript: 451 pp. Journalist-publicist recalls her newspaper career in 1982 interview.

Warren, James Lloyd La Fayette, 1805-1896. Papers 1837-1879: 3 boxes. Edited *California Farmer*. Correspondence, accounts and misc. papers. Collection guide available.

University of Southern California

• University Library, University of Southern California, Los Angeles CA 90087-0182. 213-743-6050. Open daily. Photocopy services.

Hearst Collection. 1874-1962. 4,100 bound vols: 1,064 linear ft., b/w prints: 238 linear ft., photo negatives: 158 drawers metal plates. An almost complete morgue of the various newspapers which merged in 1962 to form the *Los Angeles Herald Examiner*.

Scribes Club. 1897-   1 box: rosters, by-laws, meeting records, obituaries, etc. Club for newspapermen limited to 27 members.

COLORADO

Colorado History Museum

• Stephen H. Hart Library, Colorado History Museum, 1300 Broadway, Denver CO 80203. 303-866-2305. Katherine Kane, Dir. of Public Services and Access. 10 am-4:30 pm T-Sa. Photocopy services. Guide in repository.

Manuscript collections: 2700 linear ft.   Misc. information on Colorado journalism.

Television newsfilm: 14,500 reels from stations KOA and KMGH.

University of Colorado

• Special Collections, University Libraries, University of Colorado, Campus Box 184, Boulder CO 80309. 303-492-6144.   Nora J. Quinlan. 9 am-noon, 2-5 pm M-F. List of each collection available in repository.

Fowler, Gene, 1890-1960. Collection: 36 linear ft. Journalist with *Denver Post* in 1920s.

Cummings, Camille, 1901-1986. Collection: 24 linear ft. Society editor for *Paris Chicago Tribune* in 1920s.

Stafford, Jean, 1915-1979. Collection: 45 linear ft. Wrote for *New Yorker, New York Times*, and other publications.

CONNECTICUT

Yale University

• Manuscripts and Archives, Yale University Library, 120 High St., Box 1603A Yale Station, New Haven CT 06520. 203-432-1735. Judith Ann Schiff, Chief Research Archivist. 8:30 am-4:45 pm M-F. Collection level records on RLIN.

Acheson, Dean Gooderham, 1893-1971. Papers 1898-1978: 36 linear ft. Lawyer, author, secretary of state in Truman administration. Numerous correspondents include many journalists such as Joseph Alsop, Stewart Alsop, Eugene Rostow. RESTRICTED: Rostow files in box 71.

Anderson, Luther, 1880-1940. Papers 1899-1940: 2.75 linear ft. Far Eastern correspondent for *Chicago Daily News* 1911-1915. Correspondents include William Lyon Phelps, Sven Birger Sandzen.

Bagg, Lyman Hotchkiss, 1846-1907. Papers 1863-1907: 2 linear ft. Author, journalist. Editor of *Yale Literary Magazine* 1868-1869; author of weekly "College Chronicle" for *New York World* 1876-1882. Unpublished finding aid in repository.

Baldwin, Hanson Weightman, 1903- Papers 1929-1977: 74 linear ft. Wrote for *Baltimore Sun* 1928; *New York Times* 1929-1968. Correspondence, writings, subjects files, printed matter, special files. Correspondents including Turner Catledge, John Cowles, Clifton Daniel, Alfred A. Knopf, Adolph Ochs, James Reston, Harrison Salisbury, Arthur Hays Sulzberger, Arthur Ochs Sulzberger. Unpublished finding aid in repository.

Barth, Alan, 1906-1979. Papers 1937-1981: 5 linear ft. Reporter for *Beaumont Enterprise* 1936; *Beaumont Journal* 1937-1938; Washington correspondent for McClure Newspaper Syndicate 1938-1941; editorial writer for *Washington Post* 1949-1977; editorial writer for *Guild Reporter* 1950-1951. Correspondence; writings and subject files; biographical and personal materials; editorials. Correspondents include Eva Bittleman, Herbert Block, Malcolm Cowley, William O. Douglas, John Stirling Fisher, Abe Fortas, Fred Friendly, Felix Frankfurter, Philip Leslie Graham, Sidney Hook, Joseph McCarthy, Henry Morgenthau,

Arthur M. Schlesinger, Adlai E. Stevenson. Unpublished finding aid in repository.

Barthold, Allen Jennings, 1900- Papers 1929-1932: .5 linear ft. Correspondence and papers relating to *Courier de Boston* and its editor Paul Joseph Guerard de Nancrede. Unpublished finding aid in repository.

Bingham, Alfred Mitchell, 1905- Collection: 33 linear ft. Founder and editor of *Common Sense*. Numerous well-known correspondents. Correspondence, subject files, writings, newspapers, special files, *Common Sense*. Unpublished finding aid in repository.

Bowles, Samuel, 1826-1878. Papers 1853-1890: 1 linear ft. Editor of *Springfield Republican* 1844-1878. Numerous correspondents including Henry Adams, Henry Ward Beecher, Julia Ward Howe, Thomas Nast, Joseph Pulitzer, Whitelaw Reid. Unpublished finding aid in repository.

Buckley, William F., Jr., 1925- Papers 1951-1987: 440.25 linear ft. Founder and editor of *National Review*. Host of *Firing Line*. Unrestricted papers consist of correspondence, news releases, clippings, and subject files from Buckley's 1965 campaign for mayor of New York; letters and scrapbooks concerning *God and Man at Yale*; and videotapes and transcripts of *Firing Line*. Remaining papers are closed and may be used only with the permission of William F. Buckley, Jr. Unpublished finding aid in repository.

Byas, Hugh, 1875-1945. Papers 1928-1941: 11 microfilm reels. Wrote for *London Times, New York Times, Japan Times and Mail*, 1928-1939. Correspondents include Hanson Baldwin, Lionel Cholmondeley, Arthur Hays Sulzberger, Arthur Morgan Young. Index available.

Decision. Papers 1940-1942: .3 linear ft. Magazine 1940-1942 founded by Klaus Mann. Correspondence, drafts, legal documents, press releases, clippings. Editorial board included Stephen Vincent Benet, Louis Adamic, Horace Gregory, Robert Nathan, Ernest Boyd, Vincent Sheehan, Robert E. Sherwood. Correspondents include Marshall Field, Andre Gide, Julien Green, Christopher Isherwood, Carson McCullers, Archibald MacLeish, William S. Paley, Stephen Spender, Dorothy Thompson, Stefan Zweig, Vladimir Nabakov.

Fischer, John Sylvester, 1910-1978. Papers 1907-1980: 25 linear ft. Editor at *Harper's Magazine* 1935-1967. General correspondence, family correspondence, subject files, writings, diaries and other memorabilia, Yale files. Correspondents include Bruce Catton, Norman Cousins, Ralph Ellison, Malcolm Foster, John Kenneth Galbraith, John Gardner, Brendan Gill, Walter Kerr, Irving Kristol, Henry Luce, Willie Morris, Reinhold Niebuhr, Milo Perkins, Bertrand Russell, Arthur Schlesinger, Barbara Tuchman, Eudora Welty, Rebecca West, Tom Wolfe, C. Vann Woodward, Adlai Stevenson, John F. Kennedy, Maury Maverick, William Blair, Newton Minow, Willard Wirtz, Dean Acheson, Carl Albert, Chester Bowles, McGeorge Bundy, Frank Church, J. William Fulbright, Barry Goldwater, Hubert Humphrey, Jacob Javits, Lyndon B. Johnson, Daniel Patrick Moynihan, Edmund Muskie, Nelson Rockefeller, Dean Rusk, Harry S Truman. Unpublished finding aid available.

Fischer, Louis, 1896-1970. Papers 1929-1961: 1 linear ft. Journalist; author of numerous books and articles on Soviet Union. Family and professional correspondence and typescript drafts of four books. Unpublished finding aid in repository.

Grinnell, George Bird, 1849-1938. Papers 1886-1929: 16 linear ft. Editor of *Forest and Stream Weekly* 1876-1911. Letterbooks, correspondence, writings and photographs. Numerous correspondents including Theodore Roosevelt and William Howard Taft. Unpublished finding aid in repository.

Hale, William Harlan, 1910-1974. Papers 1915-1970: 9 linear ft. Assoc. editor, *Vanity Fair* 1932; columnist, *Washington Post* 1933-1934; editorial assoc., *Fortune* 1934-1936; Office of War Information 1941-1945; senior editor, *New Republic* 1946-1947; senior writer and editor, *Reporter* 1948-1958; managing editor, *Horizon* 1958-1963. Correspondence, writings, personal and biographical papers, topical files, printed matter. Correspondents include Max Ascoli, Bruce Bliven, Oswald Garrison Villard. Unpublished finding aid in repository.

Hale, William Bayard, 1869-1924. Papers 1888-1939: 4 linear ft. Worked for *Cosmopolitan*, the *New York World, Philadelphia Public Ledger, World's Work*. Personal papers, printed matter. Correspondents include Sigmund Freud, William Jennings Bryan, John Burroughs, Thomas Hardy, H.L. Mencken, Theodore Roosevelt, George Bernard Shaw. Unpublished finding aid in repository.

Hodgskin, Thomas, 1787-1869. Papers 1802-1903: .5 linear ft. Parliamentary reporter for *London Morning Chronicle*. Founder of *Mechanic's Magazine*. Correspondents include George Bentinck, John Bright, Henry Peter Broughm, John Campbell, Thomas Campbell, Richard Cobden, George Combe, Benjamin Disraeli. Unpublished finding aid in repository. Entire collection available on microfilm at cost.

Hooker, Richard, 1878-1964. Papers 1907-1964: .25 linear ft. Washington correspondent for *Springfield Republican* 1904-1911, literary editor 1911-1915, and editor-in-chief 1915-1922. Directed Associated Press 1927-1934. Correspondents include Ray Stannard Baker, Bernard Baruch, Samuel Bowles, Winston Churchill, Bainbridge Colby, Calvin Coolidge, Josephus Daniels, Herbert Hoover, Charles Evans Hughes, Cordell Hull, Franklin D. Roosevelt, William H. Taft, Edith Wilson, Woodrow Wilson. Unpublished finding aid in repository.

Humboldt, Charles, 1910-1964. Papers 1935-1963: 4 linear ft. Asst. Editor, *New Masses* 1934; editor, *Mainstream*, 1946; editor and publicist, Citadel Press 1948-1952; editor, *Translations* 1953. Correspondence, writings, research materials. Correspondents include Alvah Bessie, Ralph Ellison, Lillian Hellman, Kenneth Tynan, Christiana Stead, Scott Nearing, Linus Pauling. Unpublished finding aid in repository.

Kluger, Richard, 1934- Papers 1965-1986: 12 linear ft. Served in editorial capacities for *Wall Street Journal, New York Post, Forbes, New York Herald Tribune* and other publications. Correspondence, interview notes, and other materials. Unpublished finding aid in repository.

Lerner, Max, 1902- Papers 1927-1980: 46 linear ft. Editor, *Nation* 1936-1938; editorial director *PM* 1943-1948; columnist, *New York Star* 1948-1949; columnist, *New York Post*, 1949-1970s. Correspondence, speeches and writings, photographs, press clippings and memorabilia. correspondents include Dean Acheson, Edward Albee, Joseph Alsop, Bruce Bliven, Herbert Block, William F. Buckley, Norman Cousins, John Gunther, Hugh Heffner, Norman Mailer, James Reston, George Seldes, Upton Sinclair, Edmund Wilson, Katherine Graham. Unpublished finding aid available in repository.

Lippmann, Walter, 1889-1974. Robert O. Anthony collection of Walter Lippmann 1901-1978: 80 linear ft. Magazines; books; newspapers; bulletins, pamphlets and misc.; clippings; dissertations, essays, theses, seminars and study groups; correspondence relating to the collection. All known published writings by Walter Lippman. RESTRICTED: Folder 20 of Box 60 may not be photocopied without permission from Lehrman Institute. Unpublished finding aid in repository.

Printed material by and about Lippmann available on 12 reels of microfilm.

Loomis family. Loomis-Wilder family papers: includes papers of John Augustus Wilder, 1834-1870. Includes purchase papers and financial papers for the *Kansas City Journal of Commerce* 1867-1870. Special files: 2 boxes. Unpublished finding aid in repository.

Lyman family. Lyman family papers: 5 linear ft. Includes papers of Joseph Bardwell Lyman, 1829-1872, a lawyer and journalist. Correspondence, diaries, business papers, account books, court books and articles. Unpublished finding aid in repository.

Macdonald, Dwight, 1906-1982. Papers 1865-1984: 84 linear ft. Assoc. editor of *Fortune* 1929-36; editor of *Partisan Review* 1937-1943; publisher of *Politics* 1944-1949. Also wrote for *Esquire* and *New Yorker*. Correspondence, manuscripts, notes, printed material, photographs, memorabilia. Numerous correspondents including James Agee, Sherwood Anderson, W.H. Auden, Roger Baldwin, William F. Buckley, T.S. Eliot, Arnold Gingrich, Paul Goodman, Irving Howe, Irving Kristol, Henry Luce, Mary McCarthy, Norman Mailer, William Shawn, John Updike, Gore Vidal, Edmund Wilson. Unpublished finding aid in repository. RESTRICTED: Box 170 restricted until 1997; November 1985 addition restricted until processed.

McLane, John Augustus Hendrix, 1840-1893. Papers 1841-1893: 1 linear ft. Correspondence, essays, diaries, clippings and other papers of southern political independent who established independent weekly journal in Columbia SC. Correspondents include George Washington Cable, Seldon Connor, Wendell Phillips. Unpublished finding aid in repository.

Mayo, Katherine, 1868?-1940. Papers 1835-1968: 27.5 linear ft. Writer for *New York Evening Post, Atlantic Monthly, Scribner's*. Author of several books. Sometime used pen name Katherine Prence. Correspondence, diaries, writings, photographs, scrapbooks, research materials. Correspondents include Stanley Baldwin, Winston Churchill, Clarence Darrow, Walt Disney, John

Gunther, Herbert Hoover, Mark Sullivan, Charles C. Batchelder. Unpublished finding aid in repository.

Nadel, Baruch, 1926-   Papers 1929-1985: 2.75 linear ft. Author and journalist with *Yediot Aharonot.* Research files, transcribed interviews, poems, letters. RESTRICTED: Iraqi Jewish Immigration Files restricted until Jan. 1, 1991. Unpublished finding aid in repository.

Newton, Byron Rufus, 1861-1938. Papers 1882-1938: 5 linear ft. Worked at *Buffalo News* 1886-1901; Associated Press correspondent in Cuba 1898; *New York Herald* 1902-1910. Correspondence, writings, notes, printed materials, clippings, photographs, financial papers, memorabilia. Correspondents include Newton D. Baker, Charles W. Fairbanks, William G. McAdoo, William F. McCombs, Franklin D. Roosevelt, Theodore Roosevelt, Woodrow Wilson, Wilbur and Orville Wright. Unpublished finding aid in repository.

Nock, Albert Jay, 1872 or 3-1945. Papers 1892-1969: 3 linear ft. Writer and editor for *American Magazine*; writer and assoc. editor, *Nation* 1915-1919; co-editor, *Freeman* 1920-1924; author of numerous books. Correspondence and writings. Correspondents include H.L. Mencken, Ellery Sedgwick, Brand Whitlock, Newton D. Baker, Jacques Barzun, Lewis Mumford, John Dos Passos. Unpublished finding aid in repository.

Oastler, Frank Richard, 1871-1936. Papers 1912-1936: 104 linear ft. Motion picture film, prints, glass negatives and nitrate negatives.

Pearson, Drew, 1897-1969. Drew Pearson "Washington Merry-Go-Round" papers 1932-1944: 20 microfilm reels. Typed manuscripts with marginalia. Unpublished finding aid in repository.

Ranck, Than Vanneman, 1874-1947, Papers 1916-1947: 6.25 linear ft. Editor for Hearst newspapers 1906-1937. Correspondence, cables, telegrams. Includes correspondence with William Randolph Hearst, Franklin Knox, Edwin Markham. Unpublished finding aid in repository.

Reid, Ogden Rogers, 1925-   Papers: 1925-1974: 315 linear ft. Newspaper columnist and editor with *New York Herald Tribune,* 1950-1953; New York congressman, ambassador, politician. Correspondence, student papers, writings, speeches, subject files, congressional papers, clippings, photographs. Numerous correspondents including Steve Allen, Joseph Alsop, Lord Beaverbrook, Art Buchwald, Joseph R. McCarthy, Roy Cohn, Marshall Field, William Randolph Hearst, Walter Kerr, Victor Lasky, Walter Lippmann, Claire Boothe Luce, Henry Luce, John Oaks, Whitelaw Reid, William Safire, Arthur Ochs Sulzberger, Walter Winchell. RESTRICTED: Constituent case files (Series XIV, Boxes 291-313) restricted except with Ogden Reid's authorization. Acc. 87-M-38 restricted until processed. Unpublished finding aid in repository.

Reid, Whitelaw, 1837-1912. Papers 1865-1923: 2 linear ft. 9 vols. autographed letters. Journalist during Civil War who joined *New York Tribune* in 1868. Assumed control of paper in 1872. Researchers must use microfilm edition of papers and/or printed copies from microfilm. Unpublished finding aid in repository.

Robb, Walter Johnson, 1880-   Papers 1919-1969: 4 linear ft. Newspaper work and foreign news correspondent, Manila, 1918-1941; Foreign Broadcast Intelligence Service, 1943-1944; Office of War Information 1945-1946. Correspondence, writings, clippings, photographs, financial papers, memorabilia. Correspondents include Henry Andreas, Raymond L. Buell, Percy Hill, Sergio Osmena, Chick Parsons, Will Rogers, Jr. Unpublished finding aid in repository.

Sedgwick, Hubert Merrill, 1867-1950. Papers 1884-1950: .5 linear ft. Sports writer for *New Haven Palladium*, 1894-1895; for *New Haven Register* 1895, and sports editor, 1910-1918; correspondent for *New York Times*, *New York Tribune*, *Boston Transcript*, *Boston Post*, *Chicago Tribune* 1920-1944. Correspondence, clippings, memorabilia, photographs. Correspondents include Connie Mack. Unpublished finding aid in repository.

Stokes, Harold Phelps, 1887-1970. Papers 1908-1969: 9.5 linear ft. Reporter for *New York Post* 1911-1923; on editorial staff of *New York Times* 1926-1937. Free-lance author. Correspondence, diaries, memoranda, notes, writings, clippings and subject files. Correspondents include Alger Hiss, Dean Acheson, James Auchincloss, Russell Baker, Lord Beaverbrook, Francis Biddle, Turner Catledge, Jay N. Darling, Arthur Krock, Walter Lippmann, Adolph S. Ochs, James Reston, E.B. White. Unpublished finding aid in repository.

Tebbel, John William, 1912-   Papers 1948: .5 linear ft. Typescript for Tebbel's book on George Horace Lorimer and the

Saturday Evening Post published in 1948. Unpublished finding aid in repository.

Webb, James Watson, 1802-1884. Papers 1819-1890: 21 linear ft. Journalist and editor. Owner of *New York Morning Courier* and *New York World.* Correspondence, letterbooks, newspapers, diaries. Correspondents include Nicholas Biddle, James Blaine, Lewis Cass, Henry Clay, Hamilton Fish, Abraham Lincoln, William Marcy, Napoleon III, William Seward. Unpublished finding aid in repository.

Willert, Arthur, Sir, 1882-1973. Papers 1907-1973: 11 linear ft. British journalist and diplomat. Joined *London Times* in 1906; chief correspondent in U. S. 1910-1920; secretary of British War Mission in Washington and representative of Ministry of Information 1917-1918; head of News Dept. and Press Officer of British Foreign Office 1931-1935; Head of Ministry of Information Office for the Southern Region 1939-1945; author of four books. Correspondence, writings, notes, memoranda, printed matter. Correspondents include D.D. Braham, Herbert Croly, Geoffrey Dawson, Lord Northcliffe, H.W. Steed, Campbell Stuart, Robert Wilberforce, Evelyn Wrench. Unpublished finding aid in repository.

Yale University Radio Station WYBC. Records 1945-1972: 11 linear ft. Public relations materials, history of station, programming data, Ivy League network files, general office files. RESTRICTED: until 1992. Unpublished box list in repository.

Yale Daily News. Records 1890-1959: .5 linear ft. Constitution, correspondence, editing books, ledger. Unpublished folder level inventory available in repository.

DELAWARE

Historical Society of Delware

• Historical Society of Delaware, 505 Market St. Wilmington DE 19801. 302-655-7161. Constance J. Cooper, Manuscript Librarian. 1 pm-9 pm M; 9 am-5 pm T-F. Photocopy services. Inventories to collections in repository.

Higgins family. Papers: 4 linear ft. Journalist for *Baltimore Sunday Sun* late 1920s-1930s; editorial writer for *Wilmington News Journal* 1946-1970. Includes papers of Anthony Higgins, 1902-1986.

Wilson, W. Emerson, 1907-1982. Papers: 1.5 linear ft. Reporter, editor, columnist for *Wilmington News Journal* 1930-1982.

DISTRICT OF COLUMBIA

Columbia Historical Society

• Columbia Historical Society, 1307 New Hampshire Ave. N.W., Washington DC 20036. 202-785-2068. Larry Baume, Curator of Collections. 10 am-4 pm W,F,Sa. Photocopy services. See also Lawrence Baume, comp., *Guide to Research Collection* (Washington: Columbia Historical Society, 1987).

Proctor, John Clagett. Collection: 5 file drawers, 6 boxes. Journalist and writer for *Washington Star* 1928-1952. Card index available.

Suter, Jesse and Theodore Noyes. Collection: 4 file drawers. Papers of journalist Suter and managing editor Noyes for *Washington Evening Star* 1930s-1950s.

Georgetown University

• Special Collections Division, Georgetown University Library, 37th and O Streets, N. W., Washington DC 20057. 202-687-7444. Nicholas B. Scheetz, Manuscripts Librarian. 9 am-5 pm M-F. Limited photocopy services. Unpublished finding aids for most collections available in repository. See also *Special Collections at Georgetown* (Washington DC: Georgetown University, 1985).

Amrine, Michael, 1918-1974. Papers: 42 linear ft. Journalist, novelist and poet.

Downs, William R., 1914-1978. Papers: 12 linear ft. News correspondent for United Press, CBS.

Drummond, Roscoe, 1902-1983. Papers: 10.5 linear ft. Reporter, editor and columnist. Correspondents include Herbert Bayard Swope, J. Edgar Hoover, Lyndon B. Johnson.

Editorial cartoon collection. Twentieth century work by more than 25 American cartoonists. Approximately 200 cartoons in collection. Includes groups of cartoons by John Baer, Gene Basset, Oscar Cesare, Robert Clark, Bill Crawford, John Stampone, Bill Talburt, Jeff MacNelly, Tony Auth.

Emerson, Edwin, Jr., 1869-1959. Papers: 4.5 linear ft. Foreign and war correspondent for *Boston Post, New York Evening Post,*

New York Sun, Harper's Weekly, Leslie's Weekly, Collier's Weekly, Illustrirte Zeitung, New York World, Chicago News, Westminster Gazette, Black and White.

Oursler, Fulton,1893-1952. Collection: 39.5 linear ft. Writer for numerous magazines and religious broadcaster. Includes papers of Grace Perkins Oursler, d. 1955. Correspondents include H.L. Mencken, Franklin D. Roosevelt, Upton Sinclair.

Reynolds, Frank, 1923-1983. Papers: 22 linear ft. News correspondent; chief anchorman ABC World News Tonight 1978-1983.

Smith, Eric. Collection: 2,587 original editorial cartoons. Drawn for *Annapolis Capital-Gazette* and other papers. Indexed by subject and date.

Visson, Andre, 1899-   Papers: 30 linear ft. Correspondent and reporter for *Time, New York Times, Washington Post, New York Herald Tribune, Chicago Sun Times,* and other newspapers. Served on editorial staff of *Reader's Digest.*

Howard University

• Moorland-Springarn Research Center, Howard University, Washington DC 20059. 202-636-76480. Karen L. Jefferson, Curator. 9 am-1 pm, 2 pm-4:30 pm M-F. Photocopy services. Registers available in repository. See also Greta S. Wilson, *Guide to Processed Collections in the Manuscript Division of the Moorland-Springarn Research Center* (Washington, DC: Howard University, 1983).

Afro-American Newspapers Collection. ca. 1920-1964: 142.5 linear ft. Files (primarily correspondence) of publishers Carl Murphy and John H. Murphy III. RESTRICTED: Unavailable until processing is completed.

Capital Press Club. Records: 1942-   1.5 linear ft. RESTRICTED: Unavailable until processing is completed.

Carter, Jeanette, 1886-1964. Papers 1927-1964: 1.5 linear ft. Editor and manager of *Women's Voice,* magazine published in the interest of Republican policies.

Cary, Mary Ann Shad, 1823-1893. Papers 1844-1884: .5 linear ft. Editor of *Provincial Freeman,* Canadian anti-slavery publication.

Douglass, Frederick, 1817-1895. Collection 1874-1895: 6 linear ft. Founder and publisher of *North Star*. Biographical materials, correspondence, photographs.

Dunnigan, Alice A., 1906-1983. Papers: 13.5 linear ft. Chief of Washington Bureau, Associated Negro Press; first Black woman journalist to receive White House accreditation; correspondent for *Atlanta Daily World*. RESTRICTED: Unavailable until processing is completed.

Goodlet, Carlton B., 1914- Papers: 72 linear ft. Publisher of *San Francisco Sun Reporter*. RESTRICTED: Unavailable until processing is completed.

Lochard, Metz T.P. Papers ca. 1930-1970: 1.5 linear ft. Assoc. editor of *Chicago Defender*. Correspondence, writings.

Lucas, Townsend McKinley, 1930-? Collection 1948-1958: .25 linear ft. Journalist. Scrapbook with biographical data, documents, notes, clippings, photographs.

Murphy, George B., Jr., 1906-1986. Papers: 78 linear ft. Editor of *Washington Afro-American*. Files, correspondence. RESTRICTED: Unavailable until processing is completed.

Murray, Freeman Henry Morris, 1859-1950. Papers 1883-1916: 1.5 linear ft. Editor of *The Horizon, A Journal of the Color Line*. Correspondence, writings, photographs, diaries.

Payne, Ethel L., 1911- Papers: 24 linear ft. Feature writer, Washington correspondent, assoc. editor for Sengstacke Newspapers (*Chicago Daily Defender, Courier Group, Michigan Chronicle Tri-State Defender*). RESTRICTED: Unavailable until processing is completed.

Pinchback, Pinckney Benton Steward, 1837-1921. Papers 1867-1873: 1 linear ft. Includes minutes from Black organization of 1970s, The Colored Newspaper Man.

Prattis, Percival Leroy, 1895-1980. Papers 1935-1965: 13.5 linear ft. Editor of *Pittsburgh Courier*. Writings, scrapbooks, photographs. Includes correspondence of Prattis and that of Robert L. Vann, founder and editor 1910-1940. RESTRICTED: Unavailable until processing is completed.

Rapier family. Papers 1836-1883: 2 linear ft. Includes diary 1857-1859 of John H. Rapier, journalist, surgeon and world traveler.

Walker, William Otis, 1896-1981. Papers: 40.5 linear ft. Publisher of *Cleveland Call and Post.* RESTRICTED: Unavailable until processing is completed.

Library of Congress

• Manuscript Division, The Library of Congress, James Madison Building, Independence Ave., S.E., Washington DC 20540. 205-287-5387. James H. Hutson, Chief Manuscript Division. 8:30 am-5 pm M-Sa. Photocopy services. Registers for most collections available in repository. See also *National Union Catalog of Manuscript Collections* (Washington, DC: Library of Congress, 1959-).

Ackerman, Carl William, 1890-1970. Papers 1833-1970: 60,000 items. 73-50039.

Allen, Frederick Lewis, 1890-1949. Papers 1895-1949: 9,000 items. 78-10470.

Alsop, Joseph Wright, 1910-   Joseph W. and Stewart J. Alsop papers 1699-1975: 79,000 items. 77-10561.

American Press Association. Records 1890-1899: 1,300 items. 78-10769.

Arnold, Edwin, Sir, 1832-1904. Collection 1879-1883: 3 items. 83-4396.

Astor, William Waldorf, 1848-1919. Papers 1904-1910: 49 items. 78-5795.

Babbitt, Charles H. Scrapbooks 1875-1925: 3,000 items. 81-11478.

Baker, Ray Stannard, 1870-1946. Papers 1836-1947: 30,000 items. 78-11593.

Balderson, John Lloyd, 1889-1954. Papers 1915-1950: 400 items. 79-11619.

Baldwin, Hanson Weightman, 1903- Papers 1920-1977: 1,500 items. 84-61729.

Barnes, Joseph, 1907-1970. Papers 1930-1952: 5,000 items. 73-39370.

Barksdale, Ethelbert, 1824-1893. Letter 1867: 1 item. 79-115.

Barrett, John, 1866-1938. Papers 1861-1943: 50,000 items. 81-11874.

Barth, Alan, 1906-   Collection 1861-1874: 38 items. 79-935.

Beach family. Papers 1811-1962: 400 items. 82-56812.

Bennett, James Gordon, 1795-1872. Papers 1845-1934: 225 items. 75-12427.

Berry, Faith Daryl, 1939-   Papers 1975-1980: 2,500 items. 85-61711.

Beveridge, Albert Jeremiah, 1862-1927. Papers ca. 1890-1927: 98,000 items. 78-12591.

Binckley, John Milton. Papers 1816-1943: 85 items. 78-12732.

Bingham, Robert Worth, 1871-1937. Papers 1879-1974. 80-56424.

Black, Ruby Aurora, 1896-1957. Papers ca. 1930-1945: 3,500 items. 84-61716.

Blair family. Papers 1830-1968: 12,000 items. 79-12930.

Blennerhassett, Harman, 1765-1831. Papers 1755-1866: 500 items. 74-50633.

Bonsal, Stephen, 1865-1951. Papers 1890-1973: 4,500 items. 75-13193.

Bourne, William Oland. Papers 1856-1884: 1,500 items. 81-13375.

Boyd, Crosby Noyes, 1903-   Autograph collection 1791-1908: 1 vol. 75-56226.

Bradbury, William H., 1829-1900. Papers 1862-1900: 102 items. 78-56242.

Brainerd, Erastus, 1855-1922. Alaska and Klondike collection 1868-1898: 2,000 items. 79-13623.

Brant, Irving Newton, 1885-1976. Papers 1910-1977. 79-13656.

Breckinridge family. Papers 1752-1965. 79-13698.

Brenner, Anita, 1905-1974. Papers ca. 1920-1973: 120,000 items. 83-61580.

Brisbane, Arthur, 1864-1936. Letter 1909: 1 item. 79-5899.

Brissot de Warville, Jacques Pierre, 1754-1793. Notes n.d.: 31 items. 79-5075.

Brooks, Noah, 1830-1903. Letter 1898: 1 item. 79-315.

Brough, John, 1811-1865. Collection 1845-1937: 2 items. 79-320.

Broun, Heywood Campbell, 1888-1939. Collection 1912-1938: 12 items. 79-594.

Bryant, William Cullen, 1794-1878. Collection 1859-1874: 4 items. 80-2235.

Burlingame family. Papers of Anson and Edward Livermore Burlingame 1810-1936: 550 items. 78-14373.

Cadwallader, Sylvanus, 1825-1905. Papers 1849-1904: 600 items. 79-14712.

Cain, James Mallahan, 1891-1977. Papers 1901-1978: 30,000 items. 73-47399.

Carlson, Fred A., 1887-1952. Papers 1918-1952: 50 items. 79-15065.

Carpenter, Frank George, 1855-1924. Frances Carpenter collection 1875-1960: 100 items. 73-22194.

Carroll, Raymond G., 1876?-1943. Papers 1905-1935: 22 items. 81-15230.

Chandler, Joseph Ripley, 1792-1880. Letterbook 1850-1851: 1 vol. (419 pp.) 79-5834.

Chesterton, Gilbert Keith, 1874-1936. Poem 1898: 1 item. 81-1158.

Church, William Conant, 1836-1917. Papers 1862-1924: 350 items. 79-15792.

Clapp, William Warland, 1826-1891. Papers 1856-1911: 350 items. 78-15917.

Clapper, Raymond, 1892-1944. Papers ca. 1913-1944: 79,000 items. 78-15925.

Clarkson, James Sullivan, 1842-1918. Papers 1851-1917: 1,200 items. 78-16055.

Coleman, William, 1766-1829. Letters 1810-1815: 2 items. 79-548.

Colfax, Schuyler, 1823-1885. Papers 1837-1882: 160 items. 79-16394.

Collier, John Payne, 1789-1883. Letter 1840: 1 item. 79-549.

Conn, Edward Leslie, 1885-1942. Poems n.d.: 7 items. 79-562.

Corey, Herbert, 1872-1954. Papers 1847-1954: 8,700 items. 78-16915.

Craig, Elisabeth May. Journalist.

Croswell, Edwin, 1797-1871. Letter 1831: 1 item. 84-6145.

Dana, Charles Anderson, 1819-1897. Papers 1859-1882: 300 items. 79-17665.

Daniel, John Moncure, 1825-1865. Editorial 1861: 1 item. 79-1004.

Daniels, Josephus, 1862-1948. Papers 1806-1948: 331,000 items. 75-17715.

Davis, Elmer Holmes, 1890-1958. Papers 1893-1957: 7,800 items. 79-17889.

Deuel, Wallace Rankin, 1905-1974. Papers 1929-1970: 6,500 items. 81-75905.

Dixon, Frederick, 1868?-1923. Papers 1897-1923: 500 items. 77-18598.

Douglass, Frederick, 1817?-1895. Papers 1841-1967: 7,300 items. 75-11879.

Duane, William, 1760-1835. Collection 1800-1832: 14 items. 79-1193.

Dudman, Richard Beebe, 1918-   Papers 1944-1983: 14,350 items. 81-58248.

Dunn, Arthur Wallace, 1859-1926. Papers 1882-1927: 250 items. 73-51854.

Dunne, Finley Peter, 1867-1936. Correspondence 1889-1936: 160 items. 79-19208.

Eliot, George Fielding, 1894-1971. Papers 1939-1971: 5,000 items. 73-19646.

Elliot, Jonathan, 1784-1846. Correspondence 1817-1829: 300 items. 78-19695.

Emerson, T. Collection 1900: 6 vol. 81-19828.

Evans, John, b. 1824. Papers 1849-1887: 50 items. 79-5200.

Field, Eugene, 1850-1895. Journalist.

Field, Mary Katherine Keemle, 1838-1896. Note 1895: 1 item. 79-1395.

Fisk, Wilbur. Papers 1862-1865: 100 items. 78-20677.

Flanner, Janet. 1892-1978. Janet Flanner-Solita Solano papers 1870-1976: 3,000 items. 77-47084.

Forbes, Archibald, 1838-1900. Papers 1889-1898: 19 items. 79-5221.

Forney, John Wien, 1817-1881. Journalist.

Frederic, Harold, 1856-1898. Papers 1893-1897: 4,000 items. 78-21485.

Freeman, Ira Henry. Historical description 1942: 1 item. 79-5659.

Freneau, Philip Morin, 1759-1832. Letters of Philip and Peter Freneau 1800-1801: 19 items. 79-1464.

Frey, John Philip, 1871-1957. Papers 1891-1951: 28,000 items. 78-21600.

Fullam William Freeland, 1855-1926. Papers 1877-1919: 3,850 items. 70-50096.

Furman, Bess, 1894-1969. Papers 1728-1967: 47,000 items. 80-21741.

Gales, Joseph, 1786-1860. Papers of Joseph Gales and William W. Seaton 1806-1860. 81-21808.

Gardette, Charles Desmarais, 1830-1885. Papers 1842-1873. 81-21923.

Ghent, William James, 1866-1942. Papers 1876-1942: 15,000 items. 78-22699.

Gleason, Arthur Huntington, 1878-1923. Papers 1863-1931: 3,000 items. 77-18382.

Goddard, William, 1740-1817. Receipted invoice 1786: 2 items. 79-4577.

Graham, Fred Patterson, 1931-   Papers 1949-1982. 84-61617.

Grant, Hugh Gladney, 1888-1972. Papers 1924-1933: 800 items. 80-50435.

Greeley, Horace, 1811-1872. Papers 1826-1928: 1,500 items. 79-23937.

Green, Duff, 1791-1875. Papers 1716-1879: 725 items. 75-23978. Also papers 1810-1902: 25 microfilm reels. 82-60145.

Grigsby, Hugh Blair, 1806-1881. Collection 1775-1880: 13 items. 79-1587.

Guiney, Louise Imogen, 1861-1920. Papers 1884-1916: 1,500 items. 78-24323.

Gurley, John Addison, 1813-1863. Letter 1862: 1 item. 79-1596.

Gwynn, Stephen Lucius, 1864-1950. Collection 1896-1939: 5 items. 81-1228.

Hale family. Papers 1698-1916. 75-24463.

Halford, Elijah Walker, 1843-1938. Papers 1867-1928: 400 items. 73-15685.

Halpine, Charles Graham, 1829-1868. Journalist.

Harding, Warren Gamaliel, 1865-1923. Papers 1888-1923. 80-50773.

Hassett, William D., 1880-1965. Papers 1930-1945: 200 items. 78-55103.

Hawley, Joseph Roswell, 1826-1905. Papers 1638-1906. 78-25320.

Hay, John. Papers 1856-1914: 11,290 items. 78-25379.

Hazeltine, Mayo Williamson, 1841-1909. Letter 1896: 1 item. 79-5281.

Hemingway, Ernest, 1899-1961. Collection 1949: 2 items. 79-2239.

Hensley, Stewart, 1913-1976. Papers 1936-1976: 4,000 items. 81-75842.

Hill, Edwin Conger, 1884-1957. Report 1839: 1 item.

Hinds, Asher Crosby, 1863-1919. Journalist.

Hitchcock, Frank Harris, 1867-1935. Papers 1905-1935: 200 items. 78-26070.

Hood, Edwin Milton, 1858-1923. Papers 1868-1963: 750 items. 79-26435.

Hotze, Henry, 1834-1887. Papers 1861-1865: 187 items. 79-26534.

Howard, Roy Wilson, 1883-1964, Papers 1911-1966: 115,000 items. 81-26583.

Hutchings, James Mason, 1820-1902. Papers 1848-1855: 12 items. 81-26963.

Hyde, George R. Letter 1922: 1 item. 79-668.

Ingalls, John James, 1833-1900. Autograph n.d.: 1 item. 79-853.

Jarvis, Russell, 1791-1853. Papers 1816-1851: 69 items. 80-4515.

Kantor, MacKinlay, 1904-1977. Journalist.

Kauffmann, Samuel Hay, 1829-1906. Papers 1872-1896: 350 items. 81-28225.

Keating, John McLeod, 1830-1906. Papers 1866-1893: 36 items. 79-5347.

Keep, John, 1781-1866. Papers 1839-1929: 14 items. 82-28308.

Keim family. Papers 1861-1874: 20 items. 81-28340.

Kendall, Amos, 1789-1869. Papers 1835-1909: 400 items. 79-28449.

Kennan, George, 1845-1924. Papers 1840-1937: 60,000 items. 78-28456.

Kieran, John Francis, 1892-1981. Papers 1919-1981: 400 items. 85-61885.

Klein, Julius, 1901-   Collection 1960-1965: 27 items.   79-5360.

Kline, Burton, 1877-1958. Papers 1901-1954: 650 items. 73-52605.

Knoll, Rudolph, 1913-   Collection 1922-ca. 1938: 27 items. 79-5361.

Knox, Franklin, 1874-1944. Papers 1898-1954: 2,800 items. 77-28845.

Lahey, Edwin A., 1902-1969. Papers 1936-1967: 48 items. 79-3976.

Leavitt, Joshua, 1794-1873. Journalist.

Leggett, William, 1801-1839. Letters 1834-1838: 2 items. 79-2805.

Lewis, Ernest Irving, 1873-1947. Papers 1897-1944: 10,000 items. 76-12385.

Lloyd, Henry Demarest, 1847-1903. Papers 1840-1937: 52 microfilm reels. 82-59410.

Luce, Henry Robinson, 1898-1967. Papers 1917-1967. 75-30767.

Manning, Daniel, 1831-1887. Papers 1885-1921: 900 items. 79-31245.

Marble, Manton Malone, 1834-1917. Papers 1852-1969: 14,000 items. 79-31286.

Mazzini, Giuseppe, 1805-1872. La concordia: manuscript, n.d.: 1 vol. (24 pp.) 83-5704.

McKnew, Zadoc W. Papers 1834-1851: 5 items. 79-5414.

McLean, Evalyn (Walsh), 1886-1947. Papers 1886-1948: 45,000 items. 79-32318.

McMichael, Morton, 1807-1879. Papers 1834-1845: 12 items. 79-5418.

Meyer, Eugene, 1875-1959. Papers 1819-1970: 28,500 items. 82-52019.

Miller, William Henry, 1829-1870. Letters 1857-1864: 13 items. 79-3665.

Moore, Joseph Arthur, 1879-1937. Papers 1915-1927: 4,000 items. 79-33340.

Morris, George Pope, 1802-1864. Papers 1832-1862: 100 items. 82-47910.

Mulford, Prentice, 1834-1891. Letter: 1 item. 79-797.

Murdock, Victor, 1871-1945. Papers 1824-1971: 38,300 items. 77-22384.

Murrow, Edward R., 1908-1965. Papers 1927-1973. 82-60350.

National Nonpartisan League. Records 1910-1928. 80-59063.

Noyes, Crosby Stuart, 1825-1908. Letters 1867-1870: 5 items. 79-858.

O'Laughlin, John Callan, 1873-1949. Papers 1895-1949: 45,000 items. 81-35055.

O'Reilly, Henry, 1806-1886. Articles 1845-1872: 15 items. 79-879. Also correspondence 1845-1882. 80-58792.

Osborne, John, 1907-1981. Papers. 82-60400.

Parker, George Frederick, 1847-1928. Statement n.d.: 1 item. 79-910.

Patri, Angelo, 1876-1965. Papers 1904-1962: 30,000 items. 74-47167.

Pearson, Drew, 1897-1969. Papers 1947-1952: 55 items. 79-1039.

Pike, James Shepherd, 1811-1882. Collection 1849-1869: 64 items. 80-2749.

Post, Louis Freeland, 1849-1928. Papers 1864-1939: 600 items. 77-36657.

Prentice, George Dennison, 1802-1870. Letters 1831-1850: 3 items. 79-1116.

Pringle, Henry Fowles, 1897-1958. Papers 1932-1957: 7,500 items. 81-36921.

Pulitzer, Joseph, 1847-1911. Papers 1880-1924: 5,500 items. 78-37044.

Pulitzer, Joseph, 1885-1955. Journalist.

Redpath, James, 1833-1891. Papers 1861: 1 vol. (358 pp.) 80-81380.

Reid, Whitelaw, 1837-1912. Papers 1795-1946: 60,000 items. 82-65491.

Rice, Grantland, 1880-1954. Papers 1936-1954: 700 items. 83-50211.

Richardson, Albert Deane, 1833-1869. Letter 1865: 1 item. 79-1268.

Riis, Jacob August, 1849-1914. Papers 1858-1927: 2,800 items. 73-37903. Also letters 1898-1900: 2 items. 84-2392.

Ritchie, Thomas, 1778-1854. Collection 1824-1853: 400 items. 82-37929.

Rivington, James, 1724-1802. Letters 1768-1793: 2 items. 79-1288.

Roberts, Cecil Edric Mornington, 1892-   Poem 1941: 1 item. 79-3487.

Russell, Charles Edward, 1860-1941. Papers 1864-1941: 12,000 items. 79-38570.

Safire, William, 1929-   Papers 1960-1974: 65,000 items. 86-61986.

Sanborn, Franklin Benjamin, 1831-1917. Papers 1852-1879: 121 items. 79-38869.

Sargent, Nathan, 1794-1875. Letter 1840: 1 item. 79-1667.

Savage, John Godfrey, 1816-1887. Letter 1861: 1 item. 79-1676.

Saxe, John Godfrey, 1816-1887. Collection 1875-1879: 2 items. 79-1677.

Schouler, William, 1814-1872. Letters 1864: 2 items. 79-1696.

Schurz, Carl, 1829-1906. Papers 1842-1932: 23,110 items. 78-39156.

Scruggs, William Lindsay, 1836-1912. Papers 1867-1912: 1,000 items. 80-75992.

Searcher, Victor. Article 1963: 1 vol. (83 pp.) 79-5695.

Sevareid, Arnold Eric, 1912-   Papers 1930-1957: 20,500 items.

Shackford, Roland Herbert, 1908- Papers ca. 1944-1979. 83-60843.

Smalley, George Washburn, 1833-1916. Papers 1895-1902. 82-40279.

Smith, Henry Ladd, 1906-   Papers 1926-1946: 78 items. 79-3978.

Smith, Samuel Harrison, 1772-1845. Exercise Book 1787: 1 vol. (31 pp.) 82-63487.

Spring, Everett. Journalist.

Spofford, Ainsworth Rand, 1825-1908. Papers 1819-1970: 600 items. 73-40972.

Stanton, Henry Brewster, 1805-1887.   Letters 1852-1853: 6 items. 79-1823.

Stephens, Alexander Hamilton, 1812-1883. Papers 1784-1886: 27,000 items. 78-41335.

Stone, William Leete, 1792-1844. Letter 1831: 1 item. 79-1857.

Straus, Michael Wolf, 1897-1970.   Papers 1879-1968: 2,100 items. 82-47233.

Sullivan, Mark, 1874-1952.   Papers 1900-1935: 2,400 items. 78-41905.

Sweetser, Arthur, 1888-1968. Papers 1913-1963: 22,350 items. 78-42085.

Swing, Raymond Gram, 1887-1968.   Papers 1935-1963: 6,500 items. 78-42119.

Taylor, Charles Henry, 1867-1941: Letter 1895: 1 item.   82-1894.

Thayer, William Sydney, 1830-1864.   Papers 1835-1901: 600 items. 78-42689.

Tilton, Theodore, 1835-1907. Poems: 6 vol. 83-92882.

Townsend, George Alfred, 1841-1914. Papers 1865-1899. 82-43109.

Union Guard. Records. 82-82610.

Upton, William Treat, 1870-1961. Journalist.

Ursinus, Oskar. Papers 1909-1943: 4,500 items. 78-43745.

Walker, Singleton S. Papers 1824-1827: 20 items. 82-44461.

Walsh, Robert, 1784-1859, Letter 1818: 1 item. 80-2083.

Washburn, Stanley, 1878-1950. Papers 1912-1945: 1,600 items. 78-44644.

Watterson, Henry, 1840-1921. Papers 1857-1983: 7 microfilm reels. 85-61864.

Wayman, Dorothy (Godfrey), 1893-1975. Papers 1862-1971: 6,000 items. 77-39834.

Webb, James Watson, 1802-1884. Letters 1857: 3 items. 80-2111.

Weed, Thurlow, 1797-1882. Papers 1821-1882: 125 items. 78-44974.

Welles, Gideon, 1802-1878. Papers 1777-1911: 15,000 items. 78-45054.

Wentworth, Edwin Oberlin, 1833-1864. Papers 1862-1890: 120 items. 79-45088.

White, John Campbell, 1884-1967. Papers 1933-1935: 60 items. 78-55194.

White, William Allen, 1868-1944. Papers 1859-1944: 136,800 items. 78-45377.

Whiteing, Richard, 1840-1928. Letter: 1 item. 80-2288.

Wile, Frederic William, 1873-1941. Papers 1898-1941: ca. 2,000 items. 78-45674.

Woollcott, Alexander, 1887-1943. Letters 1941: 2 items. 80-2369.

Woolley, Robert Wickliffe, 1871-1958. Papers 1842-1958: 17,000 items. 78-46409.

Young, John Russell, 1840-1899. Papers 1843-1898: 28,000 items. 78-46854.

• Other collections of interest at the Library of Congress:

Alternative Press Collection. American "underground" newspapers from the mid-1960s to the present. Approximately 350 titles from twenty-six states. Located in Serial and Government Publications Division.

Meet the Press Collection. Recordings, videotapes and films of *Meet the Press*; papers of its producer Lawrence E. Spivak; related pictorial material. Spivak Papers totaled 63,800 items in 1979 and are described in an unpublished finding aid.Located in the Manuscript Division, the Motion Picture, Broadcasting, and Recorded Sound Division, and Prints and Photographs Division.

NBC Program Analysis File. Catalog guide 1939-1985: More than 632,000 cards. Air date, time, story line and credits for NBC television programs. Part of American Television and Radio Archives.

NBC Radio Collection. Broadcast recordings of NBC radio programs 1933-1970. Located in the Motion Picture, Broadcasting, and Recorded Sound Division.

National Press Club Collection. Recordings of speeches given at the National Press Club, Washington, D.C., 1952-present. Located in the Motion Picture, Broadcasting, and Recorded Sound Division.

Office of War Information Collection. Broadcast recordings, photographs, and research files. Located in the Motion Picture, Broadcasting, and Recorded Sound Division, Prints and Photographs Division, and the Archive of Folk Song.

FLORIDA

Florida State University

• Special Collections Dept. Robert Manning Strozier Library, Florida State University, Tallahassee FL 32306-2047. 904-644-3271. Susan Hamburger, Assoc. University Librarian. 9 am-6 pm M-F. Call for holiday and semester break hours. Photocopy services. Collection inventories available in repository.

Johnson, Malcolm, 1913-   Papers 1940-1978: 18,806 items. Reporter *Jacksonville Journal* 1930s; *Tallahassee Democrat*

1935-1939, editor 1954-1978; Associated Press reporter 1939-1954. Correspondence, working papers for books, political campaign materials.

Westall, William, 1834-1903. Letters 1887-1903: 172 items. Correspondence with Edmund Downey, editor and publisher of *Waterford News* who wrote novels under the name of F.M. Allen.

University of Florida

• Florida Oral History Archives, Florida State Museum, University of Florida, Gainesville FL 32611. 904-392-1721.

Weimer, Rae. Interviews. Former faculty member and dean who was editor of *PM*.

WRUF. 25 tapes documenting history of radio station.

WUFT. Tapes documenting history of television station.

• P. K. Yonge Library of Florida History, 404 Library West, University of Florida, Gainesville FL 32611. 904-392-0319. Elizabeth Alexander, Librarian. 8 am-noon, 1 pm-4:45 pm M-F. No photocopy services. Collections in NUCMUC. Contents lists for boxes available in repository. See also Elizabeth Alexander and Stephen Kerber, *A Guide to the Major Manuscript Collections of the P. K. Yonge Library of Florida History* (Gainesville: University of Florida, 1987).

Dosh, Robert N., 1886-1970. Papers 1920-1965: 1 ft. Journalist and editor of *Ocala Evening Star* and *Ocala Star Banner*.

Newton, Virgil Miller, 1904-1977. Papers 1950-1965: 28 ft. Managing editor of *Tampa Tribune* 1943-1964. Papers, scrapbooks.

Pennekamp, John D., 1897-1978. Papers 1963-1976: 1 ft. City editor and later managing editor of *Miami Herald*. Correspondence, scrapbook.

• University of Florida Archives, University Libraries, University of Florida, 450 Library East, Gainesville FL 32611. 904-392-6547. Carla M. Kemp, University Archivist. 8 am-4:30 pm. Photocopy services. Finding aids in repository.

Emig, Elmer J. Papers 1929-1955: 3 boxes. Includes unpublished manuscripts and notes on history of Florida journalism.

GEORGIA

Emory University

• Special Collections, The Robert W. Woodruff Library, Emory University, Atlanta GA 30322. 404-727-6887. Dr. Linda Matthews. 9 am-6 pm M-Sa. Photocopy services. Finding aids in repository.

Allen, Young John. Papers 1854-1924: 43 boxes. Methodist missionary to China. Founder and editor of *Wan Kwoh Kung Po*. Correspondence, diaries, notebooks, biographical data, sermons, addresses, articles, essays, other writings.

Foreman, Lauren. 2 folders 1904-1966. City editor of *Atlanta Constitution*.

Grady, Henry Woodfin. Papers 1828-1971: 5 boxes, 14 scrapbooks. Orator and journalist with *Atlanta Constitution*. Correspondence, photographs, literary manuscripts.

Hambleton, James Pinckney. Collection 1857-1893: 1 box. Newspaperman and surgeon.

Hanleiter, Cornelius R. Diary 1861-1865: 5 vols. on microfilm. Newspaperman associated with the *Southern Miscellany, Weekly Republican and Discipline, National American* which later became the *Gate City Guardian* and then the *Southern Confederacy*.

Harris, Corra May (White). Papers 1900-1934: 120 items. Author and journalist. Served as war correspondent for *Saturday Evening Post*. Manuscripts of articles, columns, short stories.

Harris, Julian Larose. Papers 1890-1968: 33 boxes. Journalist with *Atlanta Evening Herald, Atlanta Constitution, Chicago Times Herald, Atlanta Daily News, Uncle Remus Home Magazine, New York Herald, Columbus Enquirer-Sun, Chattanooga Times, New York Times*. Correspondence, articles, columns. Also in collection are papers of Harris' wife, Julia Collier, journalist and editorial writer in arts and education.

Hamphill, William Arnold. Collection ca. 1875-1900: 1 box. Founder and publisher of *Atlanta Constitution*. Record book, photocopies of letters, clippings, biographical information.

Harrison, Emily Steward, 1874-1973. Papers 1829-1979. Editor of *Southern Educational Journal* 1894-1901; woman's dept. editor *Atlanta Daily News* 1901-1902. Personal papers, writings, family papers, photographs.

Howell, Clark. Collection 1863-1965: 3 boxes. Organizer and director of Associated Press. Editor of *Atlanta Constitution.* Correspondence, scrapbooks.

Howell, Evan P. 1 folder ca. 1850-1900. Editor and publisher of *Atlanta Constitution.* Clippings, programs, letters.

Keeler, O.B. Typescript 1910-1930. Writer for *Atlanta Journal.* Typescript of "The Bobby Jones Story."

Knight, Mary Lamar. Papers ca. 1930-1970: 6 boxes. Correspondent with United Press in Paris and China. Correspondence, manuscripts, articles, clippings, scrapbooks.

Lee, Harry. Manuscript ca. 1940: 1 box. Novel *Fox in the Cloak* by editorial staff writer of *Atlanta Constitution.*

Leonard, Lewis Alexander. Papers 1820-1925: .5 box Author and newspaper editor with *Cincinnati Times-Star, Albany Times-Union.* Correspondence.

Leycester, William. Correspondence 1855-1900: ca. 100 pieces. Reporter for *London Times.*

McGill, Ralph Emerson. Papers 1853-1975: 40,000 items, 75 vols. Editor and publisher of *Atlanta Constitution.* Correspondence, writings, articles, editorials.

Martin, Harold H. Papers 1837-1975: 38 boxes. Editor with *Saturday Evening Post;* columnist with *Atlanta Constitution.* Writings, correspondence, photographs, source materials.

Mathewson, Tracy. Collection 1911-1960: 15 folders. Journalist and photographer for *Atlanta Journal Magazine, Southern Outdoors.* Correspondence, typescripts, photographs.

Mencken, H.L. (Henry Louis), 1880-1956. Correspondence 1926-1937: 252 items. Letters, post cards, telegrams and printed items from Mencken to Gretchen Hood, music teacher, opera singer and prominent social figure from Washington, D.C. Register of correspondence available in repository.

Myrick, Susan. Papers 1937-1972: 2 boxes. Journalist with *Macon Telegram. Gone with the Wind* materials and columns.

Neff, Lawrence W. Papers 1907-1960: 2 boxes. Publisher of *Banner Press* 1919-1960.

Rogers, Ernest. Collection 1918-1968: 18 boxes. Includes columns from *Atlanta Journal* 1945-1967.

Seydell, Mildred. Papers 1842-1973: ca. 30,900 pieces. Member of editorial dept of *Atlanta Georgian* 1924-1939; publisher *Seydell Quarterly* in Brussels from 1947-1967.

Sitton, Claude Fox, 1925-   Papers 1969-1983: 10 boxes. Reporter International News Service 1949-1950; United Press 1950-1955; staff of *New York Times* 1957-1968. Joined The News and Observer Publishing Co. as editorial director in 1968; also served as director and vice president of company. Since 1970 editor of *Raleigh News and Observer*. Won Pulitzer Prize in 1983. Correspondence, writings, speeches, scrapbooks.

Smith, Charles Henry (Bill Arp). Collection: ca. 50 items: 1826-1903. Georgia humorist and columnist. Correspondence, columns, etc.

Stanton, Frank Lebby, 1857-1927. Papers ca. 1885-1978: ca. 1,000 pieces. Reporter and feature writer *Savannah Morning News*; editor *Smithville News*; wrote "Just from Georgia" column for *Atlanta Constitution* ca. 1890-1926. Correspondence, poetry, scrapbooks, photographs, cartoons and drawings, clippings, biographical notes, short stories.

Styles, Carey W. Collection ca. 1870-1900: ca. 40 items. Founder of *Atlanta Constitution.* Correspondence, newspaper issues.

Woodward, Emily Barnelia. Papers 1918-1970: 11 boxes. Editor and publisher of *Vienna News* 1918-1930; contributor to *Atlanta Journal* and other publications. Founder of Georgia Press Institute.

University of Georgia

• Hargrett Rare Book and Manuscript Library, University of Georgia Libraries, Athens GA 30602. 404-542-7123. Thomas E. Camden, Head. 8 am-5 pm M-F; 9 am-5 pm Sa. Photocopy services. Unpublished collection guides available in repository.

Brown, Marel, 1899-   (Margaret Elizabeth Snow Brown; Mrs. Alex B.) Collection: 3 boxes. Poet, short story and magazine writer who was active in National League of American Pen Women. Correspondence, manuscripts, tear sheets, clippings, scrapbooks.

Daniel, Frank. Papers 1928-1979: 6 boxes. Writer and critic for *Atlanta Journal* for 40 years. Approx. 100 letters from American writer James Purdy. Correspondence, clippings, printed material, photographs. Other correspondents include James Cabell, Erskine Caldwell, Isa Glenn, Marion Montgomery, Susan Myrick, Frances Newman, Flannery O'Conner, Julia Peterkin, Jeanette Rankin, Caroline Miller Ray, Celestine Sibley.

Downes, Olin, 1886-1955. Papers ca. 1920-1955: ca. 50,000 items. Music critic for *New York Times* 1924-1955. Correspondence, manuscripts, research materials, articles, photographs. Papers of Irene Miles Downes (Mrs. Olin Downes); papers of Louisa Downes (mother of Olin Downes). Description of collection by Jean Reti-Forbes available from repository.

Drewry, John Eldridge, 1902-1983. 4 collections: ms 2272, ms 1395, ms 1734, ms 2482. Director of University of Georgia School of Journalism 1932 and dean 1940-1969. Helped established Georgia Press Institute, Georgia Radio-Television Institute, Southern Industrial Editors Institute, Georgia Scholastic Press Assoc., Georgia Collegiate Press Assoc. Helped create George Foster Peabody Awards for distinguished achievement in broadcasting. Correspondence, drafts, proofs, clippings, scrapbooks, printed material.

Howell, Clark, 1863-1936. Papers 1873-1946: 1,055 items. Editor and owner of *Atlanta Constitution.* Correspondence, clippings, photographs, notebooks, speeches. Also includes papers of E.P. Howell, his father, and Clark Howell, Jr., his son.

Smith, Lillian, 1897-1966. Papers 1928-1980: 98 boxes. Writer, editor and publisher of *South Today.* Personal and business correspondence plus drafts of books. RESTRICTED: Permission to use collection must be obtained from literary executors.

Woodward, Emily Barnelia. Collection 1916-1957: 1,769 items. Correspondence, programs, invitations, cards, speeches, radio programs, clippings, scrapbooks. Some of collection deals with Georgia Press Assoc. and Georgia Press Institute. Includes letters from Franklin D. Roosevelt, George Foster Peabody, William Allen White, Eleanor Roosevelt, Margaret Mitchell and others.

ILLINOIS

Lake Forest College

• Special Collections Dept.,Donnelley Library, Lake Forest College, Sheridan and College Rds., Lake Forest IL 60045. 312-234-3100 ext. 410. Martha Briggs, Asst. Librarian. 8:30 am-5 pm M-F and by appt. Photocopy services.

America. 1888: 7 items. Chicago literary journal 1888-1891 published by Hobart Chatfield Taylor and Slason Thompson. Includes poems and letters submitted by Charles Dudley Warner, Andrew Lang, James Whitcomb Riley and others.

Patterson, Joseph Medill, 1879-1946. Papers 1901-1950: 60 linear ft. Founder and publisher of *New York Daily News* 1919-1946, and of *Liberty Magazine* 1925-1931. Also involved with management of *Chicago Tribune* 1901-1925; *Chicago Tribune* Company and subsidiaries 1927-1946; and Chicago Tribune/New York News Syndicate 1941-1946. Correspondents include Robert R. McCormick, Eleanor Medill Patterson, Max Annenberg, Edward S. Beck, Harvey Devell, William H. Field, Roy C. Holliss, Philip A. Payne, James O'Donnell Bennett, Arthur Brisbane, Chester Gould, Floyd Gibbons, Arthur Sears Henning, Herb Martin, Carey C. Orr, Henry J. Reilly, George Seldes, Sidney Sutherland.

Orr, Carey Cassius, 1890-1967. Political cartoons 1926-1960: 11 items. Pulitzer Prize-winning cartoonist with the *Chicago Tribune.*

Northwestern University

• Northwestern University Archives, Northwestern University Library, Evanston IL 60208. 312-491-3354. Patrick M. Quinn. 8:30 am-5 pm M-F. Closed major holidays. Photocopy services. Unpublished inventories in repository. Some collections on RLIN.

Barnett, Claude, 1889-1967. Collection ca. 1950-1070: 41 boxes. Director of Associated Negro Press and World News Service. Clippings, photographs, newsletters.

Brownell, Baker, 1887-1965. Papers 1904-1965: 78 boxes. Reporter for *Chicago Tribune* and editorial writer for *Chicago Daily*

News. Correspondence, teaching files, research and publications.

University of Chicago

• Dept. of Special Collections, University of Chicago, 1100 East 57th St., Chicago IL 60637, 312-702-8705. Daniel Meyer, Asst. Curator. 8:30 am-5 pm M-F; 9 am-1 pm Sa except interims. Photocopy services. Finding aids in repository.

Commission on Freedom of the Press. Records 1944-1947: 9 boxes.

Benton, William. Papers 1900-1973: 595 boxes. Papers of U.S. Senator, advertising executive and publisher. Includes correspondence with Henry Luce and Claire Boothe Luce, Norman Cousins, Sulzberger and LaFollette families, and Dewitt Wallace.

Gunther, John. Papers 1935-1965: 122 boxes. Papers and manuscripts related to published works *Inside Europe, Inside Asia, Inside Latin America,* and others.

University of Illinois

• Archives, University of Illinois, 1408 Gregory Dr., Urbana IL 61801. 217-333-0798. Maynard Brichford, University Archivist. 8 am-5 pm M-F. Photocopy services. Finding aids in repository. See also *Guide to the University of Illinois Archives.*

Graham, Gene, 1924-   Papers 1959-1971: 2 linear ft. Correspondence, transcripts of tape recorded interviews, clippings, briefs, motions, decisions, notes, manuscripts. Correspondents include Walter Chandler, Archibald Cox, James Cummings, Maclin P. Davis, Jr., Frank Farrell, Dan Magraw, Wayne Miller, William E. Miller, Tommy Osborn, Charles Rhyne, Earl Warren, Ben Wert.

Peterson, Theodore B. Papers 1973-1979: .6 linear ft. Correspondence.

Southern Illinois University at Carbondale

• Special Collections, Morris Library, Southern Illinois University, Carbondale IL 62901. 618-453-2516. David V. Koch, Curator. 8:30 am-4:30 pm M-F. Photocopy services for works in good condition. On OCLC and ILLINET Online Catalog System.

McCoy, Ralph E. Freedom of the Press Collection 1600-1988: 10,000 pieces. English language monographs, serials, newspapers and ephemera on freedom of the press and censorship.

INDIANA

DePauw University

- Special Collections, Roy O. West Library, DePauw University, Greencastle IN 46135. 317-658-4500. Wesley Wilson, Coordinator of Archives and Special Services. 8 am-5 pm M-F; 6 pm-9:30 pm T; summer hours 8 am-4 pm M-F. Other hours by appt. Photocopy services. Finding aids in repository.

    Indiana Journalism Hall of Fame Assoc. Records 1966-1987: 2 linear ft. Correspondence, minutes, nominations, biographical sketches, photographs.

    Society of Professional Journalists/Sigma Delta Chi. Records 1920-1980: 33 linear ft. Convention proceedings, board minutes, correspondence, award entries, photographs of national society. On OCLC.

Indiana Historical Society Library

- Indiana Historical Society Library, 315 West Ohio St., Indianapolis IN 46202. 317-232-1879. Paul Brockman, Archivist. 8 am-4:30 pm M-F; 8:30 am-4 pm Sa., Sept-May. Photocopy services. Some collections on OCLC. Finding aids in repository. See also Eric Pumroy, *A Guide to Manuscript Collections of the Indiana Historical Society and Indiana State Library* (Indianapolis: Indiana Historical Society, 1986).

    Brown, Hilton Ultimus, 1859-1958. Papers 1853-1953: 7 boxes. Reporter, editor and director of *Indianapolis News*. Scrapbooks, correspondence. M 31.

    Cauthorn-Stout family. Papers 1780-1908: 4 boxes. Includes papers of Elihu Stout, publisher of *Indiana Gazette* 1804-1806 and *Western Sun* 1807-1845. Receipts, accounts and other documents relating to publishing and personal business. M 41.

    Crain, Jacob R., fl. 1830-1840. Papers 1840: 25 items. Editor of *Calumet and War Club*. Correspondence, partial list of subscribers. SC 456.

    Dowling, John, ca. 1808-1878. Papers 1827-1878: 2 boxes. Editor of *Terre Haute Wabash Courier* 1832-1841, *Jackson Southerner* 1847-1850, *Terre Haute Journal* 1861-1873;

Washington correspondent for *Boston Pilot* 1873-1878; co-publisher of *Wabash Courier* 1832-1841; editor and proprietor of *Terre Haute Express* 1842-1845. Correspondents include Clifton Allan, Thomas H. Blake, Jesse D. Bright, Charles Butler, Joseph Cable, Patrick Donahue, John Ewing, Duff Green, Edward A. Hannegan, Andrew J. Harlan, William Hendricks, William S. Holman, Richard M. Johnson, Jonathan McCarthy, Joseph G. Marshall, Henry L. Pinckney, Caleb B. Smith, John P. Usher, David Wallace, Albert S. White. M 87.

Elder, John, d. 1851. Papers 1825-1908: 1.25 linear ft. Father of John R. Elder, publisher of *Indiana Locomotive* 1848-1860 and *Indianapolis Sentinel* 1860-1864. Correspondence regarding John R. Elder's newspaper work 1840s-1860s. M93, BV 257-259.

Fuller, John Louis Hilton, 1894- Papers 1840-1962: 3 boxes. Includes letters written by Fuller's father, Hector Fuller, 1864-1934, correspondent covering the Russo-Japanese War 1903-1904 for the *Indianapolis News*. M112.

Harrison, Russell B., 1854-1936. Papers 1881-1893: 1 box. Owner of *Helena Daily Journal* 1890. M 387.

Holloway, William Robeson, 1836-1911. Papers 1824-1899: 5 linear ft. Journalist and politician. Asst. *Cincinnati Times* 1852-1857; owner and editor *Indianapolis Journal* 1864-1875; owner and founder *Indianapolis Times* 1880-1886. Correspondence, business papers. Correspondents include James G. Blaine, James Boyle, Henry V. Boynton, William M. Calkins, Schuyler Colfax, William Wade Dudley, Charles W. Fairbanks, Joseph B. Foraker, John Watson Foster, James A. Garfield, Ulysses S. Grant, Walter Q. Gresham, Charles Henry Grosvenor, Murat Halstead, Marcus A. Hanna, John M. Harlan, Benjamin Harrison, Rutherford B. Hayes, Robert R. Hitt, William McKinley, Joseph Medill, John C. New, Meredith Nicholson, Thomas C. Platt, Albert G. Porter, Whitelaw Reid, John Sherman, James N. Tyner, Lew Wallace, Charles S. Williams. M 124, BV 1478-1495, 1865-1871.

Holman-O'Brien Papers 1827-1893: 1 box. Includes letters to Lawrenceburg newspaper publisher William H. O'Brien, 1855-1933 and Dr. William H. Hunker, 1830-1898. M 368.

Hunter, William D.H., 1830-1989. Papers 1880-1885: 43 items. Proprietor of *Lawrenceburg Register* 1877-1894. Correspondence. SC 805.

Lindley, Harlow, 1875-1959. Collection 1790-1913: 3 boxes. Includes correspondence with newspapermen William Henry Smith and Delavan Smith regarding *Indianapolis News*. M 186.

Smith, Delavan, 1861-1922. Papers 1868-1921: 45 boxes. Publisher and part owner of *Indianapolis News*. Personal and business papers. Also includes business and personal papers of William Henry Smith, general manager of Western Associated Press and part owner of *Indianapolis News*. Correspondents include Charles A. Boynton, Hilton U. Brown, Jacob P. Dunn, Charles W. Fairbanks, John H. Hammond, John M. Harlan, James A. Hemenway, Victor F. Lawson, Cyrus McCormick, Medill McCormick, Jesse Overstreet, Louis F. Swift. M 255.

Smith, William Henry, 1833-1896. Papers 1816-1913: 8.5 linear ft. Reporter and editor for Cincinnati newspapers *Type of the Times*, *Commercial*, and *Gazette*; part owner of *Indianapolis News*. Business, political and historical correspondence. Internal memos, reports, financial information about Western Associated Press, the New York Associated Press, the United Press, and other press associations. Includes letters from son-in-law, Charles R. Williams, editor of *Indianapolis News*. Correspondents include Herbert Baxter Adams, William Aldrich, Joseph H. Barrett, James G. Blaine, Alden J. Blethen, Charles A. Boynton, Henry Van Ness Boynton, Erastus Brooks, Francis F. Browne, C.W. Butterfield, Zachariah Chandler, Robert C. Clowry, Shelby M. Cullum, Charles A. Dana, Lyman C. Draper, Frederick Driscoll, Thomas T. Eckert, Charles W. Fairbanks, Charles B. Farwell, John V. Farwell, Walter N. Haldeman, Murat Halstead, John M. Harlan, Rutherford B. Hayes, Webb Hayes, William R. Holloway, Henry Howe, William Dean Howells, William Henry Hurlbert, Richard Underwood Johnson, Andrew J. Kellar, Charles W. Knapp, Victor F. Lawson, John A. Logan, David R. McKee, William McKinley, Elijah B. Martindale, Joseph Medill, Harry S. New, John C. New, William Penn Nixon, Adolph S. Ochs, Joseph Pulitzer, Whitelaw Reid, William K. Rogers, Carl Schurz, John Sherman, James W. Simonton, Richard Smith, David M. Stone, Melville E. Stone, Margaret Frances Sullivan, Wager Swayne, Charles P. Taft, Henry Watterson, William H. West. M258, BV 1798-1803.

Squier, Ephraim George, 1821-1888. Papers 1842-1900: 2 boxes. Journalist, ethnologist. Newspaper editor in Albany NY, Hartford CT, Chillicothe OH. Chief editor, Frank Leslie Publishing House. Correspondents include Nathaniel P. Banks, James

Gordon Bennett, Lewis Cass, Samuel S. Cox, William Parker Cutler, Henry Winter Davis, James Dixon, Edward Everett, Hamilton Fish, Benson J. Lossing, Joel Munsell, George F. Peabody, George P. Putnam, Whitelaw Reid, Alexander Hamilton Rice, William H. Seward, Pierre Soule, Philip Henry Stanhope, Charles Sumner, George Ticknor, Nicholas Trubner, Gideon Welles. M 262.

Stuart, James Arthur, 1880-1975. Papers 1907-1965: 2 boxes. Reporter, managing editor and editor *Indianapolis Star* 1905-1960; editorial director *Rocky Mountain News* and *Denver Times* 1921-1923. Correspondents include George Ade, Irwin S. Cobb, Charles W. Fairbanks, Herbert Hoover, Kin Hubbard, Booth Tarkington, William Allen White. M 268.

Trask, George Kellogg. d. 1911. Papers 1855-1901: 41 items. Editor of railroad column for *Indianapolis Journal.* Correspondents include Elijah Walker Halford, George C. Hitt, Harry S. New. SC 1468.

Purdue University

• Public Affairs Video Archives, School of Humanities, Social Science, and Education, Purdue University, Stewart Center G-39, West Lafayette IN 47907. 317-494-9630. Robert X. Browning, Director.

C-SPAN 1987-   Archives record, preserve and distribute all programming on both channels of Cable-Satellite Public Affairs Network (C-SPAN).

University of Notre Dame

• Dept. of Special Collections, University Libraries, University of Notre Dame, 102 Hesburgh Library, Notre Dame IN 46556. 219-239-6489. 8 am-5 pm M-F. Photocopy services.

Smith, Walter W. "Red" Papers 1969-1981: 76 folders. Sportswriter for *Saint Louis Star, New York Herald,* and *New York Times.*

IOWA

Iowa State University

• Dept. of Special Collections, William Robert Parks and Ellen Sorge Parks Library, Iowa State University, Ames IA 50011. 515-294-6672. Stanley Yates, Head, Dept. of Special Collections.

8-11:50 am, 1-5 pm M-F. Photocopy services. Finding aids in repository. Collection level records on OCLC.

Anderson, Raymond F., 1888-1967. Papers 1927-1954, 1960-1966: 1 linear ft. Reporter for *Oelwein Daily Register, West Union Weekly Argus-Gazette, Cedar Rapids Gazette.* Editor for *Farm Journal* 1944-1955. Correspondence, articles, talks, writings. MS-61.

Baker, John C. Papers 1929-1980: 10 linear ft. Materials used in writing history of farm broadcasting in U.S.

Bently, Ronald C., 1899-   Papers 1926-1933, 1937-1963: 2 linear ft. Farm broadcaster.

Berry, Don L., 1880-1970. Papers 1936-1943: 2 linear ft. Editor and publisher of newspapers in Indianola IA. Correspondence, news releases, expense accounts. Correspondents include Meyers Y. Cooper, Clifford Hope, Alfred M. Landon, Harrison Spangler, Walter A. Shaeffer, Dan W. Turner, William W. Weymack, George Olmstead. MS-33.

Breth, Fred. Papers 1958-1985: 8 linear ft.

Church, Arthur B., Sr., 1896-1973. Papers. Founder of KMBC radio in 1927 and KMBC-TV in 1953 in Kansas City MO. Unprocessed.

Conn, Rex B., 1900-1975. Papers 1928-1973: 1.5 linear ft. Farm editor for *Cedar Rapids Gazette.* Correspondence, printed materials taped interview, clippings, articles. A23.

Darrow, Wayne, 1894-   Papers 1936-1958: 1 linear ft. Journalist and publisher of *Washington Farmletter.* Correspondence, clippings, pamphlets, printed matter. Correspondents include Henry A. Wallace, Claude Wickard. MS-21.

Drips, William E., 1890-1965. Papers 1934-1961: 10 folders. Journalist and agricultural broadcaster for NBC. Photographs, correspondence, clippings, printed material, scrapbooks. Correspondents include Lauren K. Smith, J.K. Russell, Henry A. Wallace, Chester C. Davis, Milton S. Eisenhower, Henry Ford II. A5.

Eyerly, Frank Rinehart. Papers 1942-1981: 4 linear ft. Joined *Des Moines Register and Tribune* in 1927; managing editor 1946-1969.

Ferguson, Elizabeth (Bess) Storm, 1897-   Papers 1927-1984: .3 linear ft. Columnist; radio broadcaster. Clippings, articles, correspondence, manuscripts.

Murphy, Donald R., 1895-1974. Papers 1950-1970: 4 linear ft. Journalist with *Wallaces Farmer* 1919-1955. MS-155.

Murphy, Zoe R., 1899-1983. Papers 1937-1969: 2.5 linear ft. Homemaking editor of *Wallaces Farmer* 1936-1974.

Plambeck, Herbert, 1908-   Papers 1936-1970: 14 linear ft. Farm broadcaster; syndicated columnist.

Risser, James. Papers 1968-1983: 7 linear ft. Pulitzer Prize-winning reporter for *Des Moines Register*. Correspondence, background materials.

Russell, J. Stuart, 1892-1960. Papers 1943, 1945-1960: 1.5 linear ft. Farm editor of *Des Moines Register and Tribune* 1925-1960. Correspondence, clippings, speeches, photographs. Correspondents include Chester Davis, Wolf Ladejinsky. MS-12.

Soth, Lauren K., 1910-   Papers 1945-1975: 19 linear ft. Editorial writer for *Des Moines Register and Tribune* 1947- . Won Pulitzer Prize for editorial writing in 1956. Correspondence, proofs, manuscripts, printed matter, photographs, articles, speeches. Correspondents include Harold F. Breimeyer, Robert K. Buck, Erwin D. Canham, Marion Clawson, Williard W. Cochrane, Joseph Dummer, Paul Engle, Orville Freeman, John Kenneth Galbraith, A.C. Hoffman, Dale Hoover, Raymond M. Hughes, Gale D. Johnson, Allan B. Kline, Alfred A. Knopf, L.G. Ligutti, George McGovern, James G. Maddox, Donald R. Murphy, Harrison E. Salisbury, Theodore W. Schultz, H. Christian Sonne, Carroll P. Streeter, George S. Talley, Frederick V. Waugh, Walter W. Wilcox. A38.

Women in Communications, Inc. Records 1961-1970: 10 folders. Correspondence, reports, membership lists, newsletters, scrapbooks, by-laws, manuals, clippings. MS-35.

Women in Communications, Inc. student chapters. Records 1910-1976: 7 linear ft. Application forms, correspondence, financial statements, annual reports. MS-103.

University of Iowa

• Special Collections Dept., University of Iowa Libraries, Iowa City IA 52242. 319-335-5921. Robert A. McCown, Head. 9 am-noon, 1-5 pm M-F. Photocopy services. Finding aids in repository.

Adler, Philip, 1902-1984. Papers 1904-1970: 49 items. Newspaperman and publisher. Correspondence, speeches, clippings. MsC 229.

Allen, Arthur Francis, 1867-1949. Papers 1913-1949: 1 ft. Editor of *Sioux City Journal.* Correspondence, speeches, clippings, scrapbook. Correspondents include Cyrenus Cole, Jay N. Darling, John W. Carey, Herbert Quick, Gilbert Hitchcock, Robert B. Wylie, Ross L. Hammond. MsC 357.

Bennett, F.R., 1825-   Memoirs Aug. 15, 1897: 44 pp. Newspaper publisher, editor and postmaster. Ms B4714 me.

Beck, Robert Knowlton, 1915-   Papers 1939-1971: 1 ft. Newspaper publisher in Centerville IA. Correspondence, clippings, photographs, speeches, subject files, scrapbook. Correspondents include Gerald Bogan, John M. Henry, Jack Miller, Leo Hoegh, James Bromwell, Karl LeCompte, Bourke Hickenlooper, Tom Martin, Jack Schroeder. MsC 394.

Booth, Thomas Eyre, 1842-1927. Papers 1875-1924: ca. 46 items. Editor and publisher of *Anamosa Eureka.* Correspondence, manuscripts, photographs, scrapbook. MsC 361.

Breen, Edward, 1899-1978. Papers 1936-1973: 2 ft. Broadcasting station executive and Iowa state legislator. Subject files, correspondence, clippings, photographs, reports. Correspondents include Guy Mark Gillette, Clyde LaVerne Herring, Nelson G. Kraschel. MsC 334.

Carey, John W., 1877-1945. Correspondence 1899-1943: ca. 228 items. Newspaper editor. Correspondents include Elbert H. Hubbard, Jay N. Darling, Herbert Quick, George C. Scott, W.D. Boies, Robert G. Cousins, Albert B. Cummins, Wallace Short, David W. Stewart, Harvey Ingham, A.B. Funk, N.E. Kendall, W.L. Harding, John P. Mulgrew, L.J. Dickinson, Louis Murphy, Clyde L. Herring, Guy M. Gillette, Cyrenus Cole, Harry L. Hopkins, Hartzell Spence, Ruth Suckow, Homer Croy. MsC 389.

Darling, Jay Norwood, 1876-1962. Papers 1909-1954: 2.5 ft. Cartoonist for *Des Moines Register.* Correspondence, speeches, articles, leaflets, clippings, scrapbooks, sketchbook. Correspondents include Bernard Baruch, Frederick Bierman, William Beardsley, Robert Blue, Gardner Cowles, Paul Cunningham, Guy Gillette, W. Earl Hall, Vincent Harrington, Bourke Hickenlooper, Herbert Hoover, Harold Ickes, Reg Manning, Conrad Nagel, Gifford Pinchot, Grantland Rice, William F. Riley, Merritt Speidel, Henry A. Wallace, William Allen White. MsC 170.

Evans, Joseph Early, 1919-1971. Papers 1935-1971: 331 items. Editorial page editor of *Wall Street Journal.* Correspondence, clippings, photographs. MsC 275.

Fairfield Daily Ledger. Records 1930-1951: ca. 3 ft. Account books, tax receipts, operating statements, advertising returns; some personal and editorial manuscripts of publisher Walter Williams, 1893-1976. MsC 155.

Hall, W. Earl, 1896-1969. Papers 1918-1969: 6 ft. Editor of *Mason City Globe Gazette.* Correspondence, subject files, editorials, speeches, radio scripts, clippings, photographs, typescript articles. Correspondents include Philip Adler, Frederick Bierman, John Cowles, Jay N. Darling, James Dolliver, Alfred Gruenther, Virgil Hancher, J. Edgar Hoover, Karl LeCompte, Hanford MacNider, Tom Martin, Conger Reynolds, Edward G. Robinson, Hartzell Spence, Dan Turner, Dixie Willson, Meredith Willson. MsC 193.

Iowa Press Women, Inc. Records 1933-1973: 2 ft. Clippings, correspondence, reports, subject files, membership records, printed material. MsC 290.

The Iowan. Records 1952-1970: 20 ft. Correspondence, manuscripts, page proofs, layouts, advertising and business records, photographs. Includes manuscripts and correspondence of Clarence Andrews, Julie McDonald and Marshall McKusick. MsC 291.

Jarnagin, William C., 1879-1971. Papers 1911-1971: 4 items. Scrapbook, clippings. Editor and publisher of *Storm Lake Pilot-Tribune.*

Kehoe, Louis, 1897-1969. Papers 1930-1969: 240 items. Lawyer and journalist. Correspondence, manuscripts, scrapbook, memoranda. MsC 219.

Meredith, Edwin Thomas, 1876-1928. Papers 1894-1928: 38 ft. Founder of Meredith Publishing Co. and U.S. Secretary of Agriculture. Correspondence, speeches, articles, scrapbooks, pamphlets, clippings, photos. Correspondents include Newton D. Baker, Bernard Baruch, Frederick E. Biermann, Smith W. Brookhart, Albert S. Burleson, Arthur Clapper, Beryl Franklin Carroll, George Washington Carver, Calvin Coolidge, Homer S. Cummings, Josephus Daniels, Jay N. Darling, John W. Davis, Lester J. Dickinson, Samuel Gompers, James W. Good, John G. Hammill, Gilbert Nelson Haugen, Clyde L. Herring, Herbert Hoover, Cordell Hull, William D. Jamieson, William M. Jardine, William S. Kenyon, Breckenridge Long, Frank O. Lowden, William G. McAdoo, Andrew W. Mellon, George Fort Milton, Eugene Meyer, Jr., Charles E. Nagel, Christian W. Ramseyer, Hollins Randolph, David L. Rockwell, Franklin D. Roosevelt, Daniel C. Roper, Daniel F. Stack, Mark Sullivan, Henry A. Wallace, Henry Cantwell Wallace, Thomas J. Walsh, Edith Bolling Wilson, Lafayette Young. MsC 121.

National Citizens Committee for Broadcasting. Records 1967-1973: 24 ft. Subject files, correspondence, photographs, clippings. Includes letters from Nicholas Johnson, Thomas P.F. Hoving.

Norris, Paul Gifford, Jr., 1904- Papers 1948-1973: 2 ft. Editor and publisher. Correspondence, subject files, speeches. Correspondents include H.R. Gross, Richard M. Nixon, Thomas E. Martin, Kenneth MacDonald, Jack Miller, Ann Landers, Sonja Egenes, Robert R. Rigler, Merle Miller, Jean Seberg, Karl M. LeCompte, Philip D. Adler. MsC 283.

Nye, Frank T., 1912-1983. Papers 1942-1983: 15 ft. Reporter and editor for *Cedar Rapids Gazette*. Correspondence, photographs, subject files. Correspondents include James E. Bromwell, John C. Culver, Jay N. Darling, John M. Henry, Bourke Hickenlooper, Harold E. Hughes, Herschel C. Loveless, Jack Miller, Robert D. Ray, Tom Riley, Fred Schwengel, David O. Shaff, Harrison Weber. MsC 437.

Moody, Clarence Wilber, 1892-1867. Papers 1932-1965: ca. 210 items. Editor of *Burlington Hawk-Eye*. Clippings, correspondence, speeches. MsC 326.

Oakville Sentinel. Records 1903-1930: 15 items. Ledgers, printing orders, cash books.

Pierce, Dante Melville, 1880-1955. Papers 1925-1945: ca. 50 items. Farm editor. Correspondents include Smith W. Brookhart, Calvin Coolidge, Lester Jesse Dickinson, Cassius Clay Dowell, Clyde L. Herring, Robert M. LaFollette, Jr., Charles A. Rawson, Christian W. Ramseyer, Thomas J.B. Robinson, Herbert Utterback, Henry A. Wallace, George W. Wilson. MsC 61.

Pownall, Dorothy Ashby. 1895-   Papers 1918-1970: 99 items. Journalist and author. Correspondence, clippings, scrapbook. MsC 259.

White, Grant, d. 1960. Papers 1931-1932: ca. 50 items. Mostly news dispatches to *Des Moines Register*. MsC 46.

Radio-Television News Directors Assoc. Records 1947-1968: 12 ft. Correspondence, minutes of board of directors, convention reports, financial records, committee files, copies of *RTNDA Bulletin*, membership files. Correspondents include Edward R. Murrow. MsC 262.

Reynolds, Conger, 1891-1971. Papers 1899-1970: ca. 11 ft. Journalist, diplomat, public relations man. Correspondence, reports, photographs, memorabilia. MsC 183.

Shearer, Brainard Hayes, 1881-1970. Papers 1901-1970: 4 ft. Editor and publisher Columbus Junction IA. Correspondence, vouchers, receipts, diaries, clippings, genealogies, photographs. MsC 242.

Shenandoah Evening Sentinel. Records 1888-1946: 57 items. Journals, ledgers, cash books, subscription lists, inventories. MsC 247.

Speidel, Merritt Charles, 1879-1960. Papers 1914-1960: 300 items. Newspaper publisher. Personal and business correspondence, clippings. Correspondents include Herbert Hoover, J. Edgar Hoover, Edmund "Pat" Brown, Earl Warren, Mark Clark, Albert C. Wedemeyer. MsC 104.

Springer, John, 1850-1937. Collection: ca. 7 ft. Advertising agent, printer and newspaper editor. Correspondence, clippings, printed matter, memorabilia. MsC 202.

Starzel, Frank, 1904-   Papers: 4 items. General manager of Associated Press. Photographs, speeches, press releases and articles in four scrapbooks. MsC 231.

Wallace, Henry, 1836-1916. Papers 1860-1924: 2.5 ft. Agricultural journalist. Correspondence, speeches, writings, photographs, clippings. MsC 180.

Wallace, Henry Cantwell, 1866-1924. Papers 1911-1930: 4,040 items. Editor of *Wallace's Farmer* and U. S. Secretary of Agriculture. Speeches, articles, correspondence, pamphlets, reports, clippings. Correspondents include Herbert Hoover, William H. Taft, Theodore Roosevelt, Gifford Pinchot, Fran Lowden, John D. Rockefeller, George Washington Carver. RESTRICTED. MsC 179.

Whitehead, Glenn E., 1892-   Papers 1924-1963: 22 items. Newspaperman and Iowa state legislator. Correspondence. MsC 237.

Zwart, Elizabeth Clarkson, 1904-1983. Papers 1925-1982: 1 ft. Columnist for *Des Moines Register*. Correspondence, photographs, diary. Correspondents include Gladys Black, Mary Koss, John M. Henry, Jay N. Darling, Louise Parker, Will C. Jumper. MsC 430.

KANSAS

Kansas State Historical Society

• Manuscripts Dept., Kansas State Historical Society, 120 W. 10th St., Topeka KS 66612. 913-296-3251. Ms. Pat Michalis, Curator. 9 am-5 pm M-F; 8 am-noon Sa. Photocopy services. Some collections may be restricted. In addition to the collections listed below, KSHS holds film footage, news scripts and other papers of three Topeka television stations (KSNT-TV, KTSB-TV, and KTKA-TV).

Brinkerhoff, Fredrick W. Collection: 9 boxes. Newspaperman, editor. Correspondents include Clyde Reed, William Allen White, Arthur Capper, Oscar Stauffer, Henry J. Allen.

Brinkley, John R. Collection: 4 boxes plus several audiotapes. Physician and radio station owner.

Bristow, Joseph L. Collection: 103 boxes. Newspaper editor and senator. Available on microfilm.

Brown, George W. Collection: 2 boxes. Newspaper editor.

Capper, Arthur. Collection: 76 boxes. Newspaperman, governor, senator. Founded Capper Publications.

Denious, Jess C. Collection: 14 boxes. Editor. Contains William Allen White material among others.

Gleed, Charles S. Collections: 55 boxes. Editor of *Kansas City Journal.*

Long, Richard M. Collection: 5 boxes. Newspaperman and editor.

Meeker, Jotham. Collection: 7 boxes and 3 vols. Pioneer missionary who brought first press to Kansas and printed first newspaper in territory in 1833. Available on microfilm.

Miller, Sol. Collection: 3 boxes and 15 vols. Editor. Includes account vols.

Morrow, Marco. Collection: 17 boxes. Asst. publisher of Capper Publications.

Stratton, Clif. Collection: 1 box. Reporter and columnist. Correspondents include Clyde Reed, Arthur Clapper.

Swayze, Oscar K. Collection: 4 boxes. Newspaperman.

Topeka Press Club. Collection: 2 boxes.

KENTUCKY

Kentucky Historical Society

• Library, Kentucky Historical Society, PO Box H, 300 Broadway, Frankfort KY 40602-2108. 502-564-3016. Mary Margaret Bell, Manuscripts Curator. 8 am-4:30 pm M-F. Appointments advisable. Photocopy services. Complete collections may not be photocopied.

Allison, Young E. 2 letters. Author and journalist.

Brown, Orlando. .4 cubic ft. Editor of *The Commonwealth* and *The Campaign*; politician. Correspondence.

Collins, Lewis and Richard. Papers: .1 linear ft. Journalists and historians.

Dana, James Green or Greene. Papers: .1 cubic ft. Editor of Frankfort newspapers *The Commentator* and *Lights and Shadows.*

LOUISIANA

Louisiana State University

• Louisiana and Lower Mississippi Valley Collections, Hill Library, Louisiana State University, Baton Rouge LA 70803. 504-888-6568. 9 am-5 pm M-F; 9 am-1 pm Sa during university semesters. Photocopy services. Manuscripts and archives on RLIN. Unpublished finding aids in repository.

Chaplin, Breazeale, and Chaplin, Natchitoches LA. Law firm records 1806-1925: 4986 items. Includes papers of lawyer, editor and U.S. Representative Phanor Breazeale 1858-1934. RESTRICTED. MS72-1549.

Dugas, Claiborne J. "Bobby", 1898-1980: 1 vol. Scrapbook. Mf. Memoirs, ca. 1909-

Taliaferro, James G. and family. Papers 1781-1934: 881 items and 11 printed vols. Judge James Govan Taliaferro, 1795-1876, published *Harrisonburg Independent.* C-15-17 Nsp.

Vignaud, Henry, 1830-1922. Papers 1862-1909: 385 items. Journalist, diplomat and historian. Correspondents include Eugene Dumez, L. Placide Canonge. C-66.

MAINE

Maine Historical Society

• Maine Historical Society, 485 Congress St., Portland ME 04101. 207-774-1822. Elizabeth S. Maule, Curator. 9 am-5 pm T,W,F; 9 am-7 pm Th; 9 am-5 pm second Sa/month. Photocopy services. Unpublished finding aids in repository.

Clark, Linda Bean. Typescript: 5 leaves. Printer and publisher of Hallowell ME. Ms 74-8.

Chapman, Leonard Bond, 1834-1915. Papers 1726-1915: 16 boxes. Newspaperman, politician, genealogist, historian. Manuscripts, clippings, genealogical and historical notes. Coll. 116.

Jenks, Eleazer Alley, 1776-1807. Day book 1801-1805: 201 leaves. Record of advertising and subscription payments of *Portland Gazette.* Ms 80-5.

Knight, Thomas E. Manuscript newspaper written by Knight to his brother-in-law James E. Bradford, Dec. 6, 1858. Ms 79.

Lovering, Frank W., d. 1969. Papers ca. 1950-1969: ca. 50 items. Journalist for various ME newspapers. Photographs, clippings. Ms 87-32.

Waldron, William H. 1 vol. Account book of newspaper publishers Waldron and Moore, Brunswick ME 1853-1855. Ms 26.

MARYLAND

Johns Hopkins University

• Special Collections, Milton S. Eisenhower Library, Johns Hopkins University, 3400 Charles St., Baltimore MD 21218. 301-338-8348. Cynthia H. Requardt, Manuscripts Librarian. 8:30 am-5 pm M-F. Photocopy services. Collections on RLIN. Unpublished finding registers in repository.

Emmert, Adolphys Dunan, 1902-1973. Papers 1923-1974: 1 linear ft. Staff member *Baltimore Sun* 1924-1972. Correspondence, clippings, cables, notebook, scrapbook, photographs, periodicals.

Freeman, Douglas Southall, 1886-1953. Papers 1902-1911: 2 linear ft. Editorial writer *Richmond Times-Dispatch* 1909-1910, 1913-1915; editor *Richmond News Leader* 1915-1949. Awarded Pulitzer Prize in 1934. Correspondence, primarily between Freeman and his parents while he was a graduate student.

Grauer, Neil-Albert, 1947-   Papers 1965-1984: 4.6 linear ft. Reporter and cartoonist *Baltimore News-American* 1970-1980. Correspondents include Jack Anderson, Russell Baker, Erma Bombeck, Jimmy Breslin, David S. Broder, Art Buchwald, William F. Buckley, Ellen Goodman, James Jackson Kilpatrick, Carl Thomas Rowan, Mike Royko, George F. Will, Richard L. Strout.

Lalley, Joseph Michael, 1896-1980. Papers 1895-1981: 14.7 linear ft. Book reviewer and editorial writer with *Washington Post* 1937-1961. Assoc. editor for *Modern Age* 1963-1980. Correspondence and writings.

Spencer, Edward, 1834-1883. Alleman Collection of Edward Spencer Papers: 3.75 linear ft. Writer and journalist with numerous publications including the *Baltimore Evening Bulletin* and *Baltimore Sun.*

Wright, Irene Aloha, 1879-1972. Collection 1906: 15 items. City editor of *Havana Daily Telegraph* during August 1906 Revolution in Cuba. Correspondence.

Maryland Historical Society

• Manuscripts Division, Maryland Historical Society, 201 West Monument St., Baltimore MD 21201. 301-685-3750. Donna Ellis, Manuscripts Librarian. 11 am-4:30 pm T-F; 9 am-4:30 pm Sa. Photocopy services. See also Avril J. M. Pedley, *The Manuscript Collections of the Maryland Historical Society* (Baltimore: Maryland Historical Society, 1968), and Richard J. Cox and Larry E. Sullivan, *Guide to the Research Collections of the Maryland Historical Society* (Baltimore: Maryland Historical Society, 1981). Unpublished finding aids in repository.

Baltimore Patriot. Account books 1847-1865: 1 box. MS. 98

Keidel, George. Papers. Includes research and correspondence with newspaper researchers on history of Maryland newspapers.

Shriver family. Papers: 2 boxes out of 52. Letters 1802-1818 from Andrew Shriver to William D. Lepper, publisher of *Pennsylvania Worhenschrift*, about subscriptions, political broadsides, political essays. MS. 750

Steiger family. Papers 1807-1887: 1 box. Newspaper articles and essays written by Hannah Van Patten in the 1880s and published in *The American Farmer* and *The Free Quill.* MS. 2501

MASSACHUSETTS

American Jewish Historical Society

• American Jewish Historical Society, 2 Thornton Rd., Waltham MA 02154. 617-891-8110. Nathan M. Kaganoff, Librarian. 8:30 am-5 pm M-Th; 8:30 am-2 pm F; 2 pm-5 pm Su. Photocopy services. Card files in repository.

American Jewish Press Assoc. Records 1945-1961: 1 linear ft. Correspondence, minutes, reports. I-62.

Jewish Culture Club. Record book 1924-1926. Members included Morris Katzeff, first president and owner of *Der Idisher Führer.* I-179.

Jewish Frontier. Anniversary speeches 1936: 12 pages. Three speeches delivered at first anniversary dinner of newspaper by Stephen S. Wise, Horace M. Kallen, Hayim Fineman. I-142.

Jewish Telegraphic Agency. 1 carton. Annual reports, minutes of board meetings, promotional and misc. material. MS-NATJ34.

Boston University

• Dept. of Special Collections, Mugar Memorial Library, Boston University, 771 Commonwealth Ave., Boston MA 02215. 617-353-3696. Dr. Harold B. Gotlieb, Director of Special Collections. 9 am-5 pm M-F. Closed holidays and Dec. 26-30. Call for appointment. See also *Special Collections at Boston University* (Boston: The Boston University Libraries, 1981). Unpublished finding aids available in repository.

Abel, Elie. 8 boxes.

Alsop, Stewart. 86 boxes.

Arnoni, M.S. 46 boxes.

Babcock, Frederic. 1 box.

Bailey, George. 4 boxes.

Bainbridge, John. 135 boxes.

Beals, Carleton. 197 boxes.

Bergquist, Laura. 47 boxes.

Biossat, Bruce. 48 boxes.

Bocca. Geoffrey. 3 boxes.

Botsford, Keith. 41 boxes.

Brackman, Arnold. 145 boxes.

Brelis, Dean. 6 boxes.

Caputo, Philip. 19 boxes.

Christy, Marian. 14 boxes. PARTIALLY RESTRICTED.

Claiborne, Craig. 62 boxes.

Cook, Alton F. 12 boxes.

Cooke, Alistair. 18 boxes.

Cutler, John Henry. 24 boxes.

De Gamez, Tana. 4 boxes.

De Toledano, Ralph. 40 boxes.

De Trevino, Elizabeth Borton. 14 boxes.

Eaton, William J. 9 boxes.

Emerson, Gloria. 21 boxes.

Epstein, Edward Jay. 24 boxes.

Fallaci, Oriana. 26 boxes. PARTIALLY RESTRICTED.

Farago, Ladislas. 61 boxes.

Fitzgerald, Frances. 48 boxes.

Fowle, Farnsworth. 10 boxes.

Freeman, Lucy. 5 boxes.

Fromm, Bella. 61 boxes.

Frye, William R. 10 boxes.

Fuller, Blair. 4 boxes.

Geyer, Georgie Anne. 3 boxes.

Gilroy, Harry D. 11 boxes.

Goldberg, Emanuel. 38 boxes.

Gould, John. 48 boxes.

Greene, Gael. 12 boxes.

Groueff, Stephane. 23 boxes.

The Guardian of Boston. 18 boxes.

Halberstam, David. 115 boxes. RESTRICTED.

Halsell, Grace. 31 boxes.

Herzog, Arthur. 32 boxes.

Hirshberg, Al. 52 boxes.

Hughes, John. 5 boxes.

Ingersoll, Ralph. 204 boxes.

James, Howard. 57 boxes.

Jennings, Gary. 4 boxes.

Kurzman, Dan. 44 boxes.

Lake, Austin. 4 boxes.

Lampe, David. 4 boxes.

Land, Myrick. 17 boxes.

Lang, Daniel. 27 boxes.

Lazar, Josette. 11 boxes.

Leacacos, John P. 32 boxes.

Lewis, Flora. 115 boxes. RESTRICTED.

Lilly, Doris. 2 boxes.

McCabe, Robert Karr. 13 boxes.

McGaffin, William. 30 boxes.

McGovern, James. 1 box.

McSweeny, William F. 1 box.

Mannes, Marya. 26 boxes.

Michelson, Herman. 1 box.

Michie, Allan A. 26 boxes.

Miller, Floyd. 12 boxes.

Moats, Alice Leonie. 55 boxes.

Moore, Raylyn. 5 boxes.

Morgan, Thomas. 82 boxes.

Muhlen, Norbert. 47 boxes.

Nobile, Philip. 3 boxes.

Peck, Graham. 3 boxes.

Pierce, Neal R. 12 boxes.

Phillips, Cabell. 27 boxes.

Poinsett, Alex. 1.5 boxes.

Popkin, Zelda. 16 boxes.

Rand, Christopher. 40 boxes.

Rather, Dan. 59 boxes. PARTIALLY RESTRICTED.

Redmont, Bernard. 18 boxes.

Reed, David. 5 boxes.

Russell, Francis. 6 boxes.

Sack, John. 18 boxes.

St. John, Robert. 40 boxes.

Samuels, Gertrude. 53 boxes.

Serantoni, Italo. Editor of *Il Tricolore*. Photograph album, business records, correspondence.

Shayton, Robert Lewis. 94 boxes.

Sheehy, Gail. 18 boxes.

Stearn, Jess. 8 boxes.

Surface, William. 2 boxes.

Swope, Herbert Bayard. 256 boxes.

Szulc, Tad. 26 boxes.

Tiede, Tom. 30 boxes.

Tregaskis, Richard. 23 boxes.

Wakefield, Dan. 40 boxes. RESTRICTED.

Wheeler, Keith. 7 boxes.

Wolfe, Linda. 5 boxes.

Yglesias, Jose. 7 boxes.

Harvard University

• Houghton Library, Harvard University, Cambridge MA 02138. 617-495-2440. Rodney Dennis, Curator of Manuscripts. 9 am-5 pm M-F. Search RLIN by name of journalist. See also *Catalogue of Manuscripts in the Houghton Library, Harvard University* (Alexandria: Chadwyck-Healey, 1986).

Massachusetts Institute of Technology

• Institute Archives and Special Collections, Massachusetts, Institute of Technology, 14N-118, Cambridge MA 02139. 617-253-5688. Helen Samuels, Institute Archivist and Head, Special Collections. 9 am-5 pm M-F. Photocopy services available. Box lists in repository. See also *Selective Guide to the Collection* (Cambridge: The Libraries, Massachusetts Institute of Technology, 1988).

de Sola, Ithiel, 1917-1984. Papers 1950-1984: 99.3 cubic ft. Political scientist; professor of communication studies. Cassette tape, correspondence, notes, speeches, reports. RESTRICTED.

MICHIGAN

Detroit Public Library

• Burton Historical Collection, Detroit Public Library, 5201 Woodward, Detroit MI 48202. 313-833-1480. Alice Dalligan, Chief. 9:30 am-5:30 pm M-T,Th-Sa; 9 am-9 pm W. Photocopy services if condition of material permits. Orders for more than 30 pages must be microfilmed. Unpublished finding aids in repository. See also Bernice Cox Sprenger, comp., *Guide to the Manuscripts in the Burton Historical Collection, Detroit Public Library* (Detroit: Burton Historical Collection, 1985).

Arnett, Judd, 1911-   Papers 1956-1967: 10 boxes. *Detroit Free Press* columnist. Letters from readers and other correspondence and papers.

Bingay, Malcolm Wallace, 1884-1953. Papers 1933-1949: 1 wallet. *Detroit Free Press* editor. Columns, speeches, typescript play, correspondence.

Catlin, George Byron, 1857-1934. Papers 1857-1892: 7 boxes. Grand Rapids and Detroit newspaperman.

Detroit Free Press. Records 1861-1913: 3 vols. Records (1861-1896) and those of Record Printing Co. (1895-1913), purchased by the *Free Press* in 1923.

Giuliano Family. Papers 1860-1964: 4 boxes. Relate to family's association with *Italian Tribune.*

Greene, Edgar Carlton "Doc," 1920-1970. Correspondence: 1964. Newspaper columnist with *Detroit News.*

Greusel, Joseph, 1837-1913. Correspondence and papers 1878-1886: 2 boxes and 2 vols. Editor of *Detroit Journal* and *Detroit Free Press*. Contains letters from Anna Katherine Greene about serial publication of her "Behind Closed Doors."

Guest, Edgar Albert, 1881-1959. Correspondence and papers 1901-1958: 66 boxes and 5 vols. Poet and *Detroit Free Press* reporter.

Holmes, John Clough, 1809-1887. Correspondence and papers 1849-1855: 1 box and 1 wallet. Contains article "Some notes respecting the pioneer newspapers of Michigan."

Holmes, Ralph, 1889-1939. Correspondence and papers 1908-1939: 9 boxes. Journalist for *Detroit Journal* and *Detroit Times*. Letters, plays, music reviews, scrapbooks.

McLauchlin, Russell Jaehne, 1894-1975. Correspondence and papers 1865-1976: 2 boxes and 9 vols. *Detroit News* music and drama critic. Biography, correspondence, photographs, works.

Michigan Chronicle. Papers 1963. Black newspaper in Detroit. Material relates to Emancipation Proclamation essay contest.

Scripps, James Edmund, 1835-1906. Correspondence and papers 1871-1896: 2 wallets. Business manager of *Detroit Tribune*; founder of *Detroit Evening News*. Includes diary.

Sheldon, John Pitts, 1792-1871. Correspondence and papers 1814-1934: 3 boxes. Founder of *Detroit Gazette*; editor of *Detroit Free Press*.

WWJ Radio Station. Papers 1920-1969: 3 boxes plus other materials. Photograph, scripts, log, a history of the station.

Michigan State University

• Archives and Historical Collections, Michigan State University, EG-13 Library, East Lansing MI 48824-1048. 517-355-2330. Dorothy Frye, Reference Archivist. Photocopy services. Computerized finding aid in repository. See also Frederick L. Honhart, Suzann M. Pyzik and Saralee R. Howard, eds., *A Guide to the Michigan State University Archives and Historical Collections* (East Lansing MI, 1976).

Crook, W. Melvin, 1914-1984. Papers 1936-1965: 3 folders and 6 vols. Sports columnist for *Rudder* and *Yachting* magazines. Personal diary, published columns.

Grenell, Judson. Autobiography 1930: 1 item. *Detroit News* reporter.

Stebbins, Cortland Bliss. Papers 1821-1940: 1.3 cubic ft. Editor *Adrian Expositor* 1844-1849 and *Lansing Republican* 1857.

West, R. Kenneth. Papers 1947-1963: 1 cubic ft. Managing editor *Lansing State Journal.* Correspondence, notes, press releases, clippings, speeches.

Wayne State University

• Archives of Labor and Urban Affairs, Wayne State University, Walter P. Reuther Library, Detroit MI 48202. 313-577-4024. Warner Pflug, Asst. Director. 9 am-5 pm M-F. Photocopy services. Inventories available in repository. See also Warner W. Pflug, *A Guide to the Archives of Labor History and Urban Affairs* (Detroit: Wayne State University Press, 1974).

Ameringer, Oscar. Papers 1909-1970: .5 linear ft. Editor of *Illinois Miner, Oklahoma Leader, American Guardian.* Correspondence, writings, photographs. Correspondents include McAlister Coleman, Eugene Debs, John Dewey, Charles Ervin, Covington Hall, Carl Sandburg, Norman Thomas, Oswald Garrison Villard, Henry Wallace.

Beffel, John. Papers 1943-54: 13.5 linear ft. Reporter, writer, editor, publicist. Correspondence, drafts, notes, clippings. Correspondents include Slim Brundage, Joseph Cohen, Paul Crouch, Harry Kelly, Walter Marshall, Rose Pesotta, Voline Vincenzo Vocirca, Ralph Chaplin, Margaret DeSilver, Max Nettlau, Matilda Robbins, Nicolas Steelink, Norman Thomas, Fred Thompson.

Benson, Herman. Papers 1944-1963: 4 linear ft. Trade union editor of *Labor Action*; editor of *Union Democracy in Action.* Correspondence, clippings, leaflets, files. Correspondents include Barry Goldwater, A.J. Hayes, John Lindsay, George Meany, Norman Thomas.

Blankenhorn, Heber. Papers 1906-1967: 7.5 linear ft. Asst. city editor *New York Evening Sun*; foreign correspondent for *Labor.* Correspondence, memoranda, notes, reports. Correspondents include Robert LaFollette, Jr., John L. Lewis, Walter Reuther, Estes Kefauver, Peter Blume.

De Caux, Len. Papers 1925-1970: 10 boxes. Asst. editor *Illinois Miner*; asst. editor *Brotherhood of Locomotive Engineers Journal*; editor *CIO News*; editor *March of Labor*. Also oral history interview.

Haessler, Carl. Papers 1916-1961: 2 linear ft. Managing editor of Federated Press 1922-1956; editor *United Auto Worker* and other local union papers. Pamphlets, leaflets, clippings, articles, radio scripts, union newspapers, oral history interview.

O'Connor, Harvey. Papers 1927-1967: 48.5 linear ft. Bureau manager for Federated Press; managing editor of *Peoples Press*; editor of *Ken*; editorial advisory board of *Nation*. Correspondents include Anne Braden, Carl Braden, Clark Foreman, Harold Golden, M. Guggenheim, O.A. Knight, Thomas W. Lamont, E.M. Livingston, Dorothy Marshall, Ernest Mazey, J.P. Morgan, James Roosevelt, Frank Wilkinson.

Vorse, Mary Heaton. Papers 1841-1966: 77 linear ft. Labor journalist. Literary manuscripts, correspondence, notes and journals, research materials, clippings, pamphlets, personal and family papers, memorabilia. Correspondents include John Dewey, John Dos Passos, Dave Dubinsky, John Edelman, Elizabeth Gurley Flynn, William Z. Foster, John F. Kennedy, John L. Lewis, Sinclair Lewis, Robert E. Peavy, Walter Reuther, Theodore Roosevelt, Lincoln Steffens.

Winn, Frank. Papers 1940-1962: 7.5 linear ft. and 37 scrapbooks. Editor of *Solidarity*.

Wolf, Herman. Papers 1924-1958: 16 linear ft. Labor editor; editor for *Bridgeport Herald*. Drafts of articles, correspondence, reports, press releases, minutes, publicity materials, clippings. Correspondents include William Benton, Chester Bowles, James B. Carey, Sidney Hillman, John W. Livingston, Edward Levinson, Claire Boothe Luce, George Meany, Henry Morgenthau, A. Philip Randolph, Victor Reuther, A.A. Ribicoff, Norman Thomas.

University of Michigan

• Michigan Historical Collections, Bentley Historical Library, University of Michigan, 1150 Beal Ave., Ann Arbor MI 48109-2113. 313-764-3482. Nancy Bartlett, Reference Archivist. 8:30 am-5 pm M-F; 9 am-noon Sa between Sept. and May. Photocopy services. Collection level descriptions on RLIN. Unpublished finding aids in the repository. See also Thomas E. Powers and William H.

McNitt, *Guide to Manuscripts in the Bentley Historical Library* (Ann Arbor: University of Michigan, 1976).

Angelo, Frank, 1914-   Papers 1953-1971: 5 boxes. Journalist with *Detroit Free Press*. Head of Michigan Associated Press Managing Editors, Michigan Press Assoc.

Averill, George R., 1893-1971. Papers 1928-1969: 2 boxes and 30 vols. Editor, publisher and owner of *Birmingham Eccentric* 1920-1961. Correspondence, clippings, speeches.

Baner, Johan G.R., 1861-1938. Papers 1914-1938: 3 boxes. Swedish-American author, poet and newspaper editor. Mostly in Swedish.

Beal, Junius E., 1860-1942. Papers 1882-1941: 15 boxes plus diaries. Editor-publisher of *Ann Arbor Courier* and *Ann Arbor Times* 1882-1904. Diaries, papers, account books.

Booth, George G., 1864-1949.   Papers 1892-1926: 1 box. Founder of Booth Newspapers, Inc., publisher of eight Michigan dailies. Manager of *Grand Rapids Evening News*. Financial and business material, correspondence.

Clarke, George W. Scrapbook 1840-1887: 1 item. Publisher of *Michigan Temperance Herald*. Editorials pasted over subscription list for newspaper.

Cook, Marshall L. and William R. Papers 1880-1945: 6 boxes and 50 vols. Brothers were editors and publishers of *Hastings Banner*. Both were leaders in state press groups.

Copeland, Royal S. 1868-1938. Papers 1892-1938: 36 boxes. Author of syndicated medical column.   Includes many photographs.

Corselius, George, 1806-1849. Diary 1833-1845: 5 vols. Editor of *Ann Arbor Western Emmigrant*; editor *Ann Arbor State Journal*.

Crosier, Edward S., d. 1891. Papers 1856: 3 items. Description of newspaper situation in Ann Arbor.

Cushing, George, 1888-   Scrapbooks and recordings 1942-1950: 2 vols plus recordings. Announcer for "In Our Opinion" radio series.

Detroit News Lansing Bureau. Scrapbooks 1931-1966. Clippings of all articles published from the bureau arranged chronologically. Index available.

Detroit Post and Tribune Co. Papers 1878-1886. 18 items. Articles of incorporation, board minutes, misc. papers.

Detzer, Karl L., 1891- Papers 1916-1967: 2 boxes. Roving editor for *Reader's Digest*. Correspondence, manuscripts, published articles.

Dexter, Samuel W., 1792-1863. Papers 1826-1844: 3 items. Founder of *Ann Arbor Western Emigrant*. Correspondence.

Engle, Cheryl. Student paper 1967: 1 item. History of newspapers on Huron, Lapeer, Sanilac and Tuscola counties. Much of information was obtained from editors in interviews and letters.

Fitzpatrick, Lee J., 1894-1971. Papers 1926-1971: 75 items. General manager of WJR radio station. Correspondence, financial reports, oral history transcripts.

Foster, Theodore, 1812-1865. Papers 1835-1862: 250 items and 5 vols. Editor of *Signal of Liberty*. Subscription list, general records, account books.

Green, Sullivan D., 1833-1889. Papers 1853-1890: 1 case and 2 vols. Correspondent for *Detroit Free Press* during Civil War. Publisher of *The Young Man's Journal*. Clippings, correspondence, leaflets, diaries.

Guest, Edgar A., 1881-1959. Papers 1908-1931: 1 box. Columnist for *Detroit Free Press* and poet. Clippings and scripts.

Hayden, Jay G., 1884- Papers 1916-1965: 8 boxes. Joined *Detroit News* in 1907; served as Washington correspondent 1915-1964. Correspondence, scrapbooks.

Hotchkiss, George W., 1831-1926. Papers 1857-1926: 4 items. Founder of *The Lumberman's Gazette*. Editor, *Bay City Evening Tribune*; president and editor of *Lumber Trade Journal*.

Jenkins, Guy H., 1888-1957. Papers 1931-1957: 1 foot. Lansing bureau chief for Booth Newspapers, Inc. Correspondence, expense accounts.

Johnson, Axel P., 1877-1952. Papers 1908-1951: 250 items. Business manager and executive for several newspapers, including *Chicago Record-Herald* 1906-1915.

Johnson, Edwin J., 1901-1968. Papers 1964-1968: 125 items. Editor-publisher of *Ironwood Daily Globe* from 1964, after twenty-five years as managing editor.

Kidd, James H., 1840-1913. Papers 1861-1910: 1 box. Publisher of *Ionia Sentinel* 1879-1913.

Knox, William Frank, 1874-1944. Papers 1901-1910: 6 boxes. Publisher of *Sault Ste. Marie Evening News*; general manager of Hearst newspapers.

Lemmer, Victor F., 1891-1974. Papers 1922-1974: 10 boxes. Publisher of *Ironwood Times*. Unpublished manuscripts, maps, photographs.

McCall, Ernest J., 1873-1950, and Almon W., 1905-1970. Papers 1897-1970: 4 boxes. Ernest published papers in Mount Pleasant and Grand Haven for 50 years; owned *Grand Haven Daily Tribune*. Son Almon joined paper in 1929. Both were active in state press associations. Correspondence, clippings.

McCallum, George P., Jr. Papers 1955-1968: 2 boxes. Manager of *Ann Arbor News*; chairman of the board of Booth Newspapers, Inc.

McNitt, William, 1948- Manuscript: 1 item. Student paper discussing role of Michigan Republican Newspaper Assoc. 1891-1916.

Marquardt, Frederic S., 1905- Papers 1934, 1942-1949, 1971: 50 items. Assoc. editor of *Philippines Free Press* 1928-1941; editor *Chicago Sun* 1941-1950.

May, Charles S., 1830-1901. Papers 1853-1861: 37 items. Michigan writer for *Toledo Blade*. Correspondence.

Michigan, University of. Broadcasting Service (formerly Bureau of Broadcasting). Papers 1913-1974: 1 case and 33 vols. Scripts, reports, records and correspondence of FM radio station WUOM and its predecessor WCBC. Log books for 1913-1914. Scripts are indexed.

Miller, Floyd J., 1886-1954, and Philip F., 1915-1970. Papers 1907-1970: 5 boxes. Editor-publishers of Oakland County *Daily Tribune*. Letters, clippings, diary kept by Floyd 1932-1954.

Moody, Blair E., 1902-1954. Papers 1928-1954: 23 boxes and 38 vols. Reporter, sports writer and Washington correspondent for *Detroit News*; also worked for *Barron's Weekly*. Correspondence, financial records, scrapbooks.

Mudge, James M., 1916-1970. Papers 1964-1970: 30 items. *Detroit Free Press* writer and press secretary to Reps. Gerald Ford and Guy Vander Jagt. Clippings, letters.

Osborn, Chase S., 1860-1949. Papers 1882-1956: 170 boxes. Owner-publisher of *Sault Ste. Marie News* 1887-1901; joint owner *Saginaw Courier-Herald* 1901-1912; Michigan governor 1911-1913. Correspondence, scrapbooks, clippings.

Perry, Stuart H., 1874-1957 and Maude E., 1891-1948. Papers 1892-1955: 3 boxes and 53 vols. Publisher of *Adrian Telegram*. Correspondence.

Powers, Perry Francis, 1875-1945. Papers: 9 items and 1 vol. Cadillac newspaper publisher and editor. Scrapbook, correspondence.

Stoneman, William H., 1904-   Papers and scrapbooks 1928-1974: 6 boxes. Foreign correspondent for *Chicago Daily News* 1928-1968.

Swinton, Stanley M., 1919-   Papers 1956-1974: 1 box. Worked 16 years for *Detroit Free Press*. Covered World War II for *Stars and Stripes*. Vice pres. and asst general manager of Associated Press.

Titus, Harold, 1888-1967.   Papers 1910-1967: 6 boxes. Freelance writer. Typescripts.

Todd, Laurence, 1882-1957. Papers 1910-1967: 1 box. Writer for *Kalamazoo Gazette* 1904-1907. Washington correspondent for *Non-Partisan Leader*, Tass and Federated Press. Diaries, correspondence, scrapbooks.

Van Koevering, Adrian, 1874-1961. Papers: 1 item and 3 vols. Publisher of *Zeeland Record*.

Vandenberg, Arthur H., 1881-1951. Papers 1917-1951: 8 boxes and 24 vols. Edited *Grand Rapids Herald* for 22 years prior to becoming United States Senator. Correspondents include Walter Lippmann, Roy Howard, Arthur Krock, Dorothy Thompson, Henry Luce.

Walsh, John K., 1887-1964. Papers 1928-1958: 1 box and 1 vol. Editor of *Kalamazoo Gazette* 1912-1964. Correspondence.

Weissert, Charles A., 1878-1947. Papers 1893-1947: 2 boxes. Kalamazoo newspaperman. Speeches, articles, notes.

White, Lee A., 1886-1971. Papers 1909-1921: 32 items. *Detroit News* executive.

White, Peter Q., 1830-1908. Papers 1848-1915: 36 boxes. State senator and businessman whose papers include correspondence with *Marquette Journal* in 1875.

Woodford, Frank B., 1903-1967. Papers 1940-1967: 3 boxes. Journalist with *Detroit Free Press* 1931-1962. Letters, manuscripts, clippings.

Wurz, Frank B., 1885-1966. Papers 1947-1966: 250 items. Editor of *Grand Rapids Herald.* Includes Newspaper Guild contracts.

MINNESOTA

Minnesota Historical Society

• Division of Library and Archives, Minnesota Historical Society, 1500 Mississippi St., St. Paul MN 55101. 612-296-6980. Dallas R. Lindgren, Head, Reference Services. 8:30 am-5 pm M-F; 9 am-1 pm Sa. Photocopy services. See also *Guide to the Personal Papers in the Manuscripts Collections of the Minnesota Historical Society* (Guide No. 1/1935), *Manuscripts Collections of the Minnesota Historical Society* (Guide No. 2/1955), and *Manuscripts Collections of the Minnesota Historical Society* (Guide No. 3/1977).

Adams, John Quincy and Cyrus Field Adams. Papers 1856-1935: 34 items. John Quincy Adams published *St. Paul Western Appeal*; C.F. Adams edited the *Chicago Appeal.* Memorabilia.

Anderson, Albert N. Papers 1936-1942, 1952-1954: 80 items. Founder and publisher of *Olberg Journal* (*Clearbrook Journal* 1902-1918) in Clearwater County MN. P951.

Brill, Hascal Russell. Family papers 1805, 1849-1964: 8.7 cu. ft. William Hascal Brill (nephew to Hascal Russell Brill) was a journalist and reporter for various St. Paul newspapers; wrote for

Newspaper Enterprise Assoc., Associated Press, and Reuter's. P813.

Le Canadien Publishing Co. Minutes October 15, 1883-October 26, 1885: 35 pp. Minutes of meetings of directors and stockholders of weekly French-language newspaper. P61.

Carle, Frank Austin. Papers 1884-1924: 3 in. Worked for *Portland Oregonian, New York Commercial-Advertiser, St. Paul Pioneer Press* (1880-1888), *Minneapolis Tribune, Minneapolis Journal* (1901-1916). Scrapbook, clippings, correspondence. Correspondents include Cass Gilbert, James J. Hill, Thomas Lowry. Alpha.

Day, Frank Arah. Papers 1889-1928: 5 boxes. Publisher of *Fairmont Sentinel* 1910-1928. Correspondents include Carlos Avery, Ignatius Donnelly, Cass Gilbert, Frank B. Kellogg, Floyd B. Olson, J.A.O. Preus, John D. Rockefeller, Jr., William D. Washburn. P307.

Day, Howard G. Papers 1889-1904: 7 items. Published *Freeborn County Standard* 1883-1914. Correspondents include Albert M. Lea, A.P. Swineford. A.D273h.

Dickerson, James Stokes. Family Papers 1839-1907: 1 box. James Spencer Dickerson (son to James Stokes Dickerson) was a journalist associated with *The Standard, Youth's Companion, Graphic* (an art and literary magazine), *Baptist Union.* Correspondence. A.D549.

Dispatch-Pioneer Press. Papers 1862-1948: 1.5 ft. Memoranda, correspondence, court and legal records, clippings, pamphlets documenting the operation of the *Pioneer Press, Dispatch, Dispatch Pioneer Press.* BC4.D6P6.

Dollenmayer, Albert. Family Papers 1865-1938: 3 ft. Reporter and correspondent for *Minneapolis Tribune* 1887-1895. Correspondents include Henry George, Jr., Dr. J.E. Bowers, Lloyd Porter, editor of *Prison Mirror,* Charles Hamblin, William Murphy, Katherine Miller. P1212.

Edgar, William Crowell. Papers 1832-1949: 6 boxes. Business manager and editor of *Northwestern Miller* 1882-1924. Published and edited *The Bellman,* a literary magazine, 1906-1919. Correspondence, clippings, manuscripts, printed matter. A.E23.

Follett, Frederic. Family Papers 1841-1912: 1 box. Newspaper publisher and postmaster in Batavia NY. Correspondence, financial papers, essays, autobiography. PORTIONS RESTRICTED. A.F667.

Gilbert, Joseph. Papers 1886-1954: 88 items. Organizer of Nonpartisan League and founder, editor, and columnist of *Midland Cooperator*. Correspondence, clippings, articles, memorabilia. Correspondents include David Douthit, Elmer A. Benson, Hubert Humphrey, Alfred Gilbert, Joseph Moravec. A.G465.

Gray, James. Family papers 1862-1960: 10 boxes. Reporter and editor for *St. Paul Pioneer* and *St. Paul Dispatch* 1920-1946; literary editor for *Chicago Daily News* 1946-1948. Reviews, articles. P494.

Hagen, Harold Christian. Papers 1923-1957: 18 ft. Journalist, businessman, U. S. Congressman. Correspondence, clippings, printed materials. A.H143.

Holley, Harvey Whitcomb, 1854-1888. Collection: 5 in. Editor for *Chatfield Republican*, construction engineer. Correspondents include George F. Potter, Horace Thompson. A.H738h.

Hudson, Horce Bushnell. Papers 1867-1917: 3.3 linear ft. Journalist and publisher associated with *Minneapolis Journal* 1885-1890, *Minneapolis Tribune* 1895-1901. Founder of Hudson Map Co. in 1895. Correspondence, research notes, clippings. Available on 6 rolls microfilm. M469.

Jaeger, Luth. Family Papers 1874-1933: 4 boxes. Editor of *The North*. Editorials, correspondence. A.J22.

Jones, Elizabeth McLeod. Reminiscences: 1 roll microfilm. Editor of *LeSueur News*, *Hutchinson Independent*, *Steward Tribune*, *Olivia Press*, *LeSueur Independent*. M100.

Jones, Stiles P. Papers 1905-1918: 5 in. St. Paul journalist. Correspondence, clippings, printed materials. A.J79.

Kirkwood, William Paul. Reminiscences: 2 folders. Journalist with *Minneapolis Tribune*, *Minneapolis Journal*. P283.

Lammon, Loren D. Papers 1932, 1954-1957: 5 in. Publisher of *Itasca Iron News* 1905-1950s. Correspondence, reminiscences, short stories. A.L234d.

Lamphere, George Nathan. Papers 1891-1906: 3 pp. and 1 scrapbook. Edited *Moorhead News*. Reminiscences, clippings.A.L237.

Lindbergh, Charles Augustus, Sr. Family Papers 1808-1971: 7.5 ft., 1 roll microfilm. Little Falls MN attorney, congressman, real estate dealer, author, publisher. PORTIONS RESTRICTED. A.L742c.

Lockhart, Andrew Francis. Papers 1920, 1937-1964: 151 items. Edited *Minnesota Union Advocate*. Correspondence, clippings, memorabilia. P607.

McKenny, Charles Richard. Family Papers 1891-1914, 1937: 36 items. Edited *North St. Paul Sentinel* Correspondence. P770.

McLain, John Scudder. Correspondence 1879-1929: 40 items. Editor for various MN newspapers. Correspondents include William C. Swearingen, Knute Nelson, Delos W. Lovelace, Oswald Garrison Billard, Cyrus Northrop, Theodore Roosevelt, Warren G. Harding, William W. Folwell, George D. Dayton. P771.

Mattson, Hans. Family Papers 1855-1939: 3 boxes. Editor of *Svenska-Amerikanaren*, Chicago 1866-1867, *Stats Tidning*; founder of *The North.* Correspondence. A.M444.

Michener, Carrol Kinsey. Family Papers 1858-1970: 6 boxes. Reporter for *Minneapolis Tribune* 1914-1917; *The Bellman* 1917-1919; editorial staff of *Northwestern Miller.* Letters, manuscripts, diaries, clippings. P1044.

Minnesotal Poll. Records 1944-1982: 139 ft. Questionnaires, tabulations, computer printouts used to produce Minnesota Poll, Metro Poll, and Metro Survey for *Minneapolis Star* and *Minneapolis Tribune* 1960-1973. Misc. files including readership and University of Minnesota surveys 1944-1974. Alpha.

Mitchell, William Bell. Family Papers 1806-1935: 5 boxes. Editor of *St. Cloud Journal Press.* Correspondence, clippings, land records. A.M682.

Neal, Eva. Family Papers 1881-1963: 5 folders. Includes information on editor John Quincy Adams. Uncataloged.

Owens, John Phillips. Book draft: 10 in. St. Paul editor. P1557.

Pearson, Albert. Papers: 1 folder. Includes history of New York City Swedish-language newspaper *Arbetaren.* P571.

Pederson, Sigurd. Papers 1911-1915, 1936, 1939: 19 items. Teacher and editor of *Tyler Journal*. Correspondents include Gunnar B. Bjornson, editor of *Minnesota Mascot*. P742.

Peterson, Hjalmar. Papers 1907-1968: 12.5 ft. Founder and editor of *Askov American*; governor, railroad commissioner. Correspondence. P1059.

Roe, Herman. Papers 1906: 3 boxes. Editor of *Northfield News*. Correspondence. P451.

Smalley, Palemon Jared. Papers 1890-1944: 1 box. Publisher and editor of *Caledonia Argus*. Correspondents include Grover Cleveland, Henry George, Robert M. LaFollette, Booker T. Washington. A.S635.

Smith, Henry Arthur. Family Papers 1820-1927: 4 boxes. Correspondent for *Kasson Republican, Dodge Center Press, Pine Island News* 1876-1878; *Mantorville Express* 1878-1881. P1553.

Underwood, Adoniram Judson. Diaries 1855-1857: 2 vols. Publisher of *Detroit (Lakes) Record*; founder *Fergus Falls Weekly Journal*. Worked on *St. Paul Pioneer, St. Anthony Express*. P528.

Valesh, Eva MacDonald. Reminiscences and biographical data 1952,1957: 72 pp; 1 reel microfilm (original at Columbia University). Reporter and labor organizer. RESTRICTED.

Wheelock, Harry M. Family Papers 1859-1939: 2.5 in. Editor of *Fergus Falls Tribune*. Letters. A.W565a.

Wheelock, Joseph Albert. Family Papers 1719-1906: 5 boxes. Correspondence concerns *St. Paul Press*. and *St. Paul Pioneer Press*. P 334.

Wimbish, Anderson H. Papers 1838: 2 boxes. Employee of *St. Paul Pioneer Press*. Correspondence, clippings, essays. A.W757.

University of Minnesota

• Eric Sevareid Library, University of Minnesota School of Journalism and Mass Communication, 120 Murphy Hall, 206 Church St. SE, Minneapolis MN 55455. 612-625-7892. Kathleen A. Hansen, Assoc. Prof. and Sevareid Librarian. 8:30 am-4:30 pm M-F. Special privilege card required for non-university users.

Sevareid, Eric. Correspondence and broadcast scripts: 31 microfilm reels. Copy of materials held at the Library of Congress.

Includes personal correspondence 1930-1959; radio and television scripts 1939-1960.

• Immigration History Research Center, University of Minnesota, 826 Berry St., St. Paul MN 55114. 612-627-4208. Joel Wurl, Curator. 8:30 am-4:30 pm M-F. Photocopy services. Comprehensive guide published 1988. Computerized finding aid in repository.

Alliance Publishing Co. (Chicago IL) Records ca. 1939-1961: 3 linear ft. Publisher of *Dziennik Zwiakowy* 1908-   and *Zgoda* 1881-   . Correspondence, cartoons, editorial material, clippings, photographs. Box inventory available.

Amerikan Uutiset. Collection: 1 in. Manuscripts and typescripts of articles by Terttu Katka, George Latvala, Matti Kantola, Paavo A. Kairemen. In Finnish.

Antonini, Luigi, 1883-1968. Papers ca. 1922-1959: 16 linear ft. Editor of *L'Operaia*, Italian language magazine sponsored by International Ladies' Garment Workers' Union Local 25. In Italian, Spanish and English. Inventory available.

Archacki, Henry, 1907-   Papers ca. 1934-1979: 80 linear ft. Sports reporter and artist for *Dziennik Zwiazokwy* (Chicago IL). Sports editor of *Poland* and *Czas* and, later, of *Nowy Swiat*. Correspondence, articles, clippings, photographs. In English and Polish. Folder level inventory available.

Argoe, Kostis Tamias, 18--?-1982. Papers 1930-1969: 5 linear ft. Greek American journalist in Chicago IL. Wrote for *The Greek Press* under the name Tzimis Brooklys. Correspondence, scrapbooks, articles, clippings. Preliminary inventory available.

Austria. Ministerium des Aussern. Records 1895-1914: 2 microfilm reels. Contain information on Hungarian-American newspapers, Slovak-American newspapers, and Slovene-American newspapers. In German. Inventory available in German.

Balogh, Dezso De A. Papers 1938-1965: 2.5 linear ft. Member of editorial board of *Kepes Magyer Magazin* in New York NY. Journals, pamphlets, clippings. In Hungarian and English. Inventory available.

Bialasiewicz, Jozef F. Papers ca. 1919-1976: .3 linear ft. Polish American newspaper editor in Chicago IL. Correspondence, financial records, clippings, reports. In Polish and English.

Bimba, Anthony, 1894-   Records 1957-1964: 1 linear ft. Editor of *Laisve* 1924-1973.   Photocopy of his autobiography.   In Lithuanian.

Caks, Raimunds. Papers ca. 1943-1980: 3 linear ft. Latvian American journalist. Correspondence, programs, publications. In Latvian.

Caselli, Alberico. Papers 1918-1947: 6 linear ft. Scrapbooks of clippings, post cards, cartoons, many from *Stampa Libera* (formerly *Il Nuovo Mundo*). In Italian and English. Folder level inventory available.

Celli, Fred. Papers ca. 1926-1972: 5 linear ft. Includes information on Italian American publishing companies. Correspondence, minutes, reports, publications. In Italian and English. Inventory available.

Chicago Foreign Language Press Survey. Records ca. 1861-1938: 67 microfilm reels. Project to translate and classify selected news articles in the foreign language press of Chicago. Participating were *Abendpost*, Danish National Committee, *Danish Times*, *Denni Hlasatel*, *Dziennik Chicagoski*, *Greek Press*, *Greek Star*, *Jewish Daily Courier*, *Jewish Daily Forward*, Jewish People's Institute, *Narod*, *Naujienos*, Polish National Alliance, Polish Roman Catholic Union of America, *Rassviet*, *Skandinaven*, *Svornost*, *Saloniki*, *Zgoda*. Project was under Works Progress Administration and Chicago Public Library. Inventory available.

Clemente, Egidio, 1899-19--? Papers ca. 1925-1970: 2.5 linear ft. Italian American editor and journalist with *La Parola del Popolo* and *Il Nuovo Mundo*. Mostly in Italian. Inventory available.

Cupelli, Alberto, 1905-   Papers ca. 1933-1973: 5 linear ft. Assoc. editor of *Il Mondo* in New York NY.   Correspondence, clippings.   Correspondents include Walter Toscanini, Angelo Guidi-Flavio, Luigi Giovanolo, John Santangelo, Mario Einaudi, Serafino Romualdi, Mario Cingolani, Fiorello LaGuardia, John D. Lodge. In English and Italian. Inventory available.

Czas Publishing Co. (Brooklyn NY) Records ca. 1925-1975: 2 linear ft. Publisher of *Czas*. In Polish and English. Inventory available.

Donnaruma, Caesar L., 1900-   Papers ca. 1928-1974: 2 linear ft.   Publisher of *La Gazzetta del Massachusetts* (later *Post-*

Gazette)in Boston MA. Records, correspondence. In English and Italian. Folder level inventory available.

Donnaruma, James V., 1874-1953. Papers 1887-1953: 3.4 liner ft. Publisher of *La Gazzetta del Massachusetts* (later *Post-Gazette*)in Boston MA. Business files, correspondence. In English and Italian.

Dundurs, Erik, 1922-1984. Papers 1949-1982: 4 linear ft. Radio talk show host. Correspondence, clippings, speeches, scrapbooks, organization files.

Egri, Lajos, 1888-1967. Papers ca. 1917-1967: 1 linear ft. Edited illustrated Hungarian weekly. Mainly in Hungarian. Folder level inventory available.

Finnish Socialist Club (Astoria OR). Records 1912-1915: 1 folder photocopies. Minutes of club which founded socialist newspaper *Toveri.* In Finnish.

Finnish Workers' Federation of the United States. Records ca. 1910-1967: 1.5 linear ft. Correspondence of Ira Gollobin and Mike Wastila 1958-1967; financial statements of Peoples' Voice Cooperative Publishing Co; various Socialist Party publications. In Finnish and English.

Grandinetti, Emilio, 1882-1964. Papers 1910-1960: 1 linear ft. Editor of *La Parola del Popolo* (Chicago IL). In Italian and English. Folder level inventory available. . .

Gualtieri, Humbert L. Papers ca. 1938: 2.5 linear ft. Editor of several Italian-language publications including *Il Proletario* (under pseudonym Enotrio Greco), *La Stampa Libera, Il Mondo, Nazioni Unite.* In Italian and English.

Harju, Walter A., 1900-19--? Papers ca. 1929-1973: 32 folders. California correspondent for *Tyomies-Enteenpain* (Superior WI). Correspondence, speeches, articles, photographs, clippings. Often wrote under the pseudonym Vincent Ignatus and John Carpenter. Mainly in English.

Horodysky, Orest Iwan, 1918-   Papers ca. 1920- : 7 linear ft. Includes newspaper clippings from *Ameryka* and *Zorya.*

Idan Uutiset. Records 1896-1899: 1 reel microfilm. Records of Idan Uutiset Publishing Co., Fitchburgh MA. Minutes document formation of *Finska Amerikanaren* (now *The Norden*). In Finnish.

Jaskolski, Alexandra, 1918-   Papers ca. 1930-1979: 4.5 linear ft. Polish American musician who edited *Gazeta Polonii.* Correspondence, diaries. In English and Polish. Inventory available.

Jaskolski, Karol T., 1908-1972. Papers ca. 1939-1973: 107 linear ft. Editor of *Kuryer Codzienny.* Founder of *Gazeta Polonii* (Boston MA). Active with Voice of America. In Polish and English. Inventory available.

Jerich, John, 1894-1973. Papers ca. 1908-   : 3.6 linear ft. Editor of *Novi Svet, Baragova Pratika,* and *Amerikanski Slovenec.* Correspondence, photographs, publications, clippings. Mainly in Slovenian.

Koski, Ernest Theodore, 1908-   Papers 1950-1983: 2 linear ft. Scrapbook including series of articles "Juuret Suomess-Elama Amerikassa (Finnish Roots-American Life). Written for *Tyomies-Enteenpain.*

Kraja, Josip, 1891-   Papers ca. 1915-1965: .5 linear ft. Publisher of several foreign language newspapers in Youngstown OH. Editor of *Hrvatska Stampa.* Owner of United Printing Co. Business records, correspondence, photographs, notebooks, clippings. In Croation and English. Preliminary inventory available.

Levchuk, Dmytro, 1900-1977. Papers 1957-1977: 10 linear ft. photocopies. Ukranian American journalist. Mainly in Ukranian. Inventory available.

Marchello, Maurice R., 1902-1973. Papers ca. 1922-1972: 2 linear ft. Journalist for *Fra Noi* and *La Tribuna* (Chicago IL). Biographical material, correspondence, manuscripts. Folder level inventory available.

Massari, Vincent, 1898-1976. Papers 1895-1976: 5 linear ft. Editor and publisher of *L'Unione,* newspaper of Columbian Federation. Biographical materials, correspondence, scrapbooks, clippings. Also includes correspondence relating to newspaper *L'Abbruzzo-Molise.* In Italian and English. Inventory available.

Mattson, Helmi Dagmar, 1890-1974. Papers 1916-1974: 3 linear ft. Prolific contributor to Finnish American newspapers, particularly *Toveritar, Tyomies Eteenpain,* and *Naisten Viiri.* Mainly in Finnish. Folder level inventory available.

Mokarzel, Mary. Papers ca. 1921-1972: 3 linear ft. Publisher of *Al-Hoda*. Correspondence, photographs, business records, advertisements. Also includes subscription lists for *Lebanese American Journal*. Correspondents include Pierre Gaymayel, William M. Kunstler, Khilil Habib-Sayegh, Leonard S. Tack, Nacib Trabulsi. Mainly in Arabic.

Molek, Ivan, 1882-1962. Papers ca. 1927-1965: 2.5 linear ft. Editor for *Prosveta* 1916-1944. Clippings, books, correspondence, photographs. In English and Slovenian.

Molinari, Alberico, 1876-1948. Papers: 1 linear ft. Founder and editor of *L'Ascesa del Proletariato* (Wilkes-Barre PA) and editor of *La Parola del Popolo* (Chicago IL). In Italian and English.

Morganti, Cesare. Papers ca. 1863-1964: 7 linear ft. Photographer and journalist in Denver CO. Clippings, correspondence, photographs. In English and Italian. Inventory available.

Nelson, Arvid, 1890-1967. Papers 1889-1967: 3 linear ft. Journalist with *Toveri*. Edited *Tyomies*. Worked for Voice of America. Correspondence, notebooks, clippings, brochures, notes, manuscripts, financial records. In Finnish and English. Folder level inventory available.

Nurczynski, Walter, ca. 1893-1962. Papers: 4.5 linear ft. Producer of radio program *Echoes of Poland* in Boston area 1937-1944. Correspondence, clippings, radio scripts, photographs. In English and Polish. Inventory available.

Nyiregynazy, Pal V., 1888-1973. Papers 1952-1975: 4 linear ft. Columnist for *Kanadai Magyarsag*. Correspondence, clippings, photographs. Mainly in Hungarian.

Orszagos Leveltar, Minisz terelnoksegi leveltar (Hungary). Records 1895-1917: 66 microfilm reels. Records of prime minister's office in Hungary including information on Slovak-American newspapers and Hungarian American newspapers.

Palandech, John R. Papers 1919-1963: 1 linear ft. Published *United Serbian*. Correspondence, pamphlets. In Serbo-Croation (Cyrillic) and English.

Paryski Publishing Co. (Toledo OH) Records ca. 1930-1960: 210 linear ft. Founded in 1889 by Antoni A. Paryski. Publisher of books, pamphlets and *Ameryka-Echo* 1889-1962. Business and editorial papers, ledgers, correspondence, mail orders, journals, editorial materials. In Polish and English. Box level inventory available.

Polish American Book Co. (Chicago IL) Records 1955-1972: 10 linear ft. Correspondence, financial records, clippings, press releases pertaining to *Polonia* and *Amerika-Echo.* Mainly in Polish.

Raivaaja Publishing Co. (Fitchburg MA) Records 1896-1966: 1 microfilm reel. Finnish-American newspaper. In Finnish.

Rasins, Nikolajs, 1915-   Papers ca. 1954-1979: 2.5 linear ft. Broadcaster. Tape recordings, clippings, correspondence, financial records. In Latvian and English. Preliminary inventory available.

Rozanski, Edward C., 1915-   Papers ca. 1940- : 43 linear ft. General manager of Alliance Printers and Publishers. Correspondence, minutes, press releases, clippings, scrapbook relating to Polish arts and press in the U.S. In Polish and English.

Saari, Onni, 1887-198-. Papers ca. 1900-1965: 3 linear ft. Editor of Finnish American and Finnish Canadian newspapers *Raivaaja, Tyomies, Sosialisti, Eteenpain* and *Vapaus.* Correspondence, materials on Finnish American press. In English and Finnish.

Sarcone, Antonio L., 1884-1964. Papers ca. 1904-1964: 1 linear ft. Editor of *The American Citizen* (previously *Il Risveglio*) in Des Moines IA. Correspondence, citations, scrapbooks, clippings, photographs. Inventory available.

Saudino, Domenico, 1888-1964. Papers 1927-1961: 2 linear ft. Contributor to *Il Corriere del Popolo* (San Francisco CA) and editor of *La Parola del Popolo* (Chicago IL). Manuscripts, diary. In Italian and English. Inventory available.

Sisca, Alessandro, 1875-1940. Papers 1893-1968: 6 linear ft. Founder of *La Follia di New York.* Correspondence, records, contracts, notebooks, clippings. Correspondents include Thomas Dewey, Fiorello LaGuardia, Enrico Caruso, William H. Taft, Dwight D. Eisenhower. Mainly in Italian.

Teresi, Matteo, 1875-197? Papers 1914-1968: 4 linear ft. Editor of *L'Araldo.* In Italian and English. Inventory available.

Thomas, Norman, 1884-1968. Papers ca. 1943-1955: 1 microfilm reel. Relate to Carlo Tresca Memorial Committee which Thomas chaired. Tresca, editor of *Il Martello,* was murdered in 1943. Press releases, clippings, correspondence. In English and Italian.

Tresca, Carlo, 1879-1943. Papers n.d.: 1 microfilm reel. Editor of *Il Proletario*, *Le Pleke*, *L'Avvenite*, and *Il Martello*.

Tyomies Society (Superior WI). Records 1903-1970: 18 linear ft. and 1 microfilm reel. Radical Finnish-American publishing company. In Finnish.

Vaskov, Milan, 1894-1970. Papers 1935-1970: 1.3 linear ft. Serbian American photoengraver. Correspondence, photographs, scrapbooks. Includes Serbian newspaper *Slobodna Rech* (Pittsburgh PA). In English and Serbo-Croatian.

Wiewiora, Joseph. Papers 1973-1979: ca. 7 linear ft. Editor of *Zgoda* (Chicago IL). Correspondence, drafts, photographs. In Polish and English.

Wiita, John, 1888-198? Papers ca. 1970-1984. Active with Finnish American- and Finnish Canadian labor press. Folder level inventory available. In Finnish and English.

Worker's Publishing Co. (Duluth MN). Records ca. 1915-1975: 4 linear ft. Correspondence, financial records, office files of Finnish newspaper *Industrialisti*. In Finnish and English. Box level inventory available.

Yogoslav (Slovenian) Radio Hour (Milwaukee WI). Scripts ca. 1942-1953: 7 linear ft. In Slovenian and English.

Zappulla, Giuseppe, 1901-   Papers ca. 1927-1973: 1 linear ft. Journalist with *La Sicilia* (New York), *Il Corriere Italiano* (Wilkes-Barre PA), *Carriere d'America* (New York), *Italamerican Magazine* (New York). Correspondents include Nino Caradonna, Arturo Giovannitti, Joseph Tusiani. In Italian and English. Inventory available.

• Silha Center for the Study of Media Ethics and Law, School of Journalism and Mass Communication, University of Minnesota, 111 Murphy Hall, 206 Church St. SE, Minneapolis MN 55455-0418. Published guide as Silha Center Report Series No 86031. For information or use contact Curator, Social Welfare History Archives, University of Minnesota Libraries, 101 Walter Library, Minneapolis MN 55455. 612-373-4420.

National News Council. Archives 1972-1984: 20 4-drawer file cabinets. Records of forum established to receive, examine and report on complaints concerning the accuracy and fairness of news reporting. Administrative records, financial records, working files, reference files, audio- and videotapes.

MISSOURI

University Of Missouri-Columbia

• Special Collections, University of Missouri-Columbia Libraries, 9th & Lowry, Columbia MO 65201. 314-882-7461. Margaret A. Howell, Head, Special Collections. 8 am-5 pm M-F. Limited photocopying permitted.

McCutcheon, John T. Collection: 235 original cartoons drawn for *Chicago Tribune.* Finding aid gives date, subject and caption of each cartoon.

MONTANA

Montana Historical Society

• Montana Historical Society, 225 N. Roberts St, Helena MT 59620. 406-444-4775. Christian Frazza, Archivist. 8 am-5 pm M-F; 9 am-4:30 pm Sa. Photocopy services. Unpublished inventories in repository.

Anderson, Don. Writings ca. 1974: .1 linear ft. Wisconsin newspaper publisher; president of Lee Newspapers of Montana. Unpublished manuscript concerns 1959 sale of seven Anaconda Co. newspapers to Lee Enterprises. RESTRICTED: Section dealing with Richard H. Morrison. SC 1211.

Annin, Jim. Reminiscence 1973: .1 cu. ft. Editor and publisher of *Columbus News* 1913-1931. SC 1711.

Baker, Thomas, 1937-   Papers 1897, ca. 1915: 2 items. Twin Bridges MT newspaperman; miner. SC 380.

Billings, Harry L. Oral history interview 1975: 30 pages. Editor of *People's Voice*; education and research director of Montana AFL-CIO. SC 1525.

Blake, Henry N., 1838-1933. Papers 1867-1911: 39 items. Editor of *Montana Post*; judge. Clippings, memorabilia. SC 438.

Draper, Charles Hiram, 1888-1972. Reminiscence 1967. Red Lodge MT newspaperman. SC 642.

Farris, James Turner, 1865-1914. Oral reminiscence 1968: 90 min. Narrated biography of Montana newspaper publisher by his son, John M. Farris. OH 40.

Fisk family, 1859-1901. Papers 1859-1901: 4.5 linear ft. Brothers owned and edited *Helena Herald*. Primarily intra-family correspondence. Manuscript collection 31.

Greenfield, Charles Diggs, Jr., 1885-1975. Oral history interviews 1970, 1971: 225 min. Helena MT reporter, writer and publicist. OH 33.

Helena Typographical Union #95. Records 1885-1973: 4.5 linear ft. Correspondence, minute books, organizational materials, subject files, financial records. Subgroup for Montana Typographical Conference 1953-1973 with correspondence of Harry Billings and Don Schmidt. MC 88. Portions available as microfilm 197.

Hocking, Thomas Joseph. Oral history interview 1968: 60 min. Owner and publisher of *Glasgow Courier* 1913-1958. OH 43.

Johnson, Thelma Abel, 1904-   Oral history interview 1984: 64 min. Discusses operation of *Chinook Opinion* 1936-1984. Summary available. OH 799.

Kennedy, Will. Papers 1862-1889: .1 ft. photocopies. Boulder MT newspaperman. SC 1659.

The Madisonian. Records 1919-1943: 1 vol. Accounts, check registers, payment lists for 13 small Madison County towns. SC 1732.

Messner, Florence L. "Peggy", 1899-   Oral history interview 1982: 90 min. Reporter for *Anaconda Herald* 1920s. Summary available. OH 413.

Mills, James H., 1837-1904. Papers 1862-1904: .6 linear ft. Editor of *Montana Post*; founder of *New Northwest*. Reminiscence, 20 diaries. MC 70.

Monroe, Bessie Kerlee, 1888-   Oral history interview 1982: 58 min. Journalist for several newspapers in Bitterroot Valley MT. Summary available. OH 425.

Moss, Gurnie Maver, 1884- Oral history interview 1970: 34 min. Publisher of *Whitefish Pilot*; Montana legislator, educator. OH 5.

O'Day, Marjory. Oral history interview 1984: 37 min. Discusses management of *Western Breeze* of Cut Bank 1955-1984. Summary available. OH 831.

Overholser, Joseph, 1911-   Oral history interview 1982: 60 min. Journalist. Summary available. OH 272.

People's Voice.   Records 1904-1967: 6.9 linear ft. Helena MT newspaper edited by H.S. "Cap" Bruce and Harry L. Billings. General correspondence, subject files. SC 40.

Rasmussen, Louise G. Eiselein, 1914-   Oral history interview 1984: 112 min. Discusses operation of *Roundup Record-Tribune* 1940s-1980s. Summary available. OH 812.

Ruder, Mel, 1914-   Oral history interview 1983: 113 min. Editor and publisher of *Hungry Horse News* (Columbia Falls MT) 1946-1978. Summary available. OH 731.

Rue, Helen Dahl. Oral history interview 1982: 120 min. Journalist with *Plentywood Herald* in 1940s. Interviewed with her husband, Roy Rue. Summary available. OH 408.

Scott, Wesley W. "Mike" 1907-   . Oral history interview 1985: 47 min. Describes operation of *Plainsman* 1938-1942. Summary available. OH 858.

Shay, Gladys Van, 1928-   Oral history interview 1983: 124 min. Discusses career at *Hungry Horse News* 1946-1976. Summary available. OH 735.

Ward, Fred J. Papers 1934-1961: .4 cubic ft. Editor and publisher of *Meagher County News*. General correspondence, financial records, account books. SC 333.

Whetstone, Dan. Papers 1953-1956: .1 linear ft. Cut Bank MT newspaper publisher and writer. Correspondence, book drafts. SC 149.

NORTH CAROLINA

Duke University

• Manuscripts Dept., William R. Perkins Library, Duke University, Durham NC 27706. 919-683-3372. 8 am-5 pm M-F; 9 am-12:30 pm Sa. Photocopy services. Finding aids in repository; collection level records of some collections on OCLC. See also Richard C. Davis and Linda Angle Miller, editors, *Guide to the Cataloged Collections in the Manuscript Dept., Perkins Library, Duke University* (Santa Barbara CA: Clio books, 1980).

Ball, William Watts. Papers 1805-1952: 28,240 items and 116 vols. Journalist with several South Carolina newspapers and editor *Charleston News and Courier* 1927-1950. Correspondence, account books, scrapbooks, photographs, diary. PORTIONS RESTRICTED.

Baker, Henry Dunster, 1873-1939. Papers 1794-1953: 272 items and 8 vols. Worked in editorial depts. of *Chicago Tribune, New York Evening Post, Commercial West.* Clippings, genealogy, printed material, pictures, volumes.

Bradshaw, Herbert Clarence. Papers: 42,000 items. Sunday feature editor. Editorial page editor *Durham Morning Herald* 1964-1974. Diaries, correspondence, notes.

Coleman, John Carrington. Papers 1924-1978: 131 items. Mississippi book collector and newspaper editor. Correspondence.

Collins, Thomas Hightower, 1910-   Papers 1950-1976: 33,000 items. Columnist. Most materials deal with "The Golden Years" and "The Senior Forum," columns on retirement. Reader mail and other correspondence, drafts, pamphlets, columns.

Dawson, Francis Warrington, I and II. Papers 1559-1963: 7,908 items and 69 vols. Father and son who were newspapermen. Papers provide information on *The News and Courier* of Charleston SC.

Harriss, Robert Preston. Papers 1927-1975: 3,569 items and 160 vols. Baltimore novelist and newspaperman. Correspondence, appointment calendars, memorandum books, publications, clippings. Correspondents include H.L. Mencken, George Bernard Shaw.

Gardner, Melzar. Papers 1833-1842: 35 items. Journalist and distribution agent for *Brother Jonathan, Democratic Review,*

Union and Messenger, Boston Quarterly Review. Publisher of *The Sunbeam.* Editor of *States Rights Republican.* Letters.

Griffin, Isabella K. Papers 1944-1947: 33 items and 1 vol. Newspaper correspondent and assoc. editor of *Democratic Digest.* Diary, clippings.

Hancock, Gordon Blaine, 1884-1970. Papers 1928-1970: 525 items. Wrote "Between the Lines" for Associated Negro Press. Correspondence, subject file, writings, clippings, photographs. Correspondents include Luther P. Jackson, P.B. Young, James E. Shepherd, Benjamin E. Mays, Guy B. Johnson, Howard W. Odum, Jessie D. Ames, Virginius Dabney. Inventory available.

Hill, Adams Sherman, 1833-1910. Papers 1859-1864: 75 items. Newspaper correspondent for *New York Tribune, Chicago Daily Tribune.* Correspondents include Whitelaw Reid, Joseph Medill, Horace White, Henry Villard, Samuel Bowles, Charles Hale, Schuyler Colfax, Horace Greeley.

Jarvis, Russell, 1791-1853. Papers 1817-1828: 7 items. Lawyer, editor, newspaper correspondent for *United States Telegraph.* Correspondents include Ashur Ware, David Henshaw. Letters.

Kirby, Ephriam, 1757-1804. Papers 1763-1878: 2,899 items and 1 vol. Includes many letters from publishers of early New England newspapers, including the *American Mercury* and the *Litchfield Weekly Monitor.*

Lander, William Hall, 1903-   Papers 1920s-1940s: ca. 700 items. Foreign correspondent for United Press International; White House correspondent 1940s. Clippings, pictures, correspondence.

Lord, Chester Sanders, 1850-1933. Papers 1887-1931: 118 items. Assoc. editor of *Oswego Advertiser.* Managing editor of *New York Sun* 1880-1913. Correspondents include Lord Northcliffe, Will Irwin, S.S. McClure, Frank A. Munsey, Adolph Ochs, William Sulzer, Chauncey M. Depew, Martin H. Glynn, Clarence Mackay, Thomas Nelson Page, Nathan Straus, Cornelius Vanderbilt, Louis Wiley.

Martin, John Sanford, 1886-1957. Papers 1917-1958: 8,586 items and 19 vols. Editor of *Winston-Salem Journal* and *Sentinel* 1912-1951. Correspondence.

Sharpe, John Allen, 1909-   Papers ca. 1928-1981: ca. 100 items. Editor of *Robesonian* in Lumberton NC. Correspondence.

Stephens, Erwin Duke, 1904-   Papers 1955-1984: 651 items and 3 vols. Owner and publisher of *Allegheny Times* of Sparta NC and *The Caswell Messenger*. Memoirs, writings.

Robinson, Magnus L. Papers 1888-1914: 33 items. Editor of *National Leader*. Letters. Correspondents include John Mitchell, Jr., editor of *Richmond Planet*, Blanche K. Bruce, Morgan Treat.

University of North Carolina at Wilmington

• Manuscripts Collection, William Madison Randall Library, University of North Carolina at Wilmington, 601 South College Rd., Wilmington NC 28403-3297. 919-395-3760. Lana D. Taylor, Reference/Special Collections Librarian. 8 am-5 pm M-F. Photocopy services.

Avery, Johnston and Virginia Hall Avery. Private papers 1916-1976: 13 boxes and 1 scrapbook. Reporter *Greensboro Daily News, New York World*; reporter and editor *Hickory Daily Record*; editor and publisher *Lenoir News-Topic*. Includes correspondence from Josephus Daniels.

NEBRASKA

Nebraska State Historical Society

• Nebraska State Historical Society, 1500 R St., Lincoln NE 68508. 402-471-4751. 10 am-5 pm M-F; 8 am-5 pm Sa. Published guide available.

Brainerd, Henry Allen

Brandsberg, George T.

Correll, Erasmus Michael

Davis, Horace M.

Fry, Edwin

Hitchcock, Gilbert M.

Howard, Edgar

Jones, Will Owen

Kline, George Washington

McCord, Gerald. Business records 1942-1946. Publisher of *Cass County Echo* and *Plattsmouth Call.*

Minney, Doris

Morton, J. Sterling

Omaha Women's Press Club

Niobarara Tribune

Parkes, John Samuel

Pierce, Charles Wilder

Renner, Frederick

Rosewater family

Sorenson, Alfred A.

Wehn family

Woods, William Henry

Wooster, Charles

Wykoff, Roy A., Jr.

NEW HAMPSHIRE

Dartmouth College

• Special Collections, Dartmouth College Library, Hanover NH 03755. 603-646-2037. Philip N. Cronenwett, Chief of Special Collections. 8 am-4:30 pm M-F. Collection described in OCLC to 1985; in RLIN, 1985-

Brown, Ernest Francis, 1903-   Papers: 7 boxes. Assoc. editor *Current History* 1930-1936; *New York Times* Sunday staff 1936-1945; senior editor *Time* 1945-1949; editor *New York Times Book Review* 1949-1970. RESTRICTED Some portions of collection may not be used without the permission of the archivist of the *New York Times* and Mr. Brown. Guide available.

Clark, John McLane, 1910-1950. Papers: 1 box. Editor *New Canaan Gazette* 1932-1934; editorial staff writer *Washington Post* 1935-1938; Nieman Fellow, Harvard University 1938-1939; editor/publisher *Clarement Daily Eagle* 1948-1950.

Gordon, George Augustus, 1827-1912. Papers: 2 boxes. Editor/publisher *Lawrence Senteniel* 1855-1856; asst. editor *Charleston Mercury* 1857-1861.

Mecklin, John Martin, 1918-1971. Papers: 11 boxes. War correspondent *Chicago Sun* 1944-1946; reporter and columnist *Rome Daily American* 1946-1947; staff writer *New York Times* 1947-1948; writer and reporter *Time* 1948-1965; assoc. editor *Fortune* 1966-1968; Board of Editors *Fortune* 1968-1971. Guide available.

NEW JERSEY

Princeton University

• Princeton University Library, 1 Washington Rd., Princeton NJ 08544. 609-452-3184. Jean F. Preston, Curator of Manuscripts. 9 am-5 pm M-F. Photocopy services.

Adler, Elmer, 1884-1962. Papers 1651-1961: 157.9 cu. ft. Personal papers plus business archives of Pynson Printers and *Colophon.* Correspondents include Arthur Sulzberger, Robert Benchley, H.L. Mencken, Alfred A. Knopf, Bennett Cerf, Dard Hunter, Rockwell Kent, John T. Winterich, Al Stanford, Willa Cather, Christopher Morley, Franklin D. Roosevelt. C0262.

Armstrong, Hamilton Fish, 1893-1973. Papers 1912-1972: 51.8 cu. ft. Editor of *Foreign Affairs.* Correspondence, clippings, documents, photographs, scrapbooks. Correspondents include Dean Acheson, Chiang Kai-shek, Winston Churchill, Archibald Carey Coolidge, David Lilienthal, Charles A. Lindbergh, Archibald MacLeish, Marshal Tito. Guide available in repository. MC002.

Attwood, William, 1919-   Manuscript 1949: .1 cu ft. Manuscript of book *The Man Who Could Grow Hair.* C0146.

Bullard, Arthur, 1879-1929. Papers 1905-1929: 9.1 cu ft. American journalist and novelist. Used name Albert Edwards. Manuscripts, correspondence, clippings, diaries, photographs. Correspondents include Malcolm Davis, Sir Horace Plunkett, Edgar Rickard, Sir Eric Drummond, Edward M. House, Woodrow Wilson, Herbert Hoover. Guide available. MC008.

Curtis, William Eleroy, 1850-1911. Papers 1874-1911: 38 cu. ft. Scrapbooks of clippings of his writings for *Chicago Record* 1874-1911. MC013.

Fischer, Louis, 1896-1970. Papers 1918-1978: 48 cu. ft. Correspondence, works, documents, financial records, film, tape and phonograph recordings, reference files, memorabilia. Correspondents include Winston Churchill, Franklin D. Roosevelt, Mohatma Gandhi, Dean Acheson, Albert Einstein, Lillian Hellman, John F. Kennedy, Arthur Koestler, Robert Oppenheimer. Guide available. RESTRICTED: Boxes 87-92 and an addition of the files of Bertha Markoosha Fischer are not available for any use until the year 2000. MC024.

Fonblanque, Albany, 1793-1872. Papers 1784-1875: .2 cu. ft. Primarily letters sent to Fonblanque as editor of *Examiner*. Correspondents include Marguerite Blessington, William Lisle Bowles, Edward Bulwer-Lytton, Rosina Lytton, George Grote, Sir George Cornewall Lewis, Lord John Russell. C0157.

Gibbons, Herbert Adams, 1880-1934. Papers 1908-1934: 13 cu. ft. Foreign correspondent. Also includes the papers of his wife, Helen Davenport Gibbons. Manuscripts, clippings, letters, scrapbooks. Correspondents include John G. Hibben, J.J. Jusserand, John J. Pershing, Margaret Deland, Rodman Wanamaker, John Wanamaker. MC0621.

Godwin, Parke, 1816-1904. Papers 1830-1900: 4.1 cu ft. Published and unpublished manuscripts. C0019.

Hotchkiss, Thomas Woodward, 1866?-1953. Papers 1891-1935: .5 cu ft. Articles, clippings, correspondence, notes. C0166.

Hutton, Laurence, 1843-1904. Papers 1817-1904: 5.6 cu ft. American drama critic. Manuscripts, correspondence, photographs, illustrations. C0021.

Phillips, David Graham, 1867-1911. Selected manuscripts 1902-1917: 4.6 cu. ft. Novels, plays, short stories, essays, articles. C0124.

Sloss, Robert Thompson. Papers 1881-1917: .3 cu ft. Journalist in London during World War I. Articles, clippings, correspondence. C0005.

Thompson, Vance, 1863-1925. Papers 1894-1925: 3.2 cu ft. Novelist, dramatist, poet, essayist, critic, editor. C0224.

We Saw It Happen. Manuscripts 1937: .6 cu ft. Manuscripts of book by 12 *New York Times* correspondents with chapters by Arthur Krock, G.E.R. Gedye, F. Raymond Daniell, Frank Nugent and Douglas Churchill, Elliott V. Bell, Ferdinand Kuhn, Russell Owen, John Kieran, William R. Conklin, Hugh Byas, Brooks Atkinson, Louis Stark. C0007.

Williams, Charles Richard, 1853-1927. Papers 1863-1927: 2.7 cu ft. Active in Associated Press 1890-1909. Correspondence, documents, memorabilia, printed material, papers of others. Correspondents include Abraham Lincoln, James A. Garfield, William T. Sherman, Benjamin Harrison, Ulysses S. Grant, William Henry Smith. C0231.

Rutgers University

• Special Collections and Archives, Rutgers University Libraries, Alexander Library, New Brunswick NJ 08903. 201-932-7510. Ruth J. Simmons, Director. 9 am-5 pm M-F; 11 am-5 pm Sa. Photocopy services. See also Herbert F. Smith, comp., *A Guide to the Manuscript Collection of the Rutgers University Library* (New Brunswick: Rutgers University Library, 1964).

Dickinson, George H. Papers 1891-1900: 147 items. Editor with *Daily America, Atlanta Journal, New York World.*

Hutchinson, Elmer T. Papers: 12 boxes. Biographical and bibliographical notes on New Jersey printers and publishers active before 1850.

Jennings, Kenneth Q. Papers: 55 boxes. Biographical and bibliographical notes on 19th and 20th century New Jersey newspapers and publishers

New Jersey Coalition for Fair Broadcasting. Papers 1973-1983: 27 boxes. Relate to New York City and Philadelphia television stations, especially WNET, and to the transfer of WOR from New York to New Jersey.

O'Neill, Harold Edgar. Papers 1907-1941: 91 items. Newspaper editor in New Brunswick NJ.

NEW YORK

Cornell University

• Dept. of Manuscripts and University Archives, Cornell University Libraries, 101 Olin Library, Ithaca NY 14853-5301. 607-255-3530. Kathleen Jacklin, Reference Archivist. 8 am-5 pm M-F; 9 am-1 pm Sa. Photocopy services. Collection level records on RLIN.

Adams, Bristow, 1875-1957. Papers 1853-1970: 15 cu. ft. Journalist, artist, forester. Worked on *The Pathfinder* 1894-1895; several Stanford University student publications; *Washington Life*; *American Spectator*. Briefly directed WPA writers' project in New York. Correspondence, articles, press releases, illustrations, clippings, posters periodicals. Correspondents include Henry G. Alsberg, Margaret Bourke-White, Sherwin Cody, Charles Collingwood, Edmund Ezra Day, A.W. Gibson, David B. Greenberg, Lester W. Herzog, David Starr Jordan, Russell Lord, Deane W. Malott, Albert R. Mann, Gifford Pinchot, Anastasia J. Romanoff, Theodore Roosevelt, Elihu Root, Harold M. Schmeck, Jr., Jacob Gould Schurman, William Howard Taft, Robert E. Treman, Peter Vischer, E.B. White, Lee A. White. Unpublished guide in repository.

Andrews, Charles Thomas, 1842-1931. Papers 1840-1922: 2.2 cu. ft. Worked for newspapers in Watkins Glen and South Bend IL. Annotated scrapbooks, correspondence.

Berry, Romeyn, 1881-1957. Papers 1636-1960: 1.6 cu. ft. Columnist, author, lawyer, farmer. Wrote "Talk of the Town" column for *The New Yorker*; articles for the *Ithaca Journal*. Correspondence, diaries, journals, drawings, photographs. Unpublished guide in repository.

Butler, William F. *Rochester Times-Union* memoranda 1927-1966: .1 cu. ft. City editor for *Rochester Times-Union*. Memoranda, clippings and related items from Frank E. Gannett and others.

Frantz, Harry Warner, 1891-1982. Papers 1905-1982: 50 cu. ft. Worked for United Press 1920-1965 (except during World War II). 425 scrapbook binders including clippings, awards, correspondence, photographs, reference files, news releases, telegrams. Volume listing available. RESTRICTED: Publication is by permission of donor until June 30, 1999 or her death, whichever date is earlier.

Gannett, Frank Ernest, 1876-1957. Papers ca. 1859-1958: 32 cu ft. Reporter for *Ithaca Journal*; worked for *Ithaca Daily News*. From 1906-1937 purchased newspapers in New York, Connecticut, New Jersey, Illinois. Correspondence, speeches, scrapbooks, articles, genealogy, notebooks. Correspondents include Raymond N. Ball, Jerome D. Barnum, Lord Beaverbrook, Neal Dow Becker, William E. Borah, Winston Churchill, John L. Collyer, George W. Crane, Edmund Ezra Day, Thomas E. Dewey, Anthony Eden, Mark Ellingson, James A. Farley, Edwin S.

Friendly, Earl Harding, William Randolph Hearst, Herbert Hoover, Harold Ickes, Alfred M. Landon, Herbert Lehman, Norman Vincent Peale, Westbrook Pegler, Raymond S. Richmond, Nelson Rockefeller, Carlos P. Romulo, Franklin D. Roosevelt, Edward A. Rumely, Jacob Gould Schurman, Harry G. Stutz, Robert A. Taft, Walter L. Todd, Frank E. Tripp, Arthur Vandenberg, David Rhys Williams, Wendell Willkie. *Guide to the Frank E. Gannett and Caroline Werner Gannett Papers* available.

Halsey family. Papers 1870-1975: 3.2 cu. ft. Francis W. Halsey held editorial positions with *Binghamton Times*, the *New York Tribune*, and, from 1880-1922, with the *New York Times* where he established the *New York Times Review of Books* in 1896. Scrapbooks of letters, clippings, photographs. Folder list available in repository.

Ithaca Journal Twenty-five Year Club. Album 1954: 1 vol. Includes historical sketch of journalism in Ithaca since 1815.

McDonald, Ruth Seely Berry, 1913-   Papers 1850-1959: 1 cu. ft. Includes letters from her father, Romeyn Berry, concerning his writing for the *Ithaca Journal.* Scrapbooks, photographs, clippings, family history. Unpublished finding aid in repository.

Singiser, Frank King, 1908-   Papers 1923-1981: 18 cu. ft. Radio and television news commentator. Scripts for newscasts, Mutual Broadcasting System programs, Wall Street Reports, Plain Table Programs, and other shows. Correspondence, scrapbooks, photographs, clippings.

Skeffington, Leo Bernard, 1892-1986. Papers 1945-1983: .8 cu. ft. and 15 tape recordings. Agriculture editor, Gannett Publications.

Spalding, Lyman. Papers 1811-1986: .4 cu. ft. Edited *Plain Truth*; established *Priesthood Exposed.* Correspondents include Thomas B. Barnum, Elihu Francis Marshall.

Stutz, Harry George, 1885-1954. Papers 1915-1954: .4 cu. ft. Editor of *Ithaca Journal.* Correspondence, awards, photographs, clippings. Correspondents include Frank E. Gannett, Howard E. Babcock, Neal Dow Becker, Frank D. Boynton, Maurice C. Burritt, Anna Botsford Comstock, Hollis E. Dann, Edmund Ezra Day, Edward R. Eastman, Felix Frankfurter, Orthon Guerlac, Robert J. Kane, Claude L. Kulp, Harry H. Love, Deane W. Malott, Veranus

A. Moore, William I. Myers, Cuthbert Pound, Ruby Green Smith, James Sullivan, Warren G. Harding, James Cox, Alfred E. Smith, Frank Thilly, Robert E. Treman, Robert H. Treman, Hendrik Willem Van Loon.

Thompson, Charles Willis. Letters 1901-1912: .1 cu. ft. Member of Washington Bureau of the *New York Times* and the *New York World.*

Van Loon, Hendrik Willem, 1882-1944. Papers 1884-1972: 35 cu. ft. Assoc. editor *Baltimore Sun* 1923-1924. Radio broadcaster. Correspondence, sketchbooks, phonograph records, photographs. In English, Dutch, German. Unpublished guide in repository.

Young, Perry Deane. Papers ca. 1968-1985: 1.2 cu. ft. Correspondent in Viet Nam. Contains material pertaining to the disappearance of war correspondents Sean Flynn and Dana Stone.

New York Public Library

• Rare Books and Manuscripts Division, Room 324, New York Public Library, Fifth Ave. and 42nd St., New York NY 10018. 212-340-0849.

Ackerman, Edward P. Papers 1867-1875: 1 vol. Journalist. Letters, autographs. 69 M30.

Aughinbaugh, William Edmund, 1870-1940. Papers 1921-1923: 1 box. Lawyer, author, editor. Foreign and export editor of *New York Commercial.*

Bacon, Edwin Munroe, 1844-1914. Correspondence 1872-1914: 2 folders. Editor of *Boston Post.*

Bennett, James Gordon, 1795-1872. Letters 1840-1851. Editor of *New York Herald.*

Bigelow, John, 1817-1911. Papers 1839-1912: 28 vol. and 36 boxes. Editor of *New York Evening Post.* Correspondence, diaries, writings. Correspondents include William Cullen Bryant, John Hay, William H. Huntington, S.J. Tilden. Inventory in repository.

Bigelow, Poultney, 1855-1954. Papers 1864-1954. Journalist, author, world traveler. Drafts, manuscripts including an unpublished biography of his father, John Bigelow, research materials, diaries, photographs, scrapbooks. Unpublished finding aid available.

Black, Alexander, 1859-1940. Papers 1881-1926: ca. 250 items. Journalist with *Brooklyn Times*; Sunday editor of *New York World*; art editor of King Features Syndicate. Correspondence, notebooks, writings.

Blair, Francis Preston, 1791-1876, and Rives, John Cook, 1795-1864. Papers 1837-1860: 7 items. Proprietors of *Washington Globe*.

Bonner, Robert, 1824-1899. Papers 1860-1899: 18 boxes. Publisher of *New York Ledger*. Letters.

Bowker, Richard Rogers, 1848-1933. Papers 1856-1958: 118 boxes, 7 cartons. Editor, publisher, journalist, business executive. Editor of *New York Evening Mail*; editor and publisher of *Publisher's Weekly* and *Library Journal*. Family correspondence, personal papers, writings, speeches, editorials, reminiscences, diaries. Container listing and alphabetical index of correspondents available.

Bryant-Godwin Papers 1804-1913. Correspondence, writings, and other personal papers of poet and newspaper editor, William Cullen Bryant, and his son-in-law and colleague, Parke Godwin. Includes records of *Evening Post* 1836-1861. Complete list of correspondents available. 87 M 15.

Calverton, Victor Francis, 1900-1940. Papers 1915-1941: ca. 6 ft. and 25 vol. Author, editor, lecturer. Correspondence, manuscripts. Inventory available.

Carruth, Hayden, 1862-1932. Papers 1853-1961: 80 vol and 19 boxes. Journalist and author. Publisher of *Estelline Bell* and *Dakota Bell*; staff member of *New York Tribune* and *Chicago Tribune*; editor of "The Drawer" at *Harper's Magazine* and "The Postscript" at *Woman's Home Companion*. Inventory available.

Church, William Conant, 1836-1917. Papers 1863-1878: 1 vol. and 8 boxes. Co-editor with his brother, Francis Pharcellus Church, of *The Galaxy*, which later merged with *The Atlantic Monthly*. Founder, editor and proprietor of *United States Army and Navy Journal*. Correspondents include Eugene Benson, Charles Astor Bristed, John Burroughs, Alice Cary, Phoebe Cary, Caroline Chesebrough, L. Clarke Davis, Rebecca Harding Davis, Annie Edwards, Paul Hamilton Hayne, Helen Hunt Jackson,

Henry James, Emma Lazarus, Justin McCarthy, Charles Reade, Robert N. Scott, Annie Moncure Seemüller, Harriett Prescott Spofford, Bayard Taylor, Henry T. Tuckerman, Richard Grant White, Walt Whitman, William Winter, Edmund Yates.

Davis, Robert Hobart, 1869-1942. Papers 1901-1942: 26 boxes. Editor, author, journalist. Fiction editor of magazines published by Frank A. Munsey Co. Correspondence, writings, clippings, photographs. Correspondents include Rex Beach, Arnold Bennett, Ambrose Bierce, Irwin S. Cobb, Charles Dana Gibson, Samuel G. Blythe, Gutzon Borglum, Charles Neville Buck, Octavius Roy Cohen, Jo Davidson, William T. Dewart, George Allen England, Geraldine Ferrar, Frederick Faust, Daniel Frohman, Arthur Hamilton Gibbs, Zane Grey, Ernest Haskell, Fannie Hurst, Richard Le Gallienne, Arthur B. Maurice, Edison Marshall, E. Phillips Oppenheim, Katharine D. Osbourne, William Sydney Porter, Mary Roberts Rinehart, Perley Poore Sheehan, Robert W. Stevenson, Ben Ames Williams. Box listing and partial listing of correspondents available.

De Casseres, Benjamin, 1873-1945. Papers 1893-1945: 30 boxes. Journalist with *New York American.* Correspondence, clippings.

Finley, John Huston, 1863-1940. Papers, 1892-1940: 115 boxes and 43 cartons. Editor of *McClure's Magazine*; assoc. editor *New York Times*. Letters, correspondents, scrapbooks. Correspondents include Brooks Atkinson, Poultney Bigelow, Arthur Krock, William Allen White, Edgar A. Bancroft, Robert Bridges, Gilbert Coolidge, Calvin Coolidge, Richard T. Ely, Hamlin Garland, Cass Gilbert, Herbert Hoover, Charles Evans Hughes, James Hazen Hyde, Robert Underwood Johnson, Jean Jules Jusserand, Franklin K. Lane, Adolph Lewisohn, George Foster Peabody, John S. Phillips, Jacob A. Riis, Nicholas Roosevelt, Theodore Roosevelt, Elihu Root, Edward Morse Shepard, Frederick Starr, Vilhjalmur Stefansson, Sir Ronald Storrs, Ida Tarbell, Henry Van Dyke. Container list available.

Flagg, Azariah Cutting, 1790-1873, Correspondence 1821-1847: 6 boxes. Journalist, politician. Correspondents include Albert Gallatin, John A. Dix, Michael Hoffman, William L. Marcy, R.H. Walworth, Silas Wright, Jr.

Fleming, Harold Manchester, 1900-1971. Papers 1917-1971: 2 boxes, 11 cartons, ca. 130 posters. Financial writer and political economist. 72 M 50.

Flint, Charles Ranlett, 1850-1934. Papers 1869-1921: 2 boxes. Includes correspondence relating to purchase of *New York Times*. Box listing available.

Ford, Gordon Lester, 1823-1891. Papers 1830-1891: 19 boxes, 1 carton, 1 folder. Founder of *Brooklyn Daily Union*. Correspondence, legal and business papers, account books. Box listing available.

Frank, Gerald. Papers 1950s: 11 boxes. Journalist and biographer. Letters, drafts, notes, galley proofs, source material, clippings. RESTRICTED: Material relating to Constance Bennett, Zsa Zsa Gabor, Sheilah Graham, Dick Haymes is closed until the death of each individual.

Frederic, Harold, 1856-1898. Correspondence 1879-1899, 1934-1935, 1945: ca. 108 items. Journalist and author. Primarily photocopies relating to running the London office of *New York Times*.

Gales, Joseph, 1786-1860, and William Winston Seaton, 1785-1866. Letters 1815-1856: 69 items. Editors of *National Intelligencer*.

Gay, Sydney Howard, 1814-1888. Papers 1837-1886: 4 vol. and 11 boxes. Correspondence, manuscripts, accountbooks of American Anti-Slavery Society and *Anti-Slavery Standard*. Box listing available.

Gilder, Joseph Benson, 1858-1936. Correspondence ca. 1880-1919: ca. 200 items. Editor of *The Critic*. Letters. Correspondent list available.

Gilder, Richard Watson, 1844-1909. Papers 1855-1916: 22 linear ft. Editor at *Scribner's Monthly* and *Century*. Correspondence, scrapbooks. Correspondent list available.

Graham, Walter B. 1878-   Papers 1907-1933: 2 boxes. Editor of *Patent and Trade Mark Review*.

Greeley, Horace, 1811-1872. Papers 1831-1873: 6 boxes. Journalist, political leader. Includes letters 1842-1871 from Greeley to Schuyler Colfax beginning when Colfax was *New York Tribune* correspondent in Indiana.

Griffin, Anthony J., 1866-1935. Papers. Founder and editor of *Bronx Independent*. Correspondence, diaries, notes, financial records.

Harding, Warren G. Letters 1916-1920: ca. 80 letters. Letters to George H. Van Fleet, manager of *Marion Star*. 41 M 79; 44 M 125.

Harvier, Ernest, 1863-1929. Papers 1867-1920: 3 boxes. Editorial writer for *New York Sun*; contributor to *New York Times*. Scrapbooks. 85 M 102.

Holland, Josiah Gilbert, 1819-1881. Papers 1834-1881: 2 boxes, 2 slipcases, 1 pkg. Editor of *Scribner's Monthly*. Letters, essays, addresses. 55 M 114; 78 M 21.

Holz, Julius. Papers 1867-1916: 1 box. Publisher of *New York Herald*. Letters, post cards. List of persons represented available. MS 69-887.

Jones, George, 1811-1891. Papers 1845-1894: ca. 300 items. Newspaper publisher. Correspondence, wills, clippings relating to policies of *New York Times* and the Tweed conspiracy. MS 76-1520.

Karsner, David Fulton, 1889-1941. Papers 1912-1929: 2 boxes. American socialist, journalist, biographer. Correspondence, articles, photographs. Correspondents include Eugene V. Debs, Theodore Debs, Katherine M. Debs, Theodore Dreiser.

King, Frederick Allen, 1865-1939. Papers 1930-1935: 2 boxes. Editor of *Literary Digest*. Correspondence, notes, clippings.

Kinsella, Thomas, 1832-1884. Scrapbook: 1 vol. Editor of *Brooklyn Daily Eagle* 1861-1884. 87 M 41.

Lenz, Charles, 1840-1914. Papers ca. 1900: .5 linear ft. Edited several German language newspapers in New York, as well as *Original Rights Magazine* and *Capital and Labor*. 86 M 53.

Livingston, Louis Joseph, 1856- Papers 1886-1931: 2 vol. Journalist and composer. Scrapbooks.

McCormick, Anne O'Hare, 1882-1954. Papers 1936-1954: 16 boxes. Editor and journalist. Correspondence, editorials, articles, columns, dispatches from *New York Times*. Unpublished inventory available.

McKelway, St. Clair, 1845-1915. Papers 1863-1948: 19 boxes and 4 pkg. Editor of *Brooklyn Eagle*. Box listing available.

Mandel, Ernest, 1885-1951. Papers 1901-1951: 3 cartons. Founder and editor of *Magyar Munkaslap.* Correspondence, writings, diary. 51 M 95.

Mencken, Henry Louis, 1880-1956. Papers, ca. 1900-1956: 52 linear ft. Letters received by Mencken. Two unpublished manuscripts RESTRICTED until Jan. 29, 1991. Correspondents listed in Betty Adler, *Man of Letters, A Census of the Correspondence of H. L. Mencken* (Baltimore: Enoch Pratt Free Library, 1969).

Mitgang, Herbert, 1920-   Papers 1937-1979: 39 boxes. Author, journalist, motion picture producer. General correspondence, *New York Times* editorial correspondence 1970-1976, clippings. RESTRICTED: Donor's or donor's lawful agent's consent required until 1991 for access to Author's League files and to correspondence and papers relating to Mitgang's editorship of *New York Times* Op-ed page.

Mok, Michael, 1889?-1961. Papers ca. 1947-ca. 1959: 2 boxes. Columnist for *New York Post.* Correspondence, business files, programs, clippings. Correspondents include Arthur Garfield Hays, Richard Halliday, Richard Rogers, John Van Druten. 61 M 50.

Mumford, Ethel Watts, 1878-1940. Papers 1900-1934: 9 boxes. Includes clippings of 1913-1914 column for *New York Evening World.* 66 M 51.

New York Associated Press. Report Jan. 5, 1875: 11 pp. General statement of operations by J.W. Simonton, general agent, to D.M. Stone, president of New York Associated Press.

New York Tribune. Papers 1870-1880: 1 box. Correspondence of managing editor Whitelaw Reid with Gordon L. Ford and others; leases; cartoons.

New York Tribune. Advertisement ledger 1855-1869: 448 pp.

Paterson, Isabel Bowler, 1886-1961. Letters 1924-1960: ca. 65 items. Author and columnist with *New York Herald Tribune.* Letters to Lincoln Fischer, fashion model and Paris editor of *Harper's Bazaar.*

Post, Helen Wilmans, 1831-1907. Scrapbook 1900-1931: 1 item. Journalist with *Overland Monthly, Chicago Express.* Founder of *The Woman's World.* Publisher of *Freedom.* Editor and publisher of *Mental Science*. Scrapbook compiled by Eugene Del Mar in 1931 as a memorial to Post. 85 M 46.

Riis, Jacob, 1849-1914. Papers 1871-1916: 7 boxes. Journalist, social reformer, photographer. Correspondence, diaries, lecture notes, photographs. 69 M 48; 70 M 24.

Raymond, Henry J., 1820-1869. Papers 1840-1897: 1 box. First editor of *New York Times*. Correspondents include Henry Bergh, Simon Cameron, Rufus Choate, Schuyler Colfax, R.H. Dana, Sr., R.H. Dana, Jr., John A. Dix, Stephen A. Douglas, Edward Everett, Hamilton Fish, Horace Greeley, John Hay, Louis Kossuth, S.P. Lyman, Charles Summer, Daniel Webster, Thurlow Weed, Henry Wilson.

Sargent, George Henry, 1867-1931. papers: 15 boxes. Journalist with *Boston Evening Transcript* 1895-1931.

Seitz, Don Carlos, 1862-1935. Papers 1882-1934: 2 vol. and 4 boxes. Journalist with *New York World*. Correspondents include Arthur Brisbane, Josephus Daniels, Frank N. Doubleday, H.L. Mencken, George Foster Peabody, Lincoln Steffens, Oswald B. Villard.

Seldes, George. Manuscript: 300 pp. Original typescript of *Freedom of the Press* with authors corrections and revisions.

Shaw, Albert, 1857-1947. Papers 1874-1947: 181 boxes, 44 vol. Editor and publisher of *Review of Reviews*. Correspondents include Albert J. Beveridge, Nicholas Murray Butler, Richart T. Ely, John H. Finley, Charles Evans Hughes, J. Franklin Jameson, Theodore Roosevelt, W.T. Snead. 85 M 30; 63 M 77; 65 M 85; 68 M 12; 68 M 23; 68 M 41.

Skinner, Constance Lindsay, 1877-1939. Papers 1876-1939: 16 boxes and 5 pkgs. Scrapbooks, clippings, notebooks.

Thompson, Ralph, 1904-1979. Papers 1929-1960: 2 boxes. Editor. Book columnist with *New York Times*. Letters. Correspondents include Ernest Hemingway, H.L. Mencken, Sean O'Casey, Ezra Pound. Listing available.

Tucker, Benjamin Ricketson, 1854-1939. Papers 1870-1960: 58 ft. Philosophical anarchist, author, editor and publisher. Editor of *Liberty*. Correspondence, manuscripts, scrapbooks. Correspondents include Steven T. Byington, Arthur C. Fifield, Joseph Labadie, Laurence Labadie, John Henry Mackay, Sidney H.

Morse, George Schum, Lincoln Steffans, Brand Whitlock. Unpublished inventory available.

Towne, Charles Hanson, 1877-1949. Papers 1891-1948: 9 boxes. Editorial asst. *Cosmopolitan*. Editor of *Smart Set, Delineator, Designer, McClure's, Harper's Bazaar*. Columnist for *New York American* 1931-1937. Correspondence, writings, financial papers, photographs, clippings. Correspondents include Richard Le Gallienne, Somerset Maugham, Royal Cortissoz, Gertrude Atherton, Fannie Hurst, Edgar Lee Masters, Zona Gale, Ellen Glasgow, Edgar P. Snow, Carolyn Wells Houghton, Theodosia P. Faulks, Marie Adelaide Belloc, Major Edward Bowes; poetry by his student J.D. Salinger. 49 M 110; 49 M 120.

Uncensored. Records 1938-1942: 13 boxes. Public affairs newsletter. Correspondence of editors Sidney Hertzberg and Cushman Reynolds, business and financial papers, notes, file of letters received by Milton S. Mayer in response to an anti-war article by him published in *Saturday Evening Post* Oct. 7, 1939. Correspondents include Charles A. Beard, Stuart Chase, John T. Flynn, C. Hartley Grattan, Frank C. Hanighen, Quincy Howe, B.W. Huebsch, George Ross Leighton, Ferdinand Lundberg, Thomas Vernon Rankin, Burton Rascoe, Porter Sargent, Oswald Garrison Villard.

Walsh, Joseph Cyrillus, 1870- Papers 1913-1947: 3 boxes and 1 vol. Editor of *Ireland*. Letters, papers, memorabilia. Box listing and index of correspondents available.

Webster, Noah, 1758-1843. Papers 1764-1843: 10 boxes and 12 vols. Lawyer, educator, editor of *American Magazine* and *New York Commercial Advertiser*. Correspondence, diaries, writings. Inventory available. Entire collection on a master negative film.

Werner, Morris R., 1897-1981. Papers 1920-1981: 5 boxes. Writer for *New Yorker*. Foreign correspondent for *Yorkshire Post* and Paris edition of *New York Herald Tribune*. Correspondents include Sir William Linton Andrews, August Belmont, Sr., Bruce Bliven, Andrew Carnegie, Gamaliel Bradford, E.E. Cummings, David B. Hill, Harry Houdini, Abraham Henry Hummel, Newbold Morris, Geoffrey Parsons, Jacob Riis, John D. Rockefeller, Jr., George Bernard Shaw, William Shawn, William L. Stone, Frank Sullivan, William Sulzer, Edmund Wilson. 81 M 11; 82 M 11; 82 M 32.

Williams, Timothy Shaler, 1862-1930. Papers 1876-1930: 8 boxes and 25 vols. Journalist in New York. Correspondence index available. 82 M 39.

Wingate, Charles Frederick, 1848-1909. Papers 1879-ca. 1902: 1 box. Editor of *Sanitary Engineer*.

World Government News, Inc. Records 1943-1952: 24 boxes, 23 cartons. Publishers of *World Government News*. General correspondence of editors Tom O. Griessmer, Hugh Nash, and Steward M. Ogilvy. Correspondents include Cass Canfield, Grenville Clark, Fyke Farmer, Georgia Lloyd, Henry Charles Usborne, Carl Van Doren. Box listing available.

New York State Library

• Manuscripts and Special Collections, New York State Library, 11th Floor, Cultural Education Center, Albany NY 12230. 518-474-4461. James Corsaro, Senior Librarian. 9 am-5 pm M-F. Photocopy services.

Bennett, James G. Deed of sale Apr. 22, 1826. Concerns establishment of *New York Courier*. 16796.

Biscoe, Walter S. Papers: 1 box. Notes, clippings relating to history of printing. SC16615.

Biscoe, Walter S. Notes on early printers and printing in Albany NY. Chiefly about Alexander and James Robertson, printers of *Albany Gazette* 1771-1772. 13244.

Bixby, George Stephenson. Papers 1872-1935: 15 boxes and 12 pkg. Lawyer and journalist. Correspondence, scrapbooks. HK12136.

Bixby family. Papers 1800-1912: 1 box. Includes correspondence relating to family's ownership of *Plattsburgh Republican.* SC16585.

Bryant, William Cullen. Letter Dec. 16, 1837: 1 pp. Concerns a meeting to discuss liberty of the press. 15831.

Carter, Nathaniel Hazeltine, 1787-1830. Letter: 2 pp. Concerns *Statesman.* 13456.

Comstock, James. Account book 1814-1819: 1 vol. Accounts for *Independent American* and *People's Watch-Tower.* 11122.

Gavit, Joseph. Newspaper records 1820-1930: 1 box. Bibliographies of newspapers of Albany NY and surrounding counties. SC17642.

Gavit, Joseph. Collection: 1 folder. Material relating to history of newspapers. SC16869.

Haines, Charles Glidden, 1792-1825. Letter Aug. 14, 1820: 3 pp. Discusses *Statesman.* 13457.

Greeley, Horace. Letter Mar. 2, 1856: 4 pp. 15639.

Reid, Whitelaw. Letter Nov. 22, 1878: 2 pp. Concerns obtaining subscribers to *Weekly Tribune.* 15810.

Public Advertiser. Scrapbook Nov. 30, 1776-June 19, 1783. SC16389.

Rosen, Hy. Cartoons 1945-   33 boxes. 1 pkg. Original political cartoons published in *Albany Times Union.* SC13603.

Schoharie County. Circuit Court. Presentation May 12, 1842: 4 pp. Concerns charges that *Helderburgh Advocate* is a public nuisance. 16582.

Smith, Christopher. Papers 1817-1903: 125 items. Includes material on *Herkimer County Journal.* HN12148.

Throop, Enos T. Letter Oct 23, 1837: 2 pp. Concerns financial aid to *Daily News.* 11324.

Tweed, William Marsh. Letter Nov. 1, 1861: 1 pp. Advice to newspaper publishers and editors against printing personal libels. 14647.

Van Benthuysen, Charles & Co. Papers 1846: 1 box. Business letters to printer of *Albany Argus.* Unpublished guide available. NZ16445.

Webster, Noah, 1758-1843. Letter Feb. 12, 1794: 4 pp. Concerns Federalist newspaper *Minerva.* 11327.

State University of New York at Binghamton

• University Library, State University of New York at Binghamton, Vestal Parkway East, Binghamton NY 13901. 607-777-4844. Marion Hanscom, Asst. Dir. for Special Collections and Fine Arts. 1-5 pm M-F. Photocopy services. Collection level records on RLIN.

Bernstein, David. Papers: 75 boxes. Journalist, editor, publisher. Correspondence, personal papers, business records.

Syracuse University

• George Arents Research Library for Special Collections, Syracuse University, Bird Library, Room 600, Syracuse NY 13244-2010. 315-423-2697 or 2585. Carolyn A. Davis, Manuscript Librarian. 8:30 am-5 pm M-F. Photocopy services. Collection level records on RLIN. Contacting Arents prior to visit is highly recommended.

Adams, Samuel Hopkins, 1871-1958. Papers 1925-1958: ca. 5 linear ft. Author and journalist. Correspondence. Correspondents include Horace B. Liveright, Bennett Cerf, Irita Van Dorn. NUC MC66-201.

Brisbane, Arthur, 1864-1936. Papers 1844-1938: ca. 6 linear ft. Newspaper editor. Correspondence, 90 scrapbooks with columns and editorials. Correspondents include Richard Harding Davis, William Randolph Hearst. NUC MC66-610.

Brown, Thomas Cook,   -1967. Papers 1929-1966: 8 linear ft. Columnist 1922-1962 for *Buffalo Courier-Express*.

Considine, Robert B., 1906-1975. Papers 1921-1966: 45 linear ft. Worked for *Washington Post, Washington Herald,* International News Service. "On the Line" radio news analysis program. Correspondence, manuscripts.

Crider, John, 1906-1966. Papers 1868-1966: 2 linear ft. Journalist with *New York Times*. Editor-in-Chief *Boston Herald*. Subject files, writings.

Forbes, Bertie Charles, 1880-1954. Papers 1892-1964: 9 linear ft. Journalist with *Rand Daily Mail, Journal of Commerce*. Business and financial editor of *New York American*. Founder of *Forbes* in 1916. Correspondence, writings, memorabilia. Correspondents include William Randolph Hearst, Herbert Hoover, Wendell Willkie.

Gilmore, Eddy Lanier King, 1907-1967. Papers: .5 linear ft. Journalist with *Atlantic Journal* 1929-1932, and *Washington Daily News* 1932-1935. Chief of Associated Press in Soviet Union 1941-1953. Correspondents include Edward R. Murrow, Casey Stengel.

Harger, Alice Rogers. Papers 1801-1881, 1920-1964: 2 linear ft. Reporter for *Los Angeles Herald* 1923-1924; writer for *New York*

Times and *Washington Star* 1929-1934. Aviation reporter for North American Newspaper Alliance 1934-1940.

Harris, Edward, 1910-1976. Papers 1928-1961: ca. 5 linear ft. *St. Louis Star Times* 1933-1940; *St. Louis Post Dispatch* 1940-1959. Correspondence, subject file, manuscripts.

Hazlett, Henry. Papers 1920-1958: 6 linear ft. Economic journalist with *New York Times, Wall Street Journal, Newsweek, Nation, American Mercury.* Correspondence, manuscripts, printed material.

Higgins, Marguerite, -1966. Papers 1935-1974: 23 linear ft. War correspondent during Korean and Vietnam wars whose work appeared in *New York Herald Tribune, Newsday, Newsweek, Time.* Subject file, correspondence, clippings, manuscripts, personal materials.

Levine, Irving R., 1922- Papers 1946-1964: 21 linear ft. Worked for *Providence Journal,* International News Service, NBC, *Times of London.* Correspondence, subject files, commentaries, articles.

Lewis, Fulton, Jr., 1903-1966. Papers 1920-1966: 90 linear ft. Worked for *Washington Herald, Buffalo Courier-Express.* Radio broadcasts for Mutual Broadcasting System included "Top of the News," "Chimney Sweep," "Your Defense Reporter." Correspondence, scripts, publications, reference and personal files. Correspondents include Bernard Baruch, Herbert Hoover.

Lewis, Fulton III. Papers 1947-1967: 2.5 linear ft. Correspondence, subject file, manuscripts and published material, continuing his father's work.

Lerner, Leo, 1907-1965. Papers 1927-1966: 34.5 linear ft. Editor and publisher of Myers Publication Co. Also held offices in Lincoln Belmont Publishing Co., Times Home Newspapers, Neighborhood Press of Chicago. Correspondence, writings, printed material.

Pearson, Drew, 1887-1969. Press releases 1945-1969: 24 linear ft.

Pegler, Westbrook, 1884-1969. Press releases 1951-1962: 4.5 linear ft.

Roosevelt, Nicholas, 1893- Papers 1846-1962: 32 linear ft. Journalist. Diaries, notes, published material. Correspondents include Winston Churchill, John Gunther, Cordell Hull, Sinclair Lewis. NUC MC68-1750.

Royster, Vermont Connecticut, 1914-   Papers 1931-1971: 14 linear ft. Editor of *Wall Street Journal.* President of American Society of Newspaper Editors. Correspondence, subject file, writings. NUC MC68-1751.

Sherrod, Robert L., 1909-   Papers 1910-1963: 25 linear ft. Journalist with several southern newspapers, *Time, Life,* and *Saturday Evening Post.* Editorial coordinator for Curtis Publishing Co.   Correspondence, subject file, writings, published material. Correspondents include Hanson Baldwin, William F. Buckley, Walter Winchell. NUC MC69-1832.

Thompson, Dorothy, 1894-1961. Papers 1917-1961: 75 linear ft. Syndicated columnist with "On the Record." Manuscripts, scripts, research materials. Correspondents include Winston Churchill, Clifton Fadiman, Newspaper Guild of America. NUC MC69-521.

University of Rochester

• Dept. of Rare Books and Special Collections, Rush Rhees Library, University of Rochester, Rochester NY 14627. 716-275-4477. Karl Kabelac, Manuscripts Librarian. 9 am-5 pm M-F. Photocopy services. Collection level records on RLIN. See also *Guide to Historical Resources in Monroe County, New York Repositories* (Ithaca: New York Historical Resources Center, Cornell University, 1980-1983). Please notify in advance of research visit.

Adams, George Matthew, 1878-1962. Papers 1899-1959: 1 box. Founder of George Matthew Adams News Service. Correspondence, photographs, printed material, biographical data, memorabilia. Correspondents include Ray Stannard Baker, Paul Jordan-Smith, Ben Hur Lampman, Rebecca McCarn, Fred S. Mathias, Bruce Barton, Henry Beston, Gelett Burgess, Edna Ferber, Hamlin Garland, George Ade, Kenneth Grahame, Edgar Guest, Haniel Long, Christopher Morley, Herbert Hoover, Theodore Roosevelt, Eleanor Roosevelt. Register available.

Cominsky, Jacob Robert, 1899-1968. Papers 1906-1968: 3 boxes. 63 pkgs. Publisher of *Saturday Review.* Correspondence with Louis Wiley of the *New York Times* and with staff and contributors of *Saturday Review*, memorabilia, photographs, testimonials, clippings, scrapbooks. Register available.

Weed, Thurlow, 1793-1882. Papers 1775-1900: 20 cu. ft., 4 reels microfilm. Politician, editor. Political and personal correspondence, financial and legal papers, broadsides, pamphlets, scrapbooks, photographs, memorabilia. Correspondents include Alvah Hunt, Millard Fillmore, Hamilton Fish, Francis Granger, Horace Greeley, Edwin D. Morgan, William H. Seward, Frederick Whittlesey, John Bigelow, Erastus Corning, Daniel Webster. Register available.

Wiley, Louis, 1859-1935. Papers 1858-1954: 20 cu. ft. Business manager of *New York Times* for 29 years. Correspondence, photographs, biographical data, memorandum books, memorabilia. Correspondents include Franklin D. Roosevelt, Walter Duranty, David Belasco, Fiorello H. LaGuardia, William Allen White, Sir Thomas Lipton, Nicholas Murray Butler, Alfred E. Smith, Edna Ferber, Andrew Mellon, William S. Hart, Carrie Chapman Catt, William E. Werner, Admiral Richard Byrd, Eleanor Roosevelt, Margaret Bourke-White, James Farley, Adolph S. Ochs, Lord Beaverbrook. Register available.

NORTH DAKOTA

State Archives and Historical Research Library

• State Archives and Historical Research Library, State Historical Society, North Dakota Heritage Center, Bismarck ND 58505-0179. 701-224-2668. David P. Gray, Deputy State Archivist. 8 am-5 pm M-F. Photocopy services. See also David P. Grey, comp., *Guide to Manuscripts* (Bismarck: State Historical Society of North Dakota, 1985).

The American Liberal. Records 1926: 1 vol. Williston ND. Account book and financial report. A304.

Bryant family. Papers 1885-1931: 4.5 ft. Includes papers of O. Frank Bryant, publisher of *Napoleon Homestead.* A132.

Dale, Alfred Samuel, 1896-1974. Papers 1921-1942: 10 ft. Includes records of *North Dakota Progressive.* Inventory available. A129.

Farmers' Independent Publishing Co. Records 1920-1963: 1 ft. Newspaper cooperative which published *McLean County Independent,* Garrison ND. Minutes of stockholders' meetings, correspondence, ledgers, financial statements. A439.

Mercer County Republican. Records 1907-1918: 1 vol. Cash ledger and subscription list. A246.

National League of American Pen Women. Records 1927, 1935-1954: 1.75 ft. State organization records and chapter records for Fargo, Medora, Bismarck, Williston. Correspondence, annual reports, newsletters, rosters, biographical sketches, scrapbooks. A65.

Nelson, Carl, 1873-1931. Papers: 6 items. Cando ND editor. Photocopies of reminiscences, poetry, articles, obituaries. B549.

Nelson, John Emil, 1883-1972. Manuscript 1958: 1 item. Editor of *Litchfield Bulletin.* Excerpts from column describing events from 1880s to 1950s. B244.

North Dakota Press Assoc. Scrapbook ca. 1915: 1 microfilm roll. A378.

North Dakota Press Women. Records 1950-1983: 1 ft. Minutes, correspondence, charter, histories, programs rosters, speeches scrapbook, photographs, membership records.

Pioneer Express. Subscription list 1906-1910: 1 vol. Pembina ND. B550.

Simons, Kenneth W., 1898-1948. Papers 1933-1951: 1.25 ft. Editor of *Bismarck Tribune.* A134.

OHIO

Cincinnati Historical Society

• Cincinnati Historical Society, Eden Park, Cincinnati OH 45202. 513-241-4622. Jonathan Dembo, Supervisor of Archives and Manuscripts. 9 am-4:30 pm Tu-Sa.

Bennett, C. Letter Apr. 12, 1849: 3 pp. Letter to B. Hough, Jr. referring to Mr. Goodman, editor of *Watchman of the Valley.*

Bethel Fair Journal. 1872. Advertising contract, subscription list, letter.

Browne, John W., 1764-1813. Letters, documents 1800-1838: 1 box.

Browne, John W., 1764-1813. Printing bills Dec. 30, 1812; Feb. 7, 1815.

Cincinnati Daily Tribune. Correspondence: 1839.

Cincinnati Enquirer. Letters and printed materials: Mar. 1956. Concerns employees vs. Roger Ferger, Pres. Includes statements by Jim Ratliff, Joel Bowlby, Joel Irwin.

Cincinnati Freie Presse Co. Records: 92 vols and 1 pkg. Correspondence, financial and subscription records.

Cincinnati Gazette. Statistics for year ending June 30, 1877. Comparisons to other Cincinnati newspapers.

Clarke, Robert, 1829-1899. Early publications west of the Alleghanies: 191 pp.

Coggeshall, William Turner. History of the Cincinnati press 1793-1851: 76 pp.

Dabney, Wendell Phillips, 1865-1952. Papers 1905-1964: 2 boxes. Register available.

Forman, Frances Marie, 1913-   Letter Mar. 3, 1970: 2 pp. Letter to Gordon Baker.

Gallagher, William Davis, 1808-1894. Letter Feb. 1881: 22 pp. Letter to C.D. Drake

Gampfer, Nelson M. Letter June 30, 1960. Letter to Cincinnati Historical Society giving history of *Hoosier Radio Announcer* published Nov. 22, 1931-June 12, 1932.

Gano, John Stites, 1766-1822. Papers 1775-1817: 3 boxes. Register available.

Hall, Virginius Cornick, 1900-1957. Speeches 1946-1952: 38 pp.

Halstead, Murat, 1829-1908. Correspondence 1851-1908: 3 boxes.

Halstead, Murat. Family papers 1875-1908: 5 boxes. Letters, telegrams, clippings, scrapbook.

Halstead, Murat, 1829-1908. Writings: 1 box.

Halstead, William Leon, 1876-   Murat Halstead: 7 pp. From "The Story of the Halsteads of the United States."

Halstead, William Leon. Unpublished manuscript: 241 pp. Biography of "Field Marshall" Murat Halstead.

Hammond, Charles, 1779-1840. Letters and documents 1800-1840: 1 reel microfilm.

Heaton, David, 1823-1870. Papers 1800-1912: .17 cu. ft. Correspondence, financial papers, deeds, mortgages, newspaper material.

Henderson, Will. Letters Feb. 26, 1923; Aug. 19, 1923. Gives early history of *Cincinnati Enquirer*.

Henry, Edward A. Cincinnati as a literary and publishing centre, 1793-1880: 15 pp.

James, John Hough, 1800-1881. Personal reminiscences of a newspaper called the *Olio*: 3 pp.

Jones, Adolphus Eberhardt, 1813-1889. Letter Sept. 3, 1862: 1 pp. Letter from Hamilton County provost marshall to C.W. Starbuck, proprietor of *Cincinnati Daily Times*, ordering it to suspend publication.

Norwood Enterprise. Account book 1908-1924: 152 pp.

Parks, Warren Wright, 1896-1982. Papers 1923-1980. Diaries, photographs, publications. Register available.

Piatt, Donn, 1819-1891. Letter Apr. 5, 1880: 2 pp. Letter to George Alfred Townsend.

Starbuck, C.W. and Co. Letter Nov.19, 1869: 1 p.

Zinn, Peter, 1819-1880. Diary June 1840-June 1842: 278 pp.

Hudson Library and Historical Society

• Archives Division, Hudson Library and Historical Society, 22 Aurora St. Hudson OH 44236. 216-653-6658. James F. Caccamo, archivist. 10 am-9 pm M-Tu,Th; 10 am-5 pm F-Sa. Photocopying of manuscripts prohibited. Write or call prior to visit.

Izant, Grace Goulder. Collection: 14 boxes, 28 scrapbooks, 4 drawers photos. Journalist with *Cleveland Plain Dealer* 1914-1917, 1940-1969.

Kent State University

• Dept. of Special Collections, Kent State University Libraries, Kent OH 44240. 216-672-2270. Alex Gildzen, Curator of Special Collections. 8 am-noon, 1 pm-5 pm M-F. Photocopy services.

Fuldheim, Dorothy, 1893-   Papers: 4 boxes. News analyst WEWS-TV, Cleveland, 1946-1984. Manuscripts, commentaries, clippings. Correspondents include I.W. Able, John H. Chafee, Lillian Gish, Hubert H. Humphrey, John S. Knight, Walter F. Mondale, Richard M. Nixon, Nelson A. Rockefeller, Seth Taft, Thomas Vail, M.C. Watters.

Hanlin, John Joseph, 1920-1976. Papers: 11 boxes. Reporter for *Lorain Journal* 1941-1947; foreign correspondent and magazine writer 1948-1960. Articles, clippings, photographs, scrapbook. Correspondents include Phoebe Lou Adams, Naomi Burton, Frank J. Lausche, Scott Meredith, Dwight Pennington, Courtland C. Smith, William D. Taylor.

Slack, Charles Wesley, 1825-1885. Papers: 12 boxes. Reporter for *Boston Journal*; editor and publisher *Boston Commonwealth* 1863-1885. Correspondents include Amos Bronson Alcott, Henry Ward Beecher, Phillips Brooks, Salmon P. Chase, Richard Henry Dana, Frederick Douglass, Ralph Waldo Emerson, William Lloyd Garrison, Thomas Wentworth Higginson, Julia Ward Howe, Wendell Phillips, Charles Sumner, Henry David Thoreau.

Ohio Historical Society

• Archives-Library Division, Ohio Historical Society, 1985 Velma Ave., Columbus OH 43211. 614-297-2510. Gary J. Arnold, Head of Research Services. 9 am-5 pm Tu-Sa. Photocopy services. Collection level records on OCLC. RESTRICTED: Collections requiring special equipment must be used with staff present and require at least 24 hours advance reservation.

AVCO-Miami: WLW Radio Collection 1936-1961: 1,555 discs. Recordings of local and national programming of Cincinnati station. AUD 42.

Arter, William Andrew, 1911-1972. Papers 1964-1972: ca. 5 ft. Advertising consultant, educator, newspaper columnist, historian. Correspondence, research files and photos for "Columbus Vignettes" column. MSS 374.

Blue Pencil Club of Ohio. Records 1961-1976: .5 ft. Correspondence, news releases, memoranda, notes, programs, speeches. MSS 753.

Buckeye Press Assoc. Minute book Feb. 4, 1926-May 16, 1930: 1 vol. Vol. 590.

Chenoweth, Doral Park, 1921-   Papers 1968-1973: .5 ft. Columnist, editor, publisher. MSS 439.

Coggeshall, William Turner, 1824-1867. Papers 1842-1868: 2 ft. Author, journalist, and U. S. Minister to Ecuador. Correspondence, articles, biographies, speeches, dispatches. MSS 115.

Comly, James Monroe Stuart, 1832-1887. Papers 1856-1926: 3 rolls microfilm. Army officer, journalist, politician. Correspondence, diaries, articles, clippings, scrapbooks. MIC 33.

Forbes, Benjamin Platt, b. 1873.   Papers 1836-1974: 9 ft. Newspaper editor and publisher and chocolate manufacturer. Correspondence, sales records, clippings, photos, scrapbooks. MSS 429.

Hassaurek, Friedrick, 1832-1885.   Papers 1849-1881: 2 ft. Lawyer, editor, politician, diplomat.   Correspondence, documents, manuscripts. MSS 113.

Hecker, June.   Diary June-Sept. 1910: 120 pp.   Newspaper columnist. VFM 3575.

Karger, Gustavus J., 1886-1924.   21 items 1908-1950. Washington correspondent for *Cincinnati Times-Star*. VFM 3036.

Kaufmann, Peter, 1800-1869.   Papers 1806-1869: 4 cu. ft. Newspaper editor. *Vaterlandsfreund* 1831; *Deutsche in Ohio und Ohio Staatzeitung* 1861-1869. Correspondence, diaries, business records. Many in German. MSS 136.

Kinder, George D., 1836-1917? Papers 1830-1903: .25 ft. Owner of *Putnam County Sentinel*. Correspondence, records, enrollment lists. MSS 19.

Locke, Robinson, 1856-1920.   Papers 1884-1931: 2 ft. Reporter for *Toledo Blade*.   Correspondence, reporters' notebooks.   MSS 234.

Long, James M. 2 vols.: 1944-1945. Associated Press dispatches from Supreme Headquarters, European theater, World War II. Vol. 108-109.

Mansfield, Edward Deering, 1801-1880. Papers 1810-1878: ca. 180 items and 7 vol. Author and editor. Correspondence, diary. Correspondents include Robert J. Breckenridge, Salmon P. Chase, Thomas Corwin, William Dennison, Jr., Rutherford B.

Hayes, William Holmes McGuffey, Henry J. Raymond, Daniel Webster. MSS 69.

Maris, Clarence. ca. 17 items ca. 1890. Notes for articles for *Ohio State Journal.* VFM 3382.

Morrow family. Papers 1806-1927: 2 ft. Josiah Morrow, 1838-1928, writer, lawyer, columnist for *Lebanon Western Star.* MSS 232.

Nationwide Communications, Inc. Records 1949-1970: 57 ft. Broadcasting Company controlling radio stations WNCI-FM and WRFD-AM. Files, newscast scripts, editorials, logbooks. MSS 377.

Ohio Legislative Correspondents Assoc. Records 1919-1960: .75 ft. Minutes, history of organization, membership roster to 1960. MSS 816.

Ohio Newspaper Assoc. Records 1927-1980: 13 ft. Subject files, documents. MSS 772.

Ohio Newspaper Women's Assoc. Records 1926-1977: .75 ft. Minutes, convention programs, correspondence. MSS 773.

Powers, Stephen. 9pp. Civil War journalist. VFM 2109.

Purdy, James L., 1793-1896. Papers 1818-1883: 3 ft. Farmer; lawyer; editor of *Mansfield Gazette.* Business and personal correspondence, registers, ledgers. MSS 229.

Rodgers, Andrew Denny, 1900-1981. Papers 1901-1980: 7.5 ft. MSS 748.

Smith, William Henry, 1833-1896. Papers 1800-1896: 8 ft. Journalist, politician, historian. Correspondence, diaries, scrapbooks, albums. Correspondents include Murat Halstead, William D. Howells, Donn Piatt, Joseph Pulitzer, Whitelaw Reid, John Sherman. MSS 2.

Tappan, Benjamin, 1773-1857. Papers 1795-1873: ca. 650 items. Bulk of correspondence is with his son, Eli Todd Tappan, a newspaper editor. MSS 326.

Tappan, Eli Todd, 1824-1888. Family papers 1824-1904: 2 ft. Correspondence. MSS 100.

Thomas, Edward Sinclair, 1891-1982. Papers 1908-1981: 5.5 ft. Naturalist, author, *Columbus Dispatch* columnist. MSS 751.

WBNS-TV Video Collection 1960s-1970s: ca. 900 reels. Columbus television documentaries. VID 1.

WOSU AM & FM Audio Collection 1967-1968: 79 reels. Recordings of historic events, prominent personalities, political campaigns, government affairs. AUD 11.

WOSU Radio Station. Records 1940-1943: .25 ft. Scripts, correspondence pertaining to Ohio history. MSS 51.

Warwick, Frank M. (Jack), 1861-1947. Misc. papers 1941-1947: 5 pieces. *Toledo Blade* staff writer. MSS 1917.

Warwick, Frank M. (Jack), 1861-1947. Manuscript: 4 pp. Partner of Warren Harding in *Marion Star*; later on editorial staff of *Toledo Blade*. Article "President Harding's story of his mother." VFM 1918.

Ohio State University

• Jerome Lawrence and Robert E. Lee Theatre Research Institute, The Ohio State University Libraries, 1430 Lincoln Tower, 1800 Cannon Dr., Columbus OH 43210-1230. 614-292-8252. Nena Couch, Curator. 8 am-5 pm M-F. Photocopy services. Collection level records on OCLC.

Edwards, Bill, 1930-1987. Collection: 14 boxes. Sports editor *Anchorage Daily News* 1963-1964; asst. sports editor *Bakersfield Californian*; wire editor and entertainment editor *Alhambra Post-Advocate*; Legit editor and creator of entertainment crossword puzzle *Daily Variety* 1966-1987. Drafts and clippings of columns, typescripts, correspondence, programs.

Radcliffe, E.B. (Ellis Brownell), 1904-1977: 8 linear ft. *Worchester Telegram* 1929; *Cincinnati Commercial Tribune* 1929-1930; *Cincinnati Enquirer* 1931-1969. Scrapbooks of columns.

Wilson, Earl, 1907-1987. Collection: 35 linear ft. *Piqua Daily Call, Columbus Dispatch,* International News Service, *Akron Beacon Journal, Washington Post* 1923-1935; *New York Post* 1935-1983; WOR-Mutual 1945. Columnist "It Happened Last Night." Drafts, interview notebooks, files, correspondence. Extensive files on Frank Sinatra, Marilyn Monroe.

• Library for Communication and Graphic Arts, The Ohio State University Libraries, Columbus OH 43210. 614-292-0538. Lucy Shelton Caswell, Curator. 8 am-5 pm M-F. Photocopy services. Collection level records on OCLC. Advance notice of visit is suggested.

Only collections with ten or more original editorial cartoons are listed. Contact the library for information about holdings of the work of political/editorial cartoonists who are not listed.

Ashley, Edward James. 16 editorial cartoons: 1979-1980. Published in the *Toledo Blade*.

Association of American Editorial Cartoonists. Archives 1956-present: ca. 12 linear ft. Correspondence, minutes, photographs. Complete run of *AAEC Notebook*. Includes oral history interviews with founding members, officers, and other members.

Baer, John M. 12 editorial cartoons: 191-?-193-? Baer is the only U. S. Congressman to have worked as an editorial cartoonist while in office.

Basset, Brian Willard, 1957-   165 cartoons: 1975-1978, 1982. Published in *OSU Lantern, Detroit Free Press, Seattle Times*.

Beard, Ned. 217 editorial cartoons: 1970s. Published in *Newark Weekly Post*.

Crawford, William H., 1913-1982. ca. 125 editorial cartoons: 1950s-1970s.   Also 41 clip files: 1939-1965.   Published in *Washington Post, Washington Daily News, Newark News*. With Newspaper Enterprise Assoc.

Dumm, Frances Edwina, 1893-   2 scrapbooks: 1915-1917. Ca. 200 editorial cartoon clippings published in *Columbus Monitor* and *Columbus Daily Monitor*. Dumm is believed to be the first woman to work full-time as a newspaper editorial cartoonist.

McCay, Winsor, 1867?-1934. 25 editorial cartoons and 75 tearsheets of editorial cartoons: 1899-1934. Part of Woody Gelman Collection.

Ireland, William Addison (Billy), 1880-1935. 25 editorial cartoons: 1912-1935 and 325 clippings: 1916-1917. Published in *Columbus Evening Dispatch.*

Kuekes, Edward Daniel, 1901-1987. 103 editorial cartoons. Published in *Cleveland Plain Dealer*. Won Pulitzer Prize in 1953.

McCutcheon, John Tinney, 1870-1987. 21 editorial cartoons: 1906-1942. Published in *Chicago Tribune*. Won Pulitzer Prize in 1932.

Osrin, Raymond Harold, 1928-   1,683 editorial cartoons: 1964-1979. Published in *Cleveland Plain Dealer.*

Payne, Eugene G. 1919-   121 editorial cartoons: 1983-1986. Published in *Charlotte Observer.* Won Pulitzer Prize in 1968.

Peters, Mike, 1943-   ca. 100 editorial cartoons: 1970s-1980s. Published in *Dayton Daily News.* Won Pulitzer Prize in 1981.

Poinier, Arthur Best, 1911-   ca. 150 editorial cartoons and 29 proofs: 1949-1979. Published in *Detroit News.*

Priggee, Milt. ca. 1,100 editorial cartoons: 1982-1987. Published in *Dayton Journal Herald.*

Stahler, Jeff. ca. 250 editorial cartoons: 1984-1985. Published in *Columbus Citizen Journal.*

Warren, L.D., 1906-   32 editorial cartoons: 1947-1978. Published in *Cincinnati Enquirer.*

Werner, Charles George, 1909-   74 editorial cartoons: most 1985. Published in *Indianapolis Star.* Won Pulitzer Prize in 1939.

White, Edward Richard (Ned), 1913-1979. 385 original editorial cartoons: 1938-1963. Published in *Akron Beacon Journal.*

Whitman, Bert. 135 editorial cartoons: 1965-1981. Published in *Phoenix Gazette.*

Willis, James Scott, 1957-   118 editorial cartoons: 1978-1986. Most published in *OSU Lantern.* Also 3 folders clippings of *Cleveland Press* cartoons.

• Rare Books and Manuscripts, The Ohio State University Libraries, 1858 Neil Ave. Mall, Columbus OH 43210. 614-292-5938. Robert A. Tibbetts, Curator. 8 am-5 pm M-F; 10 am-2 pm Sa. Photocopy services.

Bergman, Bernard Aaron, 1894-1930. Papers 1933-1978: 2.5 linear ft. Managing editor of *New Yorker* 1931-1933. Later associated with several Philadelphia papers including *Philadelphia Record* 1935-1942 and *Philadelphia Bulletin* 1961-1980. Correspondents include William Randolph Hearst, H.L. Mencken, John O'Hara, Theodore Friedman Lewis, James M. Cain, Dale Rex Coman, Morris Leopold Ernst, Ira Gershwin, Syd Hoff, Ogden Nash, S.J. Perelman, Carl Rose, Frank Sullivan, James Thurber, E.B. White, Andrew Wyeth. Guide and index available.

Creelman, James. 1859-1915. Papers: 5 boxes. Reporter, foreign correspondent *New York Herald* 1878-1896; war correspondent *New York Herald* 1894-1896; *New York Journal* 1896-1900; special correspondent and editorial writer *New York World* 1900-1906. Correspondents include James Gordon Bennett, William J. Bryan, Mary B. Bryan, William Randolph Hearst, Joseph Pulitzer.

Peninsula Library and Historical Society

• Peninsula Library and Historical Society, 6105 Riverview Rd., PO Box 236, Peninsula OH 44264. 216-657-2291. Randolph S. Bergdorf. 9 am-8 pm M-Th; 9 am-5 pm F-Sa. Photocopy services.

Bordner, Robert, 1899-1964. Collection 1920-1960: 4 drawers. Reporter, columnist *Cleveland Plain Dealer*, *Brecksville News*, *The Gristmill.*

Brown, D. Web, 1876-1974. Collection: 1 file plus prints. Political cartoonist with *Akron Beacon Journal.*

Rutherford B. Hayes Presidential Center

• Rutherford B. Hayes Presidential Center, Spiegel Grove, Fremont OH 43420. 419-332-2081. Janet L. Haas, Reference Librarian. 1:30 pm-5 pm M; 9 am-5 pm Tu-Sa. Photocopy services.

Ames, Mary Clemmer, 1839-1884. Collection: 145 pieces. Wrote for *New York Independent* 1866-1884; columnist for *Brooklyn Daily Union* 1869-1872. Correspondents include Henry Chandler Bowen, Richard Rogers Bowker, Samuel Bowles, Oliver Johnson, Horace Greeley.

Curtis, George William, 1824-1892. Papers: 8 folders plus 91 items in Hayes Papers. Editor of *Harper's Weekly* 1863-

Howells, William Dean, 1837-1920. Papers: 2 linear ft. plus 73 items in Hayes Papers. Reporter, editorial writer *Ohio State Journal* 1856-1861; editor *Atlantic Monthly* 1866-1881; editor *Cosmopolitan Magazine* 1891-1892. Correspondents include William Cullen Bryant, Samuel Langhorne Clemens, George William Curtis, Ralph Waldo Emerson, Oliver Wendell Holmes, Julia Ward Howe, Sarah Orne Jewett, Henry W. Longfellow, James Russell Lowell, Harriet B. Stowe, Rutherford B. Hayes.

Kellar, Andrew Jackson, 1835-1907. Hayes Papers: 29 pieces. Editor of *Memphis Avalanche* 1870s. Correspondents include Rutherford B. Hayes, Webb C. Hayes.

Keeler, Lucy Elliot, 1864-1930. Collection: 35 boxes. Publisher *Pot Pourri* ca. 1884; reporter *Fremont Journal* ca. 1880-1900; wrote for *Harper's Weekly, Youth's Companion, Scribner's, Atlantic Monthly* after 1900. Correspondents include Tarkington Baker, Charles R. Williams, Edward Stanwood.

Locke, David Ross, 1833-1888 and Locke, Robinson, 1856-1920. Collection: 10 boxes. David R. was a satirist and editor *Toledo Blade* 1865-1888; Robinson, editor *Toledo Blade* 1888-1920. Correspondents include Thomas Nast.

Lossing, Benson J., 1813-1891. Collection: 43 boxes. Joint editor *Poughkeepsie Telegraph* 1835; *Poughkeepsie Casket* ca. 1839. Correspondents include Lyman C. Draper, Frederic Kidder, Frank Leslie.

Mohun, Clare Hanson. Hayes Papers: 124 pieces. Used pen name of Raymonde. Washington social correspondent *Cincinnati Enquirer* 1870s.

Nast, Thomas, 1840-1902. Papers: 6 boxes. Illustrator *Frank Leslie's Illustrated News* ca. 1855-1859; *New York Illustrated News* 1859-1860; cartoonist *Harper's Weekly* 1862-1886. Correspondence mostly family and consular years. Many illustrated letters.

Nordhoff, Charles, 1830-1901. Papers: 1 folder plus ca. 40 items in Hayes Papers. Journalist and editor *Harper & Bros.* 1857-1861; managing editor *New York Evening Post* 1861-1871; Washington correspondent *New York Herald* 1874-1890. Correspondents include Charles A. Dana, Rutherford B. Hayes.

Reid, Whitelaw, 1837-1912. Papers 1 folder plus 24 items in Hayes Papers. Editor *Xenia News* 1858-1859; correspondent *Cincinnati Gazette* 1860-1868; editor-in-chief *New York Tribune* 1872-1905. Correspondents include Robert Underwood, Rutherford B. Hayes.

Snead, Austine, d. 1888. Hayes Papers: 100 pieces. Pen name of Miss Grundy. Washington social columnist *New York Daily Graphic, Washington Star, Louisville Courier Journal, Hartford Evening Post* 1870s.

University of Cincinnati

• Archives and Rare Books Dept., University of Cincinnati, 808 Blegen Library, Cincinnati OH 45221. 513-475-6459. Alice M.

Cornell, Head. 8 am-5 pm M-F. Photocopy services. Inventories available.

Basset, Gene. Warren Collection: 1 political cartoon.

Berry, Jim. Warren Collection: 15 *Berry's World* cartoons. 1965-1967.

Bierce, Ambrose, 1842-1913. Letters: 59 items. 1895-1911. RESTRICTED: Permission of Dept. necessary for use.

Dowling, Dan. Warren Collection: 6 political cartoons. *Kansas City Star* 1962, 1967, 1969.

Ficklen, Herc. Warren Collection: 6 political cartoons. *Dallas Morning News* 1969-1971.

Hamm, Jack. Warren Collection: 1 political cartoon: 1966.

Henrikson, Arthur A. Warren Collection: 6 political cartoons. Paddock Pub. 1970.

Ivey, Jim. Warren Collection: 5 political cartoons. *Orlando Sentinal Star* 1970.

Jurden, Jack. Warren Collection: 46 political cartoons. *Wilmington Evening Journal.*

McFeatters, Dale. Warren Collection: 7 political cartoons.

Maxwell, James A. Collection 1940s-1960s: 8 boxes. Articles, correspondence, books.

Morris, John Milt. Warren Collection: 25 political cartoons. Associated Press 1969-1970.

Pletcher, Eldon. Warren Collection: 19 cartoons. *New Orleans Times Picayune* 1969-1970.

Riedell, John. Warren Collection: 19 political cartoons. *Peoria Journal Star.*

Shafer, Claude. Warren Collection: 2 political cartoons. 1955.

Valtman, Ed. Warren Collection: 6 political cartoons. *Hartford Times* 1970-1971.

Wallmeyer, Dick. Warren Collection: 8 political cartoons. Register and Tribune Syndicate 1970.

Warren, L.D. Collection: 2 boxes. Political cartoons ca. 1940-1971.

Yardley, Richard Q. Warren Collection: 116 political cartoons. 1943-1970.

Western Reserve Historical Society

• Western Reserve Historical Society, 10825 East Blvd., Cleveland OH 44106. 216-721-5722. John J. Grabowski, Curator of Manuscripts. 9 am-5 pm Tu-Sa. Photocopy services. Holdings to be on OCLC by July 1990. See also Kermit J. Pike, *A Guide to Manuscripts and Archives of the Western Reserve Historical Society* (Cleveland: WRHS, 1972) and Kermit J. Pike, *A Guide to Major Manuscript Collections Accessioned and Processed by the Library of the Western Reserve Historical Society Since 1970* (Cleveland: WRHS, 1987). Finding aids available in repository.

Bellamy, Paul, 1884-1956. Papers 1907-1967: 2.6 linear ft. Editor *Cleveland Plain Dealer* 1933-1954.

Briggs, James A. Scrapbooks 1830-1887: 2 vols. Editor of *Cleveland True Democrat*; correspondent with *Cleveland Leader*.

Burrows, Jerome B. Family papers 1858-1900: .6 linear ft. Jerome S. Burrows was proprietor of *Painesville Telegraph* in late 1870s.

Curtis, William Eleroy, 1859-1911. Papers 1877-1912: 1.2 linear ft. Journalist for *Chicago Inter-Ocean* 1873-1886 and *Record Herald* 1887-1911.

Czech-American Labor News, Inc. Records 1908-1945: 4.3 linear ft. Publisher of *Americky Delnicky Listy* 1908-1953. MS 3859.

DiSantis, Anthony J. Papers 1936-1963: 4 linear ft. Labor columnist for *Cleveland Plain Dealer* 1925-1960. Clippings. MS 3790.

Donahey, James Harrison, 1875-1949. Sketches ca. 1900-1940: 100 cu. ft. Editorial cartoonist for *Cleveland Plain Dealer* 1900-1949.

Emerson, Caleb. Family papers 1795-1904: 1.8 linear ft. Caleb Emerson worked with *Western Spectator* ca. 1800-1813 and edited *Marietta Gazette* 1836.

Hodge, Orlando John, 1828-1912. Papers 1822-1913: 6 linear ft. Owner and editor of *Cleveland Sun and Voice* 1878-1888.

Howard, Nathaniel R., 1898-1980. Papers 1914-1980: 2.2 linear ft. Editor *Cleveland News* 1937-1960 and *Cleveland Plain Dealer* 1960-1963.

Kratky, John F. Papers 1964: 2 vols. Scrapbooks containing information on career of Cleveland editorial cartoonist James Harrison Donahey. MS 3543.

Sindelar, Frank, 1861-1929. Papers 1901-1929: .5 boxes. Editor of Czech-American newspaper *American.* MS 3643.

Snajdr, Vaclav, 1847-1920. Papers 1867-1954: .7 linear ft. Editor of Czech-language papers *Pkrok* 1873-1876 and *Dennice Novoveku* 1877-1910. MS 3706.

Stevens, John. Papers 1824-1875: 1.6 linear ft. Editor of *Cross & Baptist Journal.*

Wiesenfeld, Leon, 1885-1971. Papers 1911-1971: .8 linear ft. Publisher of *Jewish World* and *Jewish Voice Pictorial* 1920s to 1960s. MS 3924.

OKLAHOMA

Oklahoma State University

• Oklahoma State University Library, Stillwater OK 74078. 405-624-6313. Heather M. Lloyd, Head, General Reference Dept. By appointment 8 am-5 pm M-F. Photocopy services. Finding aids in repository.

Miller, Paul. Papers: 34 boxes. Associated Press 1932-1947. Chief Executive Officer, Gannett Corp. 1957-1978. President and Chairman Associated Press 1963-1977. Correspondents include Frank E. Gannett, Kent Cooper, Al Neuharth, Walker Stone.

Trout, Clement E. Collection: 4 linear ft. International Council of Industrial Editors 1927-1958.

University of Oklahoma

• Western History Collections, University of Oklahoma Libraries, 630 Parrington Oval, Monnet Hall Room 452, Norman OK 73019. 405-325-3641. Donald L. DeWitt, Curator. 8 am-5 pm M-F; 8 am-noon Sa. Photocopy services. See also Arrell Morgan Gibson, *A Guide to Regional Manuscript Collections...in the Division of Manuscripts, University of Oklahoma Library* (Norman: University of Oklahoma Press, 1960). Finding aids in repository.

Researchers should also contact the Herbert-Priestley Resources Center, H. H. Herbert School of Journalism and Mass Communication at the University of Oklahoma for unpublished histories of Oklahoma newspapers and unpublished biographies of prominent Oklahoma journalists.

Folsom, Lee W. Papers 1867-1910: .7 cu. ft. Newspaperman with *Indian Citizen* of Atoka, Indian Territory. Correspondence.

Harrison, Walter M. Papers 1915-1961: 10 cu. ft. Editor of *Daily Oklahoman* and owner of *North Star*. Personal and business correspondence.

Holbrook, Richard Burkey. Papers 1900-1915: 1 cu. ft. Editor of *Pawnee Dispatch*. Correspondence.

McCammon, J.D. Memoirs ca. 1900: 3 items. Journalist with various newspapers.

OREGON

Josephine County Historical Society

• Research Library, Josephine County Historical Society, 508 SW 5th St., Grants Pass OR 97526. 503-479-7827. Martha Murphy, Executive Dir. 10 am-4 pm Tu-F. Photocopy services.

Voorhies, Amos E. Collection: 600 glass negatives and 2 boxes. Publisher of *Grants Pass Courier*. RESTRICTED.

University of Oregon

• Manuscripts Collections, University of Oregon Library, 15th and Kincaid Sts., Eugene OR 97403-1299. 503-686-3068. Hillary Cummings, Curator. 8:30 am-4 pm M; 8:30 am-4:30 pm Tu-F. Photocopy services. Unpublished inventories in repository. See also Martin Schmitt, *Catalogue of Manuscripts in the University of Oregon Library* (Eugene: University of Oregon Books, 1971).

Baillie, Hugh, 1890-1966. Papers 1913-1960: 1.5 ft. Newspaperman, president and general manager United Press International 1935-1955. Manuscripts, scrapbook and correspondence, including letters from Lord Beaverbrook. Ax 631.

Berger, Josef, 1903-1971. Papers 1918-1982: 10 cu. ft. Journalist and magazine writer. Correspondence, manuscripts, speeches, memorabilia. Coll. 58.

Bloch, Kurt, 1900-1976. Papers 1919-1979: 4.9 cu. ft. Assoc. editor *Far Eastern Survey* 1938-1942; with *Fortune* 1941-1950; *Barron's* 1950-1976. Correspondence, manuscripts, articles. Partially in German. Coll. 19.

Cantwell, Robert Emmett, 1908-1978. Papers 1926-1978: ca. 38 cu. ft. Editorial staff *Time* 1935-1936; *Fortune* 1937. Assoc. editor *Time* 1938-1945. Literary editor *Newsweek* 1949-1954. *Sports Illustrated* 1956-1978. Correspondence, manuscripts, subject files. PORTIONS RESTRICTED. Coll. 20.

Coan, Philip Munson, 1879-1968. Papers 1888-1964: 1.5 ft. Reporter, chief editorial writer *New York Sun* 1906-ca. 1911. Editor-in-Chief *Evening Sun* ca. 1911-1925. Editorial writer *Brooklyn Eagle.* Manuscripts, diaries. Ax 575.

Crosby, Alexander L., 1906-1980. Papers 1921-1980: 19.3 cu. ft. Various positions *Staten Island Advance* 1929-1934. Editor *New Jersey Guide* 1936-1938; *Paterson Press* 1935-1936. News editor Federated Press 1938-1942. Correspondence, subject files, manuscripts. Coll. 13.

Ettelson, Lee, 1898-   Letters: 1 folder. Managing editor *New York American* 1926-1928. Asst. managing editor *San Francisco Examiner* 1935-1936. Editor *San Francisco Call Bulletin* 1937-1946. Letters and annotated newspapers from William Randolph Hearst. A 278.

Forman, Harrison, 1904-1978. Papers 1941-1974: 3 cu. ft. *March of Time* newsreel service. *New York Times* war correspondent in China 1932-1949. Diaries, notebooks, manuscripts, scripts, photographs. Coll. 24.

Grant, Jeanette Cole, 1892-1972. Papers 1911-1972: 11 cu. ft. *New York Times* reporter 1912-ca.1918, 1920-1925, 1928-1937. Co-founder with Harold Ross, of *New Yorker.* Correspondents include Enrico Caruso, Janet Flanner, Raoul Fleischmann, Harold Ross, James Thurber, Hawley Truax , Alexander Woollcott. Coll. 41.

Harris, William Bliss, 1900-1981. Papers ca. 1923-1977: 1 cu. ft. Editor of *Fortune* 1937-1960. Correspondence, manuscripts. Coll. 55.

Hoyem, Oliver, 1891-1965. Papers 1905-1968: ca. 12 cu. ft. Editor *Chester Wright's Labor Letter* 1934-1947. Correspondence, manuscripts, lectures, files. Coll. 46.

Littell, Robert, 1896-1963. Papers 1901-1963: 8 ft. Assoc. editor *New Republic* 1922-1927. Drama critic in New York 1927-1931. Assoc. and senior editor *Reader's Digest* 1942-1961. Letters. Ax 400.

Millard, Bailey, 1859-1941. Papers 1893-1939: 1.5 ft. Literary editor *San Francisco Call* and *San Francisco Examiner* 1890s. Managing editor *Munsey's* 1913-1914; *San Francisco Evening Bulletin* 1918-1919. Manuscripts, letters. Correspondents include Ambrose Bierce, Hamlin Garland, Jack London, Edwin Markham, Joaquin Miller, John Muir. Ax 431.

Misselwitz, Henry Francis, 1900-   Papers 1927-1946: 1.5 ft. *Kansas City Star* 1917. Far East correspondent United Press and *New York Times* 1924-1927. Staff *Japan Advertiser* 1924-1927. Manuscripts, scripts, column, journal. Ax 351.

O'Connor, Hugh, 1894-1967. Papers 1918-1967: 3 ft. Reporter *New York Sun* and *New York World* 1920s. Roving correspondent *New York Times* 1929-1943. Includes original copy and internal memoranda for *New York Times* stories. Also 470 letters 1928-1939 from Katherine Ursula Parrott. Ax 620.

Parton, Margaret, 1915-1981. Papers 1885-1981: ca. 37 cu. ft. Reporter *New York Herald Tribune* 1943-1955. Assoc. editor *Ladies Home Journal* 1955-1963. Correspondence, diaries, manuscripts, memorabilia, photographs, tape recordings. Coll. 36.

Redington, John W., 1851-1935. Papers 1880-1935: 2 ft. *Salem Oregon Statesman* 1874. Publisher *Heppner Gazette* 1883. Also published newspapers in Puyallup and Tacoma WA. Correspondence, manuscripts, clippings. Ax 93.

Soule, Isobel Walker, 1898-1972. Papers 1860-1972: 4.5 ft. Editorial board *Woman Today* ca. 1930s. Ax 774.

Thompson, Herbert Cooper, 1875-1960. Papers 1864-1960: 3 ft. Worked for San Francisco newspapers 1900-1910. Associated Press 1912-1920. Incl. 33 vol. diaries, 900 letters. Correspondents include John M. Thompson, Joseph Lane, Joaquin Miller. Ax 67.

Tolischus, Otto David, 1890-1967. Papers 1927-1966: 3 ft. International News Service ca. 1931-1933. *New York Times* foreign correspondent 1933-1941; editorial board member 1942-

1964. Manuscripts, clippings. Correspondents include Frank S. Booth, Barry Farris, Frank Mason, Arthur H. Sulzberger. Ax 368.

Tugman, William Masten, 1893-1961. Papers 1938-1959: 3 ft. *Eugene Register Guard* managing editor 1927-1950; contributing editor 1950-1955. Editor and owner *Port Umpqua Courier* 1955-1959. Correspondents include Harris Ellsworth, Guy Cordon, Wayne L. Morse, Richard L. Neuberger. Ax 607.

Watson, Morris, 1901-1972. Papers 1932-1971: 3 ft. Associated Press reporter 1929-1935. Founder of American Newspaper Guild. Ax 744.

Wheeler, Howard Duryee, 1880-1958. Typescript autobiography: 295 leaves. Editor *San Francisco Daily News* 1906-1908. Managing editor *Harper's Weekly* 1914-1915. Editor *Everybody's Magazine* 1915-1919. General manager McClure Newspaper Syndicate 1922-1926. Editor Conde Syndicate 1928-1932. Chief Editorial writer *New York Daily Mirror* 1932-1936. A 197.

Wilkinson, Kirk C. Correspondence 1934-1970: 404 letters. Art editor *Woman's Day*. Correspondents include Erik Blegvad, Edgar Garbisch, Joseph Donaldson, Jr., Ann Z. Shanks. Ax 610.

Woltman, Frederick Enos, 1905-1970. Papers 1924-1970: 13 ft. Investigative reporter *New York World-Telegram* ca. 1930-1957. Personal and professional correspondence, biographical material, clippings. Ax 768.

PENNSYLVANIA

Free Library of Philadelphia

• Print and Picture Dept., Free Library of Philadelphia, Logan Square, Philadelphia PA 19103. 215-686-5405. J.B. Post. 9 am-5 pm M-F. Photocopy services.

Political cartoons, mostly dealing with Philadelphia.

Historical Society of Western Pennsylvania

• Historical Society of Western Pennsylvania, 4338 Bigelow Blvd., Pittsburgh PA 15213. 412-681-5533. Donald L. Haggerty, Asst. Dir. for Library and Archives. 9:30 am-4:30 pm Tu-Sa. Photocopy services at discretion of staff. Finding aids in repository.

Henrici, Max, 1884-   Papers 1900-1971: 9 boxes. Worked for *Pittsburgh Press, New York Herald Tribune, Spartansburg Herald, Brooklyn Citizen, Pittsburgh Leader*. Editorial writer *Pittsburgh Sun Telegraph* 1927-1958. Columnist for *Sewickley Herald.* Diaries, scrapbooks, printed materials, clippings.

Forrest family. Papers 1860-1960: 13 boxes. Earle Robert Forrest, 1883-1969, was on the staff of *Washington Record* and *Washington Reporter*. Manuscripts, research material, personal information, correspondence, legal documents.

Swarthmore College

• Swarthmore College Peace Collection, Swarthmore PA 19081. 215-328-8557. Eleanor Barr, Acting Curator. 8:30 am-4:30 pm M-F; 9 am-noon Sa. during class sessions. Closed month of August. Photocopy services. See also *Guide to the Swarthmore College Peace Collection.*   Second ed. (Swarthmore PA: Swarthmore College, 1981).

Allen, Devere, 1891-1955. Papers 1917-1956: 42 meters. Editor of *The World Tomorrow*. Founder, editor and director of Woldover Press, established in 1933 as Nofrontier News Service. Correspondence, biographical material, manuscripts, business records, releases, clippings, photographs. Preliminary checklist available.

Burritt, Elihu, 1810-1879. Papers 1841-1958: 38 cm. Editor or publisher of *The Advocate of Peace and Universal Brotherhood* 1846; *Bond of Brotherhood* 1846-1867; *Citizen of the World* 1855-1856. Checklist available.

Dispatch News Service International. Records 1968-1973: 5 meters. Formed in Saigon to increase Western understanding of Asia. Manuscripts, news releases, articles, clippings, memoranda, financial records, photographs. Preliminary checklist available.

Innerst, J. Stuart, 1894-1975. Papers 1920-1975: 2.1 meters. Editor of *Understanding China Newsletter*. Correspondence, articles, speeches, clippings, photographs. Preliminary checklist available.

Lockwood, Belva A., 1830-1917. Papers 1878-1917: 14 cm. Edited *Peacemaker*. Correspondence, manuscripts, pamphlets, photographs.

Mead, Edwin Doak, 1849-1937. Papers 1876-1936: 2.5 meters. Edited *New England Magazine* 1889-1901. Correspondence, articles, clippings. Checklist available.

Muste, A.J., 1885-1967. Papers 1920-1967: 6.8 meters. Editor of *Liberation.* Correspondence, business papers. Checklist available.

Polnar, Murray. Papers 1963-1972: 1 meter. Editor of *Present Tense* and *Shalom.* Correspondence, legal briefs, clippings, research notes.

Sayre, John Nevin, 1884-1977. Papers 1907-1971: 20 meters. Editor *The World Tomorrow* 1922-1924; *Fellowship* 1940-1945. Correspondence, diaries, manuscripts.

Sollmann, William F., 1881-1951. Papers 1901-1951: 2 meters. Editor-in-chief *Rheinische Zeitung* 1919-1933; *Deutsche Freiheit.* Correspondence, biographical material, editorials, clippings, cartoons, typescripts. Portions in German. Checklist available.

Spencer, Anna Carpenter Garlin, 1851-1931. Papers 1830-1931: 1.2 meters. Wrote for *Providence Daily Journal.* Diary, correspondence, manuscripts, clippings, photographs.

Stöcker, Helene d. 1943. Papers 1897-1943: 1.2 meters. Published *Neue Generation* 1905-1933. Manuscript, correspondence, notes, photographs. Portions in German. Checklist available.

WIN Magazine. Collection 1971-1983. Magazine of Workshop in Nonviolence. Index, organizational minutes and correspondence, reference files, financial records, editorial guidelines.

Warren County Historical Society

• Warren County Historical Society, 210 Fourth Ave., Warren PA 16365. 814-723-1795. Derek B. McKown, Exec. Dir. 9 am-5 pm M-F. Photocopy services.

Clemons, Thomas. Collection: 14 boxes, 45 vols. Editor 1829-1879. Correspondence and business records. Index available.

SOUTH CAROLINA

Clemson University

• Special Collections, Clemson University Libraries, Clemson SC 29634-3001. 803-656-3031. Michael Kohl, Head, Special Collections. 8 am-4:30 pm M-F; Tu. until 9 pm. Photocopy services.

Bryan, Wright. Papers: 8 cu ft. Editor *Atlanta Journal* and *Cleveland Plain Dealer*; NBC News. President American Society of Newspaper Editors. RESTRICTED: Until processing completed.

Robertson, Benjamin Franklin, Jr., 1903-1943. Papers 1903-1982: 6 cu. ft. Worked for *Charleston News and Courier*, *Honolulu Star-Bulletin*, *Adelaide News*, *New York Herald Tribune*, *Anderson Independent*, Associated Press, *PM*, *Chicago Sun*. Correspondence, journals, articles, cables, novels. Correspondents include Edward R. Murrow, Lady Mary Astor, Edgar Snow, Tom Waring, Burnet R. Maybank, Roger Peace, Charles H. Busha, M.D. Klaas, Jeanne Gadsden, Mary B. Longley, Thomas Wolfe. Register available.

South Carolina Historical Society

• South Carolina Historical Society, 100 Meeting St., Charleston SC 29401-2299. 803-723-3225. 9 am-4 pm M-F; 9 am-2 pm Sa. Photocopy services. See also David Moltke-Hansen and Sallie Doscher, *South Carolina Historical Society Manuscript Guide* (Charleston: South Carolina Historical Society, 1979).

Bennett, John, 1865-1956. Papers ca. 1865-ca. 1960: ca. 40 ft. Writer and illustrator. *Light* 1890; *St. Nicholas Magazine* 1891-1935; *Saturday Review* 1925-1937. Correspondents include Tudor Jenks, A.W. Drake, Stephen Rose Benet, Bernard deVoto, Hamilton D. Mabie, Mary Mapes Dodge.

Courier. Records 1803-1809: 2 vols. Ledger and cashbook.

Lathan, Robert, 1881-1937. Papers 1898-1970: ca. 4 ft. *Columbia State* 1900-1903; *Charleston News and Courier* 1906-1927. Editor *Asheville Citizen* 1927-1937. Pulitzer Prize 1924. Correspondents include David Duncan Wallace, J.C. Hemphill, Henry Watterson, Yates Snowden, A.S. Salley, Warrington Dawson, Jr., Richard I. Manning, James F. Byrnes, Hervey Allen, Walter Lippmann, J.J. Astor, Herbert Ravenel Sass, Maurice Evans, Josephine Pinckney.

Sass, Herbert Ravenel, 1884-1958. Papers ca. 1905-1960: 24 ft. Wrote for several national magazines; columnist for *News and Courier*. Correspondence, manuscripts, clippings.

University of South Carolina

• South Caroliniana Library, University of South Carolina, Columbia SC 29208. 803-777-5183. Herbert H. Hartsook. 8:30 am-5 pm M-F; 9 am-1 pm Sa. Photocopying by staff. See also Allen H. Stokes, Jr., *A Guide to the Manuscript Collection of the South Caroliniana Library* (Columbia: University of South Carolina, 1982).

Allan, Glenn, 1899-1955. Papers: 2.5 linear ft. Columnist and editor with *Greenville Piedmont, Asheville Citizen, Atlanta Journal, New York Herald Tribune*. Editorial staff *New Yorker*. Wrote for *Saturday Evening Post.*

Aull, John Kinard, b. 1884. Collection 1912-1936: 573 items and 4 vols. Journalist.

Bass, Jack, b. 1934. Collection 1967-1978: 2,241 items. Journalist.

Billings, John Shaw. Papers: 4,083 items. *Time* national affairs editor 1929-1933; managing editor 1933-1936. Managing editor *Life* 1936-1944. Editorial director Time, Inc. publications 1944-1954. Correspondents include Henry Luce, Willard M. Kiplinger, David Lawrence, H.L. Mencken, Evelyn Waugh, Rebecca West.

Cassells, Louis Welborn, 1922-1974. Collection 1928-1974: 838 items and 12 vols.Correspondent with United Press International.

Caston, W. Thurlow. Scrapbook 1849-1850: 1 vol. Editor of *Camden Journal.*

Dawson, Francis Warrington, 1840-1889. Papers 1871-1949. Worked for *Charleston News and Courier.*

Gonzales, Narciso Gener, 1858-1903. Papers 1895-1922: 62 items. Editor of *Columbia State.*

Gonzales, William Elliott, 1866-1937. Papers 1922-1937: 1,837 items. Founder and editor *Columbia State* 1891-1913, 1922-1926; publisher 1926-1937. Manuscripts, business and personal correspondence. Correspondents include William Watts Ball, Bernard Baruch, McDavid Horton, Stanhope Sams.

Hoyt, James Allen, 1877-1959. Papers 1879-1956: 889 items. Operated *Columbia Daily Record.*

Kohn, August, 1868-1930. Papers 1882-1941: 630 items. Worked for *Columbia News and Courier.*

Lathan, Robert, 1881-1937. Papers 1901-1950: 219 items.

McKissick, James Rion, 1884-1944. Collection 1884-1944: 2,249 items and 11 vols. Editor *Greenville Piedmont.*

Quillen, Robert, 1887-1948. Papers 1906-1949: 362 mss. Editor and publisher *News and Notions*, renamed *Fountain Inn Tribune*, 1911-1943. Wrote for *Saturday Evening Post, Baltimore Evening Sun, American Magazine.* Correspondents include George Matthew Adams, Adolph S. Ochs, II, Maxfield Parrish, Alexander Woollcott.

Smoak, William Wightman, 1877-1947. Papers 1897-1947: 1,986 items. Editor and publisher *Walterboro Press and Standard* 1906-1913.

Watson, Harry Legare, 1876-1956. Papers. Editor and publisher *Greenwood Index-Journal* 1919-1956. Correspondents include James Rion McKissick, William Watts Ball, McDavid Horton, Emory Olin Watson. Financial and other records of *Index- Journal.*

Workman, William D., Jr. Collection 1921-1983: 41,075 items. Assoc. editor and editorial analyst for *Columbia State.*

TENNESSEE

University of Tennessee

• Special Collections Library, Hoskins Library, University of Tennessee, Knoxville TN 37996-4000. 615-974-4480. James B. Lloyd. 9 am-5:30 pm M-F. Photocopy services.

Cade, Dozier. Papers 1930-1955: 6 ft. AR-51.

Kenyon, Nellie. Scrapbooks 1917-1967: 9 ft. Journalist in Nashville and Chattanooga. MS-789.

Dromgoole, Miss William Allen, d. 1934. Papers 1831-1960: 3 ft. Journalist. Correspondence, journals, legal papers, manuscripts, clippings, photographs. MS-201.

Eaton, John, 1829-1906. Correspondence 1865-1881: 6 ft. Journalist with *Memphis Evening Post.* RESTRICTED. MS-18.

Ochs, Milton B., 1864-1955. Scrapbooks 1880-1955: 5 vol. MS-884.

Whitehead, Don, 1908-1981. Papers 1940-1973: 18 ft. Journalist covering World War II and Korean War. Correspondence, manuscripts, clippings, *News Sentinel* columns, photographs, scrapbooks. MS-1020.

Vanderbilt University

• Vanderbilt Television News Archive, Jean and Alexander Heard Library, Vanderbilt University, Nashville TN 37240-0007. 615-322-2927. John Lynch. Duplicate tapes available for loan.

ABC, CBS, and NBC evening news archives 1968-present. See *Television News Index and Abstracts,* monthly publication of Vanderbilt Television News Archive.

TEXAS

Dallas Historical Society

• Dallas Historical Society, PO Box 26038, Dallas TX 75226. 214-421-5136. Sarah Hunter, Curator of History. 9 am-5 pm M-F.

Dealey, G.B. Collection: ca. 20 boxes. Founded *Dallas Morning News* 1885.

Dallas Morning News. Library: 60 boxes.

Texas A & M University

• University Archives, Sterling C. Evans Library, Texas A & M University, College Station TX 77843. 409-845-1815. Charles R. Schultz, University Archivist. 8 am-5 pm M-F.

Timmons, Bascom N. Papers: 220 linear ft. being converted to microfiche. Operator of Washington, D.C. news bureau ca. 1920-1970. Inventory included in Chadwyck-Healey's *National Inventory of Documentary Sources in the United States.*

University of Texas at Arlington

• Special Collections Division, University of Texas at Arlington Libraries, PO Box 19497, Arlington TX 76019. 817-273-3393. Jane Boley or Shirley Rodnitzky. 8 am-5 pm M-F; 10 am-2 pm Sa. Photocopy services. Finding aids in repository.

Fort Worth Star-Telegram. Collection. More than 500,000 clippings 1920s-1960. Extensive photographic files.

Greene, A.C., 1923-   Papers: 7 boxes. Book editor and *Dallas Times Herald* editorial columnist 1961-1968; editorial page editor 1963-1968. Produced own show KERA-TV 1970-1971. Letters, editorials, clippings, scripts.

Rosen, Joel B., 1910-1973. Collection: 56 boxes. Original and printed cartoons collected and/or produced by Rosen. Cartoons from 48 U. S. newspapers and original cartoons by Herc Ficklen and John Knott of *Dallas Morning News.*

Ward, William Allen, 1891-1959. Papers: 56 boxes. *Dallas Morning News* 1920-1928, 1938-1959; editor of *Dallas Journal* 1929-1938.   Correspondence, manuscripts, research notes printed material.

University of Texas at Austin

• Eugene C. Barker Texas History Center, Sid Richardson Hall 2.101 General Libraries, University of Texas at Austin, Austin TX 78713. 512-471-5961. Don E. Carleton, Director. 8 am-5 pm M-Sa. See also Chester V. Kielman, *The University of Texas Archives* (Austin: University of Texas Press, 1967).

Borden, Gail R., Jr, 1801-1875. Papers 1830-1908: 6 ft. Surveyor, inventor, newspaperman, businessman, agriculturalist. Established *San Felipe Telegraph and Texas Register* 1835. Correspondence, account books, scrapbooks, newspapers.

Brown, John Henry, 1820-1895. Papers 1691-1951: 34 ft. Newspaperman on *Victoria Advocate* 1846; *Indianola Bulletin* 1848-1854; *Galveston Civilian* 1854; *Belton Democrat* 1859. Correspondence, diaries, legal documents, drawings, photographs, scrapbooks, newspapers.

Colquitt, Oscar Branch, 1861-1940. Papers 1825-1940: 48 ft. Governor, newspaper editor, railroad commissioner.

Cox, Nettie Stedman, 1855-1908. Papers 1843, 1864, 1901-1905: 1 in. Correspondence, clippings.

DeBow, J.D.B. Papers, 1855, 1865-1866: 35 items. Editor and publisher of *DeBow's Reviews.*

Douai, Adolf, 1819-1888. Papers 1819-1908: 6 in. Publisher of *San Antonio Zeitung.*   Correspondence, legal documents, clippings, pamphlets. Correspondents include Charles Anderson Dana, William Lloyd Garrison, Horace Greeley, Ferdinand Herff, Carl Schurz, Harriet Beecher Stowe, Charles Sumner.

Friei Presse Fuer Texas. Records 1870-1946: 24 ft. German language newspaper. Correspondence, legal papers, memoranda, galley proofs.

Fulton, George W., 1810-1893. Papers 1836-1911: 6 ft. Correspondence, diary, journal, clippings.

Haas, Oscar. Papers 1844-1955: 7 in. Historical and newspaper correspondent for *New Braunfels Herald.* Correspondence, business records, clippings, photographs.

Haynes, John L., 1821-1887. Papers 1846-1945: 2.5 in. Relates to political journalism in Texas 1859-1862, 1866-1869. Editorials in *Austin Intelligencer.*

Jackson, Pearl Cashwell, 1869-1928. Papers 1883, 1891-1933. President of Texas Women's Press Assoc. Correspondence, photographs, clippings.

Jones, Jesse Holman, 1874-1956. Papers ca. 1880-1965: 41.8 ft. Builder, financier, statesman, publisher of *Houston Chronicle.* Correspondence, business and financial records, notes, scrapbooks, clippings, cartoons, photographs. Material from 1930-1950 representing Jones's active service in the federal government is in the Library of Congress. Collection inventory available.

Kendall, George Wilkins, 1809-1867. Papers 1846-1850: 7 in. Newspaperman. Wrote *The War between the United States and Mexico,* considered to be the first instance of battle coverage by a foreign correspondent. Letter, diary, speech, literary productions, proofs.

Kuykendall, James Hampton, ca. 1816-1882. Papers 1822-1897: 7 in. Editor of *Texas Monument* and *Transcript.* Correspondence, diaries, journals, day books, reminiscence, biographical sketches, accounts, clippings, poems.

Lasswell, Mary Clyde Grayson Lubbock, 1905- Papers 1880-1984: 13 ft. Novelist, biographer, editorial columnist for *Houston Chronicle.* Research materials, notes, manuscripts, correspondence, legal and financial records, diaries, clippings, photographs. Collection inventory available.

Marschalk, Franklin.   Family papers 1865-1911: 3.7 ft. Newspaper publishers.   Correspondence, notes, clippings, accounts, legal papers.

Morehead, Richard M., 1913-   Papers 1946-1979: 33.8 ft. Reporter and columnist for *Dallas Morning News* ca. 1946-ca. 1978.   Clippings, research files, correspondence.   Correspondents include John Connally, James S. Cox, Price Daniel, J. Frank Dobie, W. Saint John Garwood, Beauford Jester, Lyndon Johnson, Walter Ewing Long, Erwin Perry, Allan Shivers, Logan Wilson.

Moses, Harry Bowman. Papers 1893-1947: 8 in. Reporter. Correspondence, speeches, clippings, photographs.

Navasota Leader. Ledger book 1892-1897: 1 vol.

Newcomb, James Pearson, Sr., 1837-1909.   Papers 1839-1941: 10.9 in. Editor. Letters, diary, memorandum book, clippings.

Smith, Wilford Bascom, 1884-1939.   Papers 1905-1940: 93 items.   Publisher and editor of *The Pitchfork*.   Correspondence, articles, newspapers.

Taylor, Bride Neill, 1858-1937. Papers 1893-1937: 4.3 ft. Correspondence, notes, speeches, clippings, manuscript.

Texas Siftings Publishing Co. Papers 1883-1886: 2 items. Legal document and broadside.

Texas Women's Press Assoc. Papers ca. 1900-1927: 4 in. Letters, membership lists, scrapbooks, programs, clippings.   Persons associated include Cora Milton Cross, Emma Cobb Evans, Mary Terry Gill, Mrs. J.M.F. Gill, Adele B. Looscan, Decca Lamar West.

Vincent, James Upshur.   Papers 1927-1935: 20.5 ft.   Market editor, financial editor, and farm editor for *Fort Worth Star-Telegram.* Letters, press releases, reports, clippings.

Washington, Lewis M. Henry, d. 1857. Papers 1832-1857: 42 items. Letters, certificates, literary productions.

Wilson, Walter B. Papers 1896-1939: 13.3 ft. Publisher, Journalist, printer of *Weekly Democrat* and *Daily Courier.* Letters, diaries, scrapbooks.

• Nettie Lee Benson Latin American Collection, University of Texas at Austin General Libraries, Sid Richardson Hall 1.109, Austin TX 78713-7330.   512-471-3818.   Laura   Gutierrez-Witt,   Head

Librarian. 9 am-5 pm M-F; 1-5 pm Sa. No Sa hours during summer or between quarters. Photocopy services. See also Maria G. Flores, *Mexican American Archives at the Benson Collection: a Guide for Users.* (Austin: University of Texas at Austin, 1981).

Astol, Lalo, 1906-   Papers 1913-1945: 1 manuscript, 33 photographs. Radio host at KMAC and other stations in San Antonio TX during 1940s.

Garza, Catarino E., 1859-? 1 manuscript. "'La logica de los hechos,' or sean observaciones sobre las circumstancias de los mexicanos en Tejas, desde el ano 1877 hasta 1889," Tomo I, Corpus Christi TX. Publisher *El bien publico* in Brownsville 1879, *El libre pensador,* Eagle Pass 1887, and *El Comercio mexicano* Eagle Pass 1886 and Corpus Christi 1888.

Mireles, Edmundo E., 1905-   Papers 1940-1971: 138 items. Editor *LULAC News, Texas-Mexican Gazette* Corpus Christi mid-1940s.

Munguia, Romulo, 1885-1975. Papers 1911-1975: 19 boxes. Printer, journalist, publisher of several San Antonio newspapers and magazines, including *El pueblo, La vox de Mexico, Mosaicos, Prospect Hill Inquirer.*

Rice University

• Woodson Research Center, Rice University Library, Houston TX 77251-1892. 713-527-8101, ext. 2586. Nancy L. Booth, Director. 9 am-5 pm M-F. Photocopy services. Inventories in repository.

Flint, Hallie Rienzi Johnston Russell Thomas, 1883-1965. Papers 1912-1965: 2 boxes. Wrote for *Houston Post* under pseudonym of Harriot Russell (Thomas). Clippings, correspondence, diary, scrapbook, photographs.

Johnston, Rienzi Melville, 1849-1926. Papers 1899-1927: 2 linear ft. U. S. Senator from Texas and founder of the *Houston Post.* Correspondence, printed materials, photographs.

Waggaman, Camille/Waggaman family. Collection: 3 folders. Camille Waggaman Brown hosted a radio talk show, "Around the Town with Camille Brown" in Montgomery AL for thirty-one years. Letters, memorabilia, photographs.

UTAH

University of Utah

• Manuscripts Division, Marriott Library, University of Utah, Salt Lake City UT 84112. 801-581-8864. Nancy V. Young, Head, Manuscripts Division. 8 am-5 pm M-F. Photocopy services.

Deck, Arthur C., 1908-1981. Papers 1962-1980: 4 linear ft. Executive editor of *Salt Lake Tribune* 1950-1980. President of American Society of Newspaper Editors 1973. Most papers relate to ASNE. Unpublished register available. Ms 361.

Johnson, Joseph Ellis, 1817-1882. Papers 1831-1964: 6.5 linear ft. Publisher of *The Omaha Arrow* 1854; *Huntsman's Echo* 1859-1861; *Farmer's Oracle* 1863; *Our Dixie Times*, later *Rio Virgen Times*, 1868-1869. Diaries, daybooks, broadsides, documents, newspapers. Published register available. Ms 110.

Malmquist, Orin Nebeker, 1894-1985. Oral interview 1972: 28 pages transcribed. Political writer and editor of the *Salt Lake Tribune* 1930s-1980s. See also Malmquist's speech, "The History of the *Salt Lake Tribune*," in the Westerners collection, Acc 370. Acc 564.

Webb, Lavar. Papers 1940s-1980s: 11 linear ft. Political writer for *Deseret News*. Subject files. Inventory available. Acc 968.

In addition to the collections listed above, the Division has a Communications Archive collecting records and papers from individuals associated with radio, television and the print media in the Intermountain West. Most collections received concern the business and technical side of broadcasting.

VIRGINIA

University of Virginia

• Dept. of Special Collections, Division of Manuscripts and University Archives, University of Virginia Library, Charlottesville VA 22903-2498. 804-924-3025. Michael Plunkett, Manuscripts Curator. 9 am-5 pm M-F; 9 am-1 pm Sa. Photocopy services.

Baugh, Leonidas, 1816-1884. Papers of the Baugh family 1756-1942: 9 linear ft. Publisher of *Abingdon Democrat*. Includes printing ledger. 38-104 etc.

Bradley, William E. Papers 1892-1893: ca. 70 items. Business manager of *Fredericksburg Free Lance*.

Byrd, Harry Flood, Sr., 1887-1966. Papers 1911-1965: 273 linear ft. (Papers regarding his newspaper publishing may be found in Series I Business Correspondence, 1914-1965, Boxes 1-37.) Publisher of *Winchester Star, Martinsburg Evening Journal, Harrisonburg Daily News Record*; governor of Virginia; U. S. Senator. Political papers include scattered correspondence with journalists and publishers including David Tennant Bryan, Lenoir Chambers, Virginius Dabney, Clifford Dowdey, Douglas Southall Freeman, Louis Isaac Jaffe, Arthur Krock, James Jackson Kilpatrick, Walter Lippmann, Drew Pearson, Fred Seibel, Louis Spilman. 9700.

Copeland, Walter Scott, 1856-1928. Papers 1880-1928: 2 linear ft. Editorial writer with several papers; editor and publisher of *Newport News Daily Press* and *Newport News Times Herald*. Chiefly editorial correspondence. Correspondents include Harry Flood Byrd, Sr., Josephus Daniels, Carter Glass, William Atkinson Jones, the Ku Klux Klan, John Powell, Claude Swanson, Theodore Roosevelt. 5497 etc.

Cralle, Richard Kenner, 1800-1864. Papers 1829-1869: 200 items. Newspaper editor including *Jeffersonian and Virginia Times, Washington Telegraph, Reformer, Chronicle*. 3875.

Dabney, Virginius, 1901- Papers ca. 1920-1987: 190 boxes. Pulitzer Prize-winning editor of *Richmond Times-Dispatch*. Correspondence, drafts of books. Correspondents include Sen. A. Willis Robertson, Harry Flood Byrd, Sr., Francis Pickens Miller, C. Vann Woodward. 7690 etc.

Daniel, Hawthorne, 1890- Papers 1945-1964: ca. 265 items. World War II journalist in Pacific Theater. Correspondence, manuscripts. 10409-a.

Free Lance Star Publishing Co. Records 1882-1916: 2 linear ft. Fredericksburg VA newspaper publishing firm. Ledgers, journals, cash books. 38-100.

Freeman, Douglas Southall, 1886-1953. Papers 1916-1952: ca. 9,000 items. Editor of *Richmond News Leader*. Editorial research files. 5220.

Hanes, Thomas Andrew, 1896-1972. Papers 1921-1971: 5 linear ft. Managing editor of *Norfolk Ledger Star*. Correspondents include Drew Pearson. 9863.

Harkrader, Charles Johnson, 1885-   Correspondence 1924-1964: ca. 280 items. Editor of *Bristol Herald-Courier*. Correspondence with Harry Flood Byrd, Sr., Carter Glass, Arthur Krock, James Clark McReynolds, H.L. Mencken, Drew Pearson, Claude A. Swanson. 9707 etc.

Henkel family. Papers 1805-1849: 62 items. Includes subscription list 1808-1809 to *Virginische Volksberichter* published by Ambrose Henkel. 5001-c.

Hill, Draper. Editorial cartoons 1968-1973: 15 or less. Published in *Worcester Telegram* and *Memphis Commercial Appeal*. 9864.

Hyde, Henry Morrow, 1866-   Papers 1889-1943: ca. 400 items. Staff member of *Chicago Tribune* and *Baltimore Sun*. Correspondence, diary 1931-1933, press releases, articles. Correspondents include Harry Flood Byrd, Sr., John Nance Garner, George H. Lorimer, H.L. Mencken, Sam Rayburn, Albert Ritchie. 2083, 2183, 2131, 2167.

Jaffe, Louis Isaac, 1888-1950. Papers 1917-1950: 6,500 items. Editorial correspondence files. Correspondents include Harry Flood Byrd, Sr., Virginius Dabney. 9924 etc.

Jefferson, Thomas, 1743-1826. Papers 1789-1825: includes ca. 30 letters regarding newspapers.

Kelly, C. Brian, 1935-   Papers 1959-1978: 4.5 linear ft. Staff writer for *Washington Star*. Clippings, releases, correspondence. 10566.

Kilpatrick, James Jackson, 1920-   Papers 1950-1984: 86 linear ft. Editor of *Richmond News Leader* and syndicated columnist. Office files, correspondence, articles, tapes of interviews and tv appearances, research, columns. Correspondents include William F. Buckley, Harry Flood Byrd, Sr., Harry Flood Byrd, Jr., Barry Goldwater. 6626 etc.

McClary, Jane Walker Stevenson McIlvaine, 1919-   Papers 1946-1967: 3 linear ft. *Washington Times* columnist 1929-1941. *Fortune* magazine during World War II. Co-owner and editor of *Downing Archive* 1946-1954. Drafts, proofs, correspondence.

Correspondents include Dick Francis, W. Averell Harriman, Lord Beaverbrook, Duke of Windsor, Henry Luce III. 9559-a.

MacNelly, Jeff. Editorial cartoons 1976: 15 or less. Published in *Richmond News Leader*. 1018-i.

Mencken, H.L., 1880-1956. Correspondence 1912-1949: 1 linear ft. Correspondents include Jim Tully, Upton Sinclair, Alfred Harcourt, Louis Untermeyer, Atcheson Hench, Ellen Glasgow, Gomez de Estavillo, Ludwig Lewisohn. 6253 etc.

Pierson, Charles Herbert, 1847- Papers 1874-1894: 283 items. Editor of Alliance *Necessity*. Correspondence. 38-139.

Scruggs, Philip Lightfoot, 1898- Correspondence 1930-1969: 1.5 linear ft. Editor of *Lynchburg Daily Advance*. Correspondents include Craddock Edmunds, Murrell Edmunds, Lawrence Lee, Edward R. Stettinius, Jr., Clifton Woodrum. 1390-b.

Seibel, Fred O., 1886-1969. Collection: ca. 6,000 editorial cartoons plus research and clippings files. Cartoons published in *Richmond Times-Dispatch* 1926-1968. Cartoons 1937-1945 available on microfilm M2532-2534. 2531 etc.

Spilman, Louis, 1899- Papers 1947-1970: 21 linear ft. Publisher of *Waynesboro News-Virginian*. Personal, business, political correspondence. Correspondents include Harry Flood Byrd, Sr., Harry Flood Byrd, Jr., Mills E. Godwin, A. Willis Robertson, Colgate Darden. 9833 etc.

Virginia Gazette. Daybooks 1750-1752, 1764-1766: 2 vols. Also available on microfilm M1679. Accounts. 467.

Warren Sentinel Journal. Accounts 1888-1896: 1 vol. Printing accounts of Front Royal VA newspaper. 38-103.

Wood, Art. Political cartoons 1952-1959: 625 cartoons. Published in *Richmond News-Leader*. 5235.

WRVA Radio Station. Records 1925-1963: 47 linear ft. Richmond VA station's daily files. Includes material of Larus & Brothers, Walter R. Bishop, Calvin R. Lucy. 9340.

Virginia Historical Society

• Virginia Historical Society, 428 North Boulevard, PO Box 7311, Richmond VA 23221-0311. 804-358-4901. E. Lee Shepard, Librarian. 9 am-4:45 pm daily except national holidays and holiday weekends. Photocopy services. See also Waverly K. Winfree, comp., *Guide to the Manuscript Collections of the Virginia Historical Society* (Richmond: Virginia Historical Society, 1985).

Bagby, George William, 1828-1883. Papers: ca. 5,400 items. Authur, lecturer, editor of *Petersburg Daily Courier*, *Orange Native Virginian*, and *Richmond Southern Literary Messenger*. Contributor to *Charleston Mercury* and *New Orleans Crescent*. Diaries, commonplace books, articles, essays. Correspondents include John Hampden Chamberlayne, John Esten Cooke, James Muscoe Matthews, Roger Atkinson Pryor, John Reuben Thompson, Thomas Hicks Wynne. Mss1B1463a-b; Mss2B1462b

Braxton, Henry Galt, 1881-1973. Papers: ca. 1,000 items. On staff of *Birmingham News*; later publisher and editor of *Kinston Free Press*. Includes diaries 1943-1972. In Braxton family papers Mss1B7396a.

Bryan, John Stewart, 1871-1944. Papers: ca. 910 items. Richmond VA lawyer, editor of *Richmond Times-Dispatch*; owner and publisher of *Richmond News Leader*, president of William and Mary College. Diaries, scrapbooks. Correspondents include David Tennant Bryan, Jonathan Bryan, Stewart Bryan, Harry Flood Byrd, Sr., William Howard Taft, Elbert Lee Trinkle, John Skelton Williams, Woodrow Wilson. Mss1B8405a-b; Mss5:1B8405:1; Mss5:7B8404:1-17

Bryan, Joseph, 1845-1908. Papers: ca. 500 items. Richmond VA lawyer, financier. Editor/owner of *Richmond Times* and *Richmond Times-Dispatch*. Includes indexed letterbooks. Mss1B8408a.

Carrington, William Cabell, 1821-1851. Papers: ca. 50 items. Richmond VA lawyer; editor of *Times and Compiler*. In Carrington family papers Mss1C2358g.

Chamberlayne, John Hampden, 1838-1882. Papers: ca. 450 items. Confederate veteran; lawyer; editor of *Petersburg Index*, *Norfolk Virginian*, *Richmond State*. Correspondents include George William Bagby, William Evelyn Cameron, Jubal Anderson Early. Mss1C3552a-c.

Chesterman, Evan Ragland, 1871-1931. Scrapbooks 1892-1911: 13 items. Reporter and writer for *Richmond Dispatch*, *Richmond Evening Journal*, *Richmond Times-Dispatch*. Mss5:7C4265:1-13.

Flannagan, Roy Catesby, 1897-1952. Papers: ca. 250 items. Novelist; U. S. Army officer; columnist for *Richmond News Leader*. Includes materials of his wife, Gladys Victoria Iller Flannagan, writer for *Atlanta Journal.* Mss1F6143aFA2.

Gooch, Claiborne Watts, 1791-1844. Papers: ca. 100 items. Adjutant General of Virginia; editor of *Richmond Enquirer*. In Gooch family papers Mss1Ga5906a.

Ingle, Edward. 1861-1924. Papers: ca. 352 items. Author, historian, newspaperman. Mss1IN45a.

Peninsula Enterprise. Subscription books 1906-1972: 3 vols. Accomac VA newspaper. Mss3P3782a.

Peyton, Aquila Johnson, 1837-1875. Diary 1859-1861: 1 vol. Educator; agent for *Fredericksburg Virginia Baptist.* Mss5:1P4683:1.

Virginia Publishing Co. Records 1897-1905: 7 items. Concern publication of *Warrenton Virginian.* In Marshall family papers Mss1M3587a.

VERMONT

Vermont Historical Society

• Vermont Historical Society Library, Pavilion Building, Montpelier VT 05602. 802-828-2291. Reidun D. Nuquist, Librarian. 8 am-4:30 pm M-F; 9 am-4 pm Sa. Photocopy services.

Eastman, Charles Gamage, 1816-1860. Papers: 5 boxes. Associated with *Woodstock Spirit of the Age*, 1840-1845; *Montpelier Vermont Patriot*, 1846-

Williams, Samuel, 1743-1817. Papers. Founder of *Rutland Herald.*

WASHINGTON

Eastern Washington State Historical Society

• Cheny Cowles Museum, Eastern Washington Historical Society, 2316 W. First Ave., Spokane WA 99204. 509-456-3932. Edward W. Nolan, Curator of Special Collections. 10 am-5 pm Tu-Sa. Appointment required. Limited photocopy services. See also, Edward W. Nolan, *A Guide to the Manuscript Collections in the*

Eastern Washington State Historical Society (Spokane: Eastern Washington State Historical Society, 1987).

Boyce, Edward, 1862-1941. Papers 1881-1941: 12 ft. Editor of *The Miner's Magazine* 1900-1902. Diaries, correspondence. Correspondents include Clarence Darrow, Eugene V. Debs, William D. Haywood, Charles H. Moyer, John M. O'Neill, Eamon de Valera. Ms 50.

Browne, John J., 1843-1912. Papers 1874-1906: 1.5 ft. Attorney; real estate agent; business interests in *Spokane Chronicle*. Correspondence. Ms 21.

Ferguson, Frank C., 1899-1972. Papers 1923-1966: 3 in. Reporter for *Spokane Spokesman-Review*; later city editor, assoc. editor. Clippings, correspondence. MsSC 155.

Gaylord, Myrtle, 1895-1960. Papers 1929-1960: 3 ft. Worked for *Spokane Press* until 1938; then wrote daily column, "Glimpses," for *Spokane Spokesman-Review*. Manuscripts, diary, correspondence. Ms 47.

Globe Publishing Co. 1889-1890? Papers 1889-1890: 8 pp. Published *Spokane Globe*, a daily newspaper. Articles of incorporation, by-laws, records. MsSc 86.

Marks, Callison, 1905-1969. Papers 1933-1969: 17 ft. Promotion manager with *Baltimore Sun*. After World War II, chief editorial writer for *Spokane Spokesman-Review*. Correspondence, pamphlets, reports. Ms 37.

Rice, Ben H., 1872-1957. Papers 1895-1955: 3 in. Reporter with *Spokane Spokesman-Review* 1897-1907. Correspondence, clippings. MsSC 4.

Rising, Henry, 1869-1939. Papers 1898-1937: 3 in. Joined editorial staff of *Spokane Spokesman* in 1892. Reporter for *Spokane Chronicle* in 1893, city editor in 1894, editor in 1897, editor and president in 1923. Correspondents include Gifford Pinchot, William E. Borah, Will H. Hays, William G. McAdoo, Reed Smoot, Booker T. Washington. MsSC 119.

Wasmer, Louis A., 1892-1967. Papers 1930-1967: 5 in. Pioneer in radio broadcasting in Washington. Radio stations included KHQ, KREM, KGA, KSPO and KFIO. Founded KREM television station. Publicity, letters, memorabilia. MsSC 157.

Watrous, Mable Spencer, ?-1980. Letters 1926-1932: 3 folders, 1 vol. Society editor and music critic for *Spokane Spokesman-Review*. Correspondence, scrapbook. MsSC 3.

University of Washington

• Manuscripts and University Archives Division, University of Washington Libraries, Seattle WA 98195. 206-543-1879 or 6509. Karyl Winn, Head. 8 am-noon, 1-5 pm M-F. Photocopy services. See also Marilyn Priestly, comp., *Comprehensive Guide to the Manuscripts Collection and to the Personal Papers in the University Archives* (Seattle: University of Washington Libraries, 1980).

Ault, Harry E.B., 1883-1961. Papers 1899-1953: 5 linear ft. Journalist, publisher, political activist. Editor and publisher of *Seattle Union Record*, trade union daily. Correspondence, court papers, legal documents, financial records. Unpublished inventory. See also Mary Joan O'Connell, "The *Seattle Union Record*, 1918-1928; a Pioneer Labor Daily," written as a master's thesis 1964.

Bagley, Clarence Booth, 1843-1932. Papers 1843-1932: 9 linear ft. Territorial Printer 1873-1884. Newspaper publisher 1868-1889. Correspondence, legal documents, financial records, speeches. Published inventory available.

Bone, Scott Cardelle, 1860-1936. Papers 1916-1918: .5 linear ft. Editor of *Seattle Post-Intelligencer*; Governor, Alaska Territory, 1921-1925. Scrapbook.

Brainerd, Erastus, 1855-1922. Papers 1880-1919: 3 linear ft. Editor *Seattle Post-Intelligencer* 1904-1911. Correspondence, legal documents. Published and unpublished inventories available. See also Victoria H. Livingston, "Erastus Brainerd; The Bankruptcy of Brilliance," written as master's thesis 1967.

Brown, Beriah, 1815-1900. Correspondence 1852, 1883, 1885: 4 items. Journalist. Photocopies of originals from Wisconsin Historical Society.

Brown family. (Beriah Brown, Sr., 1815-1900; Beriah Brown, Jr., 1857-1939; James H. Brown, 1871-1939; Ashmun Norris Brown, 1872-1948) Papers 1860-1940: .5 linear ft. Journalists and editors in Washington. Correspondence, clippings, ephemera. Unpublished inventory available.

Committee for an Independent P-I. Papers 1981-1982: 10.5 linear ft. Hearing transcripts, exhibits, pleadings from court case opposing the consolidation of the *Seattle Post-Intelligencer* and the *Seattle Times*.

Commission on the Freedom of the Press. Records 1944-1948: 4 linear ft. Reports and writings by Commission members; minutes, correspondence. Unpublished inventory available. See also Hilda M. Bryant, "A Free and Responsible Press: An Intellectual History of the Hutchins Commission," written as master's thesis 1968.

Cooper, Carl, 1875-1962. Papers ca. 1940-1960: 3 linear ft. City Hall reporter for *Seattle Post-Intelligencer*. Correspondence, writings, photographs, memorabilia, scrapbooks.

DeBow, Samuel P. Scrapbook 1915-1936: 1 reel microfilm. Editor of *Seattle Searchlight*; owner and manager of Seattle Searchlight Publishing Co. Correspondence, clippings.

Donahoe, Ed. Oral history interview 1973: 2 tapes. Interview with journalist, editor about 1936 *Seattle Post-Intelligencer* strike; his work as editor of *Washington Teamster*. Covers 1936-1972.

Fabbe, Harry, collector, 1899-1973. Collection 1842-1972: 4.5 linear ft. Includes subcollections: Correspondence, financial records, legal documents, subscriber lists, news releases, clippings of *Svenska Posten*, Swedish language newspaper published in Seattle. Papers of Ernst Sakrstedt, 1893-1928, Swedish-American writer, poet and journalist. Unpublished inventory available.

Forsland, Steven. Writings 1957: 2 items. Manuscripts in Swedish of articles published in *Svenska Posten*.

Freeman, Miller, 1875-1955. Papers 1911-1956: 9 linear ft. Publisher of *Pacific Fisherman* 1936-1954. Unpublished inventory available.

Garfield, Charles D., 1867-1961 Papers 1910-1960: 13 linear ft. Edited *Fur Journal*. Correspondence, diary, financial records, clippings, photographs. Unpublished inventory available.

Great Northern Daily News. Court exhibits 1916-1917: ca. 25 items. Includes copies of Japanese newspaper *Asahi News*, translations of articles from that paper.

KAYE Radio. Collection ca. 1968-1973: 19.5 linear ft. Correspondence, hearing records, legal documents, broadcast transcripts, radio program logs, clippings concerning license revocation of Puyallup WA radio station operated by Jim Nicholls, a right wing fundamentalist preacher.

Krems, Nathan. Papers, 1934-1939, 1973: 3.5 linear ft., 1 tape recorded interview and transcript. Editor of *Jewish Transcript* in late 1930s. Correspondence, writings, subject files. Tape recorded interview covers his father's publication of the *Jewish Voice*, the first Jewish newspaper in Seattle. Unpublished inventory available.

Mahaffay, Robert E., 1908-1967. Papers 1932-1967: 1.5 linear ft. Freelance writer 1932-1943. Staff correspondent *Seattle Times* 1943-1946. Publicist for West Coast Lumbermen's Assoc. 1946-1965. Unpublished inventory available.

O'Connor, Harvey. Papers 1936: ca. 25 items. Financial records, clippings about 1936 American Newspaper Guild strike against *Seattle Post-Intelligencer*.

Pettus, Terry. Papers 1935-1937, 1966, 1967: .75 linear ft. Newspaper editor, labor organizer, union official. Organized branches of American Newspaper Guild in Tacoma, Seattle, Spokane WA; Portland OR; Victoria, Vancouver, British Columbia in 1935-1937. Papers relate to strike against *Seattle Post-Intelligencer*, 1936-1937. Edited *Washington New Dealer*. Oral history interview. Unpublished inventory available.

Redington, John W. Papers 1879-1935: 1 linear ft. Pioneer, journalist, soldier. Edited *Heppner Gazet* and other newspapers. Correspondence, scrapbook. Unpublished inventory available.

Roberts, Joseph Dana, 1907-1952. Papers 1924-1949: 9 linear ft. State legislator, journalist with *The Seattle Guide* 1937-1957; *Seattlife* 1937; radio talk show "The Seattlight" 1930-1932. Unpublished inventory available.

Sakamoto, James Y. Papers 1929-1955: 9 linear ft. Publisher of *Japanese-American Courier* 1928-1942. Correspondence, speeches, writings, subject files, financial records, legal documents. Unpublished inventory available. See also "The Political Conservatism of James Sakamoto's *Japanese-American Courier*" by Mayumi Tsutakawa, written as a master's thesis 1976.

Seattle Magazine. Records 1963-1970: 66 linear ft. City magazine published by King Broadcasting Co. April 1964-December 1970. Business records, correspondence, research files. Unpublished inventory available.

Seattle Sun. Collection 1974-1982: 6 linear ft. Correspondence, minutes, financial records of weekly newspaper.

Siehoku Nippo. Records 1944-1953: 4.5 linear ft. Seattle Japanese daily newspaper. Correspondence, financial records, subscription lists, news releases, photographs. Includes correspondence of Martin K. Miyata, one of the paper's owners, about his incarceration at the Santa Fe Detention Station NM, as an alien enemy during World War II. Unpublished inventory available.

Smith, Joseph, 1873-1962. Papers 1890-1957: 9 linear ft. Journalist, political activist. Diary, reporter's notes, correspondence, articles. Unpublished inventory available.

Stone, Harold Ortho, 1881-   Papers 1918-1960: 1 reel microfilm. Journalist, advertising executive. Scrapbooks.

Strong, Anna Louise, 1885-1970. Papers 1885-1970: 19 linear ft. Political activist, author, journalist. Correspondence, legal documents, speeches and writings, literary manuscripts, notes, diary, photographs, clippings. PARTIALLY RESTRICTED Unpublished inventory available.

Svenska Posten. Records 1925-1972: 4 linear ft. Swedish-American newspaper published in Seattle. Correspondence, speeches, writings, news releases, photographs, clippings. In Swedish and English. Unpublished inventory available.

Velasco, Victorio. Papers 1920-1969: 18 linear ft. Editor and publisher *Filipino Forum.* Correspondence, reports, speeches, financial records. Microfilm copies of Filipino-American newspapers 1927-1954. PARTIALLY RESTRICTED. Unpublished inventory available.

Washington State Historical Society

• Hewitt Library, Washington State Historical Society, 315 N. Stadium Way, Tacoma WA 98403. 206-593-2830. Joy Werlink, Manuscripts Librarian. 9:30 am-5 pm Tu-Sa. Photocopy services.

Fuller, Edward, 1824-1904. Papers: 1 box. Reporter and editor. Worked on *Boston Daily Journal, Manchester Daily Mirror, Newark*

Evening Journal, Salt Lake City Daily Herald, Chicago Daily Herald, Tacoma Daily News.

Globe Publishing Co. Ledgers and papers: 3 boxes. Published *Tacoma Morning Globe* 1888-1892. Financial records and correspondence.

Perkins, Sidney Albert, 1865-1955. Papers: 3 boxes. Owner of *Daily Olympian, Olympia Daily Recorder, Bellingham Herald, Bellingham American and Reveille, Everett Herald, Aberdeen Herald, Tacoma Ledger, Tacoma Daily News.* Correspondents include William Borah, Nicholas Murray Butler, Calvin Coolidge, Thomas E. Dewey, James Forrestal, Warren G. Harding, Herbert Hoover, Charles Evans Hughes, Harold L. Ickes, Theodore Roosevelt, Elihu Root, Reed Smoot, William Howard Taft.

WISCONSIN

Milwaukee County Historical Society

• Milwaukee County Historical Society, 910 No. Third St., Milwaukee WI 53203. 414-273-8288. 9:30 am-noon, 1-4 pm M-F. Photocopy services.

Bullard, Lola. Papers 1920-1930: .5 cubic ft. Society news reporter for *Wisconsin News* and *Wisconsin State Journal.* Correspondence, clippings.

Gregory, John Goadby and family. Papers 1830-1942: 10 cubic ft. Journalist with *Milwaukee Evening Journal.*

Heath, Frederic. Papers 1903-1938: 5 cu. ft. Socialist, historian, journalist, county supervisor.

Milwaukee Press Club. Records 1871-1986: 4 cubic ft. Minutes, publications, photographs, awards.

State Historical Society of Wisconsin

• Mass Communications History Center, State Historical Society of Wisconsin, 816 State St., Madison WI 53706. 608-262-9561. Janice L. O'Connell, Director. 8 am-5 pm M-F; 9 am-4 pm Sa. Check for hours during Univ. of Wisconsin intersession and holidays. Collections on RLIN. See also *Sources for Mass Communications, Film and Theater Research: a Guide* (Madison: State Historical Society of Wisconsin, 1982).

Allen, Robert S., 1900-   Papers 1932-1942: 13 boxes and 5 vols. Author of syndicated column "Washington Merry-Go-Round." Also articles by Allen and other members of Washington bureau of *Philadelphia Record*, 1936-1942.

Allman, Norwood F., 1893-   Papers 1960-1966: 1 folder. Transcriptions of "Opinioncasts," a broadcast editorial on the Far East distributed by Broadcast Editorial Reports.

Alternative Press Centre. Records 1969-1975: 7 boxes. Non-profit collective which produced *Alternative Press Index*. Correspondence.

American Research Bureau, Inc. Television reports 1954-1955: 5 boxes. Monthly ratings.

Anderson, Donald W., 1900-1978. Papers 1890-1972: 14 boxes. Publisher of *Wisconsin State Journal* owned by the Lee Group. Correspondents include Emanuel P. and Philip D. Adler, Lee P. Loomis, William T. Evjue, Aaron Bohrod, Chester B. Bowles, Earle Stanley Gardner, Roy L. Matson, Richard M. Nixon, William Proxmire, Frederick A. Seaton, Wendell L. Willkie, Frank Lloyd Wright.

Associated Press Managing Editors Assoc. Records 1948-1973: 22 cartons. Correspondence, printed committee and story group reports, financial records, newsletters, working papers, speeches. Major files include those of Don Earl Carter, Ernest Cutts, Victor Hackler, Wendell C. Phillippi, David N. Schutz, Harry Walsh, L. Sonneborn, Gilbert P. Smith, Mason Walsh.

Association for Education in Journalism. Records 1913-1976: 50 boxes, 32 tapes. Correspondence, reports, minutes, speeches, papers, oral history interviews. Frequent additions expected.

Auer, James M., 1928-   Papers 1949-1973: 10 boxes. Editor of *Appleton Sun-Crescent* 1960-1972. Unpublished works, publicity materials, correspondence, minutes, reports. Correspondents include August Derleth.

Aukofer, Frank, 1935-   Recordings 1967: 1 tape. Interview by *Milwaukee Journal* reporter with civil rights leader Father James Groppi. Unprocessed material includes draft of *City with a Chance* (1968) and clippings and drafts of newspaper articles.

Azcarraga, Emilio, d. 1973. History: 1 folder. Biographical sketch of president of Inter-American Association of Broadcasters 1953-1954, written by Juan M. Duran.

Back, Gunnar. Recordings 1951-1953: 92 discs. Recordings of news broadcaster and director of news for WFIL/WFIL-TV, Philadelphia PA, pertaining to ABC radio series *Cross Fire* and *Lonesome Road.*

Bailey, Robert L., 1929-   Research study 1966: 1 folder. "Network Television, Patterns in Nighttime Special Programming."

Bakken, Anthony W. Correspondence 1939: 2 letters. Editor of *Rio Journal.* Correspondence from Robert M. La Follette, Jr. and William T. Evjue concerning organization of Progressive press assoc.

Bannister, Harry R., 1884-1967. Papers 1936-1967: 14 boxes, 8 tapes, 13 discs. Vice president of station relations at NBC 1952-1961. Speeches, writings, clippings, reports, biographical information. Correspondents include Martin Agronsky, Leonard Bernstein, Gerald R. Ford, J. Edgar Hoover, Lyndon B. Johnson, Allan Nevins, George W. Romney, Robert A. Taft, David C. Adams, Robert Kintner, David Sarnoff, Robert W. Sarnoff, Sylvester L. Weaver, Jr., Frank White.

Barnes, Patrick H., 1988-1969. Papers 1951, 1962: 1 box. Radio pioneer who directed public affairs for WISN/WISN-TV, Milwaukee, WI. Biographical data, script, oral history transcript.

Barton, Albert O., 1870-1974. Papers 1858-1948: 24 boxes. Assoc. editor of *Wisconsin Farmer* 1920-1929. Wrote column "Old Days" for *Capital Times.* Articles, columns, correspondence, clippings.

Baukhage, Hilmar R., 1889-1976. Papers 1906-1962: 4 boxes, 5 tapes, 26 discs. Writer; newspaperman; Washington commentator for NBC and ABC. Scripts, journals, speeches, recordings, correspondence.

Bendiner, Robert, 1909-   Papers 1934-1966: 42 boxes. Editor, writer and member of *New York Times* editorial board. Drafts, notes, research material, correspondence. Correspondents include Paul Douglas, W. Averell Harriman, Hubert H. Humphrey, Jacob K. Javits, John V. Lindsay, James Loeb, Jr., Douglas MacArthur, Mike Monroney, Joseph L. Rauh, Jr., Arthur M.

Schlesinger, Jr., Theodore Sorenson, Norman Thomas, Harry S Truman.

Benjamin, Burton, 1918-   Papers 1957-1982: 36 boxes. CBS producer, vice president, director of news; producer of television news and documentaries. Relates primarily to work on CBS documentary *The Twentieth Century* 1957-1966. Production files, publicity, distribution figures, reports, scripts, interview transcripts, research materials, narrations, reviews.

Benjamin, Philip R., 1922-1966. Papers 1934-1965: 5 boxes. *New York Times* reporter and novelist. Correspondence, financial records, diaries, notebooks, professional materials.

Benson, Alex, 1928-1974. Papers 1944-1974: 1 reel microfilm. Reporter for *New York World-Telegram and Sun* 1955-1966; *New York World-Journal-Tribune* 1966-1967. NBC producer. Biographical material, correspondence, writings, scripts.

Bergman, Jules, 1930-   Papers 1965-1974: 9 boxes. ABC news science editor. Notes, press kits, scripts.

Black, Creed C., 1925-   Papers 1943-1969: 16 boxes. Worked for *Chicago Daily News, Nashville Tennessean, Paducah Sun-Democrat, Savannah News-Press, Wilmington News-Journal.* Clippings, notebooks. Correspondents include Harry S. Ashmore, Grover Hall, C. Estes Kefauver, Robert F. Kennedy, Walter Lippmann, Richard M. Nixon, Charles H. Percy, Vermont C. Royster.

Blockman, Laurence G., Report 1944: 1 folder. "Plan for D-Day Broadcasts," preliminary report prepared by William S. Paley for Psychological Warfare Division, Allied Expeditionary Force, May 19, 1944.

Bolens, Albert D., 1861-1952. Papers 1836-1952: 3 boxes, 1 scrapbook. Conservative Republican editor and publisher of five WI newspapers including *Port Washington Star* and *Sheyboygan Statesman.* Correspondence, business papers, clippings.

Bolles, Stephen, 1866-1941. Papers 1920-1941: 7 boxes, 9 scrapbooks. Editor of *Janesville Gazette,* who served in U. S. Congress 1939-1941. Correspondence, clippings. Correspondents include William E. Borah, Calvin Coolidge, Herbert Hoover, Robert M. La Follette, Jr., David Lawrence, John J. Pershing, Franklin D. Roosevelt, William Allen White, Alexander Wiley.

Boyle, Harold V., 1911-1974. Papers 1942-1974: 8 boxes. Columnist and Pulitzer Prize-winning war correspondent who covered World War II, Korean War, Vietnam conflict for Associated Press. Correspondence, press dispatches, notes, biographical material.

Bracker, Milton, 1909-1964, and Warren, Virginia Lee. Papers 1931-1966: 3 microfilm reels. Husband-wife journalistic team. Primarily articles for *New York Times*.

Braden, Carl, 1914-1975, and Braden, Anne, 1924-   Papers 1928-1972: 97 boxes, 88 tapes, 2 discs, 5 microfilm reels, 1 film. Field organizers for Southern Conference Educational Fund and editors of *Southern Patriot*. Correspondents include James A. Dombrowski, Clark Foreman, Aubrey Williams.

Braucher, Frank, 1884-1968. Papers 1920-1968: 1 pkg. President of Periodical Publishers Assoc. and of Magazine Advertising Bureau. Primarily testimonial letters.

Bridgeman, Louis W., 1883-1960. Papers 1910-1960: 2 boxes. Reporter for *Wisconsin State Journal* 1906-1913; Associated Press 1913-1930. Correspondents include Amos P. Wilder.

Brinkley, David, 1920-   Papers 1960-1969: 10 boxes. NBC news commentator. Reactions to broadcasts of *Huntley-Brinkley Report*, *David Brinkley's Journal*, and other programs.

Broughton, Charles E., 1873-1956.   Papers 1916-1953: 15 boxes, 14 vols. Editor of *Sheyboygan Press*. Correspondence, articles, speeches, clippings. Correspondents include Robert S. Allen, Alben W. Barkley, Nicholas Murray Butler, James F. Byrnes, Raymond Clapper, Clarence A. Darrow, Joseph E. Davies, Eugene V. Debs, William O. Douglas, Dwight D. Eisenhower, James A. Farley, Hugh S. Johnson, Alfred M. Landon, Robert M. La Follette, Jr., Paul V. McNutt, George C. Marshall, Henry Morgenthau, Jr., Gaylord Nelson, Drew Pearson, Franklin D. Roosevelt, Ida Tarbell, Harry S Truman, Henry A. Wallace, Sumner Welles, Wendell L. Willkie.

Brown, Cecil, 1907-   Papers 1935-1967: 76 boxes, 16 vols, 3 discs. Journalist and news commentator for ABC, CBS, NBC and public television. Scripts, correspondence, published writings including articles for *Liberty*, *Pittsburgh Press*.

Butterfield, Charles E., 1892-1958.   Papers, 1931-1957: 3 folders. Associated Press radio and television editor. Clippings.

Correspondents include Walter L. "Red" Barber, Hans V. Kaltenvorn, Guglielmo Marconi, Mary Martin, Ed Sullivan, John Cameron Swayze, Ed Wynn.

Carnegie Commission on Educational Television. Records 1963-1967: 6 boxes, 12 tapes. Records of study which was instrumental in the establishment of the Corporation for Public Broadcasting. Correspondence, proceedings, reports, drafts. Correspondents include Lyndon Johnson, E.B. White.

Cassidy, Henry, 1910-   Papers 1945-1958: 6 boxes. NBC foreign correspondent, news executive, broadcaster. Radio scripts for *Report on Europe* 1945-1950; *Heart of the News, News of the World, World News Roundup* 1953-1955; articles for *New York Daily News* 1967-1974. Correspondents include Drew Pearson.

Cater, S. Douglass, 1923-   Papers 1959-1964: 10 boxes. Editor of *The Reporter*, special assistant to President Lyndon B. Johnson.

Chapelle, Dickey, 1918-1965. Papers 1933-1968: 20 boxes, 1 vol, 5 tapes. Correspondent, photographer, public relations consultant. Includes her work for *Look, National Geographic, Reader's Digest, Saturday Evening Post.*

Childs, Marquis W., 1903-   Papers 1919-1967: 33 boxes, 1 tape. Pulitzer Prize-winning writer and reporter for *St. Louis Post-Dispatch.* Research documents including interview notes with Winston S. Churchill, John F. Kennedy, Alfred M. Landon, Franklin D. Roosevelt. Correspondence, fan mail, *St. Louis Post-Dispatch* Washington bureau files, writings. Correspondents include Dean G. Acheson, Bruce Barton, Bernard Baruch, William Benton, Claude G. Bowers, Chester B. Bowles, Julian P. Boyd, Omar N. Bradley, James F. Byrnes, James B. Conant, Elmer Davis, Thomas E. Dewey, Paul H. Douglas, William O. Douglas, John Foster Dulles, Cyrus Eaton, T.S. Eliot, Albert Einstein, William T. Evjue, Felix Frankfurter, J. William Fulbright, John Kenneth Galbraith, Barry Goldwater, Albert A. Gore, Dag Hammarskjold, W. Averell Harriman, Lister Hill, Herbert Hoover, J. Edgar Hoover, Hubert H. Humphrey, Harold L. Ickes, Lyndon B. Johnson, Hans V. Kaltenborn, C. Estes Kefauver, John F. Kennedy, Fulton Lewis, Jr., Trygve Lie, David E. Lilienthal, Walter Lippmann, Henry Cabot Lodge, Jr., Claire Boothe Luce, H.L. Mencken, Mikhail Menshikov, Edward P. Morgan, Wayne L. Morse, Edward R. Murrow, Gaylord Nelson, Reinhold Niebuhr, Richard M. Nixon, William Proxmire, Abraham Ribicoff, Edward V. Rickenbacker, Morris H. Rubin, Dean Rusk, Adlai E. Stevenson, W. Stuart Symington, Norman M. Thomas, Harry S Truman, Arthur H. Vandenberg, Earl Warren, Sumner Welles, Wendell L. Willkie. RESTRICTED: Permission to use collection must be obtained from director, State Historical Society of Wisconsin.

Cleveland OH. Radio station WTAM. History 1955: 1 folder. History of WTAM, WTAM-FM, WNBK-TV, NBC-owned stations 1923-1955.

Clurman, Harold, 1901-   Notebooks 1945-1951: 1 box. Drama critic for *New Republic* and *The Nation.*

Codel, Martin, 1902-1973. Papers 1926-1969: 6 boxes, 30 vols. Reporter and writer on broadcasting. Includes articles written for Consolidated Press Assoc., North American Newspaper Alliance, Radio News Bureau.

Colburn, John H., 1912-   Papers 1949-1975: 9 boxes. Managing editor of *Richmond Times-Dispatch* 1949-1964; editor and publisher of *Wichita Eagle and Beacon* 1963-1972; vice president Landmark Communications, Inc. 1972-   Correspondence, clippings, speeches, statistics. PORTIONS RESTRICTED.

Collingwood, Charles C., 1917-   Papers 1952-1960: 6 boxes. Foreign correspondent; CBS news commentator. Radio scripts 1952-1959, fan mail, notes, correspondence, financial records.

Connections. Records 1967-1968: 1 box. Bi-weekly underground newspaper in Madison WI. Correspondence, budget, articles, drawings.

Cox, Kenneth, 1916-   Speeches 1964-1970: 1 box. Member of Federal Communications Commission.

Crawford, William, 1913-   Editorial cartoons 1970: 8 items.

Critchfield, Richard, 1931-   Papers 1938-1974: 24 boxes, 1 reel microfilm. Author and foreign correspondent known for his Far Eastern reporting. Correspondence, memoranda to *Washington Star* editors Burt Hoffman and Crosby C. Noyes, research files, interview notes. PARTIALLY RESTRICTED.

Crockett, Albert Stevens, 1873-   Papers 1903-1961: 1 box. Author and reporter. Correspondence, clippings.

Daly, John Charles, 1914-   Papers 1935-1967: 36 boxes, 3 discs, 8 films. Award-winning broadcaster, news executive, quiz show personality. With ABC as newsman and vice president of news, special events and public affairs 1953-1967.

Delay, Theodore S., Jr., 1915-   Dissertation 1951: 1 box. "An Historical Study of the Armed Forces Radio Service to 1946."

Denny, Ludwell, 1894-1970. Papers 1917-1959: 8 boxes, 2 reels microfilm. Associated with Scripps-Howard as editorial writer, columnist, editor 1928-1970. Correspondence, memos, notes. Correspondents include Harry Elmer Barnes, Bernard Baruch, Bruce Bliven, Chester B. Bowles, Charles R. Crane, Louis Fischer, C. Hartley Grattan, Louis M. Hacker, Roy W. Howard, Cordell Hull, Harold L. Ickes, Willard M. Kiplinger, H.L. Mencken, Frank Murphy, Marie Teresa Norton, Ralph P. Patterson, Ernest T. Pyle, Nelson A. Rockefeller, Carlos P. Romulo, Herbert Bayard Swope, Arthur H. Sulzberger, Jr., Oswald Garrison Villard, Burton K. Wheeler.

Doerfer, John C., 1904-   Papers 1953-1960: 1 folder. Member 1953-1957 and chairman 1957-1960 of Federal Communications Commission. Speeches, press releases.

Donahey, William, 1883-1970.   Papers 1914-1969: 8 boxes, 2,739 items. Some political cartoons and examples of Donahey's early work for *Cleveland Plain Dealer*. Correspondence, writings, drawings.

Dowling, Dan, 1906-   Editorial cartoons 1963-1965: 3 items.

Dreier, Alex, 1916-   Scripts 1957: 1 folder. Chicago news commentator. Editorials broadcast over NBC.

Estabrook, Robert H., 1918-   Papers 1947-1966: 7 boxes. Editorial writer, chief foreign correspondent, assoc. editor, United Nations correspondent for *Washington Post* 1946-1971; editor-publisher of *Lakeville Journal* 1971-   Correspondence, notes, reports.

Evjue, William T., 1882-1970. Papers 1905-1969: 167 boxes, 1 disc. Founder, editor, publisher of *Capital Times*. Clippings, memoranda, financial material, speeches. Correspondents include Robert S. Allen, Arthur J. Altmeyer, Herbert L. Block, Arthur Brisbane, William Jennings Bryan, John R. Commons, Leo T. Crowley, August Derleth, Irving Dilliard, William O. Douglas, Zona Gale, John Gunther, Hubert H. Humphrey, Hans

V. Kaltenborn, C. Estes Kefauver, John F. Kennedy, Robert M. La Follette, Sr., Robert M. La Follette, Jr., David E. Lilienthal, Wayne L. Morse, Gaylord Nelson, George W. Norris, Drew Pearson, Franklin D. Roosevelt, Morris H. Rubin, Carl Sandburg, Adlai E. Stevenson, Harry S Truman, Millard E. Tydings, Henry A. Wallace, Wendell L. Willkie, James A. Wechsler, Frank Lloyd Wright.

Ferber, Edna, 1887-1968. Papers 1912-1977: 29 boxes, 4 disc recordings, 1 tape recording. Journalist; novelist; playwright. Correspondence, research materials, drafts, galleys, reviews. Correspondents include H.L. Mencken, William Allen White, Alexander Woollcott.

Fischer, Ernest G., 1902-   Papers 1941-1966: 19 boxes. Associated Press correspondent and journalism educator. Press releases, dispatches, notes, correspondence. PARTIALLY RESTRICTED.

Fischer, John, 1910-   Papers 1937-1969: 18 boxes, 1 tape. Editor-in-chief *Harper's Magazine* 1953-1969. Correspondents include Walter Lippmann, Arthur M. Schlesinger, Jr., Theodore C. Sorenson, Benjamin M. Spock.

Flannery, Harry W., 1900-1975. Papers 1927-1968: 34 boxes, 806 tapes, 5 films. Foreign correspondent, news analyst, AFL-CIO radio coordinator. Articles, research materials, scripts. Correspondents include Paul H. Douglas, Arthur J. Goldberg, Hubert H. Humphrey, John F. Kennedy, Robert F. Kennedy, George Meany, Upton Sinclair, Willard Wirtz.

Fleming, Robert H. Papers 1935-1966: 5 boxes. *Milwaukee Journal* reporter, ABC news broadcaster, government official. Subject files.

Ghali, Paul, 1906?-1970. Papers 1940-1969: 13 boxes. *Chicago Daily News* Paris correspondence. Press dispatches, clippings.

Goodland, Walter W., 1862-1947. Papers 1856-1932: 1 box, 3 vols. Publisher of *Racine Times-Call* 1902-1933, Wisconsin governor 1943-1947. Personal correspondence, columns. Official papers in Wisconsin State Archives.

Goralski, Robert S., 1928-   Papers 1953-1975: 14 boxes, 1 tape. NBC Washington correspondent; public relations director for Gulf Oil. News scripts for *News on the Hour, Monitor, Today in Washington, World News Roundup, Huntley-Brinkley Report,*

NBC Nightly News, Today; correspondence, background files. RESTRICTED.

Gorrell, Henry T., 1911?-1958. Scrapbooks: 1 microfilm reel. United Press war correspondent and editor-publisher of *Veterans Report* 1946-1958.

Graebner, Walter, 1909-1976. Papers 1928-1969: 3 boxes. Journalist with *Time*, author, advertising executive. Articles, scripts, book materials. Correspondents include Winston S. Churchill, Henry R. Luce, Prince Bernhard of the Netherlands, Cardinal Francis Spellman, Harold Wilson.

Gunther, John, 1901-   Papers 1938-1944: 2 boxes, 26 discs. Author and foreign correspondent. Correspondence, contracts, annotated typescripts, radio scripts, 41 recordings of broadcasts 1942-1942.

Hall, Wilson, 1922-   Papers 1959-1973: 2 boxes. NBC foreign correspondent. Scripts, production notes for *Emphasis, Monitor, Huntley-Brinkley Report.*

Hamilton, John S., 1900-   Papers 1924-1946: 1 box. Tokyo correspondent for *London Daily Mail* 1924. Chief of night bureau, War Dept. Public Relations Bureau May 1941-Jan. 1942. With *Business Week* 1943-1946.

Harrington, Gerard. Recordings 1976: 2 tapes. Interview with New England newspaperman. Includes his experiences with William Jennings Bryan, Clarance A. Darrow, and the British War Relief Society.

Harris, T. George, 1924-   Papers 1943-1975: 39 boxes. Editor of *Time, Look, Careers Today, Psychology Today.* Correspondence, articles, editorial files, subject files. Correspondents include Harry S. Ashmore, William F. Buckley, Jr., Bennett Cerf, John Sherman Cooper, Ben Moreell, David Riesman, John Rousselot. PORTIONS RESTRICTED.

Harsch, Joseph C., 1905-   Papers 1928-1967: 37 boxes, 5 vols. Journalist and news broadcaster with CBS, BBC, NBC, *Christian Science Monitor.* Correspondence, book manuscripts, scripts, articles. Correspondents include Dean G. Acheson, David Astor, Chester B. Bowles, Omar N. Bradley, Anthony Eden, James A. Farley, John Fischer, J. William Fulbright, J.K. Lindley, Walter Lippmann, Douglas MacArthur, Harold MacMillan, Edward R. Murrow.

Harvey, Alfred S., 1891-   Recording 1950: 1 tape. Founding editor of *Milwaukee Labor Press*. Conversation with John Stroebel, Wisconsin Federation of Labor.

Hazard, Aline W., 1895-   Papers 1938-1965: 2 boxes. Broadcaster with WHA, Madison WI. Correspondence, reports, scripts, autobiography.

Hedges, William S., 1895-1978. Papers 1918-1962: 4 boxes. Broadcasting executive with NBC. Founding member of National Association of Broadcasters. Correspondence, speeches, articles, oral history interview transcript.

Henle, Raymond Z., 1899-1974. Papers 1883-1973: 16 boxes, 69 microfilm reels, 252 tapes, 31 discs. NBC news commentator and newspaper journalist. Chiefly material for *Three Star Extra*. Microfilmed scripts by Henle, Ned Brooks, Charles T. Lucey, Felix Morley, Merrill Mueller, Edward Tomlinson, Russ Ward, Albert L. Warner. Personal correspondence, financial records, social papers. Correspondents include Alben W. Barkley, Mark W. Clark, Gerald R. Ford, J. Edgar Hoover, Herbert Hoover, Hubert H. Humphrey, Richard M. Nixon, J. Howard Pew, Archibald Roosevelt. Unpublished register available.

Henry, E. William, 1929-   Papers 1955-1966: 85 boxes, 13 tapes, 1 film. FCC commissioner 1962-1963 and chairman 1963-1966. Correspondence, memoranda, working papers, testimony transcripts.

Hightower, John M., 1909-   Papers 1944-1965: 13 boxes. Pulitzer Prize-winning Associated Press correspondent and editor. Notebooks, correspondence, background files, clippings. RESTRICTED.

Hoard, Halbert L., 1861-1933. Papers 1872-1933: 14 boxes. Editor of *Jefferson County Union*. Correspondents include William Jennings Bryan, Will H. Hayes, William Mitchell, Margaret Sanger. Clippings.

Hudson Star-Observer. Records 1926-1940: 1 folder, 2 vols. Misc. financial records, physical property inventory. Personal papers of publisher Willis H. Miller.

Hull, Merlin, 1881-1953. Papers 1881-1953: 213 boxes. Editor and publisher of *Black River Falls Banner-Journal*. Politician. Correspondence.

Hungerford, Cyrus. Political cartoons ca. 1930-ca. 1950: 8 items. Published in *Pittsburgh Post-Gazette*.

Hunter, Edward, 1902-1978. Papers 1922-1960: 3 boxes. Foreign correspondent, China specialist. With International News Service 1936-1937. Editor and publisher of *Tactics* magazine.

Hunter, John Patrick, 1916- Papers 1951-1970: 2 boxes. Reporter and assoc. editor of *Capital Times*; stringer for *New York Times*. Writings, subject files. Correspondents include William F. Buckley, Jr., Otto Eisenschiml, Hubert H. Humphrey, C. Estes Kefauver, John F. Kennedy, Edward P. Morgan, Max Otto, William Proxmire, Harlow Shapley, Norman M. Thomas.

Huntley, Chet, 1911-1974. Papers 1957-1974: 16 boxes, 17 tapes. Co-anchor of NBC evening news 1956-1970. Correspondence, radio scripts, recordings. Correspondents include Orson Bean, Homer E. Capehart, Bennett Cerf, C. Douglas Dillon, Will Durant, Abba Eban, Orville E. Freeman, Dave Garroway, David Sarnoff, Walter D. Scott.

Hyatt, Donald B., 1924- Papers 1952-1973: 58 boxes, 10 films. Award-winning writer, producer and director of NBC television documentaries.

Irwin, Dilla E. Papers 1964-1966: 1 folder. Editor of *Vicksburg Citizens' Appeal*, Black community newspaper. Correspondence, minutes, clippings.

Isaacs, Edith J.R., 1878-1956. Papers 1889-1957: 1 box, 1 vol., 1 reel microfilm. Editor of *Theatre Arts* 1918-1946. Correspondents include Jacques Copeau, Paul Green, Martha Graham, Edith Hamilton, Robert Edmond Jones, D.H. Lawrence, Thornton Wilder, Stark Young.

Jacobs. Herbert. Papers 1955-1975: 1 folder and 2,000 photographs. Reporter for *Capital Times*.

Jaffe, Sam A., 1929- Papers 1947-1972: 1 box, 1 disc. News broadcaster for ABC and CBS. Correspondence, scripts, clippings.

Jones, Rogan. Letter 1957: 1 folder. Broadcasting executive. Describes his part in litigation between Associated Press and KVOS, Bellingham WA, which applied freedom of the press to radio.

Kahn, Gordon, 1902-1962. Papers 1944-1950: 1 box. Journalist and screenwriter blacklisted for his support of the Hollywood Ten. Correspondence, research files, manuscript, articles.

Kaltenborn, Hans V., 1875-1965. Papers 1883-1964: 214 boxes, 29 vols, 2 pkgs., 5 microfilm reels, 23 tapes, 556 discs, 1 film. "Dean of American Radio Commentators. Correspondence, business files, radio scripts, notebooks, manuscripts. Correspondents include Norman Angell, Chester B. Bowles, Herbert Hoover, Fannie Hurst, Fiorello La Guardia, Henrik W. van Loon, Lowell Thomas, Harry S Truman, Henry A. Wallace. Descriptive booklet "The H. V. Kaltenborn Collection" available upon request.

Katkov, Norman, 1918-   Papers 1930-1968: 34 boxes, 1 vol. Journalist for *New York World-Telegram*, North American Newspaper Alliance; writer of short stories, novels, screenplays, teleplays. Correspondence, writings, business files.

Kaufmann, Walter. Articles. 1 folder. Reporter for *Berlin Junge Welt.* Article drafts.

Kerby, Elizabeth Poe. Papers 1953-1961: 1 folder. Articles on the extent and impact of Hollywood blacklist which resulted from 1952-1953 investigations of House Un-American Activities Committee.

Kerr, Walter F., 1913-   , and Kerr, Jean, 1923-   Papers 1929-1969: ca. 50 cubic ft. Walter Kerr is a theatre critic with the *New York Herald-Tribune, New York Times, Commonwealth*; playwright. Correspondence, scripts, photographs, notes clippings, financial records. Correspondents include George Abbott, Brooks Atkinson, W.H. Auden, Ralph Bellamy, Richard Burton, Carol Channing, Barrett H. Clark, Russel Crouse, John van Druten, John Gassner, John Golden, Mordecai Gorelik, Oscar Hammerstein II, Moss Hart, Helen Hayes, Hubert H. Humphrey, Elia Kazan, Howard Lindsay, Joshua Logan, Claire Boothe Luce, Claudia McNail, Fredric March, Mary Martin, Groucho Marx, Jo Mielziner, Max Reinhardt, Richard Rogers, William Saroyan, Gloria Swanson, Tennessee Williams.

Kinoy, Ernest. Papers 1948-1966: 17 boxes. Journalist; writer for radio, television, and theatre. Correspondence, scripts.

Kiplinger, Austin H., 1918-   Papers 1951-1959: 2 boxes. News commentator and president of Kiplinger Washington Editors.

Scripts, correspondence, notes, drafts of *Kiplinger Washington Letter.*

Kirby, Edward M. Reminiscences 1964: 1 folder. Chief of Radio Branch of War Dept.'s Public Relations Bureau 1941-1945. Concerns radio broadcasting during World War II.

Knecht, Karl. Political cartoons 1930-1945: 14 items. Published in *Evansville Courier.*

Koenig, Gilbert. Papers 1920-1960: 1 folder, 1 tape. Managing editor and general manager of *Waukesha Daily Freeman.*

Kubly, Herbert, 1915-   Papers 1965-1969: 4 boxes. Author, journalist, playwright.

Lania, Leo, 1896-1961. Papers 1916-1959: 17 boxes. Journalist and propagandist Lazar Herman, who worked under pen name of Leo Lania.   Drafts, reviews, notes, writings, articles.   Correspondents include Brigid Brophy, Pearl S. Buck, Max Eastman, Lion Feuchtwanger, Granville Hicks, Hans V. Kaltenborn, Fritz Lang, Walter Lippmann, Louis P. Lochner, W. Somerset Maugham, Edgar Ansel Mowrer, Erwin Piscator, Arthur M. Schlesinger, Jr., Dorothy Thompson, Sigrid Undset.

Lasch, Robert, 1907-   Papers 1940-1971: 13 boxes, 2 vols. Editorial writer for *Chicago Sun-Times* 1942-1950; editorial writer and editorial page editor *St. Louis Post-Dispatch* 1950-1971. 1966 Pulitzer Prize. Subject files, notes, articles. Correspondents include Herbert L. Block, Marquis W. Childs, Henry Steele Commager, J. William Fulbright, Hubert H. Humphrey, Arthur M. Schlesinger, Jr., Adlai E. Stevenson, W. Stuart Symington, Joseph Pulitzer, Marshall Field III.

Laurent, Lawrence B., 1925-   Papers 1962-1964: 1 box. Radio-television editor for *Washington Post.* Articles, biographical material. Correspondents include Newton Minow, Morris S. Novik.

Lewis, Ross A. Political cartoons 1962-1966: 7 items. Published in *Milwaukee Journal.*

Lochner, Louis P., 1887-1975. Papers 1903-1972: 52 boxes, 1 pkg., 6 discs, 20 tapes. Pulitzer Prize-winning news commentator, author, foreign correspondent best known for his coverage of Nazi Germany. Correspondence, writings, diaries, subject files. Correspondents include Jane Addams, William Jennings

Bryan, Lucius D. Clay, Kent Cooper, Albert S. Crockett, Dan DeLuce, Allen W. Dulles, Hugo Eckener, Henry Ford, Pauline Frederick, Ralph J. Frantz, J. Wes Gallagher, Hugh Gibson, Alan J. Gould, William P. Gray, Dag Hammarskjold, Ernest Hanfstaegle, Hans Hinrichs, Herbert Hoover, David Starr Jordan, Hans V. Kaltenborn, Paul U. Kellogg, John F. Kennan, Henry Cabot Lodge, Prince Louis Ferdinand, Ralph O. Nafziger, Arthur H. Sulzberger, Jr, Woodrow Wilson. Unpublished register available.

Loevinger, Lee, 1913-   Papers 1963-1976: 2 boxes, 9 tapes. Member of Federal Communications Commission 1963-1968. Speeches, statements, FCC opinions.

Lowe, David, d. 1965. Papers 1960-1966: 1 box. Award-winning producer of investigative documentaries for *CBS Reports*. Scripts, research materials, photographs.

Lynch, Russell G., 1900-1979. Recording 1965: 1 tape. *Milwaukee Journal* sports and outdoor editor.

Lyon, Peter, 1915-   Papers 1884-1969: 18 boxes. Free-lance writer.   Grandson and biographer of S.S. McClure. RESTRICTED.

McBride, Joseph, 1947-   Papers 1963-1983: 106 boxes, 63 tape recordings. Film critic and writer. Drafts, research material, correspondence. RESTRICTED: Audio tapes are restricted.

McCormick, Anne O'Hare, d. 1954.   Articles 1936-1954: 4 microfilm reels.   Pulitzer Prize-winning foreign correspondent of *New York Times*. News stories.

McCormick, Robert K., 1911-   Papers 1941-1968: 10 boxes, 2 tapes.   Also available as 18 microfilm reels.   Journalist, NBC news correspondent. Interview, scripts, correspondence, subject files.

McGurn, William Barrett, 1914-   Papers 1939-1966: 9 boxes. Reporter and foreign correspondent with *New York Herald-Tribune* 1935-1966. Correspondence, memoranda, notebooks, speeches.

McMillin, Miles J., 1913-   Papers 1937-1960: 8 boxes. Editor and publisher of *Capital Times*. Clippings, article drafts, correspondence.

MacNeil, Robert, 1931-   Papers 1966-1976: 1 box. Television journalist associated with *MacNeil-Lehrer Report.* Manuscript draft, misc. biographical material.

MacVane, John, 1912-   Papers 1935-1977: 13 boxes (also available as 13 of microfilm reels), 10 tapes, 10 discs, 12 films. Radio-television news broadcaster noted for World War II and United Nations coverage. Scripts, writings. Correspondents include Dean G. Acheson, Warren P. Austin, Bernard Baruch, Omar N. Bradley, Madame Chiang Kai-Shek, Dwight D. Eisenhower, Charles De Gaulle, Andrei Gromyko, James C. Hagerty, Louis Johnson, John L. Lewis, Henry Cabot Lodge, Jr., Elmer W. Lower, Georgi M. Malenkov, Merrill Mueller, Bernard Montgomery, Richard M. Nixon, J. Robert Oppenheimer, Eleanor Roosevelt, William Sheehan, Niles Trammell.

Mason, Frank E., 1893-   Papers 1931-1945: 7 boxes. NBC vice president. Correspondence, speeches, reports.

Matson, Roy L., 1908-1960. Papers 1903-1960: 4 boxes. Editor of *Wisconsin State Journal* 1942-1960. Correspondence, articles, speeches, memorabilia, subject files.

Mickelson, Sigfried, 1913-   Papers 1947-1975: 15 boxes, 39 tapes. Broadcasting executive with CBS News 1943-1961; Time-Life Broadcast, Inc. 1961-1973. Subject files, correspondence, speeches.

Minow, Newton N., 1926-   Papers 1954-1965: 59 boxes, 25 tapes, 12 films. Federal Communications Commission chairman 1961-1963. Correspondents include William Benton, Al Capp, Emanual Celler, Martin Codel, LeRoy Collins, Everett M. Dirksen, Lawrence S. Fanning, Fred W. Friendly, Harry Golden, Arthur J. Goldberg, James C. Hagerty, Herbert Hoover, Hubert H. Humphrey, Lyndon B. Johnson, Nicholas Katzenbach, C. Estes Kefauver, John F. Kennedy, Robert F. Kennedy, Edgar Kobak, Lawrence B. Laurent, Herbert H. Lehman, Lee Loevinger, Claire Boothe Luce, Edward P. Morgan, Edward R. Murrow, Gaylord Nelson, Maurine B. Neuberger, Richard M. Nixon, William Proxmire, James Reston, Eleanor Roosevelt, Robert W. Sarnoff, David Sarnoff, Dore Schary, Arthur Schlesinger, Jr., Howard K. Smith, Merriman Smith, Lawrence E. Spivak, Frank Stanton, Sylvester L. Weaver, Jr., James A. Wechsler, Adlai E. Stevenson. RESTRICTED.

Mollenhoff, Clark R., 1921-   Papers 1936-1975: 74 boxes, 16 microfilm reels, 8 tapes. Pulitzer Prize-winning Washington correspondence, General papers, writings, subject files. Correspondents include Ezra Taft Benson, Paul H. Douglas, Gerald R. Ford, Barry Goldwater, James C. Hagerty, J. Edgar Hoover, Hubert H. Humphrey, Eliot Janeway, Lyndon B. Johnson, C. Estes Kefauver, Robert F. Kennedy, Arthur W. Krock, Robert Lasch, John L. McClellan, Raymond Moley, Karl E. Mundt, Richard M. Nixon, Drew Pearson, Westbrook Pegler, Herbert Philbrick, J. Strom Thurmond. PORTIONS RESTRICTED.

Monroe WI Radio Station WEKZ. Records 1950-1968: 3 boxes. Correspondence, program logs. Correspondents include Harold Engel, Gaylord Nelson, William Proxmire.

Morgan, Edward P., 1910-   Papers 1923-1969: 140 boxes, 100 tapes, 4 discs, 1 film. Award-winning ABC news commentator. Annotated scripts, correspondence, diaries, research files and notes, clippings.

Morin, Relman, 1907-1973. Scrapbooks 1947-1969: 3 microfilm reels. Two-time Pulitzer Prize-winning Associated Press correspondent. Clippings, correspondence, photographs. Correspondents include Kent Cooper, James C. Hagerty, Lyndon B. Johnson, Ann Landers, Adlai E. Stevenson.

Morrison, Chester L., 1900-1966. Papers 1942-1966: 3 microfilm reels. World War II correspondent for *Boston Herald*, *Chicago Sun*, *Coronet*; senior editor for *Look*. Articles, scripts, notes. PHOTODUPLICATION RESTRICTED.

Moscow, Warren, 1908-   Papers 1941-1971: 1 box. *New York Times* political reporter. Correspondence, reminiscences, articles, speeches. Correspondents include Alfred M. Landon, Herbert Bayard Swope.

Mowrer, Edgar Ansel, 1892-1977. Papers 1952-1969: 5 boxes. Pulitzer Prize-winning foreign correspondent, *Chicago Daily News* syndicated columnist, author. Reader mail.

National Association of Broadcasters. Records 1942-1975: 79 boxes, 1 tape, 1 film. Studies, surveys, correspondence, minutes. Correspondents include Hugh Beville, Paul F. Lazarsfeld, Frank Stanton. RESTRICTED.

National Association of Educational Broadcasters. Records 1925-1965: 83 boxes. Subject file, newsletters, correspondence, printed matter.

National Broadcasting Company. Records 1921-1969: 565 boxes, 3,264 discs, 21 tapes, 72 microfilm reels. Central files, office files, scripts. Includes papers of Niles Trammell, Sylvester L. Weaver, Jr., William F. Brooks, Richard A.R. Pinkham, Sidney H. Eiges, John M. Gaines, Carleton D. Smith, Ted Cott, Hamilton Shea, Doris Ann, Wade Arnold, Dorothy Culbertson, Sidney N. Strotz, Clarence N. Menser, John K. Herbert, Walter D. Scott, Charles C. Barry, Michael H. Dann, Albert L. Capstaff, William H. Fineshriber, Jr., Edward R. Madden, William S. Hedges, Davidson Taylor, William F. Brooks, Reuven Frank, Eliot Frankel, Irving Gitlin, Gerald Green, Ted Mills, Samuel Chotzinoff, Mort Abrahams. PORTIONS RESTRICTED.

National Educational Television. Records 1951-1970: 618 boxes, 2 vols., 1 tape, 5 films. Correspondence, memoranda, scripts, reports, clippings, photographs, financial records, minutes, publicity. Includes some files of John F. White.

National League of American Pen Women, Madison WI. Records 1930-1966: 4 boxes. By-laws, minutes, membership information, scrapbooks.

New York NY Radio station WRUL. Records 1961-1962: 1 folder. Miscellaneous records.

New York NY Stations WCBS/WCBS-TV. Records 1965-1978: 9 boxes, 2 tapes, 1 disc. Miscellaneous Records.

Newman, Edwin H., 1919-   Papers 1944-1974: 23 boxes. Author, NBC news commentator, drama critic. Notes, reviews, interviews, fan mail, clippings, speech materials.

Newman, Joseph, 1912-   Papers 1947-1949: 2 boxes. Journalist with *New York Herald-Tribune, U.S. News and World Report.* Articles, notes. Relate chiefly to his two years as chief of *Herald Tribune's* Moscow bureau.

Oak, Liston M., 1895-1970. Papers 1910-1970: 4 boxes. Editor of *The New Leader* 1943-1948. Economic editor of Voice of America 1948-1965. Correspondence, speeches, writings. Correspondents include Whittaker Chambers, Max Eastman, John Fischer, George Meany, Upton Sinclair, Norman M. Thomas.

Oakes, John B., 1913-   Papers 1932-1969: 6 microfilm reels. Editorial page editor of *New York Times*. General, reader and personal correspondence; subject files. Correspondence and information on Joseph Alsop, Brooks Atkinson, Roger N. Baldwin, William Benton, Daniel J. Boorstin, Chester B. Bowles, John W. Bricker, Ralph J. Bunche, Marquis Childs, Charles C. Collingwood, Henry Steele Commager, Norman Cousins, C. Douglas Dillon, Thomas Dodd, Paul H. Douglas, William O. Douglas, Morris Ernst, Robert H. Estabrook, James A. Farley, John Fischer, Felix Frankfurter, Orville E. Freeman, J. William Fulbright, John Kenneth Galbraith, John Gardner, Christian Herter, J. Edgar Hoover, Hubert H. Humphrey, Lyndon B. Johnson, Nicholas Katzenbach, C. Estes Kefauver, John F. Kennedy, Robert F. Kennedy, Martin Luther King, Jr., Julius Klein, Alfred A. Knopf, Arthur W. Krock, Robert M. La Follette, Jr., Robert Lasch, Herbert H. Lehman, David E. Lilienthal , John F. Lindsa y, Walter Lippmann, Henry Cabot Lodge, Jr., Claire Boothe Luce, Archibald MacLeish, Mike Mansfield, Joseph R. McCarthy, Newton N. Minow, Edward P. Morgan, Richard L. Neuberger, J. Robert Oppenheimer, Nelson A. Rockefeller, David Rockefeller, Winthop Rockefeller, Dean Rusk, Bertrand Russell, Arthur M. Schlesinger, Jr., R. Sargent Shriver, Jr., Howard K. Smith, Theodore C. Sorenson, Adlai E. Stevenson, Raymond Gram Swing, Barbara Tuchman, Stewart Udall, U Thant, Earl Warren, James A. Wechsler, William C. Westmoreland, Whitney Young, Max Frankel, James Reston, Harrison Salisbury. Unpublished register available.

Pacifica Foundation. Records 1949-1976: 31 boxes. Foundation sponsoring listener-sponsored broadcasting which operates four FM stations: KPFA, Berkeley CA; KPFK, Los Angeles CA; WBAI, New York NY; KPFT Houston TX. Program guides, news scripts, correspondence, personnel lists, financial information.

Pendrell, Ernest, 1913-   Papers 1939-1973: 12 boxes, 9 films. Journalist; maker of television documentaries. Shooting scripts, research interview transcripts, films, financial records, reviews relating to ABC news *Scope* and *Directions* series.

People's Video. Records 1974-1976: 3 boxes. Communications resource service providing programming for cable tv. Correspondence, minutes proposals, files.

Pierpont, Robert, 1925-   Papers 1943-1982: 8 boxes, 1 disc recording, 4 films. Journalist; CBS White House correspondent.

Reporter's notebooks, personal and biographical material, photographs.

Pitzele, Merlyn S., 1911-   Papers 1932-1968: 66 boxes, 3 tapes. Labor and economic editor 1940-1955; senior editor 1955-1957 of *Business Week*. Correspondents include William F. Buckley, Jr., Clifford P. Case, Wilbur Cohen, Paul H. Douglas, Nathan Feinsinger, James C. Hagerty, Christian Herter, Clark Kerr, Henry Cabot Lodge, Jr. Unpublished register available. PARTIALLY RESTRICTED.

Preston, James D., 1876-1959. Papers 1890-1955: 2 boxes, 7 vols. Superintendent of United States Senate press gallery 1897-1932; librarian of the Senate 1932-1957. Research notes, scrapbooks.

Price, Byron, 1891-   Papers 1901-1976: 12 boxes. Journalist and editor with Associated Press 1912-1941; director of U.S. Office of Censorship 1941-1945. Correspondence, writings, professional subject files, biographical material. Correspondents include Cecil B. de Mille, Dwight D. Eisenhower, James A. Farley, James V. Forrestal, Ernest Gruening, Dag Hammarskjold, Warren G. Harding, Herbert Hoover, J. Edgar Hoover, Cordell Hull, Harold L. Ickes, John F. Kennedy, William D. Leahey, Trygve Lie, Henry Cabot Lodge, Jr., George C. Marshall, H.L. Mencken, Drew Pearson, David Rockefeller, Nelson A. Rockefeller, Eleanor Roosevelt, Franklin D. Roosevelt, Edward R. Stettinius, Jr., Adlai E. Stevenson, Henry L. Stimson, Harry S Truman, Fred M. Vinson, Wendell L. Willkie. Unpublished register available.

The Progessive, Inc.   Records 1940-1973: 96 microfilm reels. Non-stock corporation which publishes *The Progressive*. Correspondence, drafts, memoranda. Correspondents include William Benton, Chester B. Bowles, O. Edmund Clubb, William O. Douglas, J. William Fulbright, John Kenneth Galbraith, Hubert H. Humphrey, Robert G. Lewis, Eugene J. McCarthy, George S. McGovern, Wayne Morse, Gaylord Nelson, Richard L. Neuberger, Adlai E. Stevenson, Joseph L. Rauh, Jr., Norman M. Thomas, Carleton Beals, Henry Beston, Herbert L. Block, Hal Borland, Kay Boyle, Stuart Chase, Irving Dilliard, Julius Duscha, Murray Kempton, Erwin Knoll, Ann Landers, Robert Lasch, Milton Mayer, Karl E. Meyer, Edward P. Morgan, Wilbur Munnecke, Henry Regnery, Richard Schickel, Howard K. Smith, Laurence Stern, James Warburg, James A. Wechsler, Arthur Bestor, Richard Current, Robert Hutchins, William Neumann, Russell B. Nye,

Arthur M. Schlesinger, Jr., Fred Rodell, Charles, A. Wright, Sidney Lens. Unpublished register available.

The Public Interest. Records 1964-1978: 21 boxes. Quarterly journal edited by Irving Kristol, Daniel Bell, Nathan Glazer. Manuscripts, correspondence. Includes work by Edward Banfield, Kenneth E. Boulding, Zbigniew Brzezinski, Peter Drucker, Milton Friedman, John Kenneth Galbraith, Robert L. Heilbroner, Richard Hofstadter, Samuel P. Huntington, Clark Kerr, Seymour M. Lipset, Samuel Lubell, Daniel P. Moynihan, Richard Neustadt, Robert Nisbet, Robert Oppenheimer, Talcott Parsons, David Reisman, Aaron Wildavsky, James Q. Wilson. Correspondents include Saul Bellow, S. Douglass Cater, Leo Cherne, Fred W. Friendley, Walter Lippmann, Merlyn Pitzele, James Reston, Leo Rosten, Paul S. Samuelson, Arthur M. Schlesinger, Jr. Unpublished register available. RESTRICTED.

Radical America. Records 1966-1973: 4 boxes. Correspondence, office files. Draft articles by founder-editor Paul Buhle.

Radio Executives Club of New York. Records 1944-1951: 1 box. Proceedings of television seminars in 1944, 1947, 1948, 1949.

Radio Free Europe. Research Dept. Reports 1966-1976: 38 boxes. Background and situation reports, press surveys. Indexed by subject.

Rash, Bryson, 1913-   Papers 1956-1973: 3 boxes, 5 tapes. Award-winning news broadcaster with WRC/WRC-TV. Scripts, correspondence.

Ratcliffe, Samuel K., 1868-1958. Papers 1913-1958: 2 boxes. British journalist. Diaries, articles, clippings, correspondence, biographical information.

The Reporter. Notebook 1948-1952: 1 folder. Relates to establishment and early operation of magazine edited by Max Ascoli.

Revell, Aldric, 1910-1965. Papers 1933-1957: 2 boxes. Reporter and editorial writer for *Madison Capital Times.* Correspondence, writings, biographical material. Correspondents include William T. Evjue, Glenn Davis, Robert M. La Follette, Jr., Philip F. La Follette, Frank P. Zeidler.

Riesel, Victor, 1917-   Papers 1953-1967: 1 box. Incomplete run of "Inside Labor," a syndicated column.

Robinson, Hubbell, Jr., 1904-1974. Papers 1936-1974: 2 boxes. Vice president for television programming at CBS. Scripts, speeches, articles.

Ross, Madeline Dane, 1902-1972. Papers 1914-1971: 5 boxes, 1 disc. Journalist, editor, public relations representative. Scrapbook, articles, correspondence.

Rovere, Richard H., 1915-1979. Papers 1931-1968: 17 boxes. Writer and editor with *The New Yorker* 1944- Correspondence, reports, minutes, drafts, speeches, notes, journal, engagement books, card index. Correspondents include Samuel Hopkins Adams, Algernon Blackwood, John Dos Passos, H.L. Mencken, John Kenneth Galbraith, Harry S Truman, Frederick Lewis Allen, Joseph Alsop, Stewart Alsop, Bruce Bliven, William F. Buckley, Jr., Malcolm Cowley, Babette Deutsch, James T. Farrell, James C. Hagerty, Thomas C. Hennings, Jr., Sidney Hertzberg, Granville Hicks, Richard Hostadter, Sidney Hook, Alfred Kazin, Henry Kissinger, Irving Kristol, Joseph Lash, Max Lerner, William Manchester, Henry F. May, Joseph L. Rauh, Jr., Harold Ross, Morris H. Rubin, Arthur M. Schlesinger, Jr., Rebecca West, Adam Yarmolinsky. Unpublished register available. PORTIONS RESTRICTED.

Ryskind, Morrie, 1895-1985. Papers 1927-1978: 17 folders. Reader mail of syndicated columnist for *Los Angeles Times* and Pulitzer Prize-winning playwright. Correspondents include Ezra Taft Benson, James Burnham, Barry Goldwater, Richard M. Nixon, William F. Buckley, Jr., Ronald Reagan.

Salomon, Henry J., Jr. 1917-1958. Papers 1934-1962: 3 boxes, 1 film. Creator, writer, producer of television documentaries. Business and personal correspondence, research materials, logs, biographical material. Correspondents include S.N. Behrman, Samuel Eliot Morison, Nathan M. Pusey, Robert W. Sarnoff, Romney Wheeler.

Sanders, Marlene. Papers 1969-1973: 2 boxes. News correspondent and vice president and director of documentaries for ABC. Production files for 1973 special "Population: Boom or Doom?"

Scherer, Raymond L., 1919- Recording 1964: 1 tape. Interview with NBC news correspondent in Washington and London 1947-1975.

Schickel, Richard, 1933- Papers 1958-1969: 5 boxes. Editor, film critic, freelance writer. Correspondence, research material, scripts, drafts, printed works. Correspondents include Leonard Bernstein, Richard Burton, Alexander Calder, James T. Farrell, Fred W. Friendly, Jerry Lewis, Karl A. Menninger, Leontyne Price, Robert Redford, Peter Sellers, Kurt Vonnegut.

Schoenbrun, David, 1915- Papers 1963-1970: 5 boxes, 2 tapes, 6 discs. Foreign correspondent and news broadcaster; Washington bureau chief for CBS; world affairs correspondent for Metromedia. Correspondents include McGeorge Bundy, Charles De Gaulle, Dwight D. Eisenhower, J. William Fulbright, Arthur J. Goldberg, Barry Goldwater, W. Averell Harriman, Mark Hatfield, Marvin Kalb, Edward M. Kennedy, Robert F. Kennedy, John V. Lindsay, Eugene J. McCarthy, Wayne L. Morse, Edward R. Murrow, Richard M. Nixon, George Reedy, Dean Rusk, Pierre Salinger, G. Mennen Williams, David L. Wolper.

Scott, John, 1912-1976. Papers 1955-1970: 4 boxes. Journalist and broadcasting executive. Reports prepared as special assistant to publishers of *Time*.

Scripps-Howard Newspaper Alliance. Staff articles 1949-1967: 85 microfilm reels. Prominent writers include Albert M. Colegrove, Max B. Cook, Robert Crater, Ludwell Denny, Charles Egger, Ruth Finney, Frank R. Ford, Roy W. Howard, Daniel Kidney, Ted Knap, John W. Love, James G. Lucas, Charles T. Lucey, Marshall McNeil, Fred W. Perkins, Dickson Preston, Ernest T. Pyle, Earl Richert, Robert C. Ruark, Oland D. Russell, Charles E. Scripps, Roland H. Shackford, William Philip Simms, Douglas Smith, Fred Sparks, Richard Starnes, Walker Stone, Roger Stuart, Edward Tomlinson, John Troan, Andrew Tully, Frederick Woltman. Occasional contributors include F. Lee Bailey, Bernard Baruch, Dave Beck, Bruce Catton, Claire L. Chennault, Caryl Chessman, J. Frank Dobie, Stuart Holbrook, J. Edgar Hoover, Hubert H. Humphrey, MacKinlay Kantor, John F. Kennedy, Victor Lasky, Samuel Lubell, Mickey Mantle, George Meany, Syngman Rhee, Edward V. Rickenbacker, Inez Robb, Carlos P. Romulo, Carl Sandburg, Lyle C. Wilson. Unpublished register available.

Sebring, Lewis B., Jr., 1901-1978. Papers 1901-1976: 4 boxes (also available as 13 microfilm reels). *New York Herald-Tribune* war correspondent. Later columnist with *Schenectady Union-Star*. 40 notebooks, writings, drafts of book. Correspondents include Martin Agronsky, Raymond Clapper, George Cornish, Joseph Driscoll, Frank Kelley, Joe Alex Morris, Drew Pearson, Helen Rogers Reid. PORTIONS RESTRICTED.

Sinclair, Frank, 1895-1973. Papers 1938-1964: 6 boxes. *Milwaukee Journal* reporter. Correspondence, clippings, notes.

Smith, Howard K., 1914-   Papers 1941-1963: 54 boxes, 51 films. Award-winning news analyst and foreign correspondent. Worked for ABC and CBS. Cables, dispatches, viewer mail, interview transcripts.

Smith, Merriman, 1913-1970. Papers 1942-1865: 4 boxes. Pulitzer Prize-winning United Press International journalist and author. Book drafts.

Southern Courier. Records 1965-1967: 3 microfilm reels. Weekly Montgomery AL paper founded by civil rights workers to serve the Black community. Office files.

Stone, Walker, 1904-1973. Papers 1918-1969: 28 boxes. Editor-in-chief of Scripps-Howard Newspaper Alliance. Correspondence, subject files. Correspondents include Bernard Baruch, Harry F. Byrd, Jr., Madame Chiang Kai-Shek, Raymond Clapper, Everett M. Dirksen, Paul H. Douglas, John Foster Dulles, Dwight D. Eisenhower, J. Edgar Hoover, Roy W. Howard, Jack R. Howard, Hubert H. Humphrey, Lyndon B. Johnson, John F. Kennedy, Robert F. Kennedy, Henry Cabot Lodge, Jr., James G. Lucas, Charles T. Lucey, Douglas MacArthur, Henry Morgenthau, Jr., Richard M. Nixon, Ernest T. Pyle, Sam Rayburn, Donald R. Richberg, Syngman Rhee, Carlos P. Romulo, Dean Rusk, Charles E. Scripps, Robert Scripps, Harlow Shapley, R. Sargent Shriver, Jr., William Philip Simms, Arthur E. Summerfield, W. Stuart Symington, John Troan, Arthur H. Vandenberg, Harry S Truman, Woodrow Wilson.

Stowe, Leland, 1899-   Papers 1925-1968: 23 boxes. Pulitzer Prize-winning foreign correspondent, broadcaster, lecturer, educator. Worked for *New York Herald-Tribune, Chicago Daily News.* A director of Radio Free Europe 1950-1954. Correspondents include Arthur Draper, Frank Knox, Helen Rogers Reid, Walter Lippmann.

Studies on the Left. Records 1959-1967: 25 boxes, 1 pkg. Socialist journal. Includes exchanges with authors such as Herbert Aptheker, Noam Chomsky, David Dellinger, W.E.B. Du

Bois, Philip Foner, Eugene Genovese, Thomas Hayden, Langston Hughes, Corliss Lamont, Staughton Lynd, Herbert Marcuse, C. Wright Mills, Sidney Peck, Howard Selsame, William A. Williams, C. Vann Woodward, Maurice Zeitlin.

Sullivan, Ed, 1902-1974. Papers 1920-1974: 22 boxes, 26 films. Newspaper columnist and television host-producer. Scripts, correspondence, production work, subject files, writings. Correspondents include Steve Allen, Rudolf Bing, Bing Crosby, Jimmy Durante, Dwight D. Eisenhower, Duke Ellington, J. Edgar Hoover, Lady Bird Johnson, Edward M. Kennedy, Jacqueline Kennedy, John F. Kennedy, Robert F. Kennedy, Richard M. Nixon, Louis Nizer, Ronald Reagan, Don Rickles, John D. Rockefeller, Jr., Richard Rodgers, Robert E. Sherwood, Francis Cardinal Spellman, Frank Stanton, Adlai E. Stevenson.

Swing, Raymond Gram, 1887-1968. Scripts 1943-1947: 2 boxes. Scripts of noted news analyst broadcast of Blue Network and ABC.

Talburt, Harold M., 1895-1966. Political cartoons ca. 1922-1959: 7,500 proofs. Pulitzer Prize-winning editorial cartoonist for Scripps-Howard.

Tatarian, H. Roger, 1916- Papers 1960-1972: 2 boxes. Vice president and editor of United Press International.

Taylor, Allan, 1898-1967. Papers 1927-1967: 1 boxes. Journalist with *Atlanta Constitution, Atlanta Journal, New York Times*. Articles, book reviews, theater reviews, correspondence.

Tolischus, Otto D., 1890-1967. Papers 1926-1942. Foreign correspondent who won the Pulitzer Prize for his *New York Times* coverage of pre-war Nazi Germany. Miscellaneous papers.

Tomlinson, Edward, 1892-1973. Papers 1911-1972: 12 boxes. Author, journalist, radio broadcaster. Radio scripts, writings.

Trohan, Walter, 1903- Scripts 1950-1968: 4 boxes. Editorial news scripts broadcast over WGN by *Chicago Tribune* Washington correspondent.

United States Information Agency. Voice of America. Records 1957-1961: 22 boxes. News copy, logs, indexes. Includes news analyses by Robert S. Goralski, Raymond Gram Swing.

Utley, Clifton M., 1904-1978. Papers 1930-1960: 82 boxes. News commentator specializing in foreign affairs. Scripts, correspondence.

Valeriani, Richard G., 1932-   Papers 1961-1983: 14 boxes, 1 tape recording. NBC news broadcaster. Scripts, subject files, research material.

Vorse, Mary Heaton, d. 1966. Papers 1928-1930: 2 microfilm reels. Journalist and author known for her championship of trade unionism. Correspondence, notes, dispatches to *Tass* and *New York Evening Graphic*, clippings, press releases. Original materials transferred to Wayne State University after filming.

Wales, Wellington, 1917-1966. Papers 1940-1966: 2 boxes. Reporter, editor, combat photographer. Worked for *Boston Herald, Auburn Citizen-Advertiser, Albany Knickerbocker News, New York Times*. Correspondence, educational records, writings.

Waller, Judith, 1889-1973. Interview 1951: 1 folder. Transcript of interview with public affairs director of radio station WMAQ Chicago.

Warner, Albert L., 1903-1971. Papers 1923-1969: 4 microfilm reels, 1 tape, 3 discs. Capital reporter and radio commentator. Worked for *New York Herald-Tribune* 1930-1939. Correspondence, biographical material, writings. Correspondents include John L. Lewis, George W. Romney.

Wechsler, James A., 1915-   Papers 1940-1967: 2 boxes. Columnist and editor of *New York Post*. Book drafts, memoranda. RESTRICTED.

Westin, Avram R., 1929-   Papers 1945-1970: 9 boxes, 1 tape, 10 discs. News producer and executive CBS 1947-1967; public television 1967-1969; ABC, 1969-   Scrapbooks, office files, news scripts, clippings. Correspondents include Fred W. Friendly, Richard S. Salent.

White, Roland, 1908-   Papers 1920-1962: 12 boxes. Editor of *Dubuque Leader*. Business correspondence, clippings, articles, speeches.

White House news summaries. Compilations 1969-1970: 3 boxes. Condensations of American media coverage prepared by White House staff during Nixon presidency (October 1969-July 1970). Includes occasional commentary.

Wisconsin. University-Madison. Radio Station WHA. Records 1920-1973: 1 box, 42 tapes, 14 discs. Educational station of University of Wisconsin-Madison which began broadcasting in 1919.

Wisconsin State Journal Editorial Assoc. Records 1947-1977: 3 boxes. Records of independent labor union which represented editorial and newsroom employees of *Wisconsin State Journal.* Organizational materials, constitution, minutes, correspondence, grievances, finances.

Wittner, Fred, 1909-1972. Papers 1928-1972: 14 boxes. Sports reporter with *Brooklyn Daily Eagle, The New Yorker, Sports Illustrated, American Golfer.* Founder of Fred Wittner, Co. Clippings, articles, correspondence, business records.

Wolff, Perry, 1921-   Papers 1961-1967: 1 box, 4 films. Writer-producer of television documentaries. Biographical information, correspondence, rewrites, transcripts, clippings. RESTRICTED: Use requires permission of director, State Historical Society of Wisconsin.

Work, John M., 1869-1961. Papers 1958-   : 3 boxes. Two typewritten autobiographical manuscripts by Socialist editor of *Milwaukee Leader* describing his career from ca. 1869-1942.

Yardley, Richard Q., 1902-   Editorial cartoons 1950s-1960s: 80 items. Cartoonist for *Baltimore Sun.*

Yates, Ted, 1930-1967. Scripts 1961-1967: 2 boxes. NBC-TV producer-director. Chiefly files on *David Brinkley's Journal.*

Ziemer, Gregor, 1899-   Papers 1929-1945: 16 boxes. Foreign correspondent, author, radio news commentator for WLW Cincinnati. Radio news scripts for "Background on the News' and "View of the News." Writings, correspondence, memorabilia. Correspondents include John H. Bankhead, John W. Bricker, Hans V. Kaltenborn, Lyndon B. Johnson.

Zimmerman, Louis H. Papers 1921-1928: 1 folder. Secretary-treasurer of Wisconsin Press Assoc. Drafts of organization's constitution, financial report, correspondence.

Zotos, Helen M., 1923-   Papers 1947-1967: 6 boxes. Associated Press correspondent who covered Greek Civil War. News reports, dispatches, research material. Writer for *American Magazine*; editor of Radio Free Europe's *Daily News Bulletin.*

Waukesha County Historical Museum

• Waukesha County Historical Museum, 101 West Main St., Waukesha WI 53186. 414-548-7186. Terry Becker, Research Technician. 9 am-4:30 pm M-F excluding major holidays. Photocopy services.

Waukesha County Democrat. Papers: 8 folders. Bills, subscription records, business correspondence. Some personal correspondence directed to Edward L. Spence, editor 1873-1877. M-300.

Index

Abbott, George 261
Abbruzzo-Molise, L' 180
ABC News 123, 233
ABC Radio 251
ABC/American Broadcasting Company
   251, 253, 256, 257, 260, 265,
   267, 270, 272, 273, 274
Abel, Elie 105, 160
Abendpost 178
Aberdeen Herald 249
Abingdon Democrat 238
Able, I.W. 213
Abrahams, Mort 266
Acheson, Dean 114, 116,
   117, 120, 191, 192, 254, 258,
   264
Ackerman, Carl William 125
Ackerman, Edward P. 196
Adamic, Louis 115
Adams, Bristow 194
Adams, Cyrus Field 172
Adams, David C. 251
Adams, George Matthew . . .208, 232
Adams, Henry 115
Adams, Herbert Baxter 147
Adams, John Quincy 172, 175
Adams, Phoebe Lou 213
Adams, Samuel Hopkins . . .206, 270
Addams, Jane 262
Ade, George 148, 208
Adelaide News 230
Adler, Elmer 191
Adler, Emanuel P. 250
Adler, Philip 151, 152
Adler, Philip D. 153, 250
Adrian Expositor 166

Adrian Telegram 171
Advocate of Peace and Universal
   Brotherhood, The 228
Agee, James 118
Agronsky, Martin 251, 272
Ainsworth, Edward Maddin . . . 111
Akron Beacon Journal . 216, 218, 219
Al-Hoda 181
Albany Argus 205
Albany Gazette 204
Albany Knickerbocker News . . . 274
Albany Times-Union 140, 205
Albee, Edward 117
Albert, Carl 116
Alcott, Amos Bronson 213
Aldrich, William 147
Alhambra Post-Advocate 216
Allan, Clifton 146
Allan, Glenn 231
Allegheny Times 189
Allen, Arthur Francis 151
Allen, Benjamin Shannon 105
Allen, Devere 228
Allen, Frederick Lewis 125, 270
Allen, Henry J. 155
Allen, Hervey 230
Allen, Niel R. 105
Allen, Peter C. 104
Allen, Robert S. 250, 253, 256
Allen, Steve 120, 273
Allen, Young John 139
Alliance Printers and
   Publishers 182
Alliance Publishing Company . . 177
Allison, Young E. 156
Allman, Norwood F. 250

Alsberg, Henry G. 194
Alsop, Joseph 114, 117,
   120, 125, 267, 270
Alsop, Stewart 114, 160, 270
Alta California 102
Alternative Press 137
Alternative Press Centre 250
Alternative Press Index 250
Altmeyer, Arthur J. 256
Ambrose Henkel 240
America 143
American 223
American Citizen, The 182
American Farmer, The 159
American Golfer 275
American Guardian 166
American Jewish Press Association 159
American Liberal, The 209
American Magazine 119, 203, 232, 275
American Mercury . . . 108, 188, 207
American Newspaper Guild .227, 247
American Press Association . . . 125
American Red Cross 111
American Research Bureau, Inc. . 250
American Society of Newspaper
    Editors 208, 230, 238
American Spectator 194
Americky Delnicky Listy 222
Amerika-Echo 182
Amerikan Uutiset 177
Amerikanski Slovenec 180
Ameringer, Oscar 166
Ameryka 180
Ameryka-Echo 182
Ames, Jessie D. 188
Ames, Mary Clemmer 219
Anaconda Herald 185
Anamosa Eureka 151
Anchorage Daily News 216
Anderson Independent 230
Anderson, Albert N. 172
Anderson, Alfred O. 109
Anderson, Don 184
Anderson, Donald W. 250
Anderson, Jack 158
Anderson, Luther 114
Anderson, Raymond F. 149
Anderson, Sherwood 118
Andreas, Henry 120
Andrews, Charles Thomas . . . 194
Andrews, Clarence 152
Andrews, William Linton, Sir . . . 203
Angell, Norman 261
Angelo, Frank 168

Ann Arbor Courier 168
Ann Arbor News 170
Ann Arbor State Journal 168
Ann Arbor Times 168
Ann Arbor Western Emigrant . 168, 169
Ann, Doris 266
Annapolis Captial-Gazette 123
Annenberg, Max 143
Anti-Slavery Standard 199
Antioch Ledger 102
Antonini, Luigi 177
Appeal to Reason 106
Appleton Sun-Crescent 250
Aptheker, Herbert 272
Araldo, L' 183
Arbetaren 175
Archacki, Henry 177
Argoe, Kostis Tamias 177
Argonaut 103
Argonaut Publishing Company . 102
Amrine, Michael 122
Armstrong, Hamilton Fish 191
Arnett, Judd 164
Arnold, Edwin, Sir 125
Arnold, Wade 266
Arnoni, M.S. 160
Arter, William Andrew 213
Asahi News 246
Ascesa del Proletariato, L' 181
Ascoli, Max 116, 269
Asheville Citizen 230, 231
Ashley, Edward James 217
Ashmore, Harry S. 252, 258
Askov American 176
Associated Negro Press 124,
143, 188
Associated Press 101, 102,
    106, 110, 117, 119, 154, 171,
    173, 193, 206, 214, 221, 223,
    226, 227, 230, 253, 257, 259,
    260, 265, 268, 275
Associated Press Managing Editors
    Association 250
Association for Education in
    Journalism 250
Association of American Editorial
    Cartoonists 217
Astol, Lalo 237
Astor, David 258
Astor, J.J. 230
Astor, Mary, Lady 230
Astor, William Waldorf 125
Atherton, Gertrude 203
Atkinson, Brooks .193, 198, 261, 267

Atlanta Constitution 139, 140, 141, 142, 273
Atlanta Daily News 139, 140
Atlanta Daily World 124
Atlanta Evening Herald 139
Atlanta Georgian 141
Atlanta Journal . . 140, 141, 142, 193, 230, 231, 243, 273
Atlanta Journal Magazine 140
Atlantic Journal 206
Atlantic Monthly . 118, 197, 219, 220
Attwood, William 191
Auburn Citizen-Advertiser 274
Auchincloss, James 120
Auden, W.H. 118, 261
Auer, James M. 250
Aughinbaugh, William Edmund . 196
Aukofer, Frank 250
Aull, John Kinard 231
Ault, Harry E.B. 245
Austin Intelligencer 235
Austin, Warren P. 264
Austria. Ministerium des Assern . 177
Auth, Tony 122
AVCO-Miami 213
Averill, George R. 168
Avery, Carlos 173
Avery, Johnston 189
Avery, Virginia Hall 189
Avvenite, L' 183
Ayers, Harry Mell 100
Azcarraga, Emilio 251

Babbitt, Charles H. 125
Babcock, Frederic 160
Babcock, Howard E. 195
Back, Gunnar 251
Bacon, Edwin Munroe 196
Baer, John 122
Baer, John M. 217
Bagby, George William 242
Bagg, Lyman Hotchkiss 114
Bagley, Clarence Booth 245
Bailey, F. Lee 271
Bailey, George 160
Bailey, Robert L. 251
Baillie, Hugh 224
Bainbridge, John 160
Baker, Gordon 211
Baker, Henry Dunster 187
Baker, John C. 149
Baker, Newton D. 119, 153
Baker, Ray Stannard . . 117, 125, 208
Baker, Russell 120, 158

Baker, Tarkington 220
Bakersfield Calfornian 216
Bakken, Anthony W. 251
Balderson, John Lloyd 125
Baldwin, Hanson 115, 208
Baldwin, Hanson Weightman 114, 125
Baldwin, Roger 118, 267
Baldwin, Stanley 118
Ball, Raymond N. 194
Ball, William Watts . . 187, 231, 232
Balogh, Dezso De A. 177
Baltimore Evening Bulletin 158
Baltimore Evening Sun 232
Baltimore News-American 158
Baltimore Patriot 159
Baltimore Sun 114, 158, 196, 240, 244, 275
Baltimore Sunday Sun 121
Bancroft, Edgar A. 198
Baner, Johan, G.R. 168
Banfield, Edward 269
Bankhead, John H. 275
Banks, Nathaniel P. 147
Banner Press 141
Bannister, Harry R. 251
Baptist Union 173
Baragova Pratika 180
Barber, Walter L. "Red" 254
Barkley, Alben W. 253, 259
Barksdale, Ethelbert 125
Barnes, Harry Elmer 256
Barnes, Joseph 125
Barnes, Patrick H. 251
Barnett, Claude 143
Barnum, Jerome D. 194
Barnum, Thomas B. 195
Barrett, John 126
Barrett, Joseph H. 147
Barron's Weekly 171, 225
Barry, Charles C. 266
Barth, Alan 114, 126
Barthold, Allen Jennings 115
Barton, Albert O. 251
Barton, Bruce 208, 254
Baruch, Bernard 117, 152, 153, 207, 231, 254, 256, 264, 271, 272
Barzun, Jacques 119
Bass, Jack 231
Basset, Brian Willard 217
Basset, Gene 122, 221
Batchelder, Charles C. 119
Baugh, Leonidas 238
Baukhage, Hilmar R. 251
Bay City Evening Tribune 169

BBC/British Broadcasting Company
. . . . 258
Beach family 126
Beach, Rex 198
Beal, Junius E. 168
Beals, Carleton 160, 268
Bean, Orson 260
Beard, Charles A. 203
Beard, Ned 217
Beardsley, William 152
Beaumont Enterprise 114
Beaumont Journal 114
Beaverbrook, Lord 120, 194,
    209, 224, 241
Beck, Dave 271
Beck, Edward S. 143
Beck, Robert Knowlton 151
Becker, Neal Dow 194, 195
Beecher, Henry Ward 115, 213
Beffel, John 166
Behrman, S.N. 270
Belasco, David 209
Bell, Daniel 269
Bell, Elliott V. 193
Bellamy, Paul 222
Bellamy, Ralph 261
Bellingham American and Reveille 249
Bellingham Herald 249
Bellman, The 173, 175
Belloc, Marie Adelaide 203
Bellow, Saul 269
Belmont, August, Sr. 203
Belton Democrat 234
Belville, Hugh 265
Benchley, Robert 191
Bendiner, Robert 251
Benet, Stephen Rose 230
Benet, Stephen Vincent 115
Benjamin, Burton 252
Benjamin, Philip R. 252
Bennett, Arnold 198
Bennett, C. 210
Bennett, Constance 199
Bennett, F.R. 151
Bennett, James Gordon . . 126, 148,
    196, 204, 219
Bennett, James O'Donnell 143
Bennett, John 230
Bennett, Milly 105
Benson, Alex 252
Benson, Elmer A. 174
Benson, Eugene 197
Benson, Ezra Taft 265, 270
Benson, Herman 166

Bentinck, George 117
Bently, Ronald C. 149
Benton, William 144, 167,
    254, 264, 267, 268
Berger, Josef 224
Bergh, Henry 202
Bergman, Bernard Aaron 218
Bergman, Jules 252
Bergquist, Laura 160
Berlin Junge Welt 261
Bernhard, Prince of the Netherlands
    258
Bernstein, David 206
Bernstein, Leonard 251, 271
Berry, Don L. 149
Berry, Faith Daryl 126
Berry, Jim 221
Berry, Romeyn 194, 195
Bessie, Alvah 117
Beston, Henry 208, 268
Bestor, Arthur 268
Bethel Fair Journal 210
Beveridge, Albert J. 202
Beveridge, Albert Jeremiah . . . 126
Bialasiewicz, Jozef F. 178
Biddle, Francis 120
Biddle, Nicholas 121
bien publico, El 237
Bierce, Ambrose . .104, 198, 221, 226
Bierman, Frederick 152
Biermann, Frederick E. 153
Bigelow, John 196, 209
Bigelow, Poultney 196, 198
Billard, Oswald Garrison 175
Billings, Harry L. . . . 184, 185, 186
Billings, John Shaw 231
Bimba, Anthony 178
Binckley, John Milton 126
Bing, Rudolf 273
Bingay, Malcolm Wallace 164
Bingham, Alfred Mitchell 115
Bingham, Robert Worth 126
Binghamton Times 195
Biossat, Bruce 160
Birmingham Eccentric 168
Birmingham Labor Advocate . . . 101
Birmingham News 242
Biscoe, Walter S. 204
Bishop Inyo-Register 112
Bishop, Walter R. 241
Bismarck Tribune 210
Bittleman, Eva 114
Bixby, George Stephenson 204
Bjornson, Gunnar B. 176

Black and White 123
Black River Falls Banner-Gazette . 259
Black, Alexander 197
Black, Creed, C. 252
Black, Gladys 155
Black, Ruby Aurora 126
Blackwood, Algernon 270
Blaine, James G. 121, 146, 147
Blair family 126
Blair, Francis Preston 197
Blair, William 116
Blake, Henry N. 185
Blake, Thomas H. 146
Blankenhorn, Heber 166
Blegvad, Erik 227
Blennerhassett, Harman 126
Blenthen, Alden J. 147
Blessington, Marguerite 192
Bliven, Bruce 104, 116,
117, 203, 207, 256
Bloch, Kurt 225
Block, Herbert L. 114, 117,
256, 262, 268
Blockman, Laurence G. 252
Blue Network 273
Blue Pencil Club of Ohio 213
Blue, Robert 152
Blume, Peter 166
Blythe, Samuel G. 198
Bocca, Geoffrey 160
Bogan, Gerald 151
Bohrod, Aaron 250
Boies, W.D. 151
Bolens, Albert D. 252
Bolles, Stephen 252
Bombeck, Erma 158
Bond of Brotherhood 228
Bone, Scott Cardelle 245
Bonner, Robert 197
Bonsal, Stephen 126
Boone, James Buford 101
Boorstin, Daniel J. 267
Booth Newspapers 169, 170
Booth, Frank S. 227
Booth, George G. 168
Booth, Thomas Eyre 151
Borah, William E. 194, 244, 249, 252
Borden, Gail R., Jr. 234
Bordner, Robert 219
Borglum, Gutzon 198
Borland, Hal 268
Borough, Reuben Warriner 111
Boston Commonwealth 213
Boston Daily Journal 248

Boston Evening Transcript 202
Boston Herald 206, 265, 274
Boston Journal 213
Boston Pilot 146
Boston Post 120, 122, 196
Boston Quarterly Review 188
Boston Transcript 120
Botsford, Keith 160
Boulding, Kenneth E. 269
Bourke-White, Margaret . . . 194, 209
Bourne, William Oland 126
Bouton, Stephen Miles 105
Bowen, Henry Chandler 219
Bowers, Claude G. 254
Bowers, J.E. 173
Bowes, Edward, Major 203
Bowker, Richard Rogers . . . 197, 219
Bowlby, Joel 211
Bowles, Chester B. 116, 167
250, 254, 256, 258, 261, 267,
268
Bowles, Samuel . 115, 117, 188, 219
Bowles, William Lisle 192
Boyce, Edward 244
Boyd, Crosby Noyes 126
Boyd, Ernest 115
Boyd, Julian P. 254
Boyle, Harold V. 253
Boyle, James 146
Boyle, Kay 268
Boynton, Charles A. 147
Boynton, Frank D. 195
Boynton, Henry V. 146
Boynton, Henry Van Ness 147
Bracker, Milton 253
Brackman, Arnold 160
Bradbury, William H. 126
Braden, Anne 167
Braden, Carl 167, 253
Bradford, Gamaliel 203
Bradford, James E. 157
Bradley, Omar N. . . . 254, 258, 264
Bradley, William E. 239
Bradshaw, Herbert Clarence . . . 187
Braham, D.D. 121
Brainerd, Erastus 126, 245
Brainerd, Henry Allen 189
Brandsberg, George T. 189
Brant, Irving Newton 126
Braucher, Frank 253
Braxton, Henry Galt 242
Breazeale, Phanor 157
Breckenridge, Robert J. 214
Breckinridge family 126

Brecksville News 219
Breen, Edward 151
Breimeyer, Harold F. 150
Brelis, Dean 160
Brenner, Anita 126
Breslin, Jimmy 158
Breth, Fred 149
Bricker, John W. 267, 275
Bridgeman, Louis W. 253
Bridgeport Herald 167
Bridges, Robert 198
Briggs, James A. 222
Bright, Jesse D. 146
Bright, John 117
Brill, William Hascal 172
Brinkerhoff, Fredrick W. 155
Brinkley, David 253
Brinkley, John R. 155
Brisbane, Arthur 127, 143,
    202, 206, 256
Brissot de Warville, Jacques Pierre 127
Bristed, Charles Astor 197
Bristol Herald-Courier 240
Bristow, Joseph L. 155
Broder, David S. 158
Bromwell, James 151
Bromwell, James E. 153
Bronx Independent 199
Brookhart, Smith W. 153, 154
Brooklyn Citizen 228
Brooklyn Daily Eagle 200, 275
Brooklyn Daily Union 199, 219
Brooklyn Eagle 200, 225
Brooklyn Times 197
Brooklys, Tzimis 177
Brooks, Erastus 147
Brooks, Ned 259
Brooks, Noah 127
Brooks, Phillips 213
Brooks, William F. 266
Brophy, Brigid 262
Brother Jonathan 187
Brotherhood of Locomotive Engineers
    Journal 167
Brough, John 127
Broughm, Henry Peter 117
Broughton, Charles E. 253
Broun, Heywood Campbell 127
Browder, Earl 105
Brown, Ashmun Norris 245
Brown, Beriah 102
Brown, Beriah, Jr. 245
Brown, Beriah, Sr. 245
Brown, Camille Waggaman 237

Brown, Cecil 253
Brown, Constantine 105
Brown, D. Web 219
Brown, E.C. 105
Brown, Edmund "Pat" 154
Brown, Elizabeth Churchill . . . 105
Brown, Ernest Francis 190
Brown, George W. 155
Brown, Hilton U. 147
Brown, Hilton Ultimus 145
Brown, James H. 245
Brown, John Henry 234
Brown, Louis Edgar 105
Brown, Marel 142
Brown, Margaret Elizabeth Snow 142
Brown, Orlando 156
Brown, Thomas Cook 206
Browne, Francis F. 147
Browne, John J. 244
Browne, John W. 210
Brownell, Baker 143
Bruce, Blanche K. 189
Bruce, H.S. "Cap" 186
Brundage, Slim 166
Bryan, David Tennant 239, 242
Bryan, John Stewart 242
Bryan, Jonathan 242
Bryan, Joseph 242
Bryan, Mary B. 219
Bryan, Stewart 242
Bryan, William Jennings . . .116, 219,
    256, 258, 259, 263
Bryan, Wright 230
Bryant, O. Frank 209
Bryant, William Cullen . . .127, 196,
    197, 204, 219
Brzezinski, Zbigniew 269
Buchwald, Art 120, 158
Buck, Charles Neville 198
Buck, Pearl S. 262
Buck, Robert K. 150
Buckeye Press Association 213
Buckley, William F., Jr. 115, 117, 118,
    158, 240, 258, 260, 268, 270
Buell, Raymond L. 120
Buffalo Courier-Express . . .206, 207
Buffalo News 119
Buhle, Paul 269
Bullard, Arthur 191
Bullard, Lola 249
Bulwer-Lytton, Edward 192
Bunche, Ralph J. 267
Bundy, McGeorge 116, 271
Burgess, Gelett 208

Burleson, Albert S. 153
Burlingame family 127
Burlington Hawk-Eye 153
Burnham, James 270
Burrill, Harvey 106
Burritt, Elihu 228
Burritt, Maurice C. 195
Burroughs, John 116, 197
Burrows, Jerome B. 222
Burton, Naomi 213
Burton, Richard 261, 271
Busha, Charles H. 230
Business Week 258, 268
Butler, Charles 146
Butler, Nicholas Murray . . 202, 209,
      249, 253
Butler, William F. 194
Butterfield, C.W. 147
Butterfield, Charles E. 253
Byas, Hugh 115, 193
Byington, Steven T. 202
Byrd, Harry Flood, Jr. . 240, 241, 272
Byrd, Harry Flood, Sr. . . . 209, 239,
      240, 241, 242
Byrd, Harry Floor, Sr. 239
Byrd, Richard, Admiral 209
Byrnes, James F. 230, 253, 254

C-SPAN 148
Cabell, James 142
Cable, George Washington 118
Cable, Joseph 146
Cade, Dozier 232
Cadwallader, Sylvanus 127
Cain, James M. 218
Cain, James Mallahan 127
Caks, Raimunds 178
Calder, Alexander 271
Caldwell, Erskine 142
Caledonia Argus 176
California Farmer 113
Calkins, William M. 146
Calumet and War Club 145
Calverton, Victor Francis 197
Camden Journal 231
Cameron, Simon 202
Cameron, William Evelyn 242
Campaign, The 156
Campaigne, Jameson Gilbert . . . 106
Campbell, John 117
Campbell, Thomas 117
Canadien Publishing Company, Le 173
Canfield, Cass 204

Canham, Erwin D. 150
Canonge, L. Placide 157
Cantwell, Robert Emmett 225
Capehart, Homer E. 260
Capital and Labor 200
Capital Times . . .251, 256, 260, 263
Capp, Al 264
Capper Publications 156
Capper, Arthur 155
Capstaff, Albert L. 266
Captial Press Club 123
Caputo, Philip 160
Caradonna, Nino 183
Careers Today 258
Carey, James B. 167
Carey, John W. 151
Carle, Frank Austin 173
Carlson, Fred A. 127
Carnegie Commission on Educational
      Television 254
Carnegie, Andrew 203
Carpenter, Frank George 127
Carpenter, John 179
Corriere d'America 183
Carrington, William Cabell 242
Carroll, Beryl Franklin 153
Carroll, Raymond G. 127
Carruth, Hayden 197
Carter, Don Earl 250
Carter, Jeanette 123
Carter, Nathaniel Hazeltine . . . 204
Caruso, Enrico 182, 225
Carver, George Washington . 153, 155
Cary, Alice 197
Cary, Mary Ann Shad 123
Cary, Phoebe 197
Case, Clifford P. 268
Caselli, Alberico 178
Cass County Echo 190
Cass, Lewis 121, 148
Cassells, Louis Welborn 231
Cassidy, Henry 254
Caston, W. Thurlow 231
Caswell Messenger, The 189
Cater, S. Douglass 254, 269
Cather, Willa 191
Catledge, Turner 114, 120
Catlin, George Byron 164
Catt, Carrie Chapman 209
Catton, Bruce 116, 271
Cauthorn-Stout family 145
CBS News 233
CBS Reports 263

CBS/Columbia Broadcasting System
233, 252, 253, 255, 258, 260,
264, 267, 270, 271, 272, 274
Cedar Rapids Gazette 149, 153
Celler, Emanual 264
Celli, Fred 178
Century 199
Cerf, Bennett . . . 191, 206, 258, 260
Cesare, Oscar 122
Chafee, John H. 213
Chamberlain, John 106
Chamberlayne, John Hampden . 242
Chambers, Lenoir 239
Chambers, Whittaker 106, 266
Chandler, Joseph Ripley 127
Chandler, Walter 144
Chandler, Zachariah 147
Channing, Carol 261
Chapelle, Dickey 254
Chaplin, Ralph 166
Chapman, Leonard Bond 157
Charleston Mercury 191, 242
Charleston News and Courier . . 187,
230, 231
Charlotte Observer 218
Chase, Salmon P. 213, 214
Chase, Stuart 203, 268
Chatfield Republican 174
Chattanooga Times 139
Chennault, Claire L. 271
Chenoweth, Doral Park 214
Cherne, Leo 269
Chesebrough, Caroline 197
Chessman, Caryl 271
Chester Wright's Labor Letter . . . 225
Chester, Edmund Albert 106
Chesterman, Evan Ragland . . . 242
Chesterton, Gilbert Keith 127
Chicago Appeal 172
Chicago Daily Defender 124
Chicago Daily Herald 249
Chicago Daily News . . 102, 105, 114,
144, 171, 174, 252, 257, 265,
272
Chicago Daily Tribune 188
Chicago Defender 124
Chicago Express 201
Chicago Herald 103
Chicago Inter-Ocean 222
Chicago News 123
Chicago Record 191
Chicago Record-Herald 169
Chicago Sun . . . 170, 191, 230, 265
Chicago Sun Times 123, 262

Chicago Times Herald 139
Chicago Tribune 109, 120,
143, 184, 187, 197, 217, 240,
273
Chicago Tribune/New York News
Syndicate 143
Chicherin, Georgii 109
Childs, Marquis W. . . 254, 262, 267
China Today 109
Chinese News Service 107
Chinook Opinion 185
Choate, Rufus 202
Cholmondeley, Lionel 115
Chomsky, Noam 272
Chotzinoff, Samuel 266
Christian Science Monitor . . 106, 258
Christy, Marian 160
Chronicle 239
Church, Arthur B. 149
Church, Francis Pharcellus . . . 197
Church, Frank 116
Church, William Conant . . . 127, 197
Churchill, Douglas 193
Churchill, Winston 105, 117,
118, 191, 192, 194, 208, 254,
258
Cincinnati Commercial Tribune . . 216
Cincinnati Daily Times 212
Cincinnati Daily Tribune 211
Cincinnati Enquirer 211, 212,
216, 218, 220
Cincinnati Freie Presse Company 211
Cincinnati Gazette 211, 220
Cincinnati Times 146
Cincinnati Times-Star 140, 214
Cingolani, Mario 178
CIO News 167
Citadel Press 117
Citizen of the World 228
Claiborne, Craig 160
Clapp, William Warland 127
Clapper, Arthur 153, 156
Clapper, Raymond . . . 127, 253, 272
Claremont Daily Eagle 190
Clark, Barrett H. 261
Clark, Grenville 204
Clark, John McLane 190
Clark, Linda Bean 157
Clark, Mark W. 154, 259
Clark, Robert 122
Clarke, George W. 168
Clarke, Robert 211
Clarkson, James Sullivan 127
Clawson, Marion 150

Clay, Henry 121
Clay, Lucius D. 263
Clearbrook Journal 172
Clemens, Samuel Langhorne . . . 219
Clemente, Egidio 178
Clemons, Thomas 229
Cleveland Call and Post 125
Cleveland Leader 222
Cleveland News 223
Cleveland Plain Dealer . . . 212, 217,
    218, 219, 222, 223, 230, 256
Cleveland Press 218
Cleveland Sun and Voice 222
Cleveland True Democrat 222
Cleveland, Grover 176
Clowry, Robert C. 147
Clubb, O. Edmund 268
Clurman, Harold 255
Coan, Philip Munson 225
Cobb, Irwin S. 148, 198
Cobden, Richard 117
Cochrane, Williard W. 150
Codel, Martin 255, 264
Cody, Sherwin 194
Coggeshall, William Turner .211, 214
Cohen, Joseph 166
Cohen, Octavius Roy 198
Cohen, Wilbur 268
Cohn, Roy 120
Colburn, John H. 255
Colby, Bainbridge 117
Cole, Cyrenus 151
Colegrove, Albert M. 271
Coleman, John Carrington 187
Coleman, McAlister 166
Coleman, William 128
Colfax, Schuyler 128, 146,
    188, 199, 202
Collier's 104, 110, 122
Collier, John Payne 128
Collier, Julia 139
Collingwood, Charles C. 194, 255, 267
Collins, LeRoy 264
Collins, Lewis 156
Collins, Richard 156
Collins, Thomas Hightower 187
Collyer, John L. 194
Colophon 191
Colored Newspaper Man, The . . . 124
Colquitt, Oscar Branch 234
Columbia Daily Record 232
Columbia News and Courier . . . 232
Columbia State 230, 231, 232
Columbus Citizen Journal 218

Columbus Daily Monitor 217
Columbus Dispatch 215, 216
Columbus Enquirer-Sun 139
Columbus Evening Dispatch . . . 217
Columbus Monitor 217
Coman, Dale Rex 218
Combe, George 117
Comercio mexicano, El 237
Cominsky, Jacob Robert 208
Comly, James Monroe Stuart . . 214
Commager, Henry Steele . . 262, 267
Commentator, The 156
Commercial West 187
Commerical 147
Commission on Freedom of the Press
    . . . . .144, 246
Common Sense 115
Commons, John R. 256
Commonwealth 156, 261
Comstock, Anna Botsford 195
Comstock, James 204
Conant, James B. 254
Conde Syndicate 227
Conklin, William R. 193
Conn, Edward Leslie 128
Conn, Rex B. 149
Connally, John 236
Connections 255
Connor, Seldon 118
Considine, Robert B. 206
Consolidated Press Association . 255
Cook, Alton F. 160
Cook, Marshall L. 168
Cook, Max B. 271
Cook, William R. 168
Cooke, Alistair 160
Cooke, John Esten 242
Cooley, John K. 106
Coolidge, Archibald Carey 191
Coolidge, Calvin 117, 153,
    154, 198, 249, 252
Coolidge, Gilbert 198
Cooper, Carl 246
Cooper, John Sherman 258
Cooper, Kent 223, 263, 265
Cooper, Meyers Y. 149
Copeau, Jacques 260
Copeland, Royal S. 168
Copeland, Walter Scott 239
Cordon, Guy 227
Corey, Herbert 128
Corning, Erastus 209
Cornish, George 272
Coronet 265

Corporation for Public Broadcasting
. . . . 254
Correll, Erasmus Michael 189
Correll, Henry T. 258
Corriere del Popolo, Il 182
Corriere Italiano, Il 183
Corselius, George 168
Corwin, Thomas 214
Cosmopolitan 116, 203, 219
Cotrissoz, Royal 203
Cott, Ted 266
Courier 230
Courier de Boston 115
Courier Group 124
Cousins, Norman   116, 117, 144, 267
Cousins, Robert G. 151
Cowles, Gardner 152
Cowles, John 114, 152
Cowley, Malcolm 114, 270
Cox, Archibald 144
Cox, James 196
Cox, James S. 236
Cox, Kenneth 255
Cox, Nettie Stedman 234
Cox, Samuel S. 148
Craig, Elisabeth May 128
Crain, Jacob R. 145
Cralle, Richard Kenner 239
Crane, Charles R. 256
Crane, George W. 194
Crater, Robert 271
Crawford, Bill 122, 217, 255
Creelman, James 219
Creenfield, Charles Diggs, Jr. . . 185
Crider, John 206
Critchfield, Richard 255
Critic, The 199
Crockett, Albert S. 263
Crockett, Albert Stevens 255
Croly, Herbert 121
Crook, W. Melvin 165
Crosby, Alexander L. 225
Crosby, Bing 273
Crosier, Edward S. 168
Cross & Baptist Journal 223
Cross Fire 251
Cross, Cora Milton 236
Croswell, Edwin 128
Crouch, Paul 166
Crouse, Russel 261
Crowley, Leo T. 256
Croy, Homer 151
Crozier, Brian 106
Culbertson, Dorothy 266

Cullum, Shelby M. 147
Culver, John C. 153
Cummings, Camille 113
Cummings, E.E. 203
Cummings, Homer S. 153
Cummings, James 144
Cummins, Albert B. 151
Cunningham, Paul 152
Cupelli, Alberto 178
Current History 190
Current, Richard 268
Curtis Publishing Company . . . 208
Curtis, George William 219
Curtis, William Eleroy 191, 222
Cushing, George 168
Cutler, John Henry 161
Cutler, William Parker 148
Cutts, Ernest 250
Czas 177, 179
Czas Publishing Company . . . 179
Czech-American Labor News, Inc. 222

Dabney, Virginius . . . 188, 239, 240
Dabney, Wendell Phillips 211
Daily America 193
Daily Courier 236
Daily News 205
Daily News Bulletin 275
Daily Oklahoman 224
Daily Olympian 249
Daily Tribune 170
Daily Variety 216
Dakota Bell 197
Dale, Alfred Samuel 209
Dallas Journal 234
Dallas Morning News 221, 233,
234, 236
Dallas Times Herald 234
Daly, John Charles 256
Dana, Charles A. 147, 220
Dana, Charles Anderson . . . 128, 235
Dana, James Green 156
Dana, R.H., Jr. 202
Dana, R.H., Sr. 202
Dana, Richard Henry 213
Daniel, Clifton 114
Daniel, Frank 142
Daniel, Hawthorne 239
Daniel, John Moncure 128
Daniel, Price 236
Daniell, F. Raymond 192
Daniels, Josephus 117, 128,
153, 189, 202, 239
Danish National Committee . . . 178

Danish Times 178
Dann, Hollis E. 195
Dann, Michael H. 266
Darden, Colgate 241
Darling, Jay N. 120, 151,
  152, 153, 155
Darrow, Clarence 104, 118,
  244,253, 258
Darrow, Wayne 149
David Brinkley's Journal . . .253, 275
Davidson, Jo 198
Davies, Joseph E. 253
Davis, Chester C. 149, 150
Davis, Elmer 254
Davis, Elmer Holmes 128
Davis, Glenn 269
Davis, Henry Winter 148
Davis, Horace M. 189
Davis, John W. 153
Davis, L. Clarke 197
Davis, Malcolm 191
Davis, Rebecca Harding 197
Davis, Richard Harding 206
Davis, Robert Hobart 198
Dawson, Francis Warrington . 187, 231
Dawson, Geoffrey 121
Dawson, Warrington, Jr. 230
Day, Edmund Ezra 194, 195
Day, Frank Arah 173
Day, Howard G. 173
Dayton Daily News 218
Dayton Journal Herald 218
Dayton, George D. 175
De Casseres, Benjamin 198
De Caux, Len 167
de Estavillo, Gomez 241
De Gamez, Tana 161
De Gaulle, Charles 264, 271
de Mille, Cecil B. 268
de Nancrede, Paul Joseph Guerard 115
de Sola, Ithiel 164
De Toledano, Ralph 106, 161
De Trevino, Elizabeth Borton . . . 161
de Valera, Eamon 244
Dealey, G.B. 233
DeBow's Reviews 234
DeBow, J.D.B. 234
DeBow, Samuel P. 246
Debs, Eugene V. . 166, 200, 244, 253
Debs, Katherine M. 200
Debs, Theodore 200
Decision 115
Deck, Arthur C. 238
Deland, Margaret 192

Delay, Theodore S., Jr. 256
Delineator 203
Dellinger, David 272
DeLuce, Dan 263
Democratic Digest 188
Democratic Review 187
Denious, Jess C. 155
Denni Hlasatel 178
Dennice Novoveku 223
Dennis, Jere Clemens 101
Dennis, Lawrence 106
Dennison, William, Jr. 214
Denny, Ludwell 256, 271
Denver Post 113
Denver Times 148
Depew, Chauncey M. 188
Derleth, August 250, 256
Des Moines Register 150, 151,
  154, 155
Des Moines Register and Tribune
  . . . . .149, 150
Deseret News 238
Designer 203
DeSilver, Margaret 166
Detroit (Lakes) Record 176
Detroit Evening News 165
Detroit Free Press 164, 165,
  168, 169, 171, 172, 217
Detroit Gazette 165
Detroit Journal 165
Detroit News 164, 165,
  166, 169, 171, 172, 218
Detroit News Lansing Bureau . . 168
Detroit Post and Tribune Co. . . 169
Detroit Times 165
Detroit Tribune 165
Detzer, Karl L. 169
Deuel, Wallace Rankin 128
Deutsch, Babette 270
Deutsche Freiheit 229
Deutsche in Ohio und Ohio
  Staatzeitung 214
Devell, Harvey 143
DeVoto, Bernard 104, 230
Dewart, William T. 198
Dewey, John 166, 167
Dewey, Thomas E. .182, 194, 249, 254
Dexter, Samuel W. 169
Dickerson, James Spencer 173
Dickinson, George H. 193
Dickinson, Lester Jesse 151, 153, 154
Dickson, Edward A. 112
Die Zeit (Vienna) 107
Dilliard, Irving 256, 268

Dillon, C. Douglas 260, 267
Directions 267
Dirksen, Everett M. 264, 272
DiSantis, Anthony J. 222
Disney, Walt 118
Dispatch 173
Dispatch News Service
    International 228
Dispatch-Pioneer Press 173
Disraeli, Benjamin 117
Dix, John A. 198, 202
Dixon, Frederick 128
Dixon, James 148
Dobie, J. Frank 236, 271
Dodd, Thomas 267
Dodge Center Press 176
Dodge, Mary Mapes 230
Doerfer, John C. 256
Dollenmayer, Albert 173
Dolliver, James 152
Dombrowski, James A. 253
Donahey, James Harrison . .222, 223
Donahey, William 256
Donahoe, Ed 246
Donahue, Patrick 146
Donaldson, Joseph, Jr. 227
Donnaruma, Caesar L. 179
Donnaruma, James V. 179
Donnelly, Ignatius 173
Dorrian, Cecil 107
Dos Passos, John . . . 119, 167, 270
Dosh, Robert N. 138
Douai, Adolf 234
Doubleday, Frank N. 202
Douglas, George 112
Douglas, Paul H. 251, 254,
    257, 265, 267, 268, 272
Douglas, Stephen A. 202
Douglas, William O. 114, 253,
    254, 256, 267, 268
Douglass, Frederick . . 124, 128, 213
Douthit, David 174
Dowdey, Clifford 239
Dowell, Cassius Clay 154
Dowling, Dan 221, 256
Dowling, John 145
Downes, Irene Miles 142
Downes, Louisa 142
Downes, Olin 142
Downey, Edmund 138
Downing Archive 240
Downs, William R. 122
Drake, A.W. 230
Drake, C.D. 211

Draper, Arthur 272
Draper, Charles Hiram 185
Draper, Lyman C. 147, 220
Dreier, Alex 256
Dreiser, Theodore 200
Drewry, John Eldridge 142
Drips, William E. 149
Driscoll, Frederick 147
Driscoll, Joseph 272
Dromgoole, William Allen, Miss . 232
Drucker, Peter 269
Drummond, Eric, Sir 191
Drummond, Roscoe 122
Du Bois, W.E.B. 273
Duane, William 128
Dubinsky, Dave 167
Dubuque Leader 274
Dudley, William Wade 146
Dudman, Richard Beebe 128
Dugas, Claiborne J. "Bobby" . . . 157
Dulles, Allen W. 263
Dulles, John Foster 254, 272
Dumez, Eugene 157
Dumm, Frances Edwina 217
Dummer, Joseph 150
Dundurs, Erik 179
Dunn, Arthur Wallace 128
Dunn, Jacob P. 147
Dunne, Finley Peter 128
Dunnigan, Alice A. 124
Durant, Will 260
Durante, Jimmy 273
Duranty, Walter 209
Durham Morning Herald 187
Duscha, Julius 268
Dziennik Chicagoski 178
Dziennik Zwiakowy 177

Early, Jubal Anderson 242
Eastman, Charles Gamage . . . 243
Eastman, Edward R. 195
Eastman, Max 262, 266
Eaton, Cyrus 254
Eaton, John 233
Eaton, William J. 161
Eban, Abba 260
Eckener, Hugo 263
Eckert, Thomas T. 147
Edelman, John 167
Eden, Anthony 194, 258
Edgar, William Crowell 173
Edmunds, Craddock 241
Edmunds, Murrell 241
Edwards, Albert 191

Edwards, Annie 197
Edwards, Bill 216
Egenes, Sonja 153
Egger, Charles 271
Egri, Lajos 179
Eiges, Sidney H. 266
Einaudi, Mario 178
Einstein, Albert 192, 254
Eisenhower, Dwight D. . . 182, 253,
    264, 268, 271, 272, 273
Eisenhower, Milton S. 149
Eisenschiml, Otto 260
Elder, John 146
Eliot, George Fielding 129
Eliot, T.S. 118, 254
Ellingson, Mark 194
Ellington, Duke 273
Elliot, Jonathan 129
Ellison, Ralph 116, 117
Ellsworth, Harris 227
Ely, Richart T. 198, 202
Emerson, Caleb 222
Emerson, Edwin, Jr. 122
Emerson, Gloria 161
Emerson, Ralph Waldo 213, 219
Emerson, T. 129
Emig, Elmer J. 138
Emmert, Adolphys Dunan 158
Emphasis 258
Engel, Harold 265
England, George Allen 198
Engle, Cheryl 169
Engle, Paul 150
Ephriam, Kirby 188
Epstein, Edward Jay 161
Ernst, Morris 267
Ernst, Morris Leopold 218
Ervin, Charles 166
Esquire 118
Estabrook, Robert H. 256, 267
Estelline Bell 197
Eteenpain 182
Ettelson, Lee 225
Eugene Register Guard 227
Evans, Emma Cobb 236
Evans, Henry S. 107
Evans, John 129
Evans, Joseph Early 152
Evans, Maurice 230
Evansville Courier 262
Evening Post 197
Evening Sun 225
Everett Herald 249
Everett, Edward 148, 202

Everybody's Magazine 227
Evjue, William T. 250, 251,
    254, 256, 269
Ewer, Ferdinand C. 102
Ewing, John 146
Examiner 192
Eyerly, Frank Rinehart 149

Fadiman, Clifton 208
Fairbanks, Charles W. . . .119, 146,
    147, 148
Fairfield Daily Ledger 152
Fairmont Sentinel 173
Fallaci, Oriana 161
Fanning, Lawrence S. 264
Far Eastern Survey 225
Far Easterner, The 111
Farago, Ladislas 161
Farley, James A. 194, 209,
    253, 258, 267, 268
Farm Journal 149
Farmer's Oracle 238
Farmer, Fyke 204
Farmers' Independent Publishing
    Company 209
Farrell, Frank 144
Farrell, James T. 270, 271
Farris, Barry 227
Farris, James Turner 185
Farwell, Charles B. 147
Farwell, John V. 147
Faulks, Theodosia P. 203
Faust, Frederick 198
Federal Communications Commission
    . . . . . .255, 256, 259, 263
Federated Press . .110, 167, 171, 225
Feinsinger, Nathan 268
Fellowship 229
Ferber, Edna 208, 209, 257
Ferdinand, Louis, Prince 263
Ferger, Roger 211
Fergus Falls Tribune 176
Fergus Falls Weekly Journal . . . 176
Ferguson, Elizabeth (Bess) Storm 150
Ferguson, Frank C. 244
Ferrar, Geraldine 198
Fertig, Lawrence 107
Feuchtwanger, Lion 262
Ficklen, Herc 221, 234
Field, Eugene 129
Field, Marshall 115, 120
Field, Marshall, III 262
Field, Mary Katherine Keemle . . 129
Field, William H. 143

Fifield, Arthur C. 202
Filipino Forum 248
Fillmore, Millard . . . . , . . 209
Fineman, Hayim 160
Fineshriber, William H., Jr. . . . 266
Finley, John H. 202
Finley, John Huston 198
Finney, Ruth 271
Finska Amerikanaren 180
Firing Line 115
Fischer, Bertha Markoosha . . . 192
Fischer, Ernest G. 257
Fischer, John . . 257, 258, 266, 267
Fischer, John Sylvester 116
Fischer, Lincoln 201
Fischer, Louis 116, 192, 256
Fish, Hamilton . . 121, 148, 202, 209
Fisher, Francis McCracken 101
Fisher, John Stirling 114
Fisk family 185
Fisk, Wilbur 129
Fitzgerald, Frances 161
Fitzpatrick, Lee J. 169
Flagg, Azariah Cutting 198
Flannagan, Gladys Victoria Iller . 243
Flannagan, Roy Catesby 243
Flanner, Janet 129, 225
Flannery, Harry W. 257
Fleischmann, Raoul 225
Fleming, Harold Manchester . . . 198
Fleming, Robert H. 257
Flint, Charles Ranlett 199
Flint, Hallie Rienzi Johnston Russell
        Thomas 237
Flynn, Elizabeth Gurley 167
Flynn, John T. 203
Flynn, Sean 196
Fodor, Nandor 107
Follett, Frederic 174
Follia de New York, La 182
Folsom, Lee W. 224
Folwell, William W. 175
Fonblanque, Albany 192
Foner, Philip 273
Foraker, Joseph B. 146
Forbes 117, 206
Forbes, Archibald 129
Forbes, Benjamin Platt 214
Forbes, Bertie Charles 206
Ford, Frank R. 271
Ford, Gerald R. . . 171, 251, 259, 265
Ford, Gordon Lester 199, 201
Ford, Henry 263
Ford, Henry II 149

Foreign Affairs 191
Foreign Broadcast Intelligence Service
        120
Foreman, Clark 167, 253
Foreman, Lauren 139
Forest and Stream Weekly 116
Forman, Frances Marie 211
Forman, Harrison 225
Forman, Henry James 112
Forney, John Wien 129
Forrest, Earle Robert 228
Forrestal, James V. 249, 268
Forsland, Steven 246
Fort Worth Star-Telegram . . 234, 236
Fortas, Abe 114
Fortune . . . 116, 118, 191, 225, 240
Forum World Features 106
Foster, John Watson 146
Foster, Malcolm 116
Foster, Theodore 169
Foster, William Z. 167
Fountain Inn Tribune 232
Fowle, Farnsworth 161
Fowler, Gene 113
Fra Noi 180
Francis, Dick 241
Frank A. Munsey Company . . . 198
Frank Leslie's Illustrated News . 220
Frank, Gerald 199
Frank, Reuven 266
Frankel, Eliot 266
Frankel, Max 267
Frankfurter Allgemeine Zeitung . . 101
Frankfurter, Felix .114, 195, 254, 267
Frantz, Harry Warner 194
Frantz, Ralph J. 263
Frederic, Harold 129, 199
Frederick, Pauline 263
Fredericksburg Free Lance 239
Fredericksburg Virginia Baptist . 243
Free Lance Star Publishing
        Company 239
Free Quill, The 159
Freeborn County Standard 173
Freedom 201
Freeman 119
Freeman, Douglas Southall . 158, 239
Freeman, Ira Henry 129
Freeman, Lucy 161
Freeman, Miller 246
Freeman, Orville E. . . 150, 260, 267
Fremont Journal 220
Freneau, Peter 129
Freneau, Philip Morin 129

Freud, Sigmund 116
Frey, John Philip 129
Friedman, Milton 269
Friel Presse Fuer Texas 235
Friendly, Edwin S. 195
Friendly, Fred W. 114, 264,
   269, 271, 274
Frohman, Daniel 198
Fromm, Bella 161
Fry, Edwin 189
Frye, William R. 161
Fulbright, J. William . . . 116, 254,
   258, 262, 267, 268, 271
Fuldheim, Dorothy 213
Fullam, William Freeland 129
Fuller, Blair 161
Fuller, Edward 248
Fuller, Hector 146
Fuller, John Louis Hilton 146
Fulton, George W. 235
Funk, A.B. 151
Fur Journal 246
Furman, Bess 129

Gabor, Zsa Zsa 199
Gadsby, Henry Franklin 107
Gadsden, Jeanne 230
Gaines, John M. 266
Galaxy, The 197
Galbraith, John Kenneth . . 116, 150,
   254, 267, 268, 269, 270
Gale, Zona 203, 256
Gales, Joseph 129, 199
Gallagher, J. Wes 263
Gallagher, William Davis 211
Gallatin, Albert 198
Galveston Civilian 234
Gampfer, Nelson M. 211
Gandhi, Mohatma 192
Gannett Corporation 223
Gannett Publications 195
Gannett, Frank E. . . . 194, 195, 223
Gano, John Stites 211
Garbisch, Edgar 227
Gardette, Charles Desmarais . . . 129
Gardner, Earle Stanley 250
Gardner, John 116, 267
Gardner, Melzar 187
Garfield, Charles D. 246
Garfield, James A. 146, 193
Garland, Hamlin 198, 208, 226
Garner, John Nance 240
Garner, Thomas Henry 101
Garrison, William Lloyd . . .213, 235

Garroway, Dave 260
Garwood, W. Saint John 236
Garza, Catarino E. 237
Gassner, John 261
Gate City Guardian 139
Gavit, Joseph 205
Gay, Sydney Howard 199
Gaylord, Myrtle 244
Gaymayel, Pierre 181
Gazeta Polonii 180
Gazette 147
Gazzetta del Massachusetts, La . 179
Gedye, G.E.R. 192
Genovese, Eugene 273
George Matthew Adams News Service
   208
George, Henry 176
George, Henry, Jr. 173
Georgia Collegiate Press
   Association 142
Georgia Press Association 142
Georgia Press Institute 142
Georgia Radio-Television Institute 142
Georgia Scholastic Press
   Association 142
Gershwin, Ira 218
Geyer, Georgie Anne 161
Ghali, Paul 257
Ghent, William James 129
Gibbons, Floyd 143
Gibbons, Helen Davenport 192
Gibbons, Herbert Adams 192
Gibbs, Arthur Hamilton 198
Gibson, A.W. 194
Gibson, Charles Dana 198
Gibson, Hugh 263
Gide, Andre 115
Gilbert, Alfred 174
Gilbert, Cass 173, 198
Gilbert, Joseph 174
Gilder, Joseph Benson 199
Gilder, Richard Watson 199
Gill, Brendan 116
Gill, J.M.F., Mrs. 236
Gill, Mary Terry 236
Gillette, Guy M. 151, 152
Gilmore, Eddy Lanier King . . 101, 206
Gilroy, Harry D. 161
Gingrich, Arnold 118
Giovannitti, Arturo 183
Giovanolo, Luigi 178
Gish, Lillian 213
Gitlin, Irving 266
Glasgow Courier 185

Glasgow, Ellen 203, 241
Glass, Carter 239, 240
Glazer, Nathan 269
Gleason, Arthur Huntington . . . 130
Gleed, Charles S. 156
Glenn, Isa 142
Globe Publishing Company .244, 249
Glynn, Martin H. 188
Goddard, William 130
Godwin, Mills E. 241
Godwin, Parke 192, 197
Goldberg, Arthur J. . . 257, 264, 271
Goldberg, Emanuel 161
Golden, Harold 167
Golden, Harry 264
Golden, John 261
Goldwater, Barry 116, 166,
    240, 254, 265, 270, 271
Gollobin, Ira 179
Gompers, Samuel 153
Gonzales, Narciso Gener 231
Gonzales, William Elliott 231
Gooch, Claiborne Watts 243
Good, James W. 153
Goodland, Walter W. 257
Goodlet, Carlton B. 124
Goodman, Ellen 158
Goodman, Paul 118
Goralski, Robert S. 257, 273
Gordon, David Everett 103
Gordon, George Augustus 191
Gore, Albert A. 254
Gorelik, Mordecai 261
Gould, Alan J. 263
Gould, Chester 143
Gould, John 161
Gould, Randall Chase 107
Grady, Henry Woodfin 139
Graebner, Walter 258
Graham, Fred Patterson 130
Graham, Gene 144
Graham, Katherine 117
Graham, Martha 260
Graham, Philip Leslie 114
Graham, Sheilah 199
Graham, Walter B. 199
Grahame, Kenneth 208
Grand Haven Daily Tribune . . . 170
Grand Rapids Evening News . . . 168
Grand Rapids Herald 171, 172
Grandinetti, Emilio 179
Granger, Francis 209
Grant, Hugh Gladney 130
Grant, Jeanette Cole 225
Grant, Ulysses S. 146, 193
Grants Pass Courier 224
Graphic 173
Grattan, C. Hartley 203, 256
Grauer, Neil-Albert 158
Gray, James 174
Gray, William P. 263
Great Northern Daily News 246
Greco, Enotrio 179
Greek Press 177, 178
Greek Star 178
Greeley, Horace 130, 188,
    199, 202, 205, 209, 219, 235
Green, Duff 130, 146
Green, Gerald 266
Green, Julien 115
Green, Paul 260
Green, Sullivan D. 169
Greenberg, David B. 194
Greene, A.C. 234
Greene, Anna Katherine 165
Greene, Edgar Carlton "Doc" . . . 164
Greene, Gael 161
Greensboro Daily News 189
Greenville Piedmont 231, 232
Greenwood Index-Journal 232
Gregory, Horace 115
Gregory, John Goadby 249
Grenell, Judson 166
Gresham, Walter Q. 146
Greusel, Joseph 165
Grey, Zane 198
Griessmer, Tom O. 204
Griffin, Anthony J. 199
Griffin, Isabella K. 188
Grigsby, Hugh Blair 130
Grinnell, George Bird 116
Gristmill, The 219
Gromyko, Andrei 264
Gross, H.R. 153
Grosvenor, Charles Henry 146
Grote, George 192
Groueff, Stephane 161
Gruening, Ernest 268
Gruenther, Alfred 152
Gualtieri, Humbert L. 179
Guardian of Boston, The 161
Guerlac, Orthon 195
Guest, Edgar A. 165, 169, 208
Guggenheim, M. 167
Guidi-Flavio, Angelo 178
Guild Reporter 114

Guiney, Louise Imogen 130
Gunther, John 117, 119,
144, 208, 256, 258
Gurley, John Addison 130
Gwynn, Stephen Lucius 130

Haas, Oscar 235
Habib-Sayegh, Khilil 181
Hacker, Louis M. 256
Hackler, Victor 250
Haessler, Carl 167
Hagen, Harold Christian 174
Hagerty, James C. 264, 265, 268, 270
Haines, Charles Glidden 205
Halberstam, David 161
Haldeman, Walter N. 147
Hale family 130
Hale, Charles 188
Hale, William Bayard 116
Hale, William Harlan 116
Halford, Elijah Walker 130, 148
Hall, Covington 166
Hall, Earl W. 152
Hall, Grover 252
Hall, Virginius Cornick 211
Hall, W. Earl 152
Hall, Wilson 258
Halliday, Richard 201
Halpine, Charles Graham 130
Halsell, Grace 161
Halsey, Francis W. 195
Halstead, Murat . 146, 147, 211, 215
Halstead, William Leon 211
Hambleton, James Pinckney . . . 139
Hamblin, Charles 173
Hamilton, Edith 260
Hamilton, John S. 258
Hamm, Jack 221
Hammarskjold, Dag . . 254, 263, 268
Hammerstein, Oscar, II 261
Hammill, John G. 153
Hammond, Charles 212
Hammond, John H. 147
Hammond, Ross L. 151
Hamphill, William Arnold 139
Hancher, Virgil 152
Hancock, Gordon Blaine 188
Hanes, Thomas Andrew 240
Hanfstaegle, Ernest 263
Hanighen, Frank C. 203
Hanleiter, Cornelius R. 139
Hanlin, John Joseph 213
Hanna, Marcus A. 146
Hannegan, Edward A. 146

Harcourt, Alfred 241
Harding, Earl 195
Harding, W.L. 151
Harding, Warren G. 130, 175,
196, 200, 249, 268
Hardt, Fred B. 107
Hardy, Thomas 116
Harger, Alice Rogers 206
Harju, Walter A. 179
Harkrader, Charles Johnson . . 240
Harlan, Andres J. 146
Harlan, John M. 146, 147
Harper & Bros. 220
Harper's Bazaar 201, 203
Harper's Magazine 108, 116, 197, 257
Harper's Weekly 104, 122,
219, 220, 227
Harriman, W. Averell 105, 241,
251, 254, 271
Harrington, Gerard 258
Harrington, Vincent 152
Harris, Corra May (White) 139
Harris, Edward 207
Harris, Julian Larose 139
Harris, T. George 258
Harris, William Bliss 225
Harrison, Benjamin 146, 193
Harrison, Emily Steward 140
Harrison, Russell B. 146
Harrison, Walter M. 224
Harrisonburg Daily News Record . 239
Harrisonburg Independent 157
Harriss, Robert Preston 187
Harsch, Joseph C. 258
Hart, Jeffrey Peter 107
Hart, Jerome A. 103
Hart, Moss 261
Hart, William S. 209
Hartford Evening Post 220
Hartford Times 221
Harvey, Alfred S. 259
Harvier, Ernest 200
Haskell, Ernest 198
Hassaurek, Friedrick 214
Hassett, William D. 130
Hastings Banner 168
Hatfield, Mark 271
Haugen, Gilbert Nelson 153
Havana Daily Telegraph 159
Hawley, Joseph Roswell 130
Hay, John 130, 196, 202
Hayden, Jay G. 169
Hayden, Thomas 273
Hayes, A.J. 166

Hayes, Helen 261
Hayes, Rutherford B. 146, 147, 215, 219, 220
Hayes, Webb C. 147, 219
Hayes, Will H. 259
Haymes, Dick 199
Hayne, Paul Hamilton 197
Haynes, John L. 235
Hays, Arthur Garfield 201
Hays, Will H. 244
Haywood, William D. 244
Hazard, Aline W. 259
Hazeltine, Mayo Williamson . . . 130
Hazlett, Henry 207
Hearst Collection 113
Hearst newspapers 107, 111
Hearst, William Randolph . 103, 112, 119, 120, 195, 206, 218, 219, 225
Heart of the News 254
Heath, Frederic 249
Heaton, David 212
Hecker, June 214
Hedges, William S. 259, 266
Heffner, Hugh 117
Heilbroner, Robert L. 269
Helderburgh Advocate 205
Helena Daily Journal 146
Helena Herald 185
Helena Typographical Union #95 . 185
Hellman, Lillian 117, 192
Hemenway, James A. 147
Hemingway, Ernest 131, 202
Hemphill, J.C. 230
Hench, Atcheson 241
Henderson, Alexander B. 103
Henderson, Will 212
Hendricks, William 146
Henle, Raymond Z. 259
Henning, Arthur Sears 143
Hennings, Thomas C., Jr. 270
Henrici, Max 228
Henrikson, Arthur A. 221
Henry, E. William 259
Henry, Edward A. 212
Henry, John M. 151, 153, 155
Henshaw, David 188
Hensley, Stewart 131
Heppner Gazet 247
Heppner Gazette 226
Herbert, John K. 266
Herff, Ferdinand 235
Herkimer County Journal 205
Herman, Lazar 262

Herring, Clyde L. 151, 153, 154
Herter, Christian 267, 268
Hertzberg, Sidney 203, 270
Herzog, Arthur 161
Herzog, Lester W. 194
Hibben, John G. 192
Hickenlooper, Bourke . 151, 152, 153
Hickory Daily Record 189
Hicks, Granville 262, 270
Higgins, Anthony 121
Higgins, Marguerite 207
Higginson, Thomas Wentworth . 213
Hightower, John M. 259
Hill, Adams Sherman 188
Hill, David B. 203
Hill, Draper 240
Hill, Edwin Conger 131
Hill, James J. 173
Hill, Lister 254
Hill, Percy 120
Hillman, Sidney 167
Hinds, Asher Crosby 131
Hinrichs, Hans 263
Hirschberg, Al 161
Hiss, Alger 106
Hitchcock, Frank Harris 131
Hitchcock, Gilbert 151
Hitchcock, Gilbert M. 189
Hitt, George C. 148
Hitt, Robert R. 146
Hoard, Halbert L. 259
Hocking, Thomas Joseph 185
Hodge, Orlando John 222
Hoegh, Leo 151
Hoff, Syd 218
Hoffman, A.C. 150
Hoffman, Burt 255
Hoffman, Michael 198
Hofstadter, Richard 269
Holbrook, Richard Burkey 224
Holbrook, Stuart 271
Holland, Josiah Gilbert 200
Holley, Harvey Whitcomb 174
Holliss, Roy C. 143
Holloway, William R. 147
Holloway, William Robeson . . . 146
Holman, William S. 146
Holmes, John Clough 165
Holmes, Oliver Wendell 219
Holmes, Ralph 165
Holz, Julius 200
Honolulu Star-Bulletin 230
Hood, Edwin Milton 131
Hood, Gretchen 140

Hook, Sidney 114, 270
Hooker, Richard 117
Hoosier Radio Announcer 211
Hoover, Dale 150
Hoover, Herbert 105, 107,
    117, 119, 148, 152, 153, 154,
    155, 191, 195, 198, 206, 207,
    208, 249, 252, 254, 59, 261,
    263, 264, 268
Hoover, J. Edgar 122, 152, 154,
    251, 254, 259, 265, 267, 268,
    271, 272, 273
Hope, Clifford 149
Hopkins, Harry L. 151
Horizon 116, 124
Horodysky, Orest Iwan 180
Horton, McDavid 231, 232
Hostadter, Richard 270
Hotchkiss, George W. 169
Hotchkiss, Thomas Woodward . . 192
Hotze, Henry 131
Houdini, Harry 203
Hough, B., Jr. 210
Houghton, Carolyn Wells 203
House, Edward M. 191
Houston Chronicle 235
Houston Post 237
Hoving, Thomas P.F. 153
Howard, Edgar 189
Howard, Jack R. 272
Howard, Nathaniel R. 223
Howard, Roy 171
Howard, Roy W. 256, 271, 272
Howard, Roy Wilson 131
Howe, Henry 147
Howe, Irving 118
Howe, Julia Ward . . . 115, 213, 219
Howe, Quincy 203
Howell, Clark 140, 142
Howell, Clark, Jr. 142
Howell, E.P. 142
Howell, Evan P. 140
Howells, William Dean . 147, 215, 219
Hoyem, Oliver 225
Hoyt, James Allen 232
Hrvatska Stampa 180
Hubbard, Elbert H. 151
Hubbard, Kin 148
Hudson Star-Observer 259
Hudson, Horce Bushnell 174
Huebsch, B.W. 203
Hughes, Charles Evans . . 117, 198,
    202, 249
Hughes, Harold E. 153

Hughes, John 161
Hughes, Langston 273
Hughes, Raymond M. 150
Hull, Cordell . 117, 153, 208, 256, 268
Hull, Merlin 259
Humboldt, Charles 117
Hummel, Abraham Henry 203
Humphrey, Hubert H. . 116, 174, 213,
    251, 254, 256, 257, 259, 260,
    261, 262, 264, 265, 267, 268,
    271, 272
Hungerford, Cyrus 260
Hungry Horse News 186
Hunker, William H. 146
Hunt, Alvah 209
Hunter, Dard 191
Hunter, Edward 260
Hunter, John Patrick 260
Hunter, William D.H. 146
Huntington, Samuel P. 269
Huntington, William H. 196
Huntley, Chet 260
Huntley-Brinkley Report 253,
    257, 258
Huntsman's Echo 238
Hurlbert, William Henry 147
Hurst, Fannie 198, 203, 261
Hutchings, James Mason 131
Hutchins, Robert 268
Hutchinson Independent 174
Hutchinson, Elmer T. 193
Hutton, Laurence 192
Hyatt, Donald B. 260
Hyde, George R. 131
Hyde, Henry Morrow 240
Hyde, James Hazen 198

Ickes, Harold L. 152, 195,
    249, 254, 256, 268
Idan Uutiset Publishing Company 180
Ignatus, Vincent 179
Illinois Miner 166, 167
Illustrirte Zeitung 123
Independence Inyo-Independent . 112
Independent American 204
Indian Citizen 224
Indiana Gazette 145
Indiana Locomotive 146
Indianapolis Journal 146, 148
Indianapolis News . . . 145, 146, 147
Indianapolis Sentinel 146
Indianapolis Star . . . 106, 148, 218
Indianapolis Times 146
Indianola Bulletin 234

Industrialisti 183
Ingalls, John James 131
Ingersoll, Ralph 161
Ingham, Harvey 151
Ingle, Edward 243
Innerst, J. Stuart 228
International Council of Industrial
 Editors 223
International News Service 108,
 141, 206, 207, 216, 260
Ionia Sentinel 170
Iowa Press Women, Inc. 152
Iowan, The 152
Ireland 203
Ireland, William Addision (Billy) . 217
Ironwood Daily Globe 170
Ironwood Times 170
Irwin, Dilla E. 260
Irwin, Joel 211
Irwin, Wallace 104
Irwin, Will 107, 188
Isherwood, Christopher 115
Issacs, Edith J.R. 260
Italamerican Magazine 183
Italian Tribune 164
Itasca Iron News 174
Ithaca Daily News 194
Ithaca Journal 194, 195
Ivey, Jim 221
Izant, Grace Goulder 212
Izvestiia 110

Jackson Southerner 145
Jackson, Helen Hunt 197
Jackson, Luther P. 188
Jackson, Peral Cashwell 235
Jacksonville Journal 137
Jacobs, Herbert 260
Jaeger, Luth 174
Jaffe, Louis Isaac 239, 240
Jaffe, Sam A. 260
James, Henry 198
James, Howard 162
James, John Hough 212
Jameson, J. Franklin 202
Jamieson, William D. 153
Janesville Gazette 252
Janeway, Eliot 265
Japan Advertiser 226
Japan Times and Mail 115
Japanese-American Courier . . . 247
Jardine, William H. 153
Jarnagin, William C. 152
Jarvis, Russell 131, 188

Jaskolski, Alexandra 180
Jaskolski, Karol T. 180
Javits, Jacob K. 116, 251
Jefferson County Union 259
Jefferson, Thomas 240
Jeffersonian and Virginia Times . 239
Jenkins, Guy H. 169
Jenks, Eleazer Alley 157
Jenks, Tudor 230
Jennings, Gary 162
Jennings, Kenneth Q. 193
Jerich, John 180
Jester, Beauford 236
Jewett, Sarah Orne 219
Jewish Daily Courier 178
Jewish Daily Forward 178
Jewish People's Institute 178
Jewish Telegraphic Agency . . . 160
Jewish Transcript 247
Jewish Voice 247
Jewish Voice Pictorial 223
Jewish World 223
Johnson, Axel P. 169
Johnson, Edwin, J. 170
Johnson, Gale D. 150
Johnson, Guy B. 188
Johnson, Hugh S. 253
Johnson, Joseph Ellis 238
Johnson, Lady Bird 273
Johnson, Louis 264
Johnson, Lyndon B. . . 116, 122, 236,
 251, 254, 264, 265, 267, 272,
 275
Johnson, Malcolm 137
Johnson, Nicholas 153
Johnson, Oliver 219
Johnson, Richard M. 146
Johnson, Richard Underwood . . 147
Johnson, Robert Underwood . . . 198
Johnson, Thelma, Abel 185
Johnston, Rienzi Melville 237
Jones, Adolphus Eberhardt . . . 212
Jones, Elizabeth McLeod 174
Jones, George 200
Jones, Jesse Holman 235
Jones, Robert Edmond 260
Jones, Rogan 260
Jones, Stiles P. 174
Jones, Will Owen 189
Jones, William Atkinson 239
Jordan, David Starr . . 104, 194, 263
Jordan-Smith, Paul 208
Journal de Geneve 108
Journal of Commerce 206

Jumper, Will C. 155
Jurden, Jack 221
Jusserand, J.J. 192
Jusserand, Jean Jules 198

Kahn, Gordon 261
Kai-shek, Chiang 191
Kai-Shek, Chiang, Madame .264, 272
Kaireman, Paavo A. 177
Kalamazoo Gazette 171
Kalb, Marvin 271
Kallen, Horace M. 160
Kaltenborn, Hans V. 254, 257,
    261, 262, 263, 275
Kanadai Magyarsag 181
Kane, Robert J. 195
Kanner, Heinrich 107
Kansas City Journal 156
Kansas City Journal of Commerce 118
Kansas City Star 221, 226
Kantola, Matti 177
Kantor, MacKinlay 131, 271
Karger, Gustavus J. 214
Karsner, David Fulton 200
Kasson Republican 176
Katka, Terttu 177
Katkov, Norman 261
Katzenbach, Nicholas . . .264, 267
Kauffman, Samuel Hay 131
Kaufmann, Peter 214
Kaufmann, Walter 261
KAYE Radio 247
Kazan, Elia 261
Kazin, Alfred 270
Keating, John McLeod 131
Keeler, Lucy Elliot 220
Keeler, O.B. 140
Keep, John 131
Kefauver, C. Estes 166, 252,
    254, 257, 260, 264, 265, 267
Kehoe, Louis 152
Keidel, George 159
Keim family 131
Kellar, Andrew Jackson . . .147, 219
Kelley, Frank 272
Kellogg, Frank B. 173
Kellogg, Paul U. 263
Kelly, C. Brian 240
Kelly, Harry 166
Kempton, Murray 268
Ken 167
Kendall, Amos 131
Kendall, George Wilkins 235
Kendall, N.E. 151

Kennan, George 131
Kennan, John F. 263
Kennedy, Edward M. 271, 273
Kennedy, Jacqueline 273
Kennedy, John F. 116, 167,
    192, 254, 257, 260, 264, 267,
    268, 271, 272, 273
Kennedy, Robert F. 252, 257,
    264, 265, 267, 271, 272, 273
Kennedy, Will 185
Kent, Rockwell 191
Kenyon, Nellie 232
Kenyon, William S. 153
Kepes Magyer Magazin 177
KERA-TV 234
Kerby, Elizabeth Poe 261
Kerr, Clark 268, 269
Kerr, Walter 116, 120
Kerr, Walter F. 261
Kester, Frank 103
KFIO 244
KGA 244
KHQ 244
Kidd, James H. 170
Kidder, Frederic 220
Kidney, Daniel 271
Kieran, John 193
Kieran, John Francis 132
Kilne, George Washington 189
Kilpatrick, James Jackson 158,
    239, 240
Kinder, George D. 214
King Broadcasting Company . . . 248
King Features Syndicate 197
King, Frederick Allen 200
King, Martin Luther, Jr. 267
Kinght, O.A. 167
Kinoy, Ernest 261
Kinsella, Thomas 200
Kinston Free Press 242
Kintner, Robert 251
Kiplinger Washington Letter . . . 262
Kiplinger, Austin H. 261
Kiplinger, Willard M. 231, 256
Kirby, Edward M. 262
Kirkwood, William Paul 174
Kissinger, Henry 270
Klaas, M.D. 230
Klein, Julius 132, 267
Kline, Allan B. 150
Kline, Burton 132
Kluger, Richard 117
KMAC 237
KMBC 149

KMGH 113
Knap, Ted 271
Knapp, Charles W. 147
Knecht, Karl 262
Knight, John S. 213
Knight, Mary Lamar 140
Knight, Thomas E. 157
Knoll, Erwin 268
Knoll, Rudolph 132
Knopf, Alfred A. . 114, 150, 191, 267
Knott, John 234
Know, Frank 272
Knowland, Joseph R. 103
Knox, Franklin 119, 132
Knox, William Frank 170
KOA 113
Kobak, Edgar 264
Koenig, Gilbert 262
Koestler, Arthur 192
Kohn, August 232
Koski, Ernest Theodore 180
Koss, Mary 155
Kossuth, Louis 202
KPFA 267
KPFK 267
KPFT 267
Kraja, Josip 180
Kraschel, Nelson G. 151
KREM 244
Krems, Nathan 247
Kriegs-Presseburo 107
Kristol, Irving . . 116, 118, 269, 270
Krock, Arthur 120, 171,
    192, 198, 239, 240, 265, 267
KSPO 244
Ku Klux Klan 239
Kubly, Herbert 262
Kuekes, Edward Daniel 217
Kuhn, Ferdinand 193
Kulp, Claude L. 195
Kunstler, William M. 181
Kuryer Codzienny 180
Kurzman, Dan 162
Kuykendall, James Hampton . . 235
KVOS 260

La Follette family 144
La Follette, Philip F. 269
La Follette, Robert M., Jr. . 154, 166,
    251, 252, 253, 254, 267, 269
La Follette, Robert M., Sr. . 176, 257
La Guardia, Fiorello . . . 178, 182,
    209, 261
Labadie, Joseph 202

Labadie, Laurence 202
Labor 166
Labor Action 166
Ladejinsky, Wolf 150
Ladies Home Journal 226
Lahey, Edwin A. 132
Laisve 178
Lake, Austin 162
Lakeville Journal 256
Lalley, Joseph Michael 158
Lammon, Loren D. 174
Lamont, Corliss 273
Lamont, Thomas W. 167
Lampe, David 162
Lamphere, George Nathan 175
Lampman, Ben Hur 208
Land, Myrick 162
Lander, William Hall 188
Landers, Ann 153, 265, 268
Landon, Alfred M. 149, 195,
    253, 254, 265
Lane, Franklin K. 198
Lane, Joseph 226
Lang, Andrew 143
Lang, Daniel 162
Lang, Fritz 262
Lania, Leo 262
Lansing Republican 166
Lansing State Journal 166
Lapham, Lewis H. 108
Larus & Brothers 241
Lasch, Robert . . . 262, 265, 267, 268
Lash, Joseph 270
Lasky, Victor 120, 271
Lasswell, Mary Clyde Grayson
    Lubbock 235
Lathan, Robert 230, 232
Latvala, George 177
Laurent, Lawrence B. 262, 264
Lausche, Frank J. 213
Lauzanne, Stephan Joseph Vincent 108
LaVarre, William 108
Lawrence Sentenlel 191
Lawrence, D.H. 260
Lawrence, David 231, 252
Lawrenceburg Register 146
Lawson, Victor F. 147
Lazar, Josette 162
Lazarsfeld, Paul F. 265
Lazarus, Emma 198
Le Gallienne, Richard 198, 203
Le Matin (Paris) 108
Lea, Albert M. 173
Leacacos, John P. 162

Leahey, William D. 268
Leavitt, Joshua 132
Lebanese American Journal . . . 181
Lebanon Western Star 215
LeCompte, Karl M. . . . 151, 152, 153
Lee Newspapers 184
Lee, Henry 140
Lee, Lawrence 241
Leggett, William 132
Lehman, Herbert H. . . 195, 264, 267
Leighton, George Ross 203
Lemmer, Victor F. 170
Lenoir News-Topic 189
Lens, Sidney 269
Lenz, Charles 200
Leonard, Lewis Alexander 140
Lepper, William D. 159
Lerner, Leo 207
Lerner, Max 117, 270
Leslie's Weekly 122
Leslie, Frank 147, 220
LeSueur Independent 174
LeSueur News 174
Levchuk, Dmytro 180
Levine, Irving R. 207
Levinson, Edward 167
Lewis, Ernest Irving 132
Lewis, Flora 162
Lewis, Fulton, III 207
Lewis, Fulton, Jr. 207, 254
Lewis, George Cornewall, Sir . . . 192
Lewis, Jerry 271
Lewis, John L. . . 166, 167, 264, 274
Lewis, Robert G. 268
Lewis, Ross A. 262
Lewis, Sinclair 167, 208
Lewis, Theodore Friedman 218
Lewisohn, Adolph 198
Lewisohn, Ludwig 241
Leycester, William 140
Liberation 229
Liberty 202, 253
Liberty Magazine 143
Library Journal 197
Libre pensador, El 237
Lie, Trygve 254, 268
Liepins, Olberts 108
Life 208, 231
Light 230
Lights and Shadows 156
Ligutti, L.G. 150
Lilienthal, Alfred M. 108
Lilienthal, David E. 191, 254, 257, 267

Lilly, Doris 162
Lincoln Belmont Publishing Company
. . . . 207
Lincoln, Abraham 121, 193
Lindbergh, Charles A. 191
Lindbergh, Charles Augustus, Sr. 175
Lindley, Harlow 147
Lindley, J.K. 258
Lindsay, Howard 261
Lindsay, John 166
Lindsay, John F. 267
Lindsay, John V. 251, 271
Lippmann, Walter 117, 120,
171, 230, 239, 252, 254, 257,
258, 262, 267, 269, 272
Lipset, Seymour M. 269
Lipton, Thomas, Sir 209
Litchfield Bulletin 210
Litchfield Weekly Monitor 188
Literary Digest 200
Littell, Robert 226
Liveright, Horace B. 206
Livingston, E.M. 167
Livingston, John W. 167
Livingston, Louis Joseph 200
Lloyd, Georgia 204
Lloyd, Henry Demarest 132
Lochard, Metz T.P. 124
Lochner, Louis P. 262
Locke, David Ross 220
Locke, Robinson 214, 220
Lockhart, Andrew Francis 175
Lockwood, Belva A. 228
Lodge, Henry Cabot 263
Lodge, Henry Cabot, Jr. . . .254, 264,
267, 268, 272
Lodge, John D. 178
Loeb, James, Jr. 251
Loevinger, Lee 263, 264
Logan, John A. 147
Logan, Joshua 261
London Daily Mail 258
London Daily News 111
London Morning Chronicle 117
London Times 115, 121, 140
London, Jack 226
Lone Pine Progress Citizen 112
Lonesome Road 251
Long, Breckenridge 153
Long, Haniel 208
Long, James M. 214
Long, Richard M. 156
Long, Walter Ewing 236
Longfellow, Henry W. 219

Longley, Mary B. 230
Look 254, 258, 265
Loomis, Lee P. 250
Looscan, Adele B. 236
Lorain Journal 213
Lord, Chester Sanders 188
Lord, Russell 194
Lorimer, George H. 240
Lorimer, George Horace 120
Los Angeles Herald 206
Los Angeles Herald Examiner . . 113
Los Angeles Times 102, 270
Losh, William, J. 108
Lossing, Benson J. 148, 220
Louisville Courier Journal 220
Love, Harry H. 195
Love, John W. 271
Lovelace, Delos W. 175
Loveless, Herschel C. 153
Lovering, Frank W. 158
Lowden, Fran 155
Lowden, Frank O. 153
Lowe, David 263
Lowell, James Russell 219
Lower, Elmer W. 264
Lowry, Thomas 173
Lubell, Samuel 269, 271
Lucas, James G. 271, 272
Lucas, Townsend McKinley . . . 124
Luce, Claire Boothe 120, 144,
    167, 254, 261, 264, 267
Luce, Henry 116, 118,
    120, 132, 144, 171, 231, 258
Lucey, Charles T. . . . 259, 271, 272
Lucy, Autherine 101
Lucy, Calvin R. 241
Lucy, Henry, III 241
LULAC News 237
Lumber Trade Journal 169
Lumberman's Gazette, The 169
Lundberg, Ferdinand 203
Lyman, Joseph Bardwell 118
Lyman, S.P. 202
Lynch, Russell G. 263
Lynchburg Daily Advance . . . 241
Lynd, Staughton 273
Lyon, Peter 263
Lyons, Eugene 108
Lytton, Rosina 192

Mabie, Hamilton D. 230
MacArthur, Douglas . . 251, 258, 272
Macdonald, Dwight 118
MacDonald, Kenneth 153

Mack, Connie 120
Mackay, Clarence 188
Mackay, John Henry 202
MacLeish, Archibald . . 115, 191, 267
Maclin, P. Davis, Jr. 144
MacMillan, Harold 258
MacNeil, Robert 264
MacNeil-Lehrer Report 264
MacNelly, Jeff 122, 241
MacNider, Hanford 152
Macon Telegram 141
MacVane, John 264
Madden, Edward R. 266
Maddox, James G. 150
Madison Capital Times 269
Madisonian, The 185
Magazine Advertising Bureau . . 253
Magraw, Dan 144
Magyar Munkaslap 201
Mahaffay, Robert E. 247
Mailer, Norman 117, 118
Mainstream 117
Malenkov, Georgi M. 264
Malmquist, Orin Nebeker 238
Malott, Deane W. 194, 195
Manchester Daily Mirror 248
Manchester Guardian 101
Manchester, William 270
Mandel, Ernest 201
Mann, Albert R. 194
Mann, Klaus 115
Mannes, Marya 162
Manning, Daniel 132
Manning, Reg 152
Manning, Richard I. 230
Mansfield Gazette 215
Mansfield, Edward Deering . . . 214
Mansfield, Mike 267
Mantle, Mickey 271
Mantorville Express 176
Marble, Manton Malone 132
March of Labor 167
March of Time 225
March, Fredric 261
Marchello, Maurice R. 180
Marconi, Guglielmo 254
Marcuse, Herbert 273
Marcy, William L. 121, 198
Marietta Gazette 222
Marion Star 200, 216
Maris, Clarence 215
Markham, Edwin 119, 226
Marks, Callison 244
Marquardt, Frederic S. 170

Marquette Journal 172
Marschalk, Franklin 236
Marshall, Dorothy 167
Marshall, Edison 198
Marshall, Elihu Francis 195
Marshall, George C. 253, 268
Marshall, Joseph G. 146
Marshall, Walter 166
Martello, Il 183
Martin, Harold H. 140
Martin, Herb 143
Martin, John Sanford 188
Martin, Mary 254, 261
Martin, Thomas E. 153
Martin, Tom 151, 152
Martin, William 108
Martindale, Elijah B. 147
Martinsburg Evening Journal . . . 239
Marx, Groucho 261
Mason City Globe Gazette 152
Mason, Frank 108, 227, 264
Mason, Jack 109
Massari, Vincent 180
Masters, Edgar Lee 203
Mathewson, Tracy 140
Mathias, Fred S. 208
Matson, Roy L. 250, 264
Matthews, James Muscoe 242
Mattson, Hans 175
Mattson, Helmi Dagmar 181
Maugham, Somerset 203, 262
Maurice, Arthur B. 198
Maverick, Maury 116
Maxwell, James A. 221
May, Charles S. 170
May, Henry F. 270
Maybank, Burnet R. 230
Mayer, Milton S. 203, 268
Mayfield, Sara 101
Mayo, Katherine 118
Mays, Benjamin E. 188
Mazey, Ernest 167
Mazzini, Giuseppe 132
McAdoo, William G. . . 119, 153, 244
McBride, Joseph 263
McCabe, Robert Karr 162
McCall, Almon 170
McCall, Ernest J. 170
McCallum, George P. 170
McCammon, J.D. 224
McCarn, Rebecca 208
McCarthy, Eugene J. 268, 271
McCarthy, Jonathan 146
McCarthy, Joseph R. 105, 114, 120, 267

McCarthy, Justin 198
McCarthy, Mary 118
McCay, Winsor 217
McClary, Jane Walker Stevenson
    McIlvaine 240
McClellan, John L. 265
McClure Newspaper Syndicate
    . . . . 114, 227
McClure's 198, 203
McClure, S.S. 188, 263
McCombs, William F. 119
McCord, Gerald 190
McCormick, Anne O'Hare . . 200, 263
McCormick, Cyrus 147
McCormick, Medill 147
McCormick, Robert K. 263
McCormick, Robert R. 143
McCoy, Ralph E. 144
McCullers, Carson 115
McCutcheon, John Tinney 217
McDonald, Julie 152
McDonald, Ruth Seely Berry . . . 195
McEwen, Arthur 104
McFeatters, Dale 221
McGaffin, William 162
McGill, Ralph Emerson 140
McGovern, George 150, 268
McGovern, James 162
McGuffey, William Holmes 215
McGurn, William Barrett 263
McKee, David R. 147
McKelway, St. Clair 200
McKenny, Charles Richard . . . 175
McKinley, William 146, 147
McKissick, James Rion 232
McKnew, Zadoc W. 132
McKusick, Marshall 152
McLain, John Scudder 175
McLane, John Augustus Hendrix 118
McLauchlin, Russell Jaehne . . . 165
McLean County Independent . . . 209
McLean, Evalyn 132
McMichael, Morton 132
McMillin, Miles J. 263
McNail, Claudia 261
McNeil, Marshall 271
McNitt, William 170
McNutt, Paul V. 253
McReynolds, James Clark 240
McSweeny, William F. 162
McWilliams, Carey 112
Mead, Edwin Doak 229
Meagher Country News 186
Meany, George 166, 167, 257, 266, 271

Mechanic's Magazine 117
Mecklin, John Martin 191
Medill, Joseph 146, 147, 188
Meeker, Jotham 156
Meet the Press 137
Mellon, Andres W. 153
Mellon, Andrew 209
Memphis Avalanche 219
Memphis Commercial Appeal . . . 240
Memphis Evening Post 233
Mencken, H.L. . . 104, 116, 119, 123,
    140, 187, 191, 201, 202, 218,
    231, 240, 241, 254, 256, 257,
    268, 270
Menninger, Karl A. 271
Menser, Clarence N. 266
Menshikov, Mikhail 254
Mental Science 202
Mercer County Republican . . . 210
Meredith, Edwin Thomas 152
Meredith, Scott 213
Merrill, Sedgwick, Hubert . . . 120
Messner, Florence L. "Peggy" . . 185
Metcalfe, John C. 109
Metromedia 271
Metzger, H. Peter 109
Meyer, Eugene 132
Meyer, Eugene, Jr. 153
Meyer, Karl E. 268
Miami Herald 138
Michelson, Herman 162
Michener, Carrol Kinsey 175
Michie, Allan A. 162
Michigan Associated Press Managing
    Editors 168
Michigan Chronicle 165
Michigan Chronicle Tri-State
    Defender 124
Michigan Press Association . . . 168
Michigan Republican Newspaper
    Association 170
Michigan Temperance Herald . . . 168
Mickelson, Sigfried 264
Middle East Perspective 108
Midland Cooperator 174
Mielziner, Jo 261
Millard, Bailey 226
Miller, Floyd 162, 170
Miller, Francis Pickens 239
Miller, Jack 151, 153
Miller, Joaquin 226
Miller, Katherine 173
Miller, Merle 153
Miller, Paul 223

Miller, Sol 156
Miller, Wayne 144
Miller, William E. 144
Miller, William Henry 133
Miller, Willis H. 259
Mills, C. Wright 273
Mills, James H. 185
Mills, Ted 266
Milton, George Fort 153
Milwaukee Evening Journal . . . 249
Milwaukee Journal 250, 257,
    262, 263, 272
Milwaukee Labor Press 259
Milwaukee Leader 275
Milwaukee Press Club 249
Miner's Magazine, The 244
Minerva 205
Minneapolis Journal 173, 174
Minneapolis Star 175
Minneapolis Tribune . . 173, 174, 175
Minnesota Mascot 176
Minnesota Union Advocate 175
Minney, Doris 190
Minow, Newton . .116, 262, 264, 267
Mireles, Edmundo E. 237
Misselwitz, Henry Francis . . . 226
Mitchell, John Jr. 189
Mitchell, Margaret 143
Mitchell, William 259
Mitchell, William Bell 175
Mitgang, Herbert 201
Miyata, Martin K. 248
Moats, Alice Leonie 162
Modern Age 158
Mohun, Clare Hanson 220
Mok, Michael 201
Mokarzel, Mary 181
Molek, Ivan 181
Moley, Raymond 109, 265
Molinari, Alberico 181
Mollenhoff, Clark R. 265
Mondale, Walter F. 213
Monday, Mark 109
Mondo, Il 178, 179
Monitor 257, 258
Monroe, Bessie Kerlee 186
Monroe, Marilyn 216
Monroney, Mike 251
Montana Post 185
Montgomery, Bernard 264
Montgomery, Marion 142
Montpelier Vermont Patriot . . . 243
Montrose, Sherman 109
Moody, Blair E. 170

Moody, Clarence Wilber 153
Moore, Joseph Arthur 133
Moore, Raylyn 162
Moore, Veranus A. 196
Moorhead News 175
Moravec, Joseph 174
Moreell, Ben 258
Morehead, Richard M. 236
Morgan, Edward P. 254, 260,
   264, 265, 267, 268
Morgan, Edwin D. 209
Morgan, J.P. 167
Morgan, Thomas 162
Morganthau, Henry, Jr. 272
Morganti, Cesare 181
Morgenthau, Henry 114, 167
Morgenthau, Henry, Jr. 253
Morin, Relman 265
Morison, Samuel Eliot 270
Morley, Christopher 191, 208
Morley, Felix 259
Morris, George Pope 133
Morris, Joe Alex 272
Morris, John Milt 221
Morris, Newbold 203
Morris, Willie 116
Morrison, Chester L. 265
Morrison, Richard H. 184
Morrow, Josiah 215
Morrow, Marco 156
Morse, Sidney H. 203
Morse, Wayne 227, 254, 257, 268, 271
Morton, J. Sterling 190
Mosaicos 237
Moscow, Warren 265
Moses, Harry Bowman 236
Moss, Gurnie Maver 186
Mowrer, Edgar Ansel 262, 265
Moyer, Charles H. 244
Moynihan, Daniel Patrick . . 116, 269
Mudge, James M. 171
Mueller, Merrill 259, 264
Muggerage, Malcolm 109
Muhlen, Norbert 162
Muir, John 226
Mulford, Prentice 133
Mulgrew, John P. 151
Mumford, Ethel Watts 201
Mumford, Lewis 119
Mundt, Karl E. 265
Munguia, Romulo 237
Munnecke, Wilbur 268
Munsell, Joel 148
Munsey's 226

Munsey, Frank A. 188
Murdock, Victor 133
Murphy, Carl 123
Murphy, Donald R. 150
Murphy, Frank 256
Murphy, George B., Jr. 124
Murphy, John H. III 123
Murphy, Louis 151
Murphy, William 173
Murphy, Zoe R. 150
Murray, Freeman Henry Morris . 124
Murrow, Edward R. 133, 154,
   206, 230, 254, 258, 264, 271
Muskie, Edmund 116
Muste, A.J. 229
Mutual Broadcasting System 195, 207
Myers Publication Company . . . 207
Myers, William I. 196
Myrick, Susan 141, 142

Nabakov, Vladimir 115
Nadel, Baruch 119
Nafziger, Ralph O. 263
Nagel, Charles E. 153
Nagel, Conrad 152
Naisten Viiri 181
Napoleon Homestead 209
Napoleon III 121
Narod 178
Nash, Hugh 204
Nash, Ogden 218
Nashville Tennessean 252
Nast, Thomas 115, 220
Nathan, Robert 115
Nation . 112, 117, 119, 167, 207, 255
National American 139
National Association of Broadcasters
   . . . . 259, 265
National Association of Educational
   Broadcasters 266
National Citizens Committee for
   Broadcasting 153
National Educational Television . 266
National Geographic 254
National Intelligencer 199
National Leader 189
National League of American Pen
   Women 210, 266
National News Council Archives . 184
National Nonpartisan League . . 133
National Press Club 137
National Review 107, 115
Nationwide Communications, Inc. 215
Naujienos 178

Navasota Leader 236
Nazioni Unite 179
NBC News 230, 233, 253
NBC Nightly News 258
NBC Program Analysis File 137
NBC Radio 137
NBC/National Broadcasting Company
    149, 207, 251, 252, 253, 254,
    255, 256, 257, 258, 259, 260,
    263, 264, 266, 270, 274
Neal, Eva 175
Nearing, Scott 117
Necessity 241
Neff, Lawrence W. 141
Neighborhood Press of Chicago . . 207
Nelson, Arvid 181
Nelson, Carl 210
Nelson, Gaylord 253, 254,
    257, 264, 265, 268
Nelson, John Emil 210
Nelson, Knute 175
Nettlau, Max 166
Neuberger, Maurine B. 264
Neuberger, Richard L. . 227, 267, 268
Neue Generation 229
Neuharth, Al 223
Neumann, William 268
Neustadt, Richard 269
Nevins, Allan 251
New Braunfels Herald 235
New Canaan Gazette 190
New England Magazine 229
New Haven Register 120
New Haven Palladium 120
New Jersey Coalition for Fair
    Broadcasting 193
New Jersey Guide 225
New Leader, The 266
New Masses 104, 117
New Northwest 185
New Orleans Crescent 242
New Orleans Times Picayune . . . 221
New Republic . . . 104, 116, 226, 255
New York American 198, 203,
    206, 225
New York Associated Press . . 147, 201
New York Commerical 196
New York Commerical-Advertiser
    . . . . 173, 203
New York Courier 204
New York Daily Graphic 220
New York Daily Mirror 227
New York Daily News . . . 143, 254
New York Evening Graphic 274

New York Evening Herald 103
New York Evening Mail 197
New York Evening Post . . . 118, 122,
    187, 196, 220
New York Evening Sun 166
New York Evening World 201
New York Herald 119, 139,
    148, 196, 200, 219, 220
New York Herald Tribune . . 102, 110,
    117, 119, 123, 201, 203, 207,
    226, 228, 230, 231 261, 263,
    266, 271, 272, 274
New York Illustrated News 220
New York Independent 219
New York Journal 219
New York Ledger 197
New York Morning Courier 121
New York Post 117, 120, 201, 216, 274
New York Star 117
New York Sun 122, 188, 200, 225, 226
New York Times 102, 104,
    114, 115, 120, 123, 139, 141,
    142, 148, 190, 191, 192, 195,
    196, 198, 199, 200, 201, 202,
    206, 207, 208, 209, 225, 226,
    251, 252, 253, 260, 261, 263,
    265, 267, 273, 274
New York Times Review of Books
    . . . . 190, 195
New York Tribune 120, 188,
    190, 195, 197, 199, 201, 220
New York World 114, 116, 121,
    123, 189, 193, 196, 197, 202,
    219, 226
New York World-Journal-Tribune . 252
New York World-Telegram . . 227, 261
New York World-Telegram and Sun 252
New Yorker . . . 114, 118, 194, 203,
    218, 225, 231, 270, 275
New, Harry S. 147, 148
New, John C. 146, 147
Newark Evening Journal 249
Newark Evening News 107
Newark News 217
Newark Weekly Post 217
Newcomb, James Pearson, Sr. . . 236
Newman, Edwin H. 266
Newman, Frances 142
Newman, Joseph 266
Newport News Daily Press 239
Newport News Times Herald . . . 239
News and Courier 187, 231
News and Notions 232
News and Observer Publishing Co. 141

News of the World 254
News on the Hour 257
News Sentinel 233
Newsday 207
Newspaper Enterprise Association
. . . . 109, 173
Newspaper Guild 172
Newspaper Guild of America . . . 208
Newsweek . . 106, 109, 111, 207, 225
Newton, Byron Rufus 119
Newton, Virgil Miller 138
Nicholls, Jim 247
Nicholson, Meredith 146
Niebuhr, Reinhold 116, 255
Niobarara Tribune 190
Nisbet, Robert 269
Nixon, Richard M. 109, 153,
213, 250, 252, 255, 259, 264,
265, 270, 271, 272, 273
Nixon, William Penn 147
Nizer, Louis 273
Nobile, Philip 162
Nock, Albert Jay 119
Non-Partisan Leader 171
Norden, The 180
Nordhoff, Charles 220
Norfolk Ledger Star 240
Norfolk Virginian 242
Norris, George W. 257
Norris, Paul Gifford, Jr. 153
North American Newspaper
Alliance 207, 255, 261
North Dakota Press Association . 210
North Dakota Press Women . . . 210
North Dakota Progressive 209
North St. Paul Sentinel 175
North Star 124, 224
North, The 174, 175
Northcliffe, Lord 121, 188
Northfield News 176
Northrop, Cyrus 175
Northwestern Miller 173, 175
Norton, Marie Teresa 256
Norwood Enterprise 212
Nossal, Frederick 110
Novi Svet 180
Novik, Morris S. 262
Nowy Swiat 177
Noyes, Crosby C. 255
Noyes, Crosby Stuart 133
Nugent, Frank 192
Nuovo Mundo, Il 178
Nurczynski, Walter 181
Nye, Frank T. 153

Nye, Russell B. 268
Nyiregynazy, Pal V. 181

O'Brien, William H. 146
O'Casey, Sean 202
O'Conner, Flannery 142
O'Connor, Harvey 167, 247
O'Connor, Hugh 226
O'Day, Marjory 186
O'Hara, John 218
O'Laughlin, John Callan 133
O'Neill, Harold Edgar 193
O'Neill, John M. 244
O'Reilly Henry 133
Oak, Liston M. 266
Oakes, John B. 267
Oakland Tribune 103
Oaks, John 120
Oakville Sentinel 153
Oastler, Frank Richard 119
Ocala Evening Star 138
Ocala Star Banner 138
Ochs, Adolph S. 114, 120,
147, 188, 209
Ochs, Adolph S., II 232
Ochs, Milton B. 233
Odum, Howard W. 188
Oelwein Daily Register 149
Office of War Information . . 120, 137
Ogilvy, Steward M. 204
Ohio Legislative Correspondents
Association 215
Ohio Newspaper Association . . . 215
Ohio Newspaper Women's Association
. . . . 215
Ohio State Journal 215, 219
Ohio State University Lantern
. . . . 217, 218
Oklahoma Leader 166
Olberg Journal 172
Olio 212
Olivia Press 174
Olmstead, George 149
Olson, Floyd B. 173
Olympia Daily Recorder 249
Omaha Arrow, The 238
Omaha Women's Press Club . . . 190
Operaia, L' 177
Oppenheim, E. Phillips 198
Oppenheimer, J. Robert . . . 192, 264,
267, 269
Orange Native Virginian 242
Original Rights Magazine 200
Orlando Sentinal Star 221

Orr, Carey C. 143
Orszagos Leveltar, Minisz terelnoksegi
    leveltar (Hungary) 181
Osborn, Chase S. 171
Osborn, Tommy 144
Osborne, John 133
Osbourne, Katharine D. 198
Osmena, Sergio 120
Osrin, Raymond Harold 218
Oswego Advertiser 188
Otto, Max 260
Our Dixie Times 238
Oursler, Fulton 123
Oursler, Grace Perkins 123
Overholser, Joseph 186
Overland Monthly 103, 201
Overstreet, Jesse 147
Owen, Russell 193
Owens, John Phillips 175

Pacific Fisherman 246
Pacific News 102
Pacifica Foundation 267
Paducah Sun-Democrat 252
Page, Thomas Nelson 188
Painesville Telegraph 222
Palandech, John R. 181
Paley, William S. 115, 252
Paris Chicago Tribune 113
Parker, George Frederick 133
Parker, Louise 155
Parkes, John Samuel 190
Parks, Warren Wright 212
Parola del Popolo, La 178, 179,
    181, 182
Parrish, Maxfield 232
Parrott, Katherine Ursula 226
Parsons, Chick 120
Parsons, Geoffrey 203
Partisan Review 118
Parton, Margaret 226
Paryski Publishing Company . . . 182
Patent and Trade Mark Review . . 199
Paterson Press 225
Paterson, Isabel Bowler 201
Pathfinder, The 194
Patri, Angelo 133
Patterson, Eleanor Medill 143
Patterson, Joseph Medill 143
Patterson, Ralph P. 256
Paul, Almarin Brooks 103
Pauling, Linus 117
Pawnee Dispatch 224
Payne, Ethel L. 124

Payne, Eugene G. 218
Payne, Philip A. 143
Peabody, George Foster 143, 148,
    198, 202
Peace, Roger 230
Peacemaker 228
Peale, Norman Vincent 195
Pearson, Albert 175
Pearson, Drew 119, 133,
    207, 239, 240, 253, 254, 257,
    265, 268, 272
Peavy, Robert E. 167
Peck, Graham 162
Peck, Sidney 273
Pederson, Sigurd 176
Pegler, Westbrook . . . 195, 207, 265
Pendrell, Ernest 267
Peninsula Enterprise 243
Pennekamp, John D. 138
Pennington, Dwight 213
Pennsylvania Worhenschrift . . . 159
Penzoldt, Sylvia R. 112
People's Video 267
People's Voice 186
People's Watch-Tower 204
Peoples Press 167
Peoria Journal Star 221
Percy, Charles H. 252
Perelman, S.J. 218
Periodical Publishers Association . 253
Perkins, Fred W. 271
Perkins, Milo 116
Perkins, Sidney Albert 249
Peroutka, Ferdinand 110
Perry, Erwin 236
Perry, Stuart H. 171
Pershing, John J. 192, 252
Pesotta, Rose 166
Peterkin, Julia 142
Peters, Mike 218
Petersburg Daily Courier 242
Petersburg Index 242
Peterson, Hjalmar 176
Peterson, Theodore, B. 144
Petruskevich, Ivan 110
Pettus, Terry 247
Pew, J. Howard 259
Peyton, Aquila Johnson 243
Phelps, William Lyon 114
Philadelphia Bulletin 218
Philadelphia Public Ledger 116
Philadelphia Record 218, 250
Philbrick, Herbert 265
Philippines Free Press 170

Phillippi, Wendell C. 250
Phillips, Cabell 162
Phillips, David Graham 192
Phillips, John S. 198
Phillips, Wendell 118, 213
Phoenix Gazette 218
Piatt, Donn 212, 215
Pierce, Charles Wilder 190
Pierce, Dante Melville 153
Pierce, Neal R. 162
Pierpont, Robert 267
Pierson, Charles Herbert 241
Pike, James Shepherd 133
Pinchback, Pinckney Benton Steward
. . . . 124
Pinchot, Gifford . 152, 155, 194, 244
Pinckney, Henry L. 146
Pinckney, Josephine 230
Pine Island News 176
Pinkham, Richard A.R. 266
Pioneer, The 102
Pioneer Express 102, 210
Pioneer Press 173
Piqua Daily Call 216
Piscator, Erwin 262
Pitchfork, The 236
Pittsburgh Courier 124
Pittsburgh Leader 228
Pittsburgh Post-Gazette 260
Pittsburgh Press 228, 253
Pittsburgh Sun Telegraph 228
Pitzele, Merlyn S. 268, 269
Pkrok 223
Plain Table Programs 195
Plain Truth 195
Plainsman 186
Plambeck, Herbert 150
Platt, Thomas C. 146
Plattsburgh Republican 204
Plattsmouth Call 190
Pleke, Le 183
Plentywood Herald 186
Pletcher, Eldon 221
Plunkett, Horace, Sir 191
PM 117, 138, 230
Poinier, Arthur Best 218
Poinsett, Alex 162
Poland 177
Polish American Book Company . 182
Polish National Alliance 178
Polish Roman Catholic Union of
America 178
Politics 118
Pollard, Percival 104

Polnar, Murray 229
Polonia 182
Pontanezen Duckboard 105
Popkin, Zelda 163
Port Umpqua Courier 227
Port Washington Star 252
Porter, Albert G. 146
Porter, Lloyd 173
Porter, William Sydney 198
Portland Gazette 157
Portland Oregonian 173
Post, Helen Wilmans 201
Post, Louis Freeland 133
Post-Gazette 179
Pot Pourri 220
Potter, George F. 174
Poughkeepsie Casket 220
Poughkeepsie Telegraph 220
Pound, Cuthbert 196
Pound, Ezra 202
Powell, John 239
Powers, Perry Francis 171
Powers, Stephen 215
Pownall, Dorothy Ashby 154
Prattis, Percival Leroy 124
Prence, Katherine 118
Prentice, George Dennison 133
Present Tense 229
Preston, Dickson 271
Preston, James D. 268
Preus, J.A.O. 173
Price, Byron 268
Price, Leontyne 271
Priesthood Exposed 195
Priggee, Milt 218
Pringle, Henry Fowles 133
Prison Mirror 173
Proctor, John Clagett 122
Progressive, Inc., The 268
Progressive, The 268
Proletario, Il 179, 183
Prospect Hill Inquirer 237
Prosveta 181
Providence Daily Journal 229
Providence Journal 207
Provincial Freeman 123
Proxmire, William 250, 255,
260, 264, 265
Pryor, Roger Atkinson 242
Psychology Today 258
Public Advertiser 205
Public Interest, The 269
Publisher's Weekly 197
pueblo, El 237

Pulitzer Prize 101, 141,
    143, 150, 158, 217, 218, 230,
    239, 253, 254, 259, 262, 263,
    265, 270, 272, 273
Pulitzer, Joseph 115, 134,
    147, 215, 219, 262
Punch 109
Purdy, James 142
Purdy, James L. 215
Pusey, Nathan M. 270
Putnam County Sentinel 214
Putnam, George P. 148
Pyle, Ernest T. 256, 271, 272
Pynson Printers 191

Quick, Herbert 151
Quillen, Robert 232

Racine Times-Call 257
Radcliffe, E.B. (Ellis Brownell) . . 216
Radical America 269
Radio Executives Club of New
    York 269
Radio Free Europe 110, 269, 272, 275
Radio News Bureau 255
Radio-Television News Directors
    Association 154
Raivaaja 182
Raivaajah Publishing Company . 182
Raleigh News and Observer . . . 141
Ramseyer, Christian W. . . . 153, 154
Ranck, Than Vanneman 119
Rand Daily Mail 206
Rand, Christopher 163
Randolph, A. Philip 167
Randolph, Hollin 153
Rankin, Jeanette 142
Rankin, Thomas Vernon 203
Rapier, John H. 124
Rascoe, Burton 203
Rash, Bryson 269
Rasins, Nikolajs 182
Rasmussen, Louise G. Eiselein . . 186
Rassviet 178
Ratcliffe, Samuel K. 269
Rather, Dan 163
Ratliff, Jim 211
Rauh, Joseph L., Jr. . . 251, 268, 270
Rawson, Charles A. 154
Ray, Caroline Miller 142
Ray, Robert D. 153
Rayburn, Sam 240, 272
Raymond, Henry J. 202, 215
Raymonde 220

Reade, Charles 198
Reader's Digest 108, 110,
    123, 169, 226, 254
Reagan, Ronald 270, 273
Record Herald 222
Redford, Robert 271
Redington, John W. 226, 247
Redmont, Bernard 163
Redpath, James 134
Reed, Clyde 155, 156
Reed, David 163
Reedy, George 271
Reformer 239
Register and Tribune Syndicate . 221
Regnery, Henry 268
Reid, Helen Rogers 272
Reid, Ogden Rogers 119
Reid, Whitelaw 115, 120,
    134, 146, 147, 148, 188, 201,
    205, 215, 220
Reilly, Henry J. 143
Reineger, Novella 103
Reinhardt, Max 261
Reisman, David 269
Renner, Frederick 190
Report on Europe 254
Reporter 116, 254, 269
Reston, James 114, 117,
    120, 264, 267, 269
Reuter's 173
Reuther, Victor 167
Reuther, Walter 166, 167
Revell, Aldric 269
Review of Reviews 202
Reynolds, Conger 152, 154
Reynolds, Cushman 203
Reynolds, Frank 123
Rhee, Syngman 271, 272
Rheinische Zeitung 229
Rhyne, Charles 144
Ribicoff, Abraham 167, 255
Rice, Alexander Hamilton . . . 148
Rice, Ben H. 244
Rice, Grantland 134, 152
Richardson, Albert Deane . . . 134
Richardson, James Hugh . . . 112
Richberg, Donald R. 272
Richert, Earl 271
Richmond Dispatch 242
Richmond Enquirer 243
Richmond Evening Journal . . . 242
Richmond News Leader . . .158, 239,
    240, 241, 242, 243
Richmond Planet 189

Richmond Southern Literary
  Messenger 242
Richmond State 242
Richmond Times 242
Richmond Times-Dispatch . 158, 239,
  241, 242, 255
Richmond, Raymond S. 195
Rickard, Edgar 191
Rickenbacker, Edward V. . . .255, 271
Rickles, Don 273
Riedell, John 221
Rieffel, Aristide 110
Riesel, Victor 269
Riesman, David 258
Rigler, Robert R. 153
Riis, Jacob 134, 198, 202, 203
Riley, James Whitcomb 143
Riley, Tom 153
Riley, William F. 152
Rinehart, Mary Roberts 198
Rio Journal 251
Rio Virgen Times 238
Rising, Henry 244
Risser, James 150
Risveglio, Il 182
Ritchie, Albert 240
Ritchie, Thomas 134
Rivington, James 134
Robb, Inez 271
Robb, Walter Johnson 120
Robbins, Matilda 166
Robert, Norton 109
Roberts, Cecil Edric Mornington . 134
Roberts, Joseph Dana 247
Robertson, A. Willis 239, 241
Robertson, Alexander 204
Robertson, Benjamin Franklin, Jr. 230
Robertson, James 204
Robesonian 189
Robinson, Edward G. 152
Robinson, Hubbell, Jr. 270
Robinson, Magnus L. 189
Robinson, Thomas J.B. 154
Rochester Times-Union 194
Rockefeller, David 267, 268
Rockefeller, John D. 155
Rockefeller, John D., Jr. 173,
  203, 273
Rockefeller, Nelson A. . . . 116, 195,
  213, 256, 267, 268
Rockefeller, Winthop 267
Rockwell, David 153
Rocky Mountain News 109, 148
Rodell, Fred 269

Rodgers, Andrew Denny 215
Rodgers, Richard 273
Roe, Herman 176
Rogers, Ernest 141
Rogers, Richard 201, 261
Rogers, Will, Jr. 120
Rogers, William K. 147
Romanoff, Anastasia J. 194
Rome Daily American 191
Romney, George W. 251, 274
Romualdi, Serafino 178
Romulo, Carlos P. .195, 256, 271, 272
Roosevelt, Archibald 259
Roosevelt, Eleanor 143, 208,
  209, 264, 268
Roosevelt, Franklin D. 109, 117,
  119, 123, 143, 153, 191, 192,
  195, 209, 252, 253, 254, 257,
  268
Roosevelt, James 167
Roosevelt, Nicholas 198, 207
Roosevelt, Theodore 104, 116,
  119, 155, 167, 175, 194, 198,
  202, 208, 239, 249
Root, Elihu 194, 198, 249
Roper, Daniel C. 153
Rose, Carl 218
Rosen, Hy 205
Rosen, Joel B. 234
Rosewater family 190
Ross, Harold 225, 270
Ross, Madeline Dane 270
Rosten, Leo 269
Rostow, Eugene 114
Rothermere, Lord 107
Roundup Record-Tribune 186
Rousselot, John 258
Rovere, Richard H. 270
Rowan, Carl Thomas 158
Royko, Mike 158
Royster, Vermont C. 208, 252
Rozanski, Edward C. 182
Ruark, Robert C. 271
Rubin, Morris H. 255, 257, 270
Ruder, Mel 186
Rue, Helen Dahl 186
Rumely, Edward A. 195
Rusk, Dean . 116, 255, 267, 271, 272
Russell, Bertrand 116, 267
Russell, Charles Edward 134
Russell, Francis 163
Russell, Harriot 237
Russell, Issac 104
Russell, J. Stuart 150

Russell, J.K. 149
Russell, John, Lord 192
Russell, Oland D. 271
Rutland Herald 243
Ryskind, Morrie 270
Saari, Onni 182
Sack, John 163
Sacramento Transcript 102
Safire, William 120, 134
Saginaw Courier-Herald 171
Saint Louis Herald 103
Saint Louis Star 148
Sakai, Yoneo 112
Sakamoto, James Y. 247
Sakrstedt, Ernst 246
Salem Oregon Statesman 226
Salent, Richard S. 274
Salinger, J.D. 203
Salinger, Pierre 271
Salisbury, Harrison . . 114, 150, 267
Salley, A.S. 230
Salomon, Henry J., Jr. 270
Saloniki 178
Salt Lake City Daily Herald . . . 249
Salt Lake Tribune 238
Sams, Stanhope 231
Samuels, Gertrude 163
Samuelson, Paul S. 269
San Antonio Zeitung 234
San Barbara News-Press 104
*San Felipe Telegraph and Texas
    Register* 234
San Francisco Argonaut 104
San Francisco Call 226
San Francisco Call Bulletin . . . 225
San Francisco Chronicle 103
San Francisco Daily News . . . 227
San Francisco Daily Republic . . 102
San Francisco Evening Bulletin
    . . . . .103, 226
San Francisco Examiner . . . 102, 103,
    104, 225, 226
San Francisco Sun Reporter . . . 124
San Francisco Sunday Dispatch . 102
Sanborn, Franklin Benjamin . . . 134
Sandburg, Carl 166, 257, 271
Sanders, Marlene 270
Sandzen, Sven Birger 114
Sanger, Margaret 259
Sanitary Engineer 204
Sankei Shimbun 112
Santa Barbara Daily News . . . 104
Santangelo, John 178
Sarcone, Antonio L. 182

Sargent, George Henry 202
Sargent, Nathan 134
Sargent, Porter 203
Sarnoff, David 251, 260, 264
Sarnoff, Robert W. . . . 251, 264, 270
Saroyan, William 261
Sass, Herbert Ravenel 230, 231
Saturday Evening Post 121, 139,
    140, 203, 208, 231, 232, 254
Saturday Review 208, 230
Saudino, Domenico 182
Sault Ste. Marie Evening News . . 170
Sault Ste. Marie News 171
Savage, George Walden 112
Savage, John Godfrey 134
Savannah Morning News 141
Savannah News-Press 252
Saxe, John Godfrey 134
Sayre, John Nevin 229
Schary, Dore 264
Schenectady Union-Star 271
Scherer, Raymond L. 270
Schickel, Richard 268, 271
Schlesinger, Arthur M. . 115, 116, 262
Schlesinger, Arthur M., Jr. . . . 252,
    257, 262, 264, 267, 269, 270
Schmeck, Harold M., Jr. 194
Schmidt, Don 185
Schoenberner, Franz 110
Schoenburn, David 271
Schouler, William 134
Schroeder, Jack 151
Schultz, Theodore W. 150
Schum, George 203
Schurman, Jacob Gould . . . 194, 195
Schurz, Carl 134, 147, 235
Schutz, David N. 250
Schwengel, Fred 153
Scope 267
Scopes, John 108
Scott, George C. 151
Scott, John 271
Scott, Robert N. 198
Scott, Walter D. 260, 266
Scribes Club 113
Scribner's 118, 199, 200, 220
Scripps, Charles E. 271, 272
Scripps, James Edmund 165
Scripps, Robert 272
Scripps-Howard 256
Scripps-Howard Newspaper
    Alliance 271, 272
Scruggs, Philip Lightfood 241
Scruggs, William Lindsay 135

Seaman, Henry J. 103
Searcher, Victor 135
Seaton, Frederick A. 250
Seaton, William W. 129
Seaton, William Winston 199
Seattle Guide, The 247
Seattle Magazine 248
Seattle Post-Intelligencer 245, 246, 247
Seattle Searchlight 246
Seattle Sun 248
Seattle Times 217, 246, 247
Seattle Union Record 245
Seattlife 247
Sebring, Lewis B., Jr. 271
Sedgwick, Ellery 119
Seegers, Scott 110
Seemüller, Annie Moncure 198
Segerg, Jean 153
Seibel, Fred O. 239, 241
Seitz, Don Carlos 202
Seldes, George 117, 143, 202
Sellers, Peter 271
Selsame, Howard 273
Sengstacke Newspapers 124
Sentinel 188
Serantoni, Italo 163
Setffans, Lincoln 203
Sevareid, Eric 135, 176
Seward, William 121
Seward, William H. 148, 209
Sewickley Herald 228
Seydell Quarterly 141
Seydell, Mildred 141
Shackford, Roland H. 135, 271
Shaeffer, Walter A. 149
Shafer, Claude 221
Shaff, David O. 153
Shalom 229
Shanghai Evening Post and Mercury
. . . . 107
Shanks, Ann Z. 227
Shapley, Harlow 260, 272
Sharpe, John Allen 189
Shaw, Albert 202
Shaw, George Bernard . 116, 187, 203
Shawn, William 118, 203
Shay, Gladys Van 186
Shayton, Robert Lewis 163
Shea, Hamilton 266
Shearer, Brainard Hayes 154
Sheehan, Perley Poore 198
Sheehan, Vincent 115
Sheehan, William 264

Sheehy, Gail 163
Sheldon, John Pitts 165
Shenandoah Evening Sentinel . . 154
Shepard, Edward Morse 198
Shepherd, James E. 188
Sherman, John 146, 147, 215
Sherman, William T. 193
Sherrod, Robert L. 208
Sherwood, Robert E. 115, 273
Sheyboygan Press 253
Sheyboygan Statesman 252
Shinn, Milicent Washburn 103
Shivers, Allan 236
Short, Wallace 151
Shriver, Andrew 159
Shriver, R. Sargent, Jr. . . . 267, 272
Sibley, Celestine 142
Sicilia, La 183
Siehoku Nippo 248
Signal of Liberty 169
Simms, William Philip . . . 271, 272
Simons, Kenneth W. 210
Simonton, J.W. 201
Simonton, James W. 147
Simplicissimus 110
Sinatra, Frank 216
Sinclair, Frank 272
Sinclair, Upton 104, 117, 123, 241, 257, 266
Sindelar, Frank 223
Singiser, Frank King 195
Sioux City Journal 151
Sisca, Alessandro 182
Sitton, Claude Fox 141
Skandinaven 178
Skeffington, Leo Bernard 195
Skinner, Constance Lindsay . . . 202
Slack, Charles Wesley 213
Slobodna Rech 183
Sloss, Robert Thompson 192
Smalley, George Washburn . . . 135
Smalley, Palemon Jared 176
Smart Set 203
Smedley, Agnes 101
Smith, Alfred E. 196, 209
Smith, Caleb B. 146
Smith, Carleton D. 266
Smith, Charles Henry (Bill Arp) . 141
Smith, Christopher 205
Smith, Courtland C. 213
Smith, Delavan 147
Smith, Douglas 271
Smith, Eric 123
Smith, Gilbert P. 250

Smith, Henry Arthur 176
Smith, Henry Ladd 135
Smith, Howard K.   264, 267, 268, 272
Smith, Joseph 248
Smith, Lauren K. 149
Smith, Lillian 142
Smith, Merriman 264, 272
Smith, Richard 147
Smith, Ruby Green 196
Smith, Samuel Harrison 135
Smith, Walter W. "Red" 148
Smith, Wilford Bascom 236
Smith, William Henry . 147, 193, 215
Smithville News 141
Smoak, William Wightman 232
Smoot, Reed 244, 249
Snajdr, Vaclav 223
Snead, Austine 220
Snead, W.T. 202
Snow, Edgar 203, 230
Snowden, Yates 230
Society of Professional Journalists/
    Sigma Delta Chi 145
Solano, Solita 129
Solidarity 167
Sollmann, William F. 229
Sonne, H. Christian 150
Sonneborn, L. . . . . 250 ·
Sorenson, Alfred A. 190
Sorenson, Theodore . . 252, 257, 267
Sosialisti 182
Soth, Lauren K. 150
Soule, Isobel Walker 226
Soule, Pierre 148
South Pasadena Review 112
South Today 142
Southern Confederacy 139
Southern Courier 272
Southern Educational Journal . . 140
Southern Industrial Editors
    Institute 142
Southern Miscellany 139
Southern Outdoors 140
Southern Patriot 253
Spalding, Lyman 195
Spangler, Harrison 149
Sparks, Fred 271
Spartanburg Herald 228
Speidel, Merritt 152, 154
Spellman, Francis, Cardinal .258, 273
Spence, Edward L. 276
Spence, Hartzell 151, 152
Spencer, Anna Carpenter Garlin . 229
Spencer, Edward 158

Spender, Stephen 115
Spilman, Louis 239, 241
Spivak, Lawrence E. 137, 264
Spock, Benjamin M. 257
Spofford, Ainsworth Rand 135
Spofford, Harriett Prescott 198
Spokane Chronicle 244
Spokane Globe 244
Spokane Press 244
Spokane Spokesman 244
Spokane Spokesman-Review . 244, 245
Sports Illustrated 225, 275
Spring, Everett 135
Springer, John 154
Springfield Republican 115, 117
Squier, Ephraim George 147
St. Anthony Express 176
St. Cloud Journal Press 175
St. John, Robert 163
St. Louis Post-Dispatch . 207, 254, 262
St. Louis Star Times 207
St. Nicholas Magazine 230
St. Paul Dispatch 174
St. Paul Pioneer 174, 176
St. Paul Pioneer Press 173, 176
St. Paul Press 176
St. Paul Western Appeal 172
Stack, Daniel F. 153
Stafansson, Vilhjalmur 198
Stafford, Jean 114
Stahler, Jeff 218
Stalin, Josef 105
Stampa Libera, La 178, 179
Stampone, John 122
Standard, The 173
Stanfield, Boris 110
Stanford Review 104
Stanford, Al 191
Stanhope, Philip Henry 148
Stanton, Frank 264, 265, 273
Stanton, Frank Lebby 141
Stanton, Henry Brewster 135
Stanwood, Edward 220
Starbuck, C.W. 212
Stark, Louis 193
Starnes, Richard 271
Starr, Frederick 198
Stars and Stripes 171
Starzel, Frank 154
Staten Island Advance 225
States Rights Republican 188
Statesman 204, 205
Stats Tidning 175
Stauffer, Oscar 155

Stead, Christiana 117
Stearn, Jess 163
Stebbins, Cortland Bliss 166
Steed, H.W. 121
Steele, A.T. 102
Steelink, Nicolas 166
Steffens, Lincoln 167, 202
Stengel, Casey 206
Stephens, Alexander Hamilton . . 135
Stephens, Erwin Duke 189
Sterling, George 104
Stern, Laurence 268
Stettinius, Edward R., Jr. . .241, 268
Stevens, John 223
Stevenson, Adlai E. . .115, 116, 255,
   257, 262, 264, 265, 267, 268,
   273
Stevenson, Robert W. 198
Steward Tribune 174
Stewart, David W. 151
Stimson, Henry L. 268
Stöcker, Helene 229
Stoddard, Charles Warren 104
Stokes, Harold Phelps 120
Stone, D.M. 201
Stone, Dana 196
Stone, David M. 147
Stone, Harold Ortho 248
Stone, Melville E. 147
Stone, Walker 223, 271, 272
Stone, William L. 203
Stone, William Leete 135
Stoneman, William H. 171
Storke, Thomas 104
Storm Lake Pilot-Tribune 152
Storrs, Ronald, Sir 198
Stout, Elihu 145
Stowe, Harriet Beecher 219, 235
Stowe, Leland 272
Stratton, Clif 156
Straus, Michael Wolf 135
Straus, Nathan 188
Streeter, Carroll P. 150
Strong, Anna Louise 248
Strotz, Sidney N. 266
Strout, Richard L. 158
Stuart, Campbell 121
Stuart, James Arthur 148
Stuart, Roger 271
Studies on the Left 272
Stutz, Harry G. 195
Stutz, Harry George 195
Styles, Carey W. 141
Suckow, Ruth 151

Sullivan, Ed 254, 273
Sullivan, Frank 203, 218
Sullivan, James 196
Sullivan, Margaret Frances . . . 147
Sullivan, Mark . . .110, 119, 135, 153
Sulzberger family 144
Sulzberger, Arthur 191
Sulzberger, Arthur H. 227
Sulzberger, Arthur H., Jr. . . 256, 263
Sulzberger, Arthur Hays . . . 114, 115
Sulzberger, Arthur Ochs . . . 114, 120
Sulzer, William 188, 203
Summer, Charles 202
Summerfield, Arthur E. 272
Sumner, Anna Emily 113
Sumner, Charles . . . 148, 213, 235
Sunbeam, The 188
Surface, William 163
Suter, Jesse 122
Suter, Theodore Noyes 122
Sutherland, Sidney 143
Svenska Posten 246, 248
Svenska-Amerikanaren 175
Svornost 178
Swanson, Claude 239, 240
Swanson, Gloria 261
Swayne, Wager 147
Swayze, John Cameron 254
Swayze, Oscar K. 156
Swearingen, William C. 175
Sweetser, Arthur 135
Swift, Louis F. 147
Swineford, A.P. 173
Swing, Raymond Gram 135, 267, 273
Swinton, Stanley M. 171
Swope, Herbert Bayard 122,
   163, 256, 265
Symington, W. Stuart . 255, 262, 272
Syracuse Journal 106
Szulc, Tad 163

Tack, Leonard S. 181
Tacoma Daily News 249
Tacoma Ledger 249
Tacoma Morning Globe 249
Tactics 260
Taft, Charles P. 147
Taft, Robert A. 195, 251
Taft, Seth 213
Taft, William H. 116,
   117, 155, 182, 194, 242, 249
Talburt, Bill 122
Talburt, Harold M. 273
Talcott, Parsons 269

Taliaferro, James Govan 157
Tallahassee Democrat 137
Talley, George S. 150
Tampa Tribune 138
Tan 111
Tappan, Benjamin 215
Tappan, Eli Todd 215
Tarbell, Ida 104, 198, 253
Tarkington, Booth 148
TASS 110, 171, 274
Tatarian, H. Roger 273
Taylor, Allan 273
Taylor, Bayard 198
Taylor, Bride Neill 236
Taylor, Charles Henry 135
Taylor, Davidson 266
Taylor, Hobart Chatfield 143
Taylor, William D. 213
Tebbel, John William 120
Teresi, Matteo 183
Terre Haute Express 146
Terre Haute Journal 145
Terre Haute Wabash Courier . . . 145
Texas Monument 235
Texas Siftings Publishing Company 236
Texas Women's Press
    Association 235, 236
Texas-Mexican Gazette 237
Thant, U 267
Thayer, William Sydney 135
Theatre Arts 260
Thilly, Frank 196
Thomas, Edward Sinclair 215
Thomas, Hodgskin 117
Thomas, Lowell 261
Thomas, Norman M. 166, 167,
    252, 255, 260, 266, 268
Thompson, Charles T. 110
Thompson, Charles Willis 196
Thompson, Dorothy 115, 171, 208, 262
Thompson, Fred 166
Thompson, Herbert Cooper 226
Thompson, Horace 174
Thompson, John M. 226
Thompson, John Reuben 242
Thompson, Ralph 202
Thompson, Slason 143
Thompson, Vance 192
Thoreau, Henry David 213
Three Star Extra 259
Throop, Enos T. 205
Thurber, James 218, 225
Thurmond, J. Strom 265
Ticknor, George 148
Tiede, Tom 163
Tilden, S.J. 196
Tilton, Theodore 135
Time 123, 190, 191,
    207, 208, 225, 231, 258, 271
Time, Inc. 231
Time-Life Broadcast, Inc. 264
Times and Compiler 242
Times Home Newspapers 207
Times of Havana, The 110
Times of London 207
Timmons, Bascom N. 233
Tito, Marshal 191
Titus, Harold 171
Today 258
Today in Washington 257
Todd, Carlos 110
Todd, Laurence 110, 171
Todd, Walter L. 195
Tokyo Shimbun 112
Toledo Blade . 170, 214, 216, 217, 220
Tolischus, Otto D. 226, 273
Tomlinson, Edward . . 259, 271, 273
Topeka Press Club 156
Toscanini, Walter 178
Toveri 179, 181
Toveritar 181
Towne, Charles Hanson 203
Townsend, George Alfred . . 136, 212
Trabulsi, Nacib 181
Trammell, Niles 264, 266
Transcript 235
Translations 117
Trask, George Kellogg 148
Traux, Hawley 225
Treat, Morgan 189
Tregaskis, Richard 163
Treman, Robert E. 194, 196
Treman, Robert H. 196
Tresca, Carlo 183
Tribuna, La 180
Tricolore, Il 163
Trinity Journal 103
Trinkle, Elbert Lee 242
Tripp, Frank E. 195
Troan, John 271, 272
Trohan, Walter 273
Trout, Clement E. 223
Trubner, Nicholas 148
True California 103
Truman, Harry S . . . 116, 252, 253,
    255, 257, 261, 268, 270, 272
Tuchman, Barbara 116, 267
Tucker, Benjamin Ricketson . . . 202

Tuckerman, Henry T. 198
Tugman, William Masten 227
Tully, Andrew 271
Tully, Jim 241
Turner, Dan 152
Turner, Dan W. 149
Tuscaloosa Gazette 101
Tusiani, Joseph 183
Tweed, William Marsh 205
Twentieth Century, The 252
Tydings, Millard E. 257
Tyler Journal 176
Tynan, Kenneth 117
Tyner, James N. 146
Tyomies 181, 182
Tyomies Eteenpain 181
Tyomies Society 183
Tyomies-Enteenpain 179, 180
Type of the Times 147

U.S. House of Representatives
    Un-American Activities
    Committee 109
U.S. News and World Report . . . 266
U.S. Office of Censorship 268
Udall, Stewart 267
Uncensored 203
Uncle Remus Home Magazine . . 139
Understanding China Newsletter . 228
Underwood, Adoniram Judson . . 176
Underwood, Robert 220
Undset, Sigrid 262
Union and Messenger 188
Union Democracy in Action 166
Union Guard 136
Unione, L' 180
United Auto Worker 167
United Press International . 101, 111,
    122, 140, 141, 147, 188,194,
    224, 226, 231, 258, 272, 273
United Serbian 181
United States Army and Navy
    Journal 197
United States Information Agency 273
United States Telegraph 188
Untermeyer, Louis 241
Updike, John 118
Upton, William Treat 136
Ursinus, Oskar 136
Usborne, Henry Charles 204
Usher, John P. 146
Utley, Clifton M. 274
Utterback, Herbert 154

Vail, Thomas 213
Vakit 111
Valeriani, Richard G. 274
Valesh, Eva MacDonald 176
Valtman, Ed 221
Van Benthuysen, Charles &
    Company 205
Van Doren, Carl 204
Van Dorn, Irita 206
Van Druten, John 201, 261
Van Dyke, Henry 198
Van Fleet, George H. 200
Van Koevering, Adrian 171
van Loon, Henrik W. 196, 261
Vandenberg, Arthur H. . . .171, 195,
    255, 272
Vander Jagt, Guy 171
Vanderbilt, Cornelius 188
Vaniman, Melvin 104
Vanity Fair 116
Vann, Robert L. 124
Vapaus 182
Vaskov, Milan 183
Vatan 111
Vaterlandsfreund 214
Velasco, Victorio 248
Veterans Report 258
Vicksburg Citizens' Appeal 260
Victoria Advocate 234
Vidal, Gore 118
Vienna News 141
Viereck, George Sylvester 111
Vignaud, Henry 157
Villa, Pancho 104
Villard, Henry 188
Villard, Oswald B. 202
Villard, Oswald Garrison . . .116, 166,
    203, 256
Vincent, James Upshur 236
Vinson, Fred M. 268
Virginia Gazette 241
Virginische Volksberichter 240
Vischer, Peter 194
Visson, Andre 123
Vocirca, Voline Vincenzo 166
Voice of America 180, 273
Volkov, Leon 111
Von Wiegand, Karl H. 109, 111
Vonnegut, Kurt 271
Voorhies, Amos E. 224
Vorse, Mary Heaton 167, 274
vox de Mexico, La 237

Wabash Courier 146
Waggaman, Camille 237
Wakefield, Dan 163
Waldron, William H. 158
Wales, Wellington 274
Walker, Singleton S. 136
Walker, William Otis 125
Wall Street Journal 117,
    152, 207, 208
Wall Street Reports 195
Wallace's Farmer 150, 155
Wallace, David 146
Wallace, David Duncan 230
Wallace, Dewitt 144
Wallace, Henry A. 149, 152,
    153, 154, 166, 253, 257, 261
Wallace, Henry Cantwell . . . 153, 155
Wallace, Lew 146
Waller, Judith 274
Wallmeyer, Dick 221
Walsh, Harry 250
Walsh, John K. 171
Walsh, Joseph Cyrillus 203
Walsh, Mason 250
Walsh, Robert 136
Walsh, Thomas J. 153
Walterboro Press and Standard . 232
Walworth, R.H. 198
Wan Kwoh Kung Po 139
Wanamaker, John 192
Wanamaker, Rodman 192
War Department Public Relations
    Bureau 258, 262
Warburg, James 268
Ward, Fred J. 186
Ward, Russ 259
Ward, William Allen 234
Ware, Ashur 188
Waring, Tom 230
Warner, Albert L. 259, 274
Warner, Charles Dudley 143
Warren Sentinel Journal 241
Warren, Earl . . . 144, 154, 255, 267
Warren, James Lloyd La Fayette . 113
Warren, L.D. 218, 222
Warren, Virginia Lee 253
Warrenton Virginian 243
Warwick, Frank M. (Jack) 216
Washburn, Stanley 136
Washburn, William D. 173
Washington Afro-American 124
Washington Daily News . . .206, 217
Washington Evening Star 122
Washington Farmletter 149

Washington Globe 197
Washington Herald 206, 207
Washington Life 194
Washington New Dealer 247
Washington Post 114, 116, 123,
    158, 190, 206, 216, 217, 256,
    262
Washington Record 228
Washington Reporter 228
Washington Star 122, 207,
    220, 240, 255
Washington Teamster 246
Washington Telegraph 239
Washington Times 240
Washington, Booker T. . . . 176, 244
Washington, Lewis M. Henry . . 236
Wasmer, Louis A. 244
Wastila, Mike 179
Watchman of the Valley 210
Waterford News 138
Watrous, Mable Spencer 245
Watson, Emory Olin 232
Watson, Harry Legare 232
Watson, Morris 227
Watters, M.C. 213
Watterson, Henry . . . 136, 147, 230
Waugh, Evelyn 231
Waugh, Frederick V. 150
Waukesha County Democrat . . . 276
Waukesha Daily Freeman 262
Wayman, Dorothy 136
WBAI 267
WBNS-TV 216
WCBC 170
WCBS/WCBS-TV 266
Weaver, Sylvester L., Jr. 251, 264, 266
Webb, James Watson 121, 136
Webb, Lavar 238
Weber, Harrison 153
Webster, Daniel 202, 209, 215
Webster, Noah 203, 205
Wechsler, James A. 257, 264,
    267, 268, 274
Wedemeyer, Albert C. 154
Weed, Thurlow 136, 202, 209
Weekly Democrat 236
Weekly Foreign Letter 106
Weekly Republican and Discipline 139
Weekly Tribune 205
Weimer, Rae 138
Weissert, Charles A. 172
WEKZ 265
Welles, Gideon 136, 148
Welles, Sumner 253, 255

Welty, Eudora 116
Wentworth, Edwin Oberlin 136
Werner, Charles George 218
Werner, Morris R. 203
Werner, William E. 209
Wert, Ben 144
West Union Weekly Argus- Gazette 149
West, Decca Lamar 236
West, R. Kenneth 166
West, Rebecca 116, 231, 270
West, William H. 147
Westall, William 138
Western Associated Press 147
Western Breeze 186
Western Spectator 222
Western Sun 145
Westin, Avram R. 274
Westminster Gazette 123
Westmoreland, William C. 267
WEWS-TV 213
Weymack, William W. 149
WFIL/WFIL-TV 251
WGN 273
WHA 259, 275
Wheeler, Burton K. 256
Wheeler, Howard Duryee 227
Wheeler, Keith 163
Wheeler, Romney 270
Wheelock, Harry M. 176
Wheelock, Joseph Albert 176
When family 190
Whetstone, Dan 186
White, Albert S. 146
White, E.B. 120, 194, 218, 254
White, Edward Richard (Ned) . . . 218
White, Frank 251
White, Grant 154
White, Horace 188
White, John Campbell 136
White, John F. 266
White, Lee A. 172, 194
White, Peter Q. 172
White, Richard Grant 198
White, Roland 274
White, William Allen 136, 143,
     148, 152, 155, 198, 209, 252,
     257
Whitefish Pilot 186
Whitehead, Don 233
Whitehead, Glenn E. 155
Whiteing, Richard 136
Whitlock, Brand 119, 203
Whitman, Bert 218
Whitman, Walt 198
Whittlesey, Frederick 209
Wichita Eagle and Beacon 255
Wickard, Claude 149
Wiesenfeld, Leon 223
Wiewiora, Joseph 183
Wiita, John 183
Wilberforce, Robert 121
Wilbur, Ray Lyman 104
Wilcox, Walter W. 150
Wildavsky, Aaron 269
Wilder, Amos P. 253
Wilder, John Augustus 118
Wilder, Thornton 260
Wile, Frederic William 136
Wiley, Alexander 252
Wiley, Louis 188, 208, 209
Wilkinson, Frank 167
Wilkinson, Kirk C. 227
Will, George F. 158
Willert, Arthur, Sir 121
Williams, Aubrey 253
Williams, Ben Ames 198
Williams, Charles R. 147, 220
Williams, Charles Richard 193
Williams, Charles S. 146
Williams, David Rhys 195
Williams, G. Mennen 271
Williams, John Skelton 242
Williams, Samuel 243
Williams, Tennessee 261
Williams, Timothy Shaler 204
Williams, William C. 273
Willis, James Scott 218
Willkie, Wendell L. 195, 206,
     250, 253, 255, 257, 268
Willson, Dixie 152
Willson, Meredith 152
Wilmington Evening Journal . . . 221
Wilmington News Journal 121, 122, 252
Wilson, Earl 216
Wilson, Edith 117, 153
Wilson, Edmund 117, 118, 203
Wilson, George W. 154
Wilson, Harold 258
Wilson, Henry 202
Wilson, James Q. 269
Wilson, Logan 236
Wilson, Lyle C. 271
Wilson, Philip Whitwell 111
Wilson, Richard C. 111
Wilson, W. Emerson 122
Wilson, Walter B. 236
Wilson, Woodrow 117, 119,
     191, 242, 263, 272

Wimbish, Anderson H. 176
WIN Magazine 229
Winchell, Walter 120, 208
Winchester Star 239
Windsor, Duke of 241
Wingate, Charles Frederick . . . 204
Winn, Frank 167
Winston-Salem Journal 188
Winter, William 198
Winterich, John T. 191
Wirtz, Willard 116, 257
Wisconsin Farmer 251
Wisconsin News 249
Wisconsin Press Association . . . 275
Wisconsin State Journal . . 249, 250,
  253, 264, 275
Wisconsin State Journal Editorial
  Association 275
Wise, Stephen S. 160
WISN/WISN-TV 251
Wittner, Fred 275
WJR 169
WLW 275
WLW Radio 213
WMAQ 274
WNBK-TV 255
WNCI-FM 215
WNET 193
Wolf, Herman 167
Wolfe, Linda 163
Wolfe, Thomas 230
Wolfe, Tom 116
Wolff, Perry 275
Wolper, David L. 271
Woltman, Frederick 271
Woltman, Frederick Enos 227
Woman Today 226
Woman's Day 227
Woman's Home Companion . . . 197
Woman's World, The 201
Women in Communications, Inc. . 150
Women's Voice 123
Wood, Art 241
Woodford, Frank B. 172
Woodrum, Clifton 241
Woods, William Henry 190
Woodstock Spirit of the Age . . . 243
Woodward, C. Vann . . 116, 239, 273
Woodward, Emily Barnelia . .141, 142
Woollcott, Alexander 136,
  225, 232, 257
Wolley, Robert Wickliffe 136
Wooster, Charles 190
WOR 193

WOR-Mutual 216
Worcester Telegram 240
Worchester Telegram 216
Work, John M. 275
Worker's Publishing Company . . 183
Workman, William D., Jr. 232
World Government News 204
World Government News, Inc. . . 204
World News Roundup 254, 257
World News Service 143
World Tomorrow, The 228, 229
World's Work 116
WOSU AM & FM 216
WRC/WRC-TV 269
Wrench, Evelyn 121
WRFD-AM 215
Wright, Charles A. 269
Wright, Frank Lloyd 250, 257
Wright, Irene Aloha 159
Wright, Orville 119
Wright, Orville and Wilbur . . . 104
Wright, Silas, Jr. 198
Wright, Wilbur 119
WRUF 138
WRUL 266
WRVA Radio 241
WTAM 255
WTAM-FM 255
WUFT 138
WUOM 170
Wurz, Frank B. 172
WWJ 165
WYBC 121
Wyeth, Andrew 218
Wykoff, Roy A., Jr. 190
Wylie, Robert B. 151
Wynn, Ed 254
Wynne, Thomas Hicks 242

Xenia News 220

Yale Daily News 121
Yale Literary Magazine 114
Yalman, Ahmed Emin 111
Yardley, Richard Q. 222, 275
Yarmolinsky, Adam 270
Yates, Edmund 198
Yates, Ted 275
Yediot Aharonot 119
Yglesias, Jose 163
Yorkshire Post 203
Young Man's Journal, The 169
Young, Arthur Morgan 115
Young, John Russell 137

Young, Lafayette 153
Young, P.B. 188
Young, Perry Deane 196
Young, Stark 260
Young, Whitney 267
Youth's Companion 173, 220
Yugoslav Radio Hour 183

Zappulla, Giuseppe 183
Zeeland Record 171
Zeidler, Frank P. 269
Zeitlin, Maurice 273
Zgoda 177, 178, 183
Ziemer, Gregor 275
Zimmerman, Louis H. 275
Zinn, Peter 212
Zorya 180
Zotoz, Helen M. 275
Zwart, Elizabeth Clarkson 155
Zweig, Stefan 115

About the Compiler

LUCY SHELTON CASWELL is Associate Professor and Curator of the Library of Communication and Graphic Arts at Ohio State University, where she specializes in the history of cartoon art and special collections librarianship. She is the author of a previous book, articles, and has mounted numerous exhibitions.